Singing
the
Chaos

Singing the Chaos

MADNESS AND WISDOM IN MODERN POETRY

William Pratt

University of Missouri Press
Columbia and London

Copyright © 1996 by
The Curators of the University of Missouri
University of Missouri Press, Columbia, Missouri 65201
Printed and bound in the United States of America
All rights reserved

5   4   3   2   1   00   99   98   97   96

Library of Congress Cataloging-in-Publication Data

Pratt, William, 1927–
    Singing the chaos : madness and wisdom in modern poetry / William
Pratt.
        p.   cm.
    Includes bibliographical references (p.   ) and index.
    ISBN 0-8262-1048-1 (alk. paper)
        1. American poetry—20th century—History and criticism.
    2. American poetry—19th century—History and criticism.   3. English
    poetry—History and criticism.   4. Modernism (Literature)
    I. Title.
    PS324.P73   1996
    · 809.1'041—dc20   96-6152
                                                                        CIP

∞ ™ This paper meets the requirements of the
American National Standard for Permanence of Paper
for Printed Library Materials, Z39.48, 1984.

Designer: Kristie Lee
Typesetter: BOOKCOMP
Printer and Binder: Thomson-Shore, Inc.
Typefaces: Minion, Nuptual Script

For credits, see page 337

This book is brought to publication with the generous
assistance of Miami University, Oxford, Ohio.

for my first readers:
Anne, Cullen, Stuart,
and Randall

Contents

Singing
the
Chaos

INTRODUCTION

At the low point of his fortunes in 1948, when Ezra Pound was incarcerated in the madhouse of St. Elizabeths Hospital in Washington, D.C., indicted for treason, and judged mentally incompetent to stand trial, Wyndham Lewis drafted a letter of encouragement to his old friend to tell him: "You are in a chaos. Why not face the fact and sing the chaos, songbird that you are?"[1]

This book affirms that modern poets did achieve greatness against the odds, causing a major age of poetry to flourish in an unpropitious time. It does not set out to be a complete history; it is a group of essays linked together by theme, about a period of high achievement in poetry that lasted a century, beginning in the mid–nineteenth and continuing to the mid-twentieth century, and reaching a peak roughly between 1920 and 1930, the decade after World War I. This peak was the golden age of modern poetry, precipitated by the writers within three very original and influential movements—the symbolists, the imagists, and the Fugitives—but since some of the major poets took little part in movements of any kind, I group them all together as "ironists." Yeats the Irish symbolist was the first of the major modern poets, Pound the American imagist was second, and Eliot the Anglo-American ironist was third, while the Fugitives together (so I argue) form a fourth major group of poets.

Looking back on modern poetry as a whole, we may see Baudelaire's *Les Fleurs du mal [Flowers of Evil]*, published in 1857, as the first coherent group of modern poems, while the last coherent group of modern poems may well be those Boris Pasternak published in 1957 at the end of his novel *Dr. Zhivago*, the supposed legacy of a fictional poet-doctor who survived the Russian Revolution only to die brokenhearted long afterward and to leave his poems behind as his last testament, the work of a tragic hero victimized by

---

1. Wyndham Lewis to Ezra Pound, May 1948, when Pound was at St. Elizabeths Hospital in Washington, D.C., *Pound/Lewis: The Letters of Ezra Pound and Wyndham Lewis*, ed. Timothy Materer, 247.

a totalitarian state. The past, to both of these widely separate modern poets, looked better than the present, and Baudelaire's French speaker reflected the difference tragically in the mid–nineteenth century, as did Pasternak's Russian spokesman in the mid–twentieth century.

What makes a writer most modern, then—early, middle, or late—is his opposition to his age: "Pity this busy monster manunkind / Not," E. E. Cummings advised, and W. H. Auden said, "I cannot think of a single important modern writer who is not against the age he lives in," while Donald Davidson agreed, "The artist is no longer *with* society, as perhaps even Milton, last of classicists, was. He is *against* or *away from* society, and the disturbed relation becomes his essential theme."[2] Criticizing the time in which one lives is characteristically modern, for, as Pound wrote very early in his career,

> They tell me to "Mirror my age,"
>   God pity the age if I do do it. . . .
> We ever live in the now
>   it is better to live in than sing of.[3]

And as Denis Donoghue remarked about the chief Irish poet of the age: "Yeats's wilfulness is his modernity, the poems relate themselves to our time by affronting it."[4] The paradox of modernism is that it has been most modern to be antimodern: the greatest writers, ever since the French symbolists, have been the most devastating critics of their age.

Modernism in poetry is both a positive and a negative force, then, for beginning with Baudelaire's *Les Fleurs du mal* in 1857—the first book of modern poems in any language—poets discovered that beauty could be made from ugliness, sublimity from sordidness. Their discovery resulted in the creation of great poetry in an age that was generally hostile to it, but they also discovered that the ugliness and sordidness of the world are true perceptions that poetry can mirror but cannot change; thus singing the chaos, as modern poets have tended to do, may redeem a decadent age intellectually and spiritually as great art can do, but even great art cannot transform the age socially or politically or economically into a happy time to be alive. As Yeats saw early in the twentieth century, the "growing murderousness of the world" was a fact that had to be confronted, not a trend that could be altered, and his magnificent prophetic poems picture civilization in a state of violent crisis that the poet can only suffer tragically and express eloquently, since he

2. Donald Davidson, "A Mirror for Artists," 43.

3. Ezra Pound, "Redondillas, or Something of That Sort," in *Collected Early Poems of Ezra Pound*, ed. Michael John King, 218.

4. Denis Donoghue, *Yeats*, 31–32.

has no power to reverse the trend and mend the brokenness of the world. The poet's motive for writing poetry is not revolutionary but elegiac, since he feels the same lack of unity and meaning in the modern world that Yeats had felt; Yeats later recalled, "A conviction that the world was now but a bundle of fragments possessed me without ceasing."[5]

Generally speaking, modern art and literature have seemed to share an apocalyptic vision in which the Second Fall of Man has seemed more imminent than the Second Coming of Christ. Rodin's *Gate of Hell,* Rouault's *Miserere,* and Picasso's *Guernica* are visual masterpieces that compare in their dark prophecies of evil and destructiveness in human affairs with Yeats's "Second Coming," Eliot's *Waste Land,* and Pound's *Pisan Cantos.*

But if man's creative powers in the twentieth century have seemed to mirror his destructive powers, art and literature have strangely flourished in the valley of the shadow of death: as Mallarmé said in the French symbolist period with which modern poetry began, there is the sense of "a trembling of the veil of the temple" ["une inquiétude du voile dans le temple"],[6] when the world seems thrown into the sort of chaotic darkness that surrounded Christ's crucifixion. Out of such primordial confusion, however, may come great art and literature, if artists and writers are able to "sing the chaos," that is, to express the feeling of impending apocalypse artistically, making aesthetic order out of disorder, beauty out of ugliness. It was, in fact, the goal of the French symbolist poets, starting with Gérard de Nerval and Charles Baudelaire, to bring "golden verses" out of stones and "flowers out of evil," through what Rimbaud called a "rational disordering of the senses" ["raisonné dérèglement de tous les sens"],[7] an ironic use of artistic imagination for which the philosopher Simone Weil coined the word *decreation* (meaning man's response to the original creation of the universe by God).

It was Baudelaire, in particular, who reversed the tendency to exalt and glorify the powers of man, who challenged the quasidivine faculties of reason and imagination that dominated both the previous ages, Enlightenment and romanticism, and who thus became the first great poet of modernism. He said that from childhood he had felt two conflicting impulses within him, "one toward God, the other toward Satan," and "two conflicting sensations in my heart: the horror of life and the ecstasy of life."[8] It was Baudelaire who first said of the artist of modern life that he must reveal man as a creature divided within himself, capable of the greatest good but also of the greatest

5. William Butler Yeats, *The Autobiography of William Butler Yeats,* 128.

6. Stéphane Mallarmé, "Crise de vers" (fragment), *Mallarmé: Pages choisies,* 12.

7. Rimbaud to Paul Demeny, May 15, 1871, in *Rimbaud: Complete Works, Selected Letters,* ed. Wallace Fowlie (Chicago: University of Chicago Press, 1966), 306–7.

8. Charles Baudelaire, "My Heart Laid Bare," 50.

evil, with a potential to express both the horror and the ecstasy he felt so fiercely struggling within him.

When human consciousness becomes divided, irony becomes the chief instrument for expression, since irony, from the time it was conceived by the classical Greeks, signifies doubleness of meaning, saying one thing but implying its opposite. Baudelaire, viewing himself as a radically imperfect creature who aspired to absolute perfection, insisted that the modern poet must strive to put into his works two main qualities: super-realism and irony. His "super-realism" (the French word is *surréalisme*) was a perception of the duality of existence, since it implied an inner truth beyond the senses, which was taken by the French poets who came after him to mean symbolism and by later Anglo-American poets to imply imagism. Symbolism and irony were the heritage Baudelaire bequeathed to poets through his "Flowers *from* Evil," which allowed them to order the disorder of modern life, transforming what Mallarmé called the time of "a trembling of the veil of the temple" into an age of great poetry.

Rimbaud called it "the time of the assassins": the disintegration of Western society, which he sensed prophetically long before the eruption of World War I. Without a human community of shared beliefs and sentiments, man becomes alienated from his fellow men and driven inward, where, if he is an artist, he may seek an order lacking in the world around him, becoming what Wallace Stevens called a "connoisseur of chaos" and so creating works of art that reflect an outer fragmentation of society but an inner harmony in the universe, expressed in subtle ways that often seem nonsensical or insane. Impressionism in painting and symbolism in poetry were means by which artists could express a subjective reality radically different from the objective reality outside them. To create beauty from evil as Baudelaire did with *Les Fleurs du mal* in 1857 was to make possible a poetry that produced man-made beauty out of man-made ugliness: "You have given me your mud, and I have changed it into gold," he claimed as he lyrically transformed the industrialized city of Paris.

So, as social community disintegrated and Christian faith declined, poets discovered how to restore the potential of belief through their language—a potential, that is, for readers who were capable of appreciating the new poems, for in them the religious symbols that had formerly bound men to each other were replaced by poetic symbols. Of course, as Wallace Stevens would regretfully say, aesthetic faith can only produce the satisfaction of religious faith if it is universal, and so the social function of modern poetry has been limited to the few who could understand it, not extended to the many who needed it. But the social function of poetry in any age, as Eliot thoughtfully put it, is to filter through language in many subtle ways and have its effect indirectly on readers who appreciate other literary works influenced by poetry, such as fiction, drama, and even at times journalism.

This book is indebted not only to the poets who created modern poetry but to the critics—often the poets themselves—who have interpreted it. Though there have been more schools of critics in the modern period than of poets, the New Critics (as named by John Crowe Ransom, one of the Fugitive poets) did most to make modern poetry accessible to a wide circle of readers and so performed a pioneering role of advocacy for the new poetry, especially if they were great critics as well as great poets, as was pre-eminently true of Yeats and Pound and Eliot. As Eliot wrote in 1920, "It is to be expected that the critic and the creative artist should frequently be the same person."[9] Modern poets from Baudelaire on knew that they had to be critical to be truthful, and a book about modern poetry must make use of the criticism that has flourished beside and because of that poetry, as well as offering fresh interpretations of the many major and minor poems of modernism.

The essential argument of this book is that the major modern poets and poetic movements have radically changed the shape of poetry in all major Western languages in order to play a prophetic role, expressing, by means of apparently irrational forms and ironic contrasts, insights into the supratemporal destiny of man. Such poetic truths could be dismissed as mere superstitions, fancies, or amusements by a rationally and scientifically educated audience if they were put in a more traditional metrical or logical form. In this way, poetry has tended either to replace—or, in important cases such as those of Hopkins and Eliot, to reinforce—scripture and sacred writings in our age, because its very manner implies a revelatory mode of speech, produced out of what W. H. Auden (borrowing from Coleridge) called the Primary Imagination, which recognizes supernatural events and responds to superhuman forces and beings. Starting with the French symbolist movement more than a century ago, which initiated what we now call modern (or modernist) poetry, and running through more than a century of literary history, Western poetry has followed a line of development that has linked radical experiments with poetic form—the excitement of the new, the fresh, the unprecedented—to sweepingly visionary, often disturbing, painful, and pessimistic insights into human nature.

To argue that modern poetry paradoxically glorifies the age it so profoundly criticizes, I offer this book less as a comprehensive history than as a roughly chronological sequence of essays. The essays thread their way through the four major poetic movements, with the first essay and concluding essay focused respectively on the themes of the Age of Irony and the Poet as Tragic Hero,

9. T. S. Eliot, "The Perfect Critic," in *The Sacred Wood: Essays on Poetry and Criticism*, 16.

giving some shape to the collection as a whole. It is my hope that this book will appeal to the general reader as well as to the specialist and that it will fill the need for a wide-ranging study of modern poetry that recognizes both its international and its revolutionary character, proving the truth of what Pound wrote Eliot as he returned the manuscript of *The Waste Land,* which he had drastically reduced: "It is after all a grrrreat litttttttterary period."[10]

10. Ezra Pound, *The Letters of Ezra Pound, 1907–1941,* 170.

1

THE AGE OF IRONY AND THE BEGINNING OF MODERNISM

"No age can be a great age which has not found its own genius," Ezra Pound wrote early in the twentieth century, at the beginning of the age that we think of as "modern." Now, when we find ourselves at the other end of that age, it is time to ask what this elastic term *modern* means, since it cannot go on forever meaning the same thing. Every century has its own definition of the "modern" that later centuries may choose to call by other names: Elizabethan, neoclassical, and romantic are names that have been used by later literary critics and historians to define what the major writers of the seventeenth, eighteenth, and nineteenth centuries expressed in their works. We cannot, of course, tell the next century what name to call the literature of our century; they have a perfect right to ignore all our definitions of *modern* if they choose; but we can at least try to say what name we think fits our age best, and so attempt to put our signature on literary history. Just as the Hebrew patriarch Jacob wrestled all night with the angel until it told him his true name, no longer Jacob but Israel, so we, at the latter end of the twentieth century, must wrestle with our angel, the elusive *Zeitgeist*, or Spirit of the Age, until it tells us what *modern* really means and whether it stands for a great age, after all, or one of the darker ages of human history.

Has ours been a great age or a dark age? It is tempting to call it great, as Marshall McLuhan did in his influential book *Understanding Media*, when he called the twentieth century one of the Three Great Ages of Western Man. The other two in his view were the fifth century B.C. and the thirteenth century A.D.—the heights of, respectively, classical Greek and medieval Italian civilizations, great ages in almost any historian's view of the sweep of Western civilization over the past two and a half millennia. The claim is flattering, and the prospect it opens for our age is breathtaking: Do we rival classical

Greece? Where, then, are our Sophocles and Socrates? Can we compare ourselves with medieval Italy? Where, then, are our Dante and Aquinas? In particular, what beliefs do we hold that can compare with Platonic idealism or Christian humanism, the philosophical assumptions of fifth century B.C. Athens and thirteenth century A.D. Florence? Clearly, classical Greeks and medieval Italians believed in the ultimate possibility of man's transcending himself, that man might be raised by his vision to the plane of the immortal and superhuman, to unite with the gods or with God. Do we have such high aspirations? Certainly there have been men in our century who did not shrink from playing God, but few if any have claimed to be inspired by him. More often, the voice of the twentieth century has proclaimed with the philosopher Nietzsche, "God is dead!" Our age has most often confessed not belief, but disbelief, and skeptical agnosticism would seem to be the prevailing view. Ours has been called an Age of Anxiety, but never an Age of Faith.

Yet some might say that we have held a strong positive belief in material progress; is "progressive materialism" a better phrase for what the twentieth century has believed in? And if so, is not such a belief more negative than positive, for when our age is compared to earlier ages in any respect except technological mastery, do we not suffer from a cultural inferiority complex? Against the claim of material progress must be weighed the charge of moral and cultural decay, and it is here that we must begin trying to separate the true sense of *modern* from its various false senses. One sense of *modern* is simply "new and fashionable," but what will *modern* mean when it is no longer the present but the past (and to speak of "postmodern" will only delay the answer)? In the eighteenth century, the famous contest in Jonathan Swift's *Battle of the Books* was between the Ancients and the Moderns. Those Moderns we now think of as being "neoclassical." Our own Battle of the Books has not been so much between Ancients and Moderns as between Moderns and Contemporaries; distinguishing them may lead us to a more permanent sense of what is truly "modern."

It was Stephen Spender, in his book *The Struggle of the Modern,* who first compared these terms: he defined moderns, among writers of the twentieth century, as "revolutionary traditionalists," whereas he equated contemporaries with "progressive futurists." Spender, a leading poet and critic of the mid–twentieth century, regarded such writers as William Butler Yeats, Rainer Maria Rilke, James Joyce, T. S. Eliot, Ezra Pound, and William Faulkner as moderns, while he placed such writers as George Bernard Shaw, H. G. Wells, Arnold Bennett, and C. P. Snow as contemporaries. The modern writer, he said, uses the rich human past to reveal the poverty of the present state of man, whereas the contemporary projects a progressive present state of man into a happier future state: "The contemporary belongs to the modern world, represents it in his works, and accepts the historic forces moving through it, the values of science and progress. . . . The modern is acutely conscious of the contemporary scene, but he does not accept its values. . . . modern art expresses the tension between past and present."[1]

Such a distinction between moderns and contemporaries is useful and can easily be applied to some of the recognized masterpieces of modern literature. James Joyce in *Ulysses,* for instance, used a classical Greek myth to illuminate twentieth-century Dublin, paralleling the adventures of Leopold and Molly Bloom and Stephen Dedalus with the Homeric hero Ulysses, his wife, Penelope, and their son, Telemachus. Joyce meticulously carried out this parallel, as serious readers of *Ulysses* know, for the purpose of tragicomic irony: to point up the absurdity of the comparison between human struggles in a mechanized urban environment, where the Cave of the Winds becomes a newspaper office and Circe's Island becomes a brothel, with the human struggles against nature and the gods in Homer's *Odyssey,* thus revealing the poverty of the present state of man. If we put beside Joyce's revolutionary yet traditional novel, so scathing in its use of the past to criticize the present, such a popular work as Shaw's play *Pygmalion* (even better known in its musical version, *My Fair Lady*), we can see how Shaw uses the Greek myth of Pygmalion and Galatea—the sculptor whose statue of a perfect woman comes to life—to show how easily miracles may be performed in a scientific age. Whereas it took the power of the goddess Aphrodite to transform a statue into a woman in the Greek myth, in Shaw's play Professor Higgins and his skilled assistant, Colonel Pickering, in their up-to-date linguistics laboratory, are able to convert Eliza Doolittle speedily from a "draggletail guttersnipe" to a duchess. Shaw was a highly successful comic dramatist, and a better artist than his American musical heirs, for he did not tack on a conventional happy ending to his play, but his comedy for all its humor contains little irony. Professor Higgins is openly admired for his feat of transforming a flower-girl into a duchess by simply improving her English accent, and at the end of the play he is the dispassionate scientist who detaches himself from the emotions of love he has aroused in Eliza during her transformation, and he tells her quite plainly to go packing and look for a young man her own age to marry. Higgins is a clever, pragmatic technician who carries off his human miracle as if he were dividing cells or atoms in a laboratory, and Shaw as the creator of this contemporary Pygmalion implies that modern man is better able to perform miracles than were ancient heroes or gods and that modern woman can rise from the bottom to the top of society simply by changing her surroundings and her accent, acquiring the necessary education to make herself a lady.

1. Stephen Spender, *The Struggle of the Modern,* 77–79.

What such a comparison between Joyce and Shaw shows is that the characteristically "modern" treatment of the relation of past to present, of ancient myth to present reality, is one of ironic contrast, showing a degeneration rather than a progression, while the "contemporary" relation of past to present moves in the opposite direction, demonstrating the progress and improvement of man, and making the present seem the best possible age to live in—except for the future, when men may become even more rational and efficient. Joyce's Bloom is clearly fallen from the heroism of Ulysses into a comic antiheroism, becoming in the transformation a rather pathetic but laughable figure somewhat like Charlie Chaplin's movie tramp, while Shaw's Higgins is not only cleverer than Pygmalion but less sentimental and more the master of his own fate, more like an intellectual Superman. Shaw's hero may seem superior to Joyce's until we ask ourselves whether Higgins in his assumed superiority engages our sympathy as much as Bloom in his unassuming helplessness. In Shaw's Brave New World, as T. S. Eliot once tellingly observed, "Morality consists in working to forward the happiness of future generations, 'happiness' of a not remarkably spiritualized kind." But, as Eliot went on to point out, "It is important not only that we should try to want the right things for the future. It is important also that we should have just as much respect for ourselves; and remember that we, as human beings, are just as valuable as the men of the future." So Shaw, even at his best (and *Pygmalion* is certainly one of his best plays), seemed to Eliot to be a rather limited social optimist, while he viewed Joyce as a profound moral realist.

An equally pertinent comparison could be made between Eliot's *Waste Land* as a "modern" epic and such a "contemporary" epic as *The Bridge,* by Hart Crane. For in *The Waste Land,* the city life of London is portrayed as a contrasting texture of past and present, in which the present is being continually thrown into bold and shocking relief by allusion to and parody of the past. Eliot thus "modernizes" Andrew Marvell:

> But at my back in a cold blast I hear
> The rattle of the bones, and chuckle spread from ear to ear.

And he "modernizes" Oliver Goldsmith:

> When lovely woman stoops to folly and
> Paces about her room again, alone,
> She smoothes her hair with automatic hand,
> And puts a record on the gramophone.

These echoes of the past, when lovers pledged to be true to each other till death, are ironically contrasted with the casual adulteries of the present;

spiritless modern people, Eliot implies, are not aware of how dead they already are. *The Waste Land* is thus not only myth but reality, the tragedy being that no one takes it seriously—no one, that is, except the poet and his reader.

But put it beside *The Bridge* and the difference is immediately apparent. Crane's poem is another epic of the modern city, in which London is replaced by New York; it was written soon after Eliot's poem and in direct response to it (as we know from Crane's letters) and was meant to be an expression of positive faith in the city and all it means—the Machine Age, America past, present, and future. Crane chose the Brooklyn Bridge as his major symbol because he regarded it as an engineering triumph that had aesthetic and even religious significance, a "harp and altar of the fury fused" whose "curveship" might somehow "lend a myth to God." Crane wanted passionately to believe in the creative possibilities of an urban industrial environment, but found that he was unable to sustain this belief throughout his poem and that he could hold it only in certain isolated passages, while in others he lapsed into a bitter irony. Again, Crane's poem might seem as preferable to Eliot's poem as Shaw's play is to Joyce's novel, if the purpose of literature is to cast human experience in a positive light. Time, however, has proved Eliot's devastating criticism of the modern city increasingly relevant, while Crane's optimism about the modern city did not even last through the writing of his poem. We read *The Waste Land* at the end of the century with a sense still of its devastating truthfulness about the moral and spiritual state of man, while we read *The Bridge* with a sense that Crane's major symbol deserted him, his subconscious pessimism about the modern city having become more truthful than his conscious optimism about it. All four works are masterpieces in their way, but two are "modern," while two are—at least in intention—"contemporary." Eliot's epic poem and Joyce's epic novel—finished almost simultaneously in 1922, the vintage year of modernism—seem more and more the central masterpieces of the age, while Crane's counter-epic, like Shaw's super-mythical drama, suffers from its positive message about the progressive materialism of the age. As Allen Tate wrote sympathetically after Crane's tragic suicide in 1930, "Far from 'refuting' Eliot, Hart Crane's whole career is a vindication of Eliot's major premise: that the integrity of the individual consciousness has broken down."[2]

However much modernism may mean to us, then, as we near the end of the twentieth century, it is a temporal term that will eventually have to be replaced by some other term; the only uncertainty is what that term may be. It cannot be replaced by a term as patently derivative and illogical as *postmodernism: late modernism* describes much more accurately the period we are in just now, when modernism is inevitably losing force, but when

2. Allen Tate, "Hart Crane," in *Essays of Four Decades,* 321.

no new force, or power of inspiration, has yet made its appearance. Of the terms that might be reasonable substitutes someday for *modernism,* those most closely linked with modern poetry are *symbolism* and *imagism,* while those most closely tied to modern fiction are *realism* and *naturalism,* and one of these terms may in time replace *modernism* as a descriptive label for twentieth-century literature. We might even recall the suggestion of Edmund Wilson, in his pioneering critical survey of modern literature, *Axel's Castle: A Study in the Imaginative Literature of 1870 to 1930,* that symbolism converged with naturalism in certain major works, and so might "symbolic naturalism" perhaps be a name for modernism?

Perhaps. At the moment, we can only speculate about what posterity may choose to call our age, but I think a good case can be made for calling it the Age of Irony, since it can be claimed that irony has been involved in the style and the attitude of most of the great modern writers, whether they were symbolists or imagists, realists or naturalists, poets or novelists. One influential modern poet and critic, John Crowe Ransom, even went so far as to maintain that "irony may be regarded as the ultimate mode of the great minds. . . . it implies a rejection of romantic forms and formulas. . . . Irony is the rarest of the states of mind, because it is the most inclusive; the whole mind has been active in arriving at it, both creation and criticism, both poetry and science."[3] So let me tentatively propose that a twentieth-century Age of Irony could as logically follow the nineteenth-century Age of Romance as the latter followed the eighteenth-century Age of Reason, or neoclassicism. Such a succession of literary styles in three centuries—from neoclassicism to romanticism to ironism—has at least some symmetry to recommend it and sets up a kind of dialectical evolution that makes the three movements complementary to each other, balancing instead of canceling each other out.

In his essay "Tradition and the Individual Talent," T. S. Eliot pictured just such a chain of creative minds linking civilization together, providing an active and regenerative notion of tradition, but he also recognized that no age, however great, can become permanent. We know this truth instinctively, yet we always want to believe that our own age is the exception—that it alone will last forever—just as every individual wants to believe that he alone is immortal. Eliot believed that every age has something unique to contribute to the whole of human culture, something that has never existed before and will never exist again with the same distinctness and the same intensity, and he held that though each significant age cannot endure in itself, it does become a permanent part of the whole fabric of culture, which makes up what we call the Humanities.

3. John Crowe Ransom, editorial, *Fugitive* 4, no. 2 (June 1925): 64.

T. E. Hulme, the philosopher-poet who was one of the founders of imagism, anticipated Eliot's insight into culture by theorizing early in the twentieth century in "Romanticism and Classicism":

> A particular convention or attitude in art has a strict analogy to the phenomena of organic life. It grows old and decays. It has a definite period of life and must die. All the possible tunes get played on it and then it is exhausted; moreover its best period is its youngest. Take the case of the extraordinary efflorescence of verse in the Elizabethan period. All kinds of reasons have been given for this—the discovery of the new world and the rest of it. There is a much simpler one. A new medium had been given them to play with—namely, blank verse. It was new and so it was easy to play new tunes on it.[4]

Hulme's observation helps to define what is new in our age, when the discoveries of symbolism and then of imagism led to an extraordinary flowering of *vers libre*, or free verse. We can feel confident that because of that flowering—the creation of a new style in which masterpieces were created—modernism, however we finally define it, will outlive the age in which it was invented.

Modernism thus means irony and it also means free verse. And it means internationalism. Modernism looms impressively over a hundred years of literary history, from Baudelaire's *Les Fleurs du mal* and Flaubert's *Madame Bovary* in 1857 to Pasternak's *Dr. Zhivago* in 1957, reaching its peak in 1922, with Eliot's *Waste Land* and Joyce's *Ulysses*. It has been an international literary movement from beginning to end, passing from French to English to German to Russian. These four European languages have contributed their share of masterpieces to modernism, and no one can study modern literature thoroughly without some acquaintance with each of them. Conclusive evidence of the international character of modernism is the amount of translation it has inspired and the amount of cross-cultural influence that has occurred along the way. Symbolism, realism, and naturalism were all originally French literary movements, but all have become naturalized in other languages, so that it is quite possible to speak of English, German, or Russian symbolism, realism, and naturalism, as well as of French.

One important movement that was not originally French is imagism, but the English and American writers who invented imagism in London in about 1910 were strongly influenced by the French symbolists, so much so that René Taupin, the French scholar who wrote the fullest study of the subject, *The*

---

4. T. E. Hulme, "Romanticism and Classicism," in *Speculations*, 121–22.

Influence of French Symbolism on Modern American Poetry, argued that through the imagists it came to pass that "American poetry spoke French."[5]

Certainly no period of literary history since the Renaissance has shown as much interlingual influence as the period of modernism. The extensive use of foreign languages accounts for much of the notable complexity and obscurity of the major works of modernism, and the central influence of a gifted linguist such as Ezra Pound comes largely from his ability to translate, quote, and paraphrase from languages other than his native English (or his native American). Historically, modernism has spoken an international language compounded from a variety of sources, ancient as well as modern, and even including a language as remote as Chinese.

Modernism is international and interlingual, therefore, and it is also theoretical, for there has never been an age when literary theory was as much a part of the very fabric of literature as in the modern period, nor when writers have as often been practicing critics as well as poets or novelists. Hugh Kenner was not joking when, in *The Pound Era*, he defined *symbolism* as "Scientific Romanticism," although combining science and romance had seemed an impossibility before Baudelaire, Mallarmé, Verlaine, Rimbaud, and Valéry wrote down their theories, often in poetic form. Baudelaire's sonnet "Correspondences" is the first touchstone of French symbolism, and it is both a poem and a theory of poetry in one. In it, Baudelaire speaks of nature as "a living temple," where man walks through "a forest of symbols" that communicate to him by the correspondence of visible and invisible realities, inspiring him to "sing the transports of the senses and the soul." It was Baudelaire whom Eliot later called the first modern poet in any language because he was able to transform the dehumanized landscape of the industrial city into a metaphor for human suffering, to see it, in Baudelaire's own words, as "steeped in an atmosphere of the marvelous." Baudelaire maintained that the two supreme poetic qualities, "super-realism and irony," were both derived from man's fallen nature, his double identity driving him in two contrary directions at the same time—one toward God, the other toward Satan.

The resolution of this inherent duality in man was the poetic symbol, and it was Mallarmé who first used the term *symboliste* to stand for the new theory of poetry. In the symbolist decade of the 1880s in Paris, Mallarmé wrote his famous pronouncement, "To name an object is to do away with three-quarters of the enjoyment of the poem, which is derived from the satisfaction of guessing little by little: to suggest it, to evoke it—that is what charms the imagination." This technique of indirect suggestion was for Mallarmé the means by which the poet could induce in his readers' minds "the delicious joy

---

5. René Taupin, *The Influence of French Symbolism on Modern American Poetry*, 245.

of believing that they are creating," and so make the reader himself participate in the process by which the poem expresses meaning.[6] It was Verlaine who, also in the symbolist decade, wrote the ultimate theoretical poem, called simply "L'Art poétique" ["The Art of Poetry"], where he spoke of the need for "Music, always more music," for "not color but Nuance," and urged the poet to "take rhyme and wring its neck"—in short, he licensed all sorts of experiments with verse form and sound quality, thus encouraging his younger friend Rimbaud to attempt what Rimbaud called a "rational disordering of the senses" in order to achieve new poetic effects. By the end of the nineteenth century, the French symbolists had radically altered the shape, sound, and meaning of poetry, and their example excited the imaginations of poets in other languages, most notably Yeats, who came to Paris in the 1890s with his friend Arthur Symons to be introduced into Mallarmé's circle, and who in 1900 wrote the major essay "The Symbolism of Poetry."

Yeats, with his Irish religious and mythological background, saw the French symbolists as opening new possibilities for poets, in his words, to "overcome the slow dying of men's hearts," to "lay their hands upon men's heartstrings again," and to make poetry "the garment of religion as in old times." He felt they had demonstrated how to blend sounds and colors to evoke fleeting yet distinct emotions, how to create delicate rhythms that put the reader in a "state of perhaps real trance, in which the mind liberated from the pressure of the will is unfolded in symbols," and how to express shades of meaning that would otherwise remain unknown, because "you cannot give a body to something that moves beyond the senses, unless your words are as subtle, as complex, as full of mysterious life, as the body of a flower or of a woman."[7] Yeats was profoundly influenced by the French symbolists during the rest of his poetic career, for he came to write poetic theories in verse as well as in prose (following their example), he quoted Mallarmé in his essays ("the new sacred book of which all the arts, as someone has said, are beginning to dream") and in his *Autobiography* (the second section's title is "The Trembling of the Veil"), and he even modeled one of his most strikingly personal later poems on one of Mallarmé's poems: "A Coat" closely resembles "La Marchande d'habits" ["The Old-Clothes Woman"].

When Yeats translated a brief French symbolist poem into an Irish symbolist poem, he stripped off his whole array of Celtic mythology to achieve a new poetic realism. What Yeats learned for himself from the symbolists, Pound learned for a whole generation of poets, by building the imagist movement in English poetry on the foundation of French symbolism. Perhaps it would

6. Mallarmé, "Sur l'évolution littéraire," quoted in *Mallarmé: Pages choisies,* 10.
7. William Butler Yeats, "The Symbolism of Poetry" (1900), in *Essays and Introductions,* 164.

be truer to say that in imagism Pound and his fellow poets fused poetic symbolism with prose realism, because the example of Flaubert, the father of French realism, was as important to Pound as was the example of the symbolist poets. In fact, Pound criticized the indefiniteness, or what he called the "softness," of some symbolist poetry, and praised the concreteness, or what he called the "hardness," of particular symbolists such as Laforgue and Corbière. He also criticized the wordiness of some French poetry and praised the terseness of Flaubert's prose. His definition of the *image* was "that which presents an intellectual and emotional complex in an instant of time," which was to be achieved by a combination of directness, brevity, and "the sequence of the musical phrase, not in sequence of a metronome"—in other words, free verse.

The theory of imagism was more definite than that of symbolism, and so was the poetry that resulted from it: instead of thinking of the poem as a complex symbol, imagists conceived it as a simple image, brief and vivid, the expression of a single moment of time. According to D. H. Lawrence, who joined the imagists after Pound had left them, the purpose of the new poetry was to capture the immediacy of the "one realm we have never conquered: the pure present." But all the imagists remained aware of their debt to the symbolists, which Pound doubly acknowledged in 1914 by bringing out the first imagist anthology under the French title *Des Imagistes* and by publishing an essay in which he declared his belief in " 'an absolute rhythm,' a rhythm, that is, in poetry which corresponds exactly to the emotion or shade of emotion to be expressed" and "a like belief in a sort of permanent metaphor, which is, as I understand it, 'symbolism' in its profounder sense." René Taupin would later sum up the close relation between the symbolists and the imagists by saying that "between the 'image' of the Imagists and the 'symbol' of the Symbolists there is a difference only of precision."[8]

Poets have been fairly evenly divided between symbolists and imagists in the century of modernism because in addition to Yeats, major poets such as Wallace Stevens and Hart Crane have had a strong symbolist vein in their poetry, as has Dylan Thomas, and I would even claim that Hopkins, who was a contemporary of Verlaine and Mallarmé, while not being influenced by them, intuitively paralleled their theories by his doctrines of "inscape" and "sprung rhythm," which are comparable to "symbol" and "free verse." A similar claim can be made that Emily Dickinson anticipated imagism with her brief, irregular lyrics and that she expressed something close to Pound's belief that "the proper and perfect symbol is the natural object" when she wrote to Thomas Wentworth Higginson in a letter of 1863, "I was thinking

8. Taupin, *Influence of French Symbolism*, 93.

today, as I noticed, that the 'Supernatural' was only the Natural disclosed."
During the imagist decade from 1910 to 1920, the original imagist group
included along with Pound his friend H. D., Hilda Doolittle, who had come
to London from Philadelphia, and his other friend William Carlos Williams,
who stayed in Philadelphia but continued to send him poems. H. D. and
Williams both remained true to the imagist style in their poetry, even when
they wrote longer poems, because in principle imagism could be extended to
any length by linking brief images together in a chain, as Eliot did superbly
in *The Waste Land* and as Williams did through the five books of *Paterson*
and the five sections of his late poem *Of Asphodel, That Greeny Flower*. But
in addition to those who were close to Pound in the imagist decade, other
major poets who belong to the imagist line include D. H. Lawrence, Marianne
Moore, E. E. Cummings, and Archibald MacLeish. And as Amy Lowell would
say, if Stephen Crane had been born a little later, he would certainly have
been known as an imagist—both for his poetry and for his prose. Yes, in
prose, too, because in fact, there are symbolist and imagist novels as well as
poems: Edmund Wilson long ago recognized Proust and Joyce as symbolist
novelists, and he might have included Faulkner if he had written the book
a decade later than 1930; just as certainly, it seems to me, Stephen Crane,
Sherwood Anderson, and Ernest Hemingway were prose imagists, not simply
American realists and naturalists. As Wallace Stevens observed about William
Carlos Williams, "Imagism is not something superficial. It obeys an instinct.
Moreover, Imagism is an ancient phase of poetry. It is something permanent."[9]
"Imagistic realism" might therefore be as good a phrase for modernism as
"symbolic naturalism."

But the full meaning of modernism seems to be that we are living in an
Age of Irony, when free verse, internationalism, symbolism, and imagism
all converge in the new literary style. The writers who have criticized our
age most profoundly are the most truly modern, from the symbolists to the
imagists, and the ironic self-criticism embodied masterfully in Joyce's *Ulysses*
and Eliot's *Waste Land* are the keys to modern sensibility. Spender traced
the origin of what he called "the struggle of the modern" to the literary
movement that started in the first decade of the century, saying, "The aims of
the imagist movement in poetry provide the archetype of a modern creative
procedure,"[10] and since imagism was the metamorphosis in another language
of French symbolism, modernism may be regarded as a continuation from
the symbolists to the imagists.

When modernism arose, the elusive Spirit of the Age directed a deep
undercurrent of moral criticism against the tide of material progress that

9. Wallace Stevens, "Rubbings of Reality," in *Opus Posthumous*, 258.
10. Spender, *The Struggle of the Modern,* 110.

has dominated the twentieth century, and as Yeats put it in the unforgettably ironic refrain of his memorial to the martyred Irish patriots in "Easter 1916": "A terrible beauty is born." The "terrible beauty" of modernism is expressed in poetry and the other arts, a reflection, it seems, of the violent age we have lived through, with its two world wars and many lesser wars, with its splitting of the atom and unleashing of a power of nature unknown to any previous age. It is not a pretty vision, nor a reassuring one, but it is a truthful one, because the modern is not the contemporary, being *against* the time, not *with* it.

Of course, a sense of the modern age as an Age of Irony derives from literature and art, not from science, which has been the dominant mode of knowledge in our age, but the "terrible beauty" of modernism may be as true as any of the physical theories of the universe by which we have mastered natural forces and unleashed them. No less a scientist than Werner Heisenberg, the theoretical physicist whose uncertainty principle raised doubts among scientists about whether a completely accurate quantification of matter is ever possible, mused in his book *Physics and Philosophy:*

> Are the different styles of art an arbitrary product of the human mind? . . . The style arises out of the interplay between the world and ourselves, or more specifically between the spirit of the time and the artist. The spirit of a time is probably as objective as any fact in natural science, and this spirit brings out certain features of the world which are even independent of time, are in this sense eternal.[11]

If calling modernism the Age of Irony fits the twentieth century better than calling it the Age of Progress, perhaps the vision shared by poets is as true as any scientific theory. Perhaps, also, if the modern vision of "terrible beauty" compares with the greatest human visions of the past, the expression of that vision in works of high literary merit has made the twentieth century a great age rather than a dark age to live in.

11. Werner Heisenberg, *Physics and Philosophy,* 109.

2

FRENCH SYMBOLISM AND THE ORIGIN OF MODERN POETRY

To have been present at the birth of modern poetry, one would have had to be living in Paris in 1857, when Charles Baudelaire published *Les Fleurs du mal*—and was immediately prosecuted for obscenity and forced to remove some of the more shocking poems. The official censors clearly disapproved of this new poetry, but many writers greeted it as did Victor Hugo, who wrote approvingly to Baudelaire, "Monsieur, vous créez un frisson nouveau" ["Sir, you give us a new thrill"]. It was not until the next century that T. S. Eliot would offer the ultimate tribute: "Baudelaire is indeed the greatest exemplar of *modern* poetry in any language, for his verse and language is the nearest thing to a complete renovation that we have experienced."[1]

Les Fleurs du mal was indeed the first book of modern poetry. It scandalized the reading public of that day quite as much as Eliot's *Waste Land* scandalized a later generation, in 1922, and for many of the same reasons. Both Baudelaire's book and Eliot's long poem contained descriptions of modern life that were repugnant to any reader's sense of decency. They reflected the people's general boredom with life, the pursuit of novelty for its own sake, the sordidness of urban scenes, and the perversity of human behavior. But worst of all, to readers of refined sensibility, they implied that men and women were somehow responsible for the ugliness that surrounded them, that they were involved inescapably in a common human guilt. Not just *some* men and women, not an abstraction such as "Society," but everyone alive:

1. T. S. Eliot, "Baudelaire," in *Selected Essays*, 377. The sentence from Hugo is well enough known to French readers to be quoted under the word *frisson* in *Le Petit Robert* dictionary, by Paul Robert (Paris: Société du Nouveau Littré, 1969), 750.

> Tu le connais, lecteur, ce monstre délicat,
> —Hypocrite lecteur,—mon semblable,—mon frère!
>
> [You know him, reader, this delicate monster,
> —Hypocritical reader—my likeness—my brother!]

These lines accosted the reader from the first poem in Baudelaire's book, "Au Lecteur" ["To the Reader"], and they accosted him again, in an altered context, at the end of the opening section of Eliot's *Waste Land:*

> "That corpse you planted last year in your garden,
> "Has it begun to sprout? Will it bloom this year?
> "Or has the sudden frost disturbed its bed?
> "O keep the Dog far hence, that's friend to men,
> "Or with his nails he'll dig it up again!
> "You! hypocrite lecteur!—mon semblable,—mon frère!"

When Eliot called Baudelaire "the greatest exemplar of *modern* poetry in any language," he was not thinking primarily of the shock the poems produced, but of the fact that "actually Baudelaire is concerned, not with demons, black masses, and romantic blasphemy, but with the real problem of good and evil."[2] However decadent—some even called it satanic—Baudelaire's poetry may have appeared at first glance, its lasting effect was to convince readers of the reality of evil in the human heart, the certitude of human guilt. This effect, coming in the midst of a Romantic age when men were desperately seeking to convince themselves of the natural goodness of man, was salutary, and for it Baudelaire was publicly prosecuted by the indignant French bourgeoisie but elevated at the same time almost to sainthood by the French poets who followed him—the *poètes maudits* [damned poets], as they were called by Verlaine, who founded the symbolist school in Paris in about 1880.

It was not for his moral perception alone that Baudelaire was admired: to the practicing poet, that was less important than his technical achievement. To the poets who started the symbolist school in the 1880s, especially to their presiding genius, Stéphane Mallarmé, Baudelaire had been the discoverer of new poetic laws. They were drawn toward the richness of his language, with its complex metaphors and its sudden ironies, its powerful sensuality that seemed to spring from a source deeper than the senses. In particular, they centered their attention on his famous sonnet "Correspondences," where

---

2. Eliot, "Baudelaire," in *Selected Essays,* 378.

> L'homme y passe à travers des forêts de symboles
> Qui l'observent avec des regards familiers.
>
> [Man wanders there through forests of symbols
> Which observe him with insinuating eyes.]

The very word *symbolist* may have originated in these lines, for they imply that symbolic meaning lies hidden within every common object. Moreover, as the poem develops its theme with increasing sonority and eloquence, the symbolic power of words becomes an extension of the senses into a realm where

> Les parfums, les couleurs et les sons se répondent.
>
> [Odors, colors, and sounds correspond.]

It is through the correspondence of different sense experiences that the symbolic meaning of poetry is released, and ordinary language becomes resonant with the divine harmony of the universe:

> Comme l'ambre, le musc, le benjoin et l'encens,
> Qui chantent les transports de l'esprit et des sens.
>
> [Like amber, musk, benjamin, incense,
> Which sing the transports of the soul and the sense.]

The doctrine of symbolism contained in this poem has been called *synesthesia,* "the harmony or equilibrium of sensations,"[3] but whatever name may be given to it, it is a doctrine illustrated in all French symbolist poetry. What made this poetry "symbolist" rather than simply "symbolic" was the deliberate juxtaposition of things, or sensations, or words not normally associated with each other to create an initially jarring effect like certain metaphors of the English metaphysical poets, but not to expound them by rational argument, as the metaphysical poets often did. Rimbaud, for example, wrote a long poem about a "drunken boat" and a sonnet in which he described the colors of vowels; Mallarmé wrote an astonishing visionary poem about "a throw of the dice," and Laforgue wrote a series of tragicomic "Complaints," including "A Complaint of the Moon" and "A Complaint of the Pianos Heard in the

---

3. I. A. Richards and C. K. Ogden, *The Foundations of Aesthetics.* For a discussion of the doctrine of *synesthesia,* see chap. 14.

Better Neighborhoods." These were not spoofs, but serious, indeed brilliant, poems, proving that poetic imagination was capable of synthesizing the most disparate materials of experience into meaningful combinations. Freedom of imagination was a symbolist prerogative, and Rimbaud—the youngest and brashest of them all, who gave up poetry entirely at the age of nineteen— even spoke of attempting "a rational disordering of the senses," with the aim of arriving at the beginning of all creation and recovering the primal spontaneity of God.

He did not succeed, needless to say, but the very audacity with which he used his imagination was a symbolist influence on all poets that followed. Baudelaire had once spoken of the mission of artists as being none other than to "discover the obscure laws by virtue of which they have created, and to extract from this study a set of precepts whose divine aim is infallibility in poetic creation."[4] Baudelaire cannot be said to have accomplished his aim any more than Rimbaud did, but the symbolists as a school of poets penetrated further into the mysteries of the creative process than any group of poets had ever done before. They were originally impelled to this task, interestingly enough, by Edgar Allan Poe (an American influence on the French symbolists before the French symbolists influenced American poets), who, in a self-analytical essay that Baudelaire himself translated into French, had once tried to show how "The Raven," his best-known poem, "proceeded, step by step, to its completion with the precision and rigid consequence of a mathematical problem."[5] Saying of Poe that he subjected inspiration to method and analysis, Baudelaire held that the artist is best when he both feels and analyzes his feelings, and this was the position the symbolists took throughout their movement. It was perhaps Mallarmé, and later Valéry, who carried critical intelligence farthest into poetry, seeking by indirect suggestion rather than by direct statement to produce a sense of ambiguity, like a faintly traced outline, to lead readers to experience what Mallarmé called "cette joie délicieuse de croire qu'ils créent" ["the delicious joy of believing that they are creating"].[6] All the Symbolists sought in some way to make the creative process manifest in their poetry so that the reader might share in it and derive a new and more intimate satisfaction from poetry.

The French symbolists, then, became the first modern poets by providing a new theory and practice of poetry, which included as principal elements: 1) a moral perception of the prevalence of evil in modern urban life, the poet assuming the role of fallen man, called by Jules Laforgue "the ordinary lost soul of the capital"; 2) a technical ability to bring beauty out of ugliness by

---

4. Charles Baudelaire, *The Mirror of Art: Critical Studies*, x.
5. Edgar Allan Poe, "The Philosophy of Composition," in *The Portable Edgar Allan Poe*, 552.
6. Stéphane Mallarmé, "Sur l'évolution littéraire," quoted in *Mallarmé: Pages choisies*, 10.

resolving the repugnant surface complexity of modern experience into inner harmonies of poetic language; and 3) an aesthetic urge to lay bare the mysteries of poetic creation within the poem itself. The combined effect of these qualities was little short of earthshaking, for it brought poetry to a new stage of self-consciousness. As one French critic summed it up: "The moment arrives, in the course of the 19th Century, when poetry begins to take consciousness of itself as poetry. . . . I believe that what has happened to French poetry since Baudelaire has a historical importance equal in the domain of art to that of the greatest epochs of revolution and renewal of physics and astronomy in the domain of science."[7]

Thus, Baudelaire began a new kind of poetry, and modernism was the eventual result of it. The poetic tradition of symbolism that stems from Baudelaire has been transmitted into the poetry of all major European languages—not only the French, through the work of Verlaine, Rimbaud, Mallarmé, and Valéry, but also the German, especially through the work of Rainer Maria Rilke; the Russian, through the work of Boris Pasternak and others; and the English, through a variety of accents: the Irish of William Butler Yeats, the Welsh of Dylan Thomas, and the American of Wallace Stevens and Hart Crane, not to mention the Anglo-American of Ezra Pound and T. S. Eliot.

It was Eliot who gave the most credit to the symbolist influence on modern poetry, when he declared that

> in the second half of the nineteenth century the greatest contribution to European poetry was certainly made in France. I refer to the tradition which starts with Baudelaire, and culminates in Paul Valéry. I venture to say that without this French tradition the work of three poets in other languages—and three very different from each other—I refer to W. B. Yeats, to Rainer Maria Rilke, and if I may, to myself—would hardly be conceivable.[8]

Modern poetry thus has been as international as the age in which it was created, and the call that Ezra Pound issued early in the century for a new European renaissance was answered, especially in poetry. At least one critic, Georges Poulet, in his *Studies in Human Time,* has claimed for Baudelaire that

> Just as the discovery of Copernicus changed the aspect of the cosmic universe, so the final thought of Baudelaire reversed the aspect of the interior world. It becomes a world without fixed relationships; a world essentially transitory; a world of contingencies in which the creature watches himself pass from

---

7. Jacques Maritain, *The Situation of Poetry,* 42.
8. T. S. Eliot, *Notes towards the Definition of Culture,* 115.

the grotesque to the sublime, from ecstasy to debauchery, from fatigue to
drunkenness, from corruption to salvation.[9]

Such a complicated state of self-consciousness is precarious and difficult to
maintain for any length of time, of course, since it contains destructive as
well as creative possibilities. Poetry expressing such a consciousness must be
sophisticated and complex, plumbing the depths as well as the heights of inner
experience. Beginning with Baudelaire and the French symbolists, poets have
envisioned man as a polarity of opposites from the sublime to the ridiculous,
with the poet himself as the ironic or tragic hero of his poem.

An additional consequence of French symbolist experiments with poetic
technique was the perception that a given language might be inadequate to
express the invisible reality of things, the hidden harmony of the universe.
Hence French poets often used foreign words in their poetry: Baudelaire
liked the English word *spleen* better than any French equivalent for anger,
and Gérard de Nerval used a Spanish title for his most famous sonnet, "El
Desdichado" ["The Luckless One"]; Mallarmé used the English word *steamer*
in his poem "Brise marine" ["Sea Breeze"], and Laforgue wrote of "albums" in
which he could find pictures of the Wild West. Similarly, Pound's use of many
foreign tongues in *Hugh Selwyn Mauberley* or the *Cantos,* or Eliot's mingling
of other languages with English in *The Waste Land,* implies that there is more
to be expressed than one language can convey. The invention of new words
by a poet signifies that ordinary language is inadequate for his purpose, the
poet's duty being always, as Eliot once put it, "to his *language.*" According to
Eliot, "the structure, the rhythm, the sound, the idiom of a language, express
the personality of the people who speak it," thus "making people more aware
of what they feel."[10] Whether a poet uses foreign words or invents new words,
he is stretching the range of articulated experience, the known territory of the
mind, but he is at the same time demonstrating how experience continually
outruns the capacity of language to express meaning, showing that there are
mental frontiers that have to be crossed again and again in the effort to extend
human consciousness, but that ultimately silence exceeds speech, because the
unknown always outreaches the known.

If the modern age is an age of extreme verbalism, then, it is also an age
of extreme reticence, a time when writers have attempted to express the
inexpressible, and have proved that it is, after all, impossible to say everything.
Perhaps one of the final lessons of modern literature is that silence sometimes
speaks louder than words, for one result of the radical experiments with

9. Georges Poulet, *Studies in Human Time,* 277–78.
10. Eliot, "The Social Function of Poetry," in *On Poets and Poetry,* 8–9.

words has been to show that the amount of implied meaning contained in a poem, even the spaces around the words, which Mallarmé called "the white spaces" on a page, may be as important as the words themselves. And it does seem that the very effort to compress more and more meaning into words produces large areas of white space surrounding very little black space, making us aware as we read of the silences between the sounds. The elliptical technique of fiction, leaving deliberate gaps in the narrative, has its equivalent in the imagist technique in poetry, which creates a mosaic of separate and discrete fragments that hang together without transitions, in apparent disjunction but implicit unity, or sometimes simply lets the words speak of the silence beyond them, as in "The White Horse," by D. H. Lawrence:

> The youth walks up to the white horse, to put its halter on
> and the horse looks at him in silence.
> They are so silent they are in another world.

The origin of the theory that language can speak through silence comes from the French symbolists, who used words much as the impressionist painters used color, creating a discontinuous surface with an underlying unity, thus leaving the missing link between sensed experiences to be furnished by the imagination of the viewer or reader, whose participation in the work of art produces in the minds of readers what Mallarmé spoke of as "the delicious joy of believing that they are creating." It was Mallarmé who, in "Un Coup de dés" ["A Throw of the Dice"], projected words into empty space, dramatizing the gaps between words that signify the unknown territory beyond speech, Pascal's "eternal silence of the infinite spaces," and it was also Mallarmé who conceived of the poet as "musician of silences" in his short poem "Saint":

> At the window ledge concealing
> The ancient sandalwood gold-flaking
> Of her viol dimly twinkling
> Long ago with flute or mandore
>
> Stands the pallid Saint displaying
> The ancient missal page unfolding
> At the Magnificat outpouring
> Long ago for vesper and compline:
>
> At that monstrance glazing lightly
> Brushed now by a harp the Angel
> Fashioned in his evening flight
> Just for the delicate finger

Tip which, lacking the ancient missal
Or ancient sandalwood, she poises
On the instrumental plumage,
Musician of silences.
(translated by Hubert Creekmore)[11]

We are not told the name of the "pallid Saint" in this poem, but since she is playing a musical instrument, we may guess that it is Saint Lucy, the patron saint of musicians, and since we know that Mallarmé, like Walter Pater, placed music highest among the arts (and Pater wrote that "all art constantly aspires towards the condition of music"), we can assume that he is asking her to bless poets as she has musicians, and that he is praying to her to give him the harp of the angel, as depicted in the medieval illuminated manuscript of the Magnificat, or Hymn to the Virgin Mary, which she appears to be holding up to the eye of the reader, so that the poet, like her, may become the "musicien du silence," or "musician of silence." Knowing that Mallarmé was a disciple of Baudelaire, who placed the sonnet "Correspondences" at the center of his symbolist poetics, we can take the poem to be an expression of the poet's ambition to echo in the music of his poem the corresponding unheard music of the angels—a silence pregnant with sound.

Mallarmé's disciple, Paul Valéry, the last great French symbolist, performed a variation on this theme in his poem "Le Bois amical" ["The Friendly Wood"]:

Meditations pure were ours
Side by side, along the ways;
We held each other's hand without
Speaking, among the hidden flowers.

Alone we walked as if betrothed,
Lost in the green night of the fields;
We shared this fruit of fairy reels,
The moon, to madmen well disposed.

And then, we were dead upon the moss,
Far, quite alone, among the soft
Shades of this intimate, murmuring wood;

And there, in the vast light aloft,
We found ourselves with many a tear,

11. *An Anthology of French Poetry from Nerval to Valéry in English Translation*, ed. Angel Flores (New York: Doubleday Anchor, 1958), 151.

> O my companion of silence dear!
> (translated by Vernon Watkins)[12]

Again, we are not given the identity of the female figure in the poem, but we assume that she and the poet are in love "as if betrothed," and that they are both in communion with nature, inside "this intimate, murmuring wood," but what passes between them is a wordless communication that is sad, because they are mortal, "dead upon the moss," but also sweet, because they become "companions of silence" in the wood, "dear" to each other through what they share silently, which spoken words would only violate and disenchant. Valéry once said that poetry attempts to express in words what sighs, kisses, and tears express bodily, that is, the strongest human emotions, and in "The Friendly Wood" he implies that the deepest feelings of love are conveyed speechlessly, as the lovers hold hands in the dark silence of a forest at night, where even the flowers are "hidden" and the light of the moon above them barely illuminates "the green night of the fields." The only sound is that of the "murmuring wood," which appears, with its faintly rustling leaves, to be drawing the two "companions of silence" together, much as the angel in Mallarmé's poem is the "musician of silence" to the listening poet. Each of these characteristic French symbolist poems seems to make the silence speak, though the message is imagined as wordless in itself—an unheard music, or an unspoken love.

Among the chief inheritors of symbolism outside of France were Yeats and Rilke, and the poems of both the Irish and the German poet are full of this language of silence. One of Yeats's shortest and most memorable poems, in fact, is called "After Long Silence":

> Speech after long silence; it is right
> All other lovers being estranged or dead,
> Unfriendly lamplight hid under its shade,
> The curtains drawn upon unfriendly night,
> That we descant and yet again descant
> Upon the supreme theme of Art and Song:
> Bodily decrepitude is wisdom; young
> We loved each other and were ignorant.

The silence here, as in Valéry's poem, is between lovers, but lovers who have long ago parted and who now, grown old, meet each other again: the silence thus comes out of the memory of past love, not out of a dark wood. What brings them together, it seems, is the departure of those they have loved, either by estrangement or by death, and they find themselves in touch this time, not

12. Ibid., 271–72.

through love, but through "bodily decrepitude"—that curse of old age, which Yeats railed against so vehemently in his later poems, but which here he views with surprising calm, because it has conferred upon the two aging lovers a wisdom they never had when they were young and passionately in love. After long silence, they are able to speak, and they do so gladly—"That we descant and yet again descant" conveys both a delight in their conversation and a certain musical counterpoint in what they say, as if they were performing something like a Bach fugue on "the supreme theme of Art and Song." The theme itself is moving and tragic—wisdom is the compensation for the kind of love they have lost with age, and though they would not trade this wisdom for the ignorance of youthful passion, they are aware of what they have lost as well as what they have gained in trading the wisdom of age for the passion of young love. The poem has a bittersweet quality that is both anguishing and consoling, and the silence is as eloquent as the speech.

There is silence everywhere in Rilke's poetry, early and late, and he often seems to speak out of a deep well of solitude in which the voices he hears are not human voices but the voices of the angels, as in his *Duino Elegies,* or the voice of the semi-divine poet Orpheus in his *Sonnets to Orpheus,* but nowhere is the silence more eloquent than in his early poem about "the singing of things," where the voices come from those mute objects of the physical world that have no human language and that only a very attentive listener can hear:

> I'm so much afraid of the words of men,
> for people say with the gravest sound
> that here is a House, and there is a Hound,
> and here is Beginning, and there is the End.
>
> I'm afraid of their wit, of their smiles and nods;
> they know all things, what was and will be;
> a mountain to them isn't heavenly;
> the grass in their gardens grows greener than God's!
>
> I will keep them away; I will say: let me be.
> I so love to hear the singing of things.
> And they interfere; to them, nothing sings.
> These people murder all things for me.
>   (my translation)

Rilke is expressing a fear that human words not only may fail to convey meaning, but can actually destroy it, because men become so preoccupied with themselves, with the purely human realm of experience, that they are insensitive to the nonhuman creatures around them and thus are unaware of the wholeness of being that exists in silence outside the range of human consciousness. Much of Rilke's poetry is concerned with animals and flowers and other natural objects whose existence is threatened by men's tendency either to ignore them or to convert them to human uses and so to desecrate them. No modern poet has entered more feelingly into the nonhuman realm than Rilke, who could write about a caged panther in the Jardins des Plantes in Paris as if he were actually inside the skin of the beast, or could make the wooden animals on the carousel in the Luxembourg Gardens seem more alive than the children who rode on them, or could take up the lyre of Orpheus and draw all the wild creatures of the forest to him—including in his late poems even a mythological animal, the unicorn, whose existence depends entirely on the imagination of those who believe in it.

Rilke sang of the *Weltinnenraum*, the inner space of the world, where death and life are intertwined, and where the invisible gives meaning to the visible. These dramatic moments of silent communication and mystical union are among the profoundest expressions in modern poetry, as they have been in the great poetry of the past, and they can be found in abundance in the twentieth century. I have mentioned Eliot and Pound, Mallarmé and Valéry, Yeats and Rilke and D. H. Lawrence, and there are others whose poetry contains these dramatic moments when the language of silence eloquently speaks. I think, for instance, of the love poem by E. E. Cummings that begins:

> somewhere i have never traveled, gladly beyond
> any experience, your eyes have their silence

and ends:

> the voice of your eyes is deeper than all roses)
> nobody, not even the rain, has such small hands

And I think of Hart Crane's final poem, "The Broken Tower," with its concluding image of a tower within the heart that will replace the broken towers of the world:

> And builds, within, a tower that is not stone
> (Not stone can jacket heaven)—but slip
> Of pebbles—visible wings of silence sown
> In azure circles, widening as they dip
>
> The matrix of the heart, lift down the eye
> That shrines the quiet lake and swells a tower . . .
> The commodious, tall decorum of that sky
> Unseals her earth, and lifts love in its shower.

The silence in the eyes, or the visible wings of silence in the heart, are expressions of a love that transcends words, even though the words are a mirror, like the legendary mirror in which the lady sees the unicorn. Or I think of Allen Tate's fine late poem, "The Swimmers," an autobiographical poem about his horrified witness, as a young boy, of the lynching of a black man in Kentucky, which ends:

> Alone in the public clearing
> This private thing was owned by all the town,
> Though never claimed by us within my hearing.

The dramatic moment of silence here is a communication of unspoken guilt, linking the people of a small town together in a shame that they were too humiliated to utter, but that is remembered by them in later years beyond anything that was spoken at the time. And there is a similar moment of unspoken guilt in Robert Penn Warren's poem "The Ballad of Billie Potts," which also tells a horrifying tale, of a son who is murdered by his parents without their knowing who he is, until the moment of silent recognition comes between them:

> And so they sit and breathe and wait
> And breathe while the night gets big and late
> And neither of them gives move or stir
> And she won't look at him and he won't look at her.

Guilt and fear can be emotions as powerful as love, and they, too, must often be expressed wordlessly because speech would not be adequate for such a sense of supernatural terror, brought on by the unmentioned but harrowing thought of eternal damnation.

These examples could be multiplied, but in the poetry of the twentieth century silence is often more eloquent than speech at the dramatic moment when tongues are tied by overpowering emotion. If the French symbolists invented silence as a form of speech, they also invented free verse. Just as poetic imagery becomes conventionalized, and needs to be refreshed with new metaphors, so does poetic meter, and there is a need in each age for a renewal of form as well as of meaning. In English poetry, the iambic-pentameter line was a fresh innovation in Shakespeare's day but had by the late nineteenth century lost most of its vitality. Then the French symbolists began experimenting with free verse with brilliant success, as in the lyrics of Verlaine and the "Complaints" of Laforgue, and in time they demonstrated that an irregular and shifting rhythm is best suited to the description of inner impressions and moods. As Verlaine theorized in "The Art of Poetry," there was a need to "moderate Rhyme a little more," and to try for

> Music, always more music!
> Let your verse be the winged thing
> We feel soaring from a soul on its way
> To other loves in other heavens.

Like Debussy's preludes, often based on symbolist poems, the lyrics of Verlaine and Mallarmé change as swiftly and unpredictably in their rhythm as does the mind itself. Pound would go on in his imagist phase to advise poets to "compose in the sequence of the musical phrase, not in sequence of a metronome," much as Verlaine advised in "The Art of Poetry." The theory was one of *organic form* in poetry, more difficult to practice than any regular meter, for as T. E. Hulme pointed out, "It is a delicate and difficult art, that of evoking an image, of fitting the rhythm to the idea, and one is tempted to fall back into the comforting and easy arms of the old, regular metre, which takes away all the trouble for us." Hulme said that though he searched for models in English poetry—and he, like Pound and other imagist poets, was well aware of Walt Whitman's example—he was unable to find the right rhythm for his poetic images "until I came to read the French *vers-libre* which seemed to exactly fit the case."[13] Hulme, whom Eliot credited with writing "two or three of the most beautiful poems in the language," made excellent use of free verse in his imagist poems, including "The Poet," which portrays the poet at work:

> Over a large table, smooth, he leaned in ecstasies
> In a dream.
> He had been to woods, and talked and walked with trees.
> Had left the world
> And brought back round globes and stone images,
> Of gems, colors, hard and definite.
> With these he played, in a dream
> On the smooth table.

The poet as Hulme sees him finds his symbols in mineral nature, as Baudelaire found his in "forests of symbols," and he contemplates their shapes, colors, and textures until he makes them into mental images that mirror the elemental beauty of nature, so that he can play with them in his dreams, the

---

13. T. E. Hulme, "A Lecture on Modern Poetry" (first given to the Poets Club in London in 1908 or 1909), published in London in 1938; reprinted in Hulme, *Further Speculations,* 74, 68.

outer material world becoming through verbal mediation the inner world of thought.

One way to understand the continuity between French symbolism and Anglo-American imagism is as a regeneration of poetic language, first in French and later in English. Both seem to have started with the intuition that, as Hulme put it, modern art "no longer deals with heroic action, it has become definitely and finally introspective, and deals with expression and communication of momentary phases in the poet's mind."[14] What the symbolists meant by *symbol* is very much like what the imagists meant by *image,* except that with the latter the subject was briefer in duration and "harder," or more concrete, in expression. Both schools acknowledged the duality of human experience, and both tried to make contact by means of words with an invisible reality beyond visible appearances. The main difference between their achievements was that while the symbolists moved in the direction of the "pure poem" and the language of silence, risking more and more subjective expression, the imagists moved in the direction of realism and concreteness, toward more objective expression. The chief principle guiding the imagists was that "images in verse are not mere decoration, but the very essence of an intuitive language,"[15] and so they relied on the expressive power of things seen, rather than on the suggestive power of things unseen, as favored by the symbolists.

To say that the main influence of the French symbolists on English poetry came through the imagists is to consider imagism as a movement that did not end in 1917, when the third and last of Amy Lowell's *Some Imagist Poets* appeared, but that carried on into a second stage under the leadership of T. S. Eliot and the further work of the Fugitives. For it was Eliot's poetry, more than any other's, which increased the symbolist influence on English and American poetry and at the same time broadened the dimensions of imagism into the ironic and metaphysical. It may be said that until Eliot began publishing his poems, there was no explicitly religious attitude in imagism, whereas after his work had made its impression, this attitude became more and more explicit—particularly after 1922, when *The Waste Land* exploded like a time bomb on postwar Europe and America. The effect of this one poem by Eliot on all the poetry that followed has been inestimable, and surely Pound did not exaggerate in hailing it as "the justification of the modern movement in poetry." *The Waste Land* may well be seen as the point at which the symbolist and imagist movements converged, for it is a poem constructed almost entirely out of images, connected not by plot but by an underlying

14. Ibid., 72.
15. T. E. Hulme, "Romanticism and Classicism," in *Further Speculations,* 135.

myth that gives the whole poem its powerful symbolic force. No poem of the symbolists, and certainly no poem of the imagists before this one, carried such an overwhelming load of implied meaning. The multiple ambiguities and ironies of the poem place it squarely within the symbolist tradition, while the economy and concreteness of the language—greatly increased by Ezra Pound's editing of it—show the full effect of imagist concentration. Insofar as *The Waste Land* stands at the center of modern poetry in all languages, and there is much evidence that it does, it is the best witness to the continuity between French symbolism and Anglo-American imagism.

3

HOPKINS'S *INSCAPE* AND RILKE'S *WELTINNENRAUM*

"But there is more peace, and it is the holier lot, to be unknown than to be known," Gerard Manley Hopkins once wrote,[1] and he often communicated his preference for anonymity to his friend Robert Bridges, his classmate at Oxford who later became poet laureate of England. By a strange irony of literary history, Bridges is now better known as the editor of Hopkins's poetry, which he brought out of obscurity and published in 1918, than as a poet in his own right. But at the time Hopkins wrote to him, Bridges was publicly identified as a poet, while Hopkins's only public role was as a Roman Catholic priest, and, later, as professor of classics at University College Dublin: Hopkins was never known in his lifetime as a poet. The choice was partly his own, though he had tried to have some poems published, without success; his poetry was of a singularity that his friend Bridges liked but deplored, and it could be said that Hopkins, like his American contemporary Emily Dickinson, was too original for his time.

It seems evident to us that Hopkins was very much in advance of his time, a truly modern poet though he lived in the Victorian age of Tennyson and Browning, when the poetry of his friend Bridges was much more acceptable than his. Now Bridges appears to be a faded late Victorian, at best, without even the staying power of Swinburne, while Hopkins is one of the most original poets ever to write in the English language. If Hopkins had any real contemporaries, they were the French symbolists rather than the English Victorians, for his poetry is full of the sort of verbal and rhythmic invention

---

1. Gerard Manley Hopkins to R. W. Dixon, October 29, 1881, quoted in Hopkins, *The Oxford Authors: Gerard Manley Hopkins*, 249.

that made the French symbolists the first school of modern poets, and his creation of "inscape" and "sprung rhythm" are permanent additions to the vocabulary essential to understanding poetry—not just Hopkins's poetry. Furthermore, Hopkins created poems that are symbolist in nature, syntactically complex and dense with ambiguity and irony, making them difficult to paraphrase or even to comprehend. As he wrote once in a letter, responding to criticism of his obscurity as a poet: "Plainly if it is possible to express a subtle and recondite thought on a subtle and recondite subject in a subtle and recondite way, and with great felicity and perfection, in the end, something must be sacrificed . . . and this may be the being at once . . . intelligible." Hopkins might well be called an English symbolist, though since he anticipated the later imagists—his notion of "inscape" being a forerunner of the image and his notion of "sprung rhythm" a precursor of free verse—his true position may best be seen as somewhere between the symbolists and the imagists, a position he may be said to share with just one other major modern poet, the German Rainer Maria Rilke. Hopkins of course knew nothing of either symbolism or imagism, since both came after him, but he anticipated them by incorporating symbolist as well as imagist principles in his poetry, and he would probably have agreed with something Ezra Pound later said: "To break the pentameter, that was the first heave" (Canto 81). Pound was talking about the direction that he and other imagists took in experimenting with English verse form in the early twentieth century; Hopkins, in the late nineteenth century, was the first poet after Whitman to depart from strict pentameter, and his tightly controlled "sprung rhythm" bore more resemblance to the imagists' kind of free verse than to Whitman's long, loose lines.

Hopkins knowingly, indeed stubbornly, cultivated the technical ingenuity criticized by his friends and fellow poets Bridges and Coventry Patmore (another late Victorian poet whom he knew at Oxford), and if he felt condemned to poetic obscurity, he consciously courted the condition that led him to write in virtual isolation. His most original terms, *inscape* and *sprung rhythm*, apt for the poetry he was writing, separated him from other poets, and he deliberately—one might even say defiantly—went on with his experiments in the face of strong criticism. As he wrote to Bridges in 1879, four years after finishing his first great stylistic triumph, "The Wreck of the Deutschland," and after giving up his vain search for an editor who would publish it:

> No doubt my poetry errs on the side of oddness. . . . But as air, melody, is what strikes me most of all in music and design in painting, so design, pattern, or what I am in the habit of calling *inscape* is what I above all aim at in poetry. Now it is the virtue of design, pattern, or inscape to be

distinctive and it is the vice of distinctiveness to become queer. This vice I cannot have escaped.[2]

Such an assertion on Hopkins's part may sound like the typical eccentric English individualist who insists on having his own way regardless of what others think of him, yet he was really a highly principled individualist who regarded poetry as the expression of a distinctive identity in every created being or thing. Here again, he differed from Whitman's kind of American individualism, which was both egotistical and nationalistic in its aggressive self-assertion, for Hopkins believed that his innovations were not simple self-expression but a fulfillment of the will of God that everything be itself and not anything else. Hopkins's inscape was a consciousness not simply of his own uniqueness, but of the uniqueness of everything in the universe, animate or inanimate.

Certainly the most important event in Hopkins's short life of forty-five years was his conversion to Roman Catholicism in 1866, the year before he graduated from Oxford. He had been a fairly conventional Anglican until that time, like the rest of his family, and it was a great and permanent shock to them when he was received into the Roman church by none other than John Henry Cardinal Newman, whose Oxford Movement had so much affected Hopkins as a classical scholar that he decided to defy the family and become a Catholic, following the same course of faith that Newman himself had followed, from nominal Protestant to devout Catholic. Thus Hopkins's choice even as a student led to his first painful isolation, from his own family. His later choices to become a priest and teacher publicly, and a poet only privately, were made with the full consciousness that he had defied his family already and so isolated himself, in his vocation as well as his avocation, for the remainder of his life.

Probably Hopkins's lonely career as a poet of radical originality stems from the earlier decisions he made; but certainly his theory of poetry depended on his understanding of Christian faith, as unorthodox in its way as his poetry. Hopkins's unconventionality was so ingrained in his life and character by the time he began writing poetry seriously again in 1875 (he had burned all his earlier poems as an act of self-sacrifice when he entered the Jesuit order in 1867) that it could almost be said he could not help being original.

Hopkins himself, however, felt that his departures from convention were consistent with Christian doctrine, as he understood it. He took as his master teacher not Newman, whom Hopkins knew and respected as an eminent Victorian thinker and religious poet, but the medieval philosopher Duns

2. Notes to *The Poems of Gerard Manley Hopkins,* 240.

Scotus, called "the subtle doctor" for his divergence from the more orthodox medieval Catholic philosopher Thomas Aquinas. Hopkins was especially
drawn to the teaching of Duns Scotus that the soul of man and of all created
things is revealed in its *haeccitas,* or "thisness," which makes it one of a kind
and distinguishes it from every other creature of God. We find in Hopkins's
writings a number of affirmations of his principle that "inscape is the very
soul of art," connected in his mind with the belief that each poem should
be as distinctively individual as each creature, and that Scotus's *haeccitas*
applied to human creations as well as divine creation. Thus his understanding
of Christian faith and his understanding of poetry were both linked to the
existential principle that what men are and what they do are the same, so that
to be oneself and to act according to one's nature is to be what God intended
each of us to be. He expressed this understanding in his prose writings as well
as in his poetry, saying once in prose:

> . . . when I consider my selfbeing, my consciousness and feeling of myself,
> that taste of myself, of *I* and *me* above and in all things, which is more
> distinctive than the taste of ale or alum, more distinctive than the smell of
> walnutleaf or camphor, and is incommunicable by any means to another
> man . . . Nothing else in nature comes near this unspeakable stress of pitch,
> distinctiveness, and selving, this selfbeing of my own. . . . searching nature I
> taste *self* but at one tankard, that of my own being.[3]

In his poetry, the equivalent expression may be found in one of his best-
known—though untitled—sprung-rhythm sonnets:

> As kingfishers catch fire, dragonflies draw flame;
>   As tumbled over rim in roundy wells
>   Stones ring; like each tucked string tells, each hung bell's
> Bow swung finds tongue to fling out broad its name;
> Each mortal thing does one thing and the same:
>   Deals out that being indoors each one dwells;
>   Selves—goes itself; *myself* it speaks and spells,
> Crying *What I do is me: for that I came.*
>
> I say more: the just man justices;
>   Keeps grace: that keeps all his goings graces;
> Acts in God's eye what in God's eye he is—
>   Christ. For Christ plays in ten thousand places,

---

3. "Spiritual Exercises," in *Sermons and Devotional Writings of Gerard Manley Hopkins,*
reprinted in Hopkins, *The Oxford Authors: Gerard Manley Hopkins,* 282.

Lovely in limbs, and lovely in eyes not his
To the Father through the features of men's faces.

This poem embodies *inscape* more explicitly than his other sonnets, for instead of expressing a single intuition of individuality, as in the autumn landscape of "Hurrahing in Harvest" or the kestrel riding the air in "The Windhover," Hopkins perceives multiple incarnations as he watches, first, the kingfisher diving for fish—changing "fish" to the near-rhyme "fire" to stress the light flashing from the bird rather than its downward motion—then the dragonfly gliding over water—"drawing flame" again emphasizes the quality of light emitted by the winged insect in its horizontal flight—then the ringing of a stone as it strikes the walls of a well, the plucking of a stringed instrument, and the swinging of the clapper inside a bell as it sounds its note. All of these manifestations of individuality in nature are summed up in the selfhood of each creature and thematically distilled into the italicized but irregular phrase "*What I do is me*" ("I am what I do" would be a more normal way of expressing that thought). Hopkins's ingenuity in making a verbal phrase— "What I do"—equal a pronoun—"me"—is no greater than his ingenuity in making each of the earlier "inscapes" a consonantal rhyme between noun or adjective and verb: the *kingf*isher *c*atches *f*ire, the *dragonfly draws flame*, the stones *r*ing in *r*oundy wells, the *t*ucked string *t*ells, and the h*ung* b*e*ll's *b*ow sw*ung* can "fling out broad its name"—in other words, the action of each thing in nature, both animate and inanimate, *names* the thing, or writes its signature and establishes its identity. All of this rush of activity happens within the octave of an Italian sonnet, leading in the sestet to Hopkins's concentration on human "inscapes"—the noun-and-verb combinations of "the just man" who "justices" and the graceful man who "keeps grace" by making "all his goings graces." The full meaning of inscape is reserved for the end of the sonnet, where it becomes a manifestation of God's will that everyone and everything in the universe should have its own name and its own self, and that the word *Christ* should stand for all creation. Hopkins is hereby asserting his faith in the doctrine of Incarnation, that "the Word became flesh and dwelt among us, full of grace and light," just as he had read it in the beginning of the Gospel according to St. John.

Hopkins's belief in Incarnation is translated into the inscapes of his individual poems by means of his second original invention, "sprung rhythm." Essentially, Hopkins wanted every poem to have its own rhythmical as well as visual inscape, making it distinct from every other poem, as created things are distinct from each other. Hopkins had been called the "Star of Balliol" by Benjamin Jowett, the revered teacher and translator of Greek at Oxford, and he knew classical poetry thoroughly, so that it was his independent judgment of English poetry that most of it up to his time had been written in what he called "running rhythm," that is, in the normal metrical pattern of English verse. Hopkins, like Whitman before him and Pound after him, intuitively felt that enough English poetry had already been written in regular meters, and that it was time for a new departure in rhythm. But whereas Whitman used the long, loose cadence of free verse, which owed much to the poetic prose of the King James version of the Bible, and Pound started out by translating from a variety of foreign languages to make new poems in English, Hopkins started with what he thought was already audible in English poetry, in nursery rhymes and in common speech, the "sprung rhythm" that is musical but not metrical, depending on stressed and unstressed syllables that do not form a regular pattern of repeated beats and pauses.

In a long letter to his brother written in 1885, near the end of his life (he died of typhoid fever in Dublin in 1889), Hopkins made what is probably his fullest explication of sprung rhythm, saying in response to a complimentary letter about his poetry:

> I am sweetly soothed by your saying that you cd. make any one understand my poem by reciting it well. That is what I always hoped, thought and said; it is my prime aim.
>
> Every art then and every work of art has its own play or performance. The play or performance of a stage-play is the playing it on the boards, the stage: reading it, much more writing it, is not its performance. . . . Poetry was originally meant either for singing or reciting . . . the true nature of poetry, the darling child of speech, of lips and spoken utterance: it must be spoken; *till it is spoken it is not performed,* it does not perform, is not itself. *Sprung rhythm gives back to poetry its true soul and self. . . . sprung rhythm makes verse stressy;* it purges it to an emphasis as much brighter, livelier, more lustrous than the regular but commonplace emphasis of common rhythm as poetry in general is brighter than common speech. . . . I must however add that to perform it quite satisfactorily is not at all easy, I do not say I could do it; but this is nothing against the truth of the principle maintained. A composer need not be able to play his violin music or sing his songs. Indeed the higher wrought the art, clearly the wider severance between the parts of the author and the performer.
>
> Neither of course do I mean my verse to be recited only. True poetry must be studied. As Shakespeare and all great dramatists have their maximum effect on the stage but bear to be or must be studied at home before or after or both, so I should wish it to be with my lyric poetry.
>
> . . . the natural performance and delivery belonging properly to lyric poetry, which is speech, has not been enough cultivated, and should be. When performers were trained to do it (it needed the rarest gifts) and audiences to appreciate it, it would be, I am persuaded, a lovely art. . . .

With the aid of the phonograph each phrase could be fixed and learnt by heart like a song.[4]

One may judge from this letter that Hopkins wished all his poems to be read aloud, so that the distinctive rhythms he had carefully wrought in them could be heard, and thus it is clear that he understood *sprung rhythm* to mean a more complex and pleasing harmony of sounds than would be possible if he had written his poems in regular meters, or "running rhythm." Saying as he does, "*Sprung rhythm gives back to poetry its true soul and self,*" is very close to saying, "Inscape is the very soul of art," so that, putting them together, one may deduce that Hopkins intended inscape and sprung rhythm to be as closely associated as the content and the form of each poem he wrote. Just as Hulme and Pound would later insist that the image must be matched by free verse in the composition of poems of the imagist type, so Hopkins anticipated their theory of poetry by his own matching of inscape with the appropriate sprung rhythm.

To say how Hopkins made his new rhythmic principle work in his poetry is not easy, because it involves some scansion of his poetry, and scansion, or metrical analysis, is as foreign to readers of poetry in our age as is memorizing poems: we have almost forgotten how to hear a poem with our ears; we see it instead with our eyes, thus leaving out half of the magic of poetry, which consists of a blending of sound and sense, of the visual and the aural properties of words. Hopkins was a word-musician who wrote English with his ears as well as his eyes, and in insisting to his brother, "*Sprung rhythm gives back to poetry its true soul and self,*" he must have meant that making poetry "stressy," as sprung rhythm did, would call attention to its sound; he clearly felt that the sound of English poetry was being heard less and less by readers even in his own lifetime.

To translate a poem like "As kingfishers catch fire, dragonflies draw flame" into sprung rhythm is to recognize first of all that it is outwardly an Italian sonnet, one of the most familiar forms of poetry since the Renaissance, honored by Milton and Wordsworth as well as many other poets in English, and that its standard fourteen lines are divided, like all Italian sonnets, into stanzas of eight lines (the octave) and six lines (the sestet), with the conventional rhyming pattern of *abbaabba cdcdcd*. Where Hopkins departs from the standard form is inwardly, that is, in the variations of rhythm from line to line, and it was his theory that what he called a "sprung" effect was created when an existing rhythm was deliberately countered, usually by adding

---

4. Hopkins to his younger brother, Edward, 1885, published in the *London Times Literary Supplement*, December 8, 1972, p. 1571.

stresses to the line to make it more emphatic or "stressy." The normal meter of the Italian sonnet in English is the same as for the English sonnet, that is, iambic pentameter. Hopkins immediately begins altering this meter as he starts his sonnet, so that even the first line is irregular:

As kíngfishers cátch fíre, drágonflíes dráw fláme

giving eight rather than five stresses to the ear, or octameter rather than pentameter, and the remaining lines are also generally irregular, though there are exceptions, as in the second line:

As túmbled óver rím in róundy wélls

where the normal iambic pentameter is maintained, but after the first line has created a different expectation. Also, this second line runs over into the third line, and the third line into the fourth, by the force of meaning, causing a run-on, or, in Hopkins's vocabulary, a "rove-over" effect:

Stónes ríng; líke éach túcked stríng télls, éach húng béll's

which gives every syllable in the line a stress, making it a ten-beat, or decameter, line (unheard of in English poetry before Hopkins), followed by:

Bów swúng fínds tóngue to flíng out bróad its náme

where there are now seven stresses following the run-on line, leading to a next line of perfectly regular iambic pentameter:

Each mórtal thíng does óne thing ánd the sáme

Thus in the space of five lines, Hopkins has created sprung effects in three of the lines by making them "stressy," and thereby set off the two regular pentameter lines as if they were the variation rather than the norm. Adding to the metrical effects are a number of internal rhymes, the most conspicuous of which are the "chime-rhymes," which Hopkins learned from Welsh poetry. Chime-rhymes are proximate repetitions of a word or phrase, as in "*Selves—*
goes *itself; myself,*" and "*just* man *just*ices," and "Acts *in God's eye* what *in God's eye* he is," and "*Christ.* For *Christ* plays in ten thousand places." The combination of stressy lines and internal chime-rhymes makes Hopkins's Italian sonnet unlike any other that was ever written, and the result of sprung

rhythm in it is to enhance and "instress" (another good Hopkins word) meaning with deliberate sound effects. Since some of Hopkins's finest poems are
sprung-rhythm sonnets, including the miraculous "The Windhover," where
the kestrel's motion of hovering in the air is somehow echoed in the rhythm of
the lines, to demonstrate the effects of sprung rhythm in a single sonnet such
as "As kingfishers catch fire, dragonflies draw flame" is enough to prove the
value of Hopkins's experiments. His somewhat unorthodox Christian or Sco-
tist belief was translated directly into the unorthodox inscapes or incarnations
of his poems, giving his English symbolism an explicit religious reference that
is only vaguely implied in French symbolism. Nonetheless, he was a symbolist
as well as an imagist before his time, by virtue of the concreteness of his
subjectivity, just as was the German poet Rainer Maria Rilke.

     As the soul of a language is its poetry, Rilke is the soul of German poetry.
Any poetry in a foreign language has a certain seductive charm, appealing to
us more immediately sometimes than poetry in our own language, probably
because we are too aware of the impurities in our native tongue—the clichés,
the vulgarities, the profanities of common speech—to be able to read it with
full attention to the poetry in itself, whereas we can do so more readily
in a language not tarnished by daily use. The great value that the study of
Greek and Latin has is that it allows speakers of other languages to acquire
an appreciation of style in its purest form, one of the perennial values of
comparative literature.

     I was smitten by Rilke the first time I read him, although I knew very little
German then; I still know little German, but I know Rilke well enough to risk
translating him into English—and the translations that follow, for better or
for worse, are all mine. "The poem," as Wallace Stevens once said, "reveals
itself only to the ignorant man," meaning there is a pleasure in it that defies
rational analysis, requiring us to be as innocent as children, opening our eyes
to the wonders contained in words while their meaning filters through as
best it can. T. S. Eliot had this elemental fact about poetry in mind when
he wrote, in *The Use of Poetry and the Use of Criticism,* that the meaning of
a poem is only a sop to the reader, "to keep his mind diverted and quiet,
while the poem does its work upon him: much as the imaginary burglar is
always provided with a bit of nice meat for the house-dog." In their common
use, words are no more than a useful means of communication, but in their
poetic use, words are mirrors of an invisible reality, of what Plato called the
Ideas, or Ideal Forms, behind appearances, and of what Christians call the soul
or spirit, the incarnation of God, the Word made flesh. Rilke was neither a
Platonist nor a Christian, in the strictly orthodox sense, but he was essentially
a religious poet, who would have agreed with W. H. Auden that "there is only
one thing that all poetry must do: it must praise all it can for being and for
happening." Rilke once described the task of the poet as "this intimate and

lasting conversion of the visible into an invisible,"[5] and in one of his poems he described the poet's mission as he understood it:

> Poet, what's your business? I praise.
> What, in these murderous, barbaric days,
> You still believe in miracles? I praise.
> But where, in this monotony of greys,
> Are faces you can recognize? I praise.
> And who, in these bewildering displays
> Of masks and costumes, is yourself? I praise.
> And both the violent and silent ways
> Of storm and star are yours? Because I praise.

Rilke's poetic praise crosses the language barrier with what seems an irresistible force, but while Rilke expresses the soul of German poetry, he also expresses the soul of modern poetry. He wrote in an age that he characterized as murderous and barbaric, that Eliot symbolized as *The Waste Land,* an age when, as Yeats described it in "The Second Coming," "Mere anarchy is loosed upon the world."

Thus Rilke can be understood better in the context of modern poetry than in the context of German poetry, for he was truly international, sharing the feeling Baudelaire expressed in his preface to *Les Fleurs du mal,* "The world has taken on a thickness of vulgarity that raises a spiritual man's contempt to the violence of a passion." Like Baudelaire, Rilke expressed the existential loneliness of man alienated from other men, from nature, and from God. He was profoundly a poet of solitude. But in his solitude he was never wholly alone; his is an inclusive, rather than an exclusive, loneliness, which plumbs the depths of selfhood and finds a universal center of gravity. All modern poets are in some sense solipsists; lacking a unifying belief that binds men together in a community, poets are forced inward and must begin with their unique personal existence as the only given. We have the example of Yeats that by a heroic effort the poet may convert his private life, with all its foibles and failures, into great poetry, forcing his reader by necessity to be interested in everything that interested him: Irish Nationalism, folklore, theosophy, Byzantine civilization—even "the foul rag-and-bone shop of the heart." Yeats made a dramatic struggle out of his own peculiar destiny as an individual, constructing poetry out of the belief expressed in his *Autobiography*

---

5. Wallace Stevens, *Opus Posthumous,* 160; T. S. Eliot, *The Use of Poetry and the Use of Criticism,* 151; W. H. Auden, "Making, Knowing, and Judging," in *The Dyer's Hand* (New York: Random House, 1962), 60; Rilke, letter to Witold von Hulewicz, November 13, 1925, in *Selected Letters of Rainer Maria Rilke,* ed. Harry T. Moore, 390.

that "I shall, if good luck or bad luck make my life interesting, be a great poet; for it will be no longer a matter of literature at all."[6] But Rilke, forced inward like Yeats, requires us to know very little about his private life; he built a kingdom within, revealed an interior universe, explored what he called the *Weltinnenraum*, "world-inner-space," which gradually expanded from the finite and personal to the infinite and universal. As he said in another early poem:

> I live my life in a widening ring
> of circles curving toward everything.
> Maybe the last one will never be drawn.
> But I will go on. And on. And on.
>
> I girdle God, and a Gothic tower,
> I span a whole millennium.
> But still I'm not sure: Am I falcon? Storm-shower?
> Or even, perhaps, a great poem?

The circle of Rilke's inner experience grew as his poetry developed, becoming less subjective and more objective poem by poem, until he seemed most conscious of himself when he was most conscious of something outside himself. The inwardness that he expressed became a property not merely of his own being but of all being, a shared interiority of subject and object. In terms of the historical movements of modern poetry, Rilke grew from a symbolist into an imagist. What chiefly influenced this growth was his encounter with Paris as a city ("A human landscape emerges here," he wrote in a letter of 1907,[7] five years after he arrived in Paris), and the artistic influence of Auguste Rodin, a sculptor completely dedicated to his craft. The poetry of the *Frühe Gedichte [Early Poems]* and *Das Stundenbuch [The Book of Hours]*, which emerged from his childhood in Prague and his travels to Germany and Russia, is moody and meditative, subjective and personal, while the poetry of *Das Buch der Bilder [The Book of Images]* and the *Neue Gedichte [New Poems]*, which emerged from his experience of Paris in the first decade of the twentieth century, is starkly realistic and solid, objective and impersonal, making each subject appear to shine with its own inner light.

It is remarkable how Rilke, schooled in German romantic poetry and German idealist philosophy, came to write with such concreteness. He was

6. Baudelaire, "Preface to the Flowers," in *The Flowers of Evil*, ed. Marthiel Mathews and Jackson Mathews (New York: New Directions, 1955), xviii; Yeats, *The Autobiography of William Butler Yeats*, 69.

7. Quoted in *Rainer Maria Rilke*, by E. M. Butler (Cambridge: Cambridge University Press, 1946), 184.

helped by his reading of Baudelaire, which showed him that the modern city is rich in poetic subjects, and by his observation of Rodin, who showed him, as he said in his monograph on the sculptor, that "his art was not built upon a great idea, but upon a minute, conscientious realization, upon the attainable, upon a craft."[8] What the poetry of Baudelaire and the sculpture of Rodin had in common was their portrayal of the nobility of human suffering. Rilke said of Rodin, "To discover in all lusts and all crimes, in all trials and all despair, an infinite reason for existence is a part of that great longing that creates poets," and he knew that Rodin's great sculptural masterpiece, "The Gate of Hell," was based on Baudelaire as well as on Dante.

But whatever his influences, the mastery was Rilke's own achievement. There is no better example of his mature style than the famous "Panther":

The Panther
In the Botanical Gardens, Paris

His sight has been so beaten by the bars,
it is exhausted, and can barely see.
Bewildered by a thousand bars he stares
into the blankness of reality.

The steady padding of his silken pace
narrows, as if circling for the kill;
as if he danced for strength about a place
where stands in stupefaction some huge will.

But then his inner eyelid, soundlessly,
flickers—and beyond its lucent screen,
an image fills the quiet-muscled body,
enters the heart, and ceases to be seen.

Rilke seems in this poem to *become* the panther, pacing in his cage in the menagerie of the Jardin des Plantes in Paris. The world outside the bars is canceled into nothingness, and only the inner world of the cage is real. There, the panther moves with lithe animal grace, his hunting instinct focused on a vacant space in the middle of the floor, where a "huge will" holds him entranced in a hypnotic "dance for strength." The poem begins in the panther's cage, and moves inside the panther's body, behind his eyes, where the almost imperceptible movement of the membrane under the eyelid allows a single image to pass deep into his consciousness and then disappear in the chambers

---

8. Rainer Maria Rilke, *Rodin,* 10.

of his heart. What image? It may be the jungle habitat from which he came, or his mate, with whom he shared natural freedom once, before he was captured and brought to the zoo. We can guess at, but cannot be sure of, what the panther sees, and it is the ambiguity of the final image that opens our eyes to the mystery of the panther's being: he is no dumb animal, but an intelligent creature like ourselves, who also hold a mystery in our hearts that we feel but cannot define. We realize that like the panther we are creatures of a will greater than ourselves, which has created us and placed us in the cage of our bodies, from which we, too, long to escape. The sympathy—no, it is empathy, complete identification—Rilke feels for the panther is felt for the human species as well, and a unity of being is established between the animal kingdom and man.

What Rilke has done for man and beast in his poems—not only the panther, but also the gazelle, the swan, the flamingo—he has done for creature and thing in other poems, allowing an equally full penetration to occur between animal and plant, or between organic and inorganic beings. There are his flower and fruit poems—the anemone, the rose, the apple, the orange—or his seasonal poems—the marvelous sequence of autumn poems, especially, or his poems to rivers and springs and mirrors—any one of them would do as an example of his kinship with nonthinking things. But best of all are his sculpture poems, where the lessons he learned from Rodin are most evident— in particular, the celebrated "Archaic Torso of Apollo":

> The god's unheard-of head we cannot know,
> nor see the apple-ripeness of his eyes.
> His body is a candelabra, though,
> from which his gaze, borne downward, still will rise,
>
> still deeply shining. Otherwise the arc
> of bending breastbone could not blind you so;
> a smile could not reach through the curving, dark,
> soft loin, to the genitals, and glow.
>
> This stone would otherwise be only stone,
> a stunted pillar shouldering the air—
> instead of this translucent, leonine
>
> body, from whose edges light is torn
> as if it were a star: now, everywhere
> is filled with seeing. You must be reborn.

In this poem, Rilke has entered into solid stone, a fragment of marble sculpture preserved from the Greek classical age, perhaps from the studio of Phidias or

Praxiteles, where Greek sculpture reached its full perfection of living form. And he has chosen only a remnant, the torso of a statue deprived of its magnificent head and graceful limbs, so that he must not only describe but reconstitute the original, replacing missing stone with words and images. He begins with what is no longer visible, the noble head with its protuberant and all-seeing eyes, the mirrors of a divine intelligence. He then proceeds to show these invisible eyes looking out from every contour of the marble torso, like a candelabra shining from within the body—the breast, the loins, the shoulders, the skin, all that gives life and strength and generative power to the god. Finally, these invisible eyes seem to look directly at the beholder, till the air is filled with seeing, and a divine command comes forth: "Du musst dein Leben ändern," literally, "You must change your life," but the spirit of it is Christian and is, I think, better understood as "You must be reborn." The sense of the god's imperative surely is "You must see with Apollo's eyes"; that is, the gazer is impelled to see through the stone to its inner being, an immortal god. Once again, as with the panther, the effect is that what is inside the statue is inside man—seeing a divine gaze within the broken stone, he is conscious of a divine presence within himself: he is "reborn" to a new sense of his life.

In his later poems, particularly the stupendous *Duino Elegies,* Rilke moved even farther into invisible realms, which he called "the angelic orders," becoming mystical, at times almost impenetrable. Yet he did not lose his grasp of the real world, as we know from the poems that came immediately after the *Duino Elegies,* the *Sonnets to Orpheus.* In one of his letters to his patroness, Princess Marie von Thurn und Taxis-Hohenlohe, the owner of Duino Castle, Rilke described the process of poetic creation as "the return journey from infinity, on which you encounter all the honest, earthly things."[9] This description anticipates his movement from the *Duino Elegies* to the *Sonnets to Orpheus,* where once more he is in touch with the earth and the tangible world, but sees it from a perspective beyond it, so that substance seems converted into essence, the visible into the invisible, lyrically and exuberantly. The "singing of things" that he yearned to hear in an early poem is fully expressed in these late sonnets. Each one is a miracle in its way, but perhaps the most miraculous of all is the sonnet about the unicorn (*Sonnets to Orpheus,* pt. 2, no. 4), that legendary beast that could only be seen by a pure virgin (as only a pure-hearted knight could see the Holy Grail) and then only indirectly, in a reflecting mirror:

> O this is he: the beast that never lived.
> But they seemed unaware of any lack—

9. *Selected Letters of Rainer Maria Rilke, 1902–1926,* trans. and ed. R. F. C. Hull, 181.

his bearing, and the carriage of his neck,
the very light of his still eyes—they loved.

He never was. But of their love they made
a perfect creature. And they gave it room.
And in the room, unhaltered, unafraid,
he raised his head and barely did presume

to be. They fed him, not on ears of corn,
but always on the possibility
of being, and he gained such strength he grew

a horn out of his head. A single horn.
And to a maiden bore it whitely through
the silver mirror, and in her was he.

Here, even more than in his Apollo poem, Rilke has created the seen from the unseen. The unicorn has no reality except in the eyes of those who love him, and through their love he becomes "a perfect creature," calm and strong in the "possibility of being." Moreover—and this is the finest touch—he grows his single horn as an expression of trust, a symbol of inner truth, the fulfillment of a spiritual love that needs no physical proof. Rilke said in a letter written after he composed the poem that "no Christ-parallel is meant by the unicorn; but all love of the non-proven, the non-palpable, all belief in the worth and reality of whatever our soul has created and lifted up out of itself through the centuries." Rilke's lifelong cultivation of *Weltinnenraum* has its culmination in this poem, where the interior universe is revealed through human love and seems to fill the air with light. Rilke wrote in a letter that the artist "yearns to cultivate and perfect his inner world so that it may one day hold all external things, the very stars even, poised in the balance and, as it were, equated."[10] Surely no modern poet in any language has surpassed Rilke in making his unique private experience accessible to others, creating an inner reality that seems to radiate being, to see through existence to essence.

In one of his early stories in *Stories of the Loving God,* Rilke told of a grave digger who said that he buried men down here as other men "bury God up there." The narrator replies, "The God who has fled from us out of the heavens will return to us out of the earth." Rilke seems to have spent his life fulfilling this prophecy, for in his poetry the sense of divine immanence, of the Word of God made flesh, is conveyed over and over again. But whereas in his early

10. *Selected Letters of Rainer Maria Rilke,* ed. Harry T. Moore, 360; Rilke to Rosa Schobloch, September 24, 1908, in *Selected Letters of Rainer Maria Rilke, 1902–1926,* trans. and ed. R. F. C. Hull, 172.

poems he frequently mentioned God by name, in his later poems he seldom mentioned God. He did not need to, for in these poems all existence becomes holy, and a new incarnation is revealed in which the creator and the created become one.

4

Two Pre-Imagists
Emily Dickinson and Stephen Crane

It is a phenomenon of literary history that some writers seem to anticipate the next age, making their work appear, in retrospect, more a part of the future than of their own time. So it was with Dryden, whose verse satires in the late seventeenth century anticipated the neoclassicists, causing him to be grouped with writers of the eighteenth century such as Pope, Swift, and Johnson, rather than with contemporaries such as Milton. And so it was with Burns, who looked forward to the romantics of the nineteenth century when in the late eighteenth century he wrote his love poems and visions, placing him more with Wordsworth and Coleridge and Keats, the romantic poets who came after him, than with Samuel Johnson, the neoclassicist who was his older contemporary. The Spirit of the Age moves in unpredictable cycles, and writers may be inspired to a new sense of style well ahead of its emergence as a movement.

Such was the case with Emily Dickinson and Stephen Crane, two American writers who in the late nineteenth century wrote short lyrics that were precise in diction, free in form, and vivid in imagery, remarkably like the new poetic form of imagism that dominated the early twentieth century, when modernism was taking over as a literary movement. Like Hopkins in England, Dickinson and Crane in America were more like modern poets than romantic or Victorian poets, although they themselves wrote in isolation, never suspecting that their unconventional poems might foreshadow a new literary epoch. Dickinson published almost nothing during her lifetime and never had the satisfaction of being recognized for what she now appears to us to be—a major poet and the forerunner of a new poetic style. Stephen Crane published his "lines," as he called them, in the last decade of the nineteenth century, but he found a much readier audience for his prose fiction, especially his classic war novel, *The Red Badge of Courage,* than for his poetry, which did not fit any definition of poetry until the imagists came along a decade after his early death in 1900 and made his kind of short, concrete, free-verse lyric the touchstone of the modern style.

Besides being ahead of her time, Dickinson was one of the most private poets who ever lived, choosing to lead a phenomenally secluded life, showing her poems to few others, willing to die without being recognized as the poet she would posthumously become. The miracle is that her poetry even survived to be acclaimed as the work of genius. Born in the quiet New England college town of Amherst, Massachusetts, in 1830, she belonged to one of the town's first families, yet she chose not to be a public figure, preferring instead the intimacy of her home and garden. Her grandfather was one of the founders of Amherst College, her father and her brother both served it as treasurers, and her family members were pillars of the Congregational church across the street from the Dickinson homestead, but "she mastered life by rejecting it," as Allen Tate wrote in an appreciative essay about her in the twentieth century. Totally unknown as a poet in her own day, she provided an example of the alienated artist that Tate and his fellow Fugitives could respond to long after her death, despite the regional differences otherwise separating southerners from a New Englander. She had little formal education beyond high school, spending just a year at the South Hadley Female Seminary (later Mount Holyoke College) before returning to her home in Amherst, and never leaving it afterward except for brief trips with her father to Boston, Philadelphia, and Washington. Some readers of Dickinson's poetry have persisted in seeing her as an unwilling victim of male dominance and puritan morality, potent influences in both her family and her town, but the evidence of her poetry confirms Tate's opinion that "all pity for Miss Dickinson's 'starved life' is misdirected. Her life was one of the richest and deepest ever lived on this continent."[1]

It is her poetry above all that shows how rich a life she lived in the voluntary confinement of her house and garden. It is a poetry without titles, written for herself alone, yet full of enigmatic hints that she knew she might someday have a larger audience:

> This is my letter to the World
> That never wrote to Me—
> The simple News that Nature told—
> With tender Majesty
>
> Her Message is committed
> To Hands I cannot see—

1. Allen Tate, "Emily Dickinson," in *Essays of Four Decades,* 286.

For love of Her—Sweet—countrymen—
Judge tenderly—of Me

There is a charming coyness in these lines, suggesting that the shy New England woman would respond to outsiders if only she were invited. When she did write to an editor once, he found her a curious combination of audacity and concealment, since she sent him poems for comment but hid her signature in an inner envelope. Thomas Wentworth Higginson, as editor of the *Atlantic Monthly* in Boston, had announced his interest in unpublished authors, but was unprepared for this one, whose singularity was apparent from the first and yet whose unconventionality was too great for him to overcome by publishing the poems she sent him. In time he would help to edit not only these poems but also some of the nearly 2,000 tiny, handwritten poems that posthumously survived, tucked away in her desk to be discovered by her sister, which could only be published years after she was "called back," as her tombstone in the Amherst Cemetery reads, in 1886. Higginson coedited only a fraction of them, and he made editorial changes to regularize their meter and rhyme, removing some of their idiosyncratic punctuation and peculiarly apt diction, but the 1,775 poems and fragments that were eventually published read now like a set of imagist poems composed long before there was any definition of imagist poetry into which her tight, irregular lyrics could fit.

Every attempt to find some influence on her life that might have prompted her to write poetry has failed, and though it is known that she wrote the largest number of poems—over 300, or almost one poem a day—in 1862, when the American Civil War was raging, she was seemingly as oblivious to it as to any other event that occurred outside the little world of her house and garden in Amherst. What happened there, however, often seemed momentous in her view:

There's a certain Slant of light
Winter Afternoons—
That oppresses, like the Heft
Of Cathedral Tunes—

Heavenly Hurt, it gives us—
We can find no scar,
But internal difference,
Where the Meanings, are—

None may teach it—Any—
'Tis the Seal Despair—
An imperial affliction
Sent us of the Air—

When it comes, the Landscape listens—
Shadows—hold their breath—
When it goes, 'tis like the Distance
On the look of Death—

What exactly has she seen? It is not an easy question to answer, despite the long familiarity of readers with this poem, but there is no doubt that the poem begins with something perceived, that like the imagists she worked from outer experience to an inner mood, from the objective and visible world outside her to the subjective consciousness inside her. In this poem the natural is nothing more exceptional than the quality of light on a winter day, but what she makes of it is supernatural, for in her mind it is associated with such disparate phenomena as organ music heard in a church, shadows on a landscape, and a dead person's eyes—all oppressive to her spirit, arousing in her a premonition of her own death. The poem is about a physical experience that causes metaphysical tremors in her soul, the sort of insight into some unseen reality beyond appearances that must have been in her mind when she wrote to Higginson, "Nature is a Haunted House, but Art—a house that tries to be haunted."[2] All of Dickinson's best poems have this duality about them that comes from a duality perceived in nature; starting from the known, she reached into the unknown, for, as she put it once in a letter, "It is true that the unknown is the largest need of the intellect, though for it, no one thinks to thank God."[3]

The unknown enters all Dickinson's poems, through their haunting imagery and free use of language: she was as experimental in her way as the later imagists. She chose uneven meters and odd rhymes, not writing completely free verse but writing hymn-like stanzas with unexpected rhythmic twists in them, and sometimes leaving the final shape of a poem indeterminate, with words that she had not yet fixed in place—posing cruxes for later editors, who often find them unresolvable, but opening up possibilities of expression that she apparently did not want to close. In one extreme instance, to be found in the three-volume Complete Edition that Thomas H. Johnson compiled from her manuscripts, she left a poem in two separate versions, one complete and one with numerous variations. It is as if, having invented an original poem about butterflies, Dickinson were not satisfied with the complete version she first wrote, but wanted to perform her own variations on it, and did so

2. Quoted by Denis Donoghue in his essay "Emily Dickinson," in *Six American Poets,* ed. Allen Tate (Minneapolis: University of Minnesota Press, 1965), 16.

3. Dickinson to her cousins, Louise and Frances Norcross, August 1876, in *Letters of Emily Dickinson,* ed. Mabel Loomis Todd (New York: Grosset and Dunlap, 1963), 237.

delightfully, without ever settling on a finished second version. The pleasure for the reader is in seeing the same subject in both its finished and unfinished form:

533[4]

Two Butterflies went out at Noon—
And waltzed upon a Farm—
Then stepped straight through the Firmament
And rested, on a Beam—

And then—together bore away
Upon a shining Sea—
Though never yet, in any Port—
Their coming, mentioned—be—

If spoken by the distant Bird—
If met in Ether Sea
By Frigate, or by Merchantman—
No notice—was—to me—

The poem is one of the 300-odd she wrote in 1862, and it is original and satisfying as it stands. She pictures a pair of adventurous butterflies in a zigzag flight—what else can "waltzed upon a Farm" mean?—that goes beyond the visible world, "through the Firmament" (a biblical word for the sphere of fixed stars that in ancient times was thought to form a boundary of the universe) and into space, the "shining Sea" or "Ether Sea" of imagined gas, where the butterflies disappear for good, never reaching any "port" or passing any ships that might observe them, and so the speaker of the poem (she warned Higginson in one of her letters, "When I state myself, as the representative of the verse, it does not mean me, but a supposed person") is left wondering where the butterflies might have gone, being unable to see them any longer but imagining that they are still sailing somewhere out in space. In its first finished version, then, the poem seems light and happy, with just a hint at the end that the butterflies might have flown too far and so become not simply invisible but dead.

The unedited 1878 version of the same poem, which Dickinson left behind to puzzle editors and readers, is even more interesting, with all its alternate readings exposed on the page:

---

4. The poems are numbered here as in Thomas H. Johnson's complete edition of *The Poems of Emily Dickinson.*

Two Butterflies went out at Noon
And waltzed upon a Farm
And then espied circumference
Then overtook
And caught a ride with him
And took a Bout with him
Then lost themselves and found themselves
            staked   lost
            chased   caught
In eddies of the sun
    Fathoms in
In rapids of
    Gambols with
                of
For Frenzies of
    Antics in
            with
Till Rapture missed them
            missed her footing
            missed Peninsula
    Gravitation chased them
                humbled
                ejected
                foundered
                grumbled
Until a Zephyr pushed them
                chased
                flung
                spurned
                scourged
And Both were wrecked in Noon
                drowned
                Quenched
                whelmed
And they were hurled from noon—

To all surviving Butterflies
Be this Biography—
Example—and monition—
To entomology—

The unfinished poem starts off by describing the same pair of wandering
butterflies, but before the first stanza is over, it has veered into a more

obscure territory than the earlier version, since "circumference" is both a more abstract and more mathematical boundary than "Firmament," and the butterflies appear to be enjoying their adventure into outer space, since they either "caught a ride" or "took a Bout" with "circumference," beyond the limits of the universe. In the second stanza, they appear to go wild, for Emily Dickinson gave free rein to her imagination and visualized the butterflies' motion as a reckless game being played with the sun, until suddenly a wind blows hard on their fragile wings and they are "wrecked in Noon"—or else "drowned" or "Quenched" or "whelmed" or "hurled from noon"—that is to say, whatever verb one chooses, they are destroyed finally at midday. For a finale, Dickinson wrote an entirely new stanza to end the poem, one in which a mock-serious moral is addressed to "all surviving Butterflies," admonishing them not to follow the disastrous example of the wayward butterflies who flew too far. The unfinished version has a more humorous tone than the finished version, since the flight of the butterflies in the second stanza is not so much described as caricatured, and after the reader has followed all the deliriously active verbs of flight, there is a lesson to be learned, but one that is not to be taken too seriously, since the learned words *Biography* and *entomology* are for people more than for butterflies. Beware, she says, of leading a reckless life that brings an early death—her poem about butterflies has become a garden version of the myth of Icarus flying too near the sun and falling into the sea.

Which of the two versions is the better poem? Both are excellent, but the reader is tempted to choose the unfinished over the finished version, since it has more freedom, more fancy, and more humor in it than the earlier poem. What makes it especially appealing is the range of possibilities it affords, leaving the reader in the enviable position of the author, still undecided, enjoying the opportunity of trying out all the words without having to make up his mind, the sort of active participation that the French symbolist Mallarmé thought was the highest possibility a poet could offer to his readers, "the delicious joy of believing that they are creating." In this unfinished poem, her alternatives all seem good ones, and readers can turn them over in their minds indefinitely, never being forced to make the choice the poet herself refused to make.

It is to Emily Dickinson's lasting credit that she left behind as many memorable poems about death as any single poet. "I am glad to find that advancing life brings this power of imagining the nearness of death," she wrote in a letter of 1874. She struck the death knell early in "I never lost as much but twice" (no. 49), and later described "An ecstasy of parting / Denominated 'Death'" (no. 71); she first observed the death of others in "I like a look of Agony / Because I know it's true" (no. 241) and then faced the thought of her own death in "To die—takes just a little while— / They say it doesn't hurt" (no. 255) and "I felt a Funeral in my Brain" (no. 280). The death poem most familiar to readers is a late one, "Because I could not stop for Death / He kindly stopped for me" (no. 712), which personifies death as a gentleman who calls for her in a chariot, the "kindly" bridegroom who takes her unsuspectingly to her grave, but does not cause her any pain, for she has been dead for centuries, she says, yet it "seems shorter than the Day— / I first surmised the Horses' Heads / Were toward Eternity."

The portrait of death is beguiling, but no more striking than her more realistic portrayal of death in "I heard a Fly buzz—when I died" (no. 465). In this short but arresting poem, death is transformed into a single fly, which so dominates the scene with its buzzing noise that nothing else seems to matter to the dying person. She sees the mourners around her, drying their eyes and holding their breath, waiting for death ("the King") to come and claim her; she makes out her last will and testament ("Signed away / What portion of me be / Assignable") but leaves her self alone to face death in the shape and sound of the fly, whose "Blueuncertain stumbling Buzz" comes "Between the light— and me—" and blocks out all the visible light from the windows, then even the invisible light in her brain: "I could not see to see" implies not only that she has lost the vision in her eyes but that she is no longer conscious of any light; a complete and all-engulfing darkness has settled inside her at the end. Or has it? The reader follows the poet's description of death beyond the point where the fly can be seen or heard, that is, into apparent oblivion, yet who can be speaking the poem, if not the dying person? Emily Dickinson manages to treat her own death with characteristic ambiguity: "I heard a Fly buzz—when I died" holds such fascination because in it she seems to pursue the physical experience of death to its uttermost limit, beyond human consciousness, and yet the words are those of a person who must be alive, both before the poem and after it. She speaks of death before it happens, but takes the viewpoint of one to whom it has already happened, and so her short poem performs a feat of imagination unequaled by any other death poem, however long it might be.

If Emily Dickinson was a poet who anticipated the imagists by her brevity, her unconventionality, her realistic imagery of nature and death, Stephen Crane anticipated them by the way he could sum up his whole philosophy of life in a few unforgettable lines:

> A man said to the universe:
> "Sir, I exist!"
> "However," replied the universe,
> "The fact has not created in me
> A sense of obligation."

Crane's lines are even more irregular than Dickinson's, a freer kind of verse than she wrote, since they are without meter or rhyme, but they are equally memorable in presenting the one-sided dialogue between man and the universe, exposing the human figure as he futilely asserts his importance before the blank gaze of an indifferent nature. The situation would be pathetic, except that it is saved by ironic humor, expressed in the ridiculous contrast between the fierce pride of man and the sublime unconcern of the universe. Thus in a single short poem Crane epitomized the new viewpoint of natural determinism, derived from scientists such as Darwin who preceded him, but in a new poetic form like that of the imagists who succeeded him.

It was in 1924, after the imagists had made their impact, that Amy Lowell wrote an introduction to *The Works of Stephen Crane,* in which she affirmed: "So short a time as twelve years after his death, a type of poetry extremely like Crane's came into being. By all rights, he should have been its direct parent, but he was not, simply because most of the practitioners of it had based themselves upon French precedent." He was, she said, a leader before his time, and he died too soon, of tuberculosis in 1900, before he had reached the age of twenty-nine. But the poetry he wrote in a few short years, during the last decade of the nineteenth century, came into its own when the imagists made their experiments count in the second decade of the twentieth century. It was a vindication of his poetry, and one that Crane seems to have anticipated, for he wrote: "I suppose I ought to be thankful to 'The Red Badge,' but I am much fonder of my little book of poems, 'The Black Riders.' The reason, perhaps, is that it was a more ambitious effort. My aim in it was to comprehend the thoughts I have had about life in general, while 'The Red Badge' is a mere episode in life, an amplification."[5]

Crane's whole literary career lasted less than a decade, but in that period he made an indelible mark with both his poetry and his fiction, for his extreme originality was recognized from the moment he visited the writer and editor Hamlin Garland in 1893. Crane was only twenty-two; his year at Syracuse University had proved him a better baseball player than student, and he was trying to become a journalist in New York, where, as he admitted, "of all human lots for a person of sensibility that of an obscure free lance in literature or journalism is, I think, the most discouraging." He went to see Garland in hopes of making literature rather than journalism his career, and Garland helped him so much that Crane became an international celebrity within two years, publishing in 1895 both *Black Riders and Other Lines* and *The Red Badge of Courage,* and going to England to live in proximity to the master writers in whose company he belonged, Joseph Conrad and Henry James.

---

5. Stephen Crane, *Stephen Crane: An Omnibus,* 628.

In Garland's detailed account of Crane's visit to his Manhattan office (put in a memoir called "Stephen Crane, A Soldier of Fortune" for the *Saturday Evening Post* in 1900, shortly after Crane's death at the age of twenty-eight), we have one of the fullest descriptions ever given of the creative process at work in an artist:

One day he appeared in my study with his outside pockets bulging with two rolls of manuscript. As he entered he turned ostentatiously to put down his hat, and so managed to convey to my mind an impression that he was concealing something. His manner was embarrassed, as if he had come to do a thing and was sorry about it.

"Come now, out with it," I said. "What is the roll I see in your pocket?"

With a sheepish look he took out a fat roll of legal cap paper and handed it to me with a careless, boyish gesture. . . .

I unrolled the first package, and found it to be a sheaf of poems. I can see the initial poem now, exactly as it was then written, without a blot or erasure, almost without punctuation, in blue ink. It was beautifully legible and clean of outline.

It was the poem which begins: "God fashioned the ship of the world carefully."

I read this with delight and amazement. I rushed through the others, some thirty in all, with growing wonder. I could not believe they were the work of the pale, reticent boy moving restlessly about the room.

"Have you any more?" I asked.

"I've got five or six all in a little row up here," he quaintly replied, pointing to his temple. "That's the way they come—in little rows, all made up, ready to be put down on paper."

"When did you write these?"

"Oh! I've been writing five or six every day. I wrote nine yesterday. I wanted to write some more last night, but those 'Indians' wouldn't let me. They howled over the other verses so loud they nearly cracked my ears. You see, we all live in a box together, and I've no place to write, except in the general squabble. They think my lines are funny. They make a circus of me." All this with a note of exaggeration, of course. . . .

When Crane came next day he brought the first part of a war story which was at that time without a name. The first page of this was as original as the verses, and it passed at once to the description of a great battle. . . .

"Did you do any more 'lines'?"

He looked away bashfully.

"Only six."

"Let me see them."

As he handed them to me he said: "Got three more waiting in line. I could do one now."

"Sit down and try," I said, glad of his offer, for I could not relate the man to his work.

He took a seat and began to write steadily, composedly, without hesitation or blot or interlineation, and so produced in my presence one of his most powerful verses. It flowed from his pen as smooth as oil. . . .

His was a singular and daring soul, as irresponsible as the wind. He was a man to be called a genius, for we call that power genius which we do not easily understand or measure. I have never known a man whose source of power was so unaccounted for.[6]

If Garland found Crane unaccountable, Crane gave his own account of the source of his power in one of his shortest poems:

> Many red devils ran from my heart
> And out upon the page.
> They were so tiny
> The pen could mash them.
> And many struggled in the ink.
> It was strange
> To write in this red muck
> Of things from my heart.

Crane found evil in his own heart and believed it was his inspiration; "It seems a pity that art should be a child of pain," he once wrote, "and yet I think it is." His fiction is filled with pain—caused by war in *The Red Badge of Courage,* or shipwreck in *The Open Boat,* or frontier violence in *The Blue Hotel* and "The Bride Comes to Yellow Sky." In his short poems there is the constant apprehension that men might meet with violence from others and the greater apprehension that they might *do* violence to others:

> A man feared that he might find an assassin;
> Another that he might find a victim.
> One was more wise than the other.

A poem as short as this one, only three lines long, makes heavy demands on the reader, as Pound knew when he wrote his imagist touchstone "In a Station of the Metro" more than a decade after Crane's death, but if the lines are arresting enough, the reader will reflect on them until their meaning is clear, and in this instance, it is clear that the man who fears the violence within himself is

---

6. Appendix to *Stephen Crane: Letters,* 303–5.

"more wise," that is, more honest with himself, than the man who fears the violence of others. The assumption that man is the source of evil, and that the perception of evil in his own heart is the source of poetic inspiration, is a major theme of all Stephen Crane wrote, both poetry and fiction, and it links him with Eliot and the Fugitives as well as with Pound and the imagists. His writing is fundamentally pessimistic, full of self-accusation and a penetrating irony that leaves little hope for mankind.

Of all Stephen Crane's poems, "War Is Kind" is the most distinctive, since it has a more symmetrical free-verse form than his other poems and since it is a sort of miniature *Red Badge of Courage,* condensing the horror of war into a few scenes and couching it in a searing irony that the refrain communicates repeatedly. The form of this poem is a combination of three brief scenes of death and sorrow in free verse and two battle scenes in strongly accented tetrameter, like three sketches of the suffering caused by war away from the battlefield and two marching hymns for the soldiers on the battlefield. The tone of the poem is heavily ironic throughout, with its constant refrain "War is kind," countered by the first scene, of a man being killed and falling from his horse while his sweetheart mourns him, the second scene, of a man caught in a death agony in the "yellow trenches" (sickening color!) while his infant weeps, and then the final scene, of a mother's grief as she stands over her son's coffin, her heart reduced to a button on his shroud. The two battle hymns present the rattling sound of drums, and the men go marching to their deaths while the battle-god grins above their corpses, with the dazzling sight of a regimental flag flying its proud red and gold eagle crest over the soldiers, who file into death like sheep, learning ironic lessons about "the virtue of slaughter" and "the excellence of killing" as they contribute their own bodies to the "field where a thousand corpses lie."

Stephen Crane, like Emily Dickinson, wrote some remarkable pre-imagist poems during his brief literary career from 1893 to 1900. His poems are highly original, with their free-verse form, their brevity, their hard realistic imagery, and their frequent use of understatement and irony. Though the painful truths of his poetry may have been overshadowed by the powerful impressionism of his fiction, Crane himself believed that his poetry was the more important creation because it was more universal. Both Dickinson and Crane were fine poets who anticipated the imagists by exemplifying the short, experimental poem focused on a single poetic image or succession of images, and so they seem prophetic voices now.

5

AN IRISH SYMBOLIST
William Butler Yeats

Yeats's *Responsibilities:* The Ironist Ascending

"A Coat," from the volume *Responsibilities,* which Yeats published in 1914, marks the midpoint in Yeats's career, when he looked in the mirror of his imagination and took off his old style in order to put on his new style. The man who had once dreamed of an Irish fairyland was waking up to the world outside, no longer shielding himself from it but meeting it head-on, fashioning a poetic style that would illuminate himself and his time as in a lightning flash and would enable him to write those gripping later poems in which history is entangled with myth and all human experience seems starkly exposed to view, "riddled with light." It was the only way he could grow as an artist from his youthful idealism, so ardently and appealingly Irish in its preoccupations and its aims, into his more mature, more tragic and cosmopolitan, visionary realism. It was a painful but necessary phase of his development, a soul-stripping phase, which, while it coincided with the imagist movement toward concentration of imagery and directness of expression, was essentially Yeats's own inevitable coming of age. His motto for the volume was "In dreams begin responsibilities," a paradoxical statement that seems to signify "When dreams end, responsibilities begin."

As "A Coat" tells us, Yeats had become increasingly critical of himself and disillusioned with others, and he needed to purge himself of those romantic yearnings for an ideal past so characteristic of his *Celtic Twilight* period so that he could face up to what he recognized as the modern artist's responsibility: to reintegrate, by the power of imagination, the recalcitrant materials of a civilization that seemed to be rapidly disintegrating around him. He was preparing himself in *Responsibilities* for the heroic synthesis of history and myth that is so magnificently realized in the later poems.

Yeats made a penetrating analysis of this period of his self-transformation in a speech he gave in Chicago at a banquet held by *Poetry* in his honor. It was delivered in 1914, the year *Responsibilities* was published, and most of the poems in this sixth collection of his work had first appeared in the pages of *Poetry* (nineteen poems out of thirty-two), where Ezra Pound had placed them, side by side with poems by himself and by other younger American and English contemporaries of Yeats. As an Irish poet who was going on fifty and already renowned, Yeats was having the rejuvenating experience of being adopted by a new generation of international poets who were strongly oriented toward current French art and literature, and his exhilaration is evident in his banquet speech in Chicago, as he took a long look back over his whole poetic career of twenty-five years, from 1889, when his first poems appeared in *Crossways*, until 1914 and *Responsibilities*:

> When I was younger, and was beginning to write in Ireland, there was all around me the rhetorical poetry of the Irish politicians. The younger writers rebelled against that rhetoric; there was too much of it and to a great extent it was meaningless. When I went to London I found a group of young lyric writers who were also against rhetoric. We formed the Rhymers' Club; we used to meet and read our poems to one another, and we tried to rid them of rhetoric.
>
> But now, when I open the ordinary American magazine, I find that all we rebelled against in those early days—the sentimentality, the rhetoric, the "moral uplift"—still exist here. Not because you are too far from England but because you are too far from Paris.
>
> It is from Paris that nearly all the great influences in art and literature have come, from the time of Chaucer until now. Today the metrical experiments of French poets are overwhelming in their variety and delicacy. The best English writing is dominated by French criticism; in France is the great critical mind.
>
> The Victorians forgot this; also, they forgot the austerity of art and began to preach. When I saw Paul Verlaine in Paris, he told me that he could not translate Tennyson because he was "too Anglais, too noble"—"when he should be broken-hearted he has too many reminiscences."
>
> We in England, our little group of rhymers, were weary of all this. We wanted to get rid not only of rhetoric but of poetic diction. We tried to strip away everything that was artificial, to get a style like speech, as simple as the simplest prose, like a cry of the heart. . . .
>
> Real enjoyment of a beautiful thing is not achieved when a poet tries to teach. It is not the business of a poet to instruct his age. His business is merely to express himself, whatever that self might be. I would have all American poets keep in mind the example of François Villon.

So you who are readers should encourage young American poets to strive
to become very simple, very humble. Your poet must put the fervor of his
life into his work, giving you his emotions before the world, the evil with
the good, not thinking whether he is a good man or a bad man, or whether
he is teaching you. A poet does not know whether he is a good man. If he is
a good man, he probably thinks he is a bad man.

Poetry that is naturally simple, that might exist as the simplest prose,
should have instantaneousness of effect, provided it finds the right audience. You may have to wait years for that audience, but when it is found
instantaneousness of effect is produced.[1]

Yeats had found his audience, all right, a new audience for a new style. He
had found it by eliminating qualities from his poetry that readers had grown
accustomed to over many years—abstract thought, sentiment, moralizing,
patently poetic language, easy rhymes and rhythm—all that made his early
poetry so hauntingly beautiful. What he was putting in its place were the
qualities evident in "A Coat"—conversational speech, irregular rhythms and
imperfect rhymes, startlingly frank imagery, and above all a searching honesty
and humility of tone.

Yeats acknowledged that he was helped in his process of self-transformation
by the younger poets he had met, and by one of them in particular, as
mentioned in his banquet speech in Chicago: "We rebelled against rhetoric,
and now there is group of younger writers who dare to call us rhetorical.
When I returned to London from Ireland, I had a young poet go over all
my work with me to eliminate the abstract. This was an American poet, Ezra
Pound." Pound's service had been personal and practical, performed during
the two previous winters, of 1913 and 1914, while the poets were sharing Stone
Cottage, a country house in Sussex, where according to Yeats's account in a
letter they talked about his poetry at length: "To talk over a poem with him is
like getting you to put a sentence into dialect," he wrote to Lady Gregory. But
according to Pound's account, they were doing much more: "Mostly reading
aloud. Doughty's Dawn in Britain and so on. And wrangling, you see. The
Irish like contradiction. He tried to learn fencing at forty-five, which was
amusing. He would thrash around with the foils like a whale. He sometimes
gave the impression of being even worse an idiot than I am."[2]

Besides this personal help from a young American poet and critic, Yeats
received help of a more indirect kind from an older group of poets and
critics, the French symbolists. Though Yeats confessed in a letter, "Of French

1. William Butler Yeats, Uncollected Prose, vol. 2, 412–13.
2. Ezra Pound, interview by Donald Hall in Writers at Work: The "Paris Review" Interviews,
ed. George Plimpton, 2d ser., 43.

Symbolism I never had any detailed or accurate knowledge," he learned much through his friend Arthur Symons, author of *The Symbolist Movement in Literature*, and later from Pound as well. The only French symbolist he mentioned by name was Paul Verlaine, whom he had met in Paris in the 1890s, but he learned much from Stéphane Mallarmé, who was the leader of the symbolists as Pound was of the imagists. Yeats quoted phrases of Mallarmé prominently in his *Autobiography*, notably from "The Trembling of the Veil" and "The Sacred Book of the Arts," and he probably modeled "A Coat" on a short lyric by Mallarmé called "La Marchande d'habits" ["The Old-Clothes Woman"].

If Yeats did consciously borrow the clothes-stripping image from Mallarmé, he used it for a different purpose, since the clothes in "A Coat" are metaphorical; they are the whole array of Irish mythology Yeats had adopted in his early poetry. His poem is a self-dramatization of stylistic change: he is casting off the old, rhetorical, ornate style of "embroideries out of old mythologies" for a new, simple, realistic style of "walking naked." The themes of the French peom and Irish poem are contrasting, but the imagery and brevity make them alike, and the tone is one of irony in both poems. The sudden juxtaposition of the clothed and naked figures of the poet is common to both and owes something to the art of striptease; Mallarmé reveals the nude statue of a Greek god beneath his clothes, while Yeats reveals a symbolic nakedness of style as he walks out of his mythological dress. Both poems are shocking in their humor, and there is a further twist of irony in Yeats's poem, which becomes clear if we remember his theory of the Self and the Mask, and recognize that the Self is the "coat" of romanticism he is abandoning, while the Mask is the naked state of modernism he is adopting. In his poem, Yeats depicts himself as both romantic and modern, moving from one style to another with the ease of a dancer disrobing on stage before the startled eyes of the audience. "A Coat" was a liberating poem for Yeats, since it showed him moving resolutely in a single stride from one poetic age to the next.

There is a historical argument involved in this interpretation of the poem, for if Yeats regarded himself as one of "the last romantics," as he says in another poem, the significance of his change of style might seem to be only from one phase of romanticism to another, his Self and his Mask two different aspects of the same romantic Ego. Some critics view Yeats as a later romantic, though others view him as modern in his later phase, a great poet who visibly moved from one period style to another. Though he was a romantic by temperament, Yeats was instinctively self-critical, and the process of remaking his style was highly self-conscious, as much a rational act as an intuitive one, and in the later poetry he was much more the modernist, or what Stephen Spender has called the Revolutionary Traditionalist, than he was in his earlier poetry. The Mask, or Opposing Self, prevails in the later poetry, with its accompanying dualism, and if he was still romantic at that time, it was in Hugh Kenner's definition of symbolism as "Scientific Romanticism." The term *ironist* is simplest, however, and it takes in the greater complexity of Yeats's later style, which, in *Responsibilities,* is reflected by a heightened self-criticism, a tendency to unmask himself and let all his faults be seen, not to appear in the guise of an Irish mythical hero like Oisin or Cuchulain or Aengus or Fergus, but as a real man who quarrels with his age and condemns it, but at the same time criticizes himself and sees himself as a slightly ridiculous figure.

Yeats's gift for self-mockery shows itself brilliantly in the later poems, as his gift for self-heroism had shown itself earlier; he becomes more and more inclined to scoff at his own seriousness and to cut himself down to human scale. If Blake was a great example to him earlier, Swift became a great example to him later, and he read widely in history and philosophy, spending part of his time with Pound at Stone Cottage reading the works of Voltaire. In intellectual range, Yeats tried consciously to emulate Dante in his later poetry and to take the whole range of European culture—not simply the Irish—into his work, striving for the breadth of Renaissance learning in his effort to reach a unified view of history. *Responsibilities* marks the turning-point in Yeats's career, because the modern ironist emerges out of the romantic idealist in this volume, as the poet steps naked out of his embroidered coat.

Earlier in 1914 Yeats and Pound had paid tribute to an older English poet, Wilfred Scawen Blunt, and on that occasion Yeats had spoken self-analytically as he did at the later *Poetry* banquet in his honor in Chicago. His remarks were printed in the February 2, 1914, issue of the *Egoist,* which Pound also edited, and were a frank appraisal of the state of poetry as Yeats saw it at the time he published *Responsibilities.* Addressing Blunt, he said:

> When you published your first work, sir, it was the very height of the Victorian period. The abstract poet was in a state of glory. One no longer wrote as a human being with an address, living in a London street, having a definite income, and a definite tradition, but one wrote as an abstract personality. One was expected to be very much wiser than other people. The only objection to such a conception of the poet is that it was impossible to believe that he had existed. This abstraction was the result of the un-real culture of Victorian romance. . . . We are now at the end of Victorian romance—completely at an end. One may admire Tennyson, but one cannot read him. The whole movement is over, but the work that survives is this work which does not speak out of the life of an impossible abstract poet, but out of the life of a man who is simply giving the thoughts which he had in some definite situation of life, or persuades us that he had; so that behind his work we find some definite impulse of life itself. If I take up today some of the things that interested me in the past, I find that I can no longer

use them. They bore me. Every year some part of my poetical machinery suddenly becomes of no use. As the tide of romance recedes I am driven back simply on myself and my thoughts in actual life.[3]

Pound was in the audience for both of these frank self-appraisals by Yeats, and he must have taken them to heart, for it was he who invented the title "The Later Yeats" for his review of *Responsibilities* in the May 1914 issue of *Poetry*,[4] where the speech by Yeats also appeared along with some of his poems, including "A Coat." It was not only Pound who showed that he appreciated the change Yeats was making in his poetry, but Eliot did also. After Yeats's death in 1939 Eliot gave a lecture at the Abbey Theatre in Dublin in which he placed the Irish poet at the pinnacle of modern poets in all languages and placed *Responsibilities* at the center of Yeats's work, praising him as "one of those few whose history is the history of their own time, who are part of the consciousness of an age that cannot be understood without them."[5]

Though Pound and Eliot both praised the later style of Yeats that could first be clearly perceived in *Responsibilities,* they did so from different perspectives. To Pound, it showed a firmer control of the poet's language, increased clarity and precision: "one has felt his work becoming gaunter, seeking greater hardness of outline," Pound said, and he cited as the major example of the "manifestly new note in his later work" the poem called "The Magi," which he praised for its "quality of hard light." Serious readers of Yeats have become so accustomed to reading this poem in the light of *A Vision,* and seeing it in its appointed place on the gyres of history, with its prophecy of an impending supernatural event, a new Annunciation, with the Apocalyptic Beast of the Second Coming waiting in the desert to come slouching forth to Bethlehem to be born, that it is difficult to see it as Pound saw it when it first came out, simply a brilliant new poem to "fill the mind with a noble profusion of sounds and images," and to fulfill "the highest function of art." Pound's view of poetic history was highly colored by the stylistic changes that were occurring at the time, especially in the work of his fellow imagists, and he saw in "The Magi" a fusion of symbolism and imagism, for he asked, "Is Mr. Yeats an Imagiste?" and answered, "No, Mr. Yeats is a symbolist, but he has written *des Images.*" To Pound, Yeats was the bridge between these two major poetic movements, and he rated Yeats highly for that reason. He did not pay particular attention to the religious symbolism of the poem, especially in its shocking final line, where the faces of the Magi look for a new annunciation and see it not as the traditionally tender nativity scene, with the babe in the manger adored by its

3. Quoted in the *Egoist* (February 2, 1914): 57; also in Yeats, *Uncollected Prose,* vol. 2.

4. Ezra Pound, "The Later Yeats," in *The Literary Essays of Ezra Pound,* 378–81.

5. T. S. Eliot, "Yeats," in *On Poets and Poetry,* 295–308.

parents, but as its opposite: "The uncontrollable mystery on the bestial floor." The ironic contrast in the poem between conventional religious imagery and a scene of menacing violence is part of what Pound must have meant when he spoke of "the quality of hard light" in the poem.

Eliot took a more retrospective view in his lecture on Yeats in 1940, after the poet's death and twenty-six years after Pound's essay. Whereas Pound's response was to the technical achievement represented by *Responsibilities*, Eliot responded to the moral achievement. He had never been, like Pound, a disciple of Yeats, and had only gradually learned to appreciate what he called the "extraordinary development" of Yeats from an admired older poet to an active contemporary poet. In Eliot's view, "to have accomplished what Yeats did in the middle and later years is a great and permanent example— which poets-to-come should study with reverence—of what I have called the Character of the Artist: a kind of moral, as well as intellectual, excellence." He could see that excellence emerging, he said, as early as 1904, in such poems as "The Folly of Being Comforted" (also one of Pound's favorites) and "Adam's Curse," both from *In the Seven Woods*, where "something is coming through, and in beginning to speak as a particular man he is beginning to speak for man." The excellence was clearer to Eliot's mind in the short poem "Peace," in *The Green Helmet* of 1910. "But it is not fully evinced until the volume of 1914, in the violent and terrible epistle dedicatory of *Responsibilities*," Eliot went on to say, and he quoted the lines from "Pardon, Old Fathers":

> Pardon that for a barren passion's sake
> Although I have come close on forty-nine,
> I have no child, I have nothing but a book,
> Nothing but that to prove your blood and mine.

Eliot's comment on this poem was simply that "the naming of his age in the poem is significant. More than half a lifetime to arrive at this freedom of speech. It is a triumph." Eliot chose a poem full of people to single out, while Pound chose a poem full of images. "Pardon, Old Fathers" contains Yeats's own genealogy, projected on a heroic scale, and sees two centuries of strong-willed ancestors looking down on him and being disappointed in him for not producing sons to carry on the line, "nothing but a book." It is the poet measuring himself against his family line, admitting that he has not lived up to it as yet and asking pardon for the barrenness of his life so far. There is in this self-portrait the tone of modesty that Yeats advocated in his speech, but it is not without its note of irony as well, for Yeats put the poem at the beginning of a new collection of which he was justifiably proud. Yeats was a complex enough personality to express humility and pride at the same time, and he was certainly aware that he was adding the new vocation of poet to the ancestral line of merchant, scholar, soldier, skipper, and trader. The "pardon" he asks is also a high claim for himself, and Eliot must have taken note of that claim in calling the poem a "triumph" of Yeats's newly won "freedom of speech," since it implies a contrast of barrenness and creativity in its final lines.

To the list of qualities that characterize Yeats's later style—simplicity, honesty, humility, hardness of imagery, intellectual and moral strength—irony can be added, though neither Pound nor Eliot mentioned it. Perhaps it was too obvious for them to mention, something they took for granted, as we take passionate emotion for granted in romantic poetry. Yeats certainly retained his romantic passion, but he refined and tempered it with his intellect, and where passion contended with intellect, the modern note was struck, as in most of the poems in *Responsibilities*. Most, but not all: if we were to make a catalogue of the thirty-two poems in the volume, according to whether they seem early or late, romantic or modern, we might come out with a table that has, on one side, three long poems, and on the other, twenty-nine shorter poems, nearly half of which fall into three main groupings: the Hugh Lane, or Irish Gallery, poems (5); the Beggar poems (4); and the Maud and Iseult Gonne poems (5). Such a list is useful in showing that the longer narrative poems are more in continuity with his early style, the shorter lyrics—many of which are short enough to be imagist poems—with his later style, and there are far more of the latter than the former. Furthermore, the longer poems have little irony, the shorter ones more. If a similar test were applied to Yeats's previous volume, *The Green Helmet*, published in 1910, at least half seem to be early, while in the volume before that, *In The Seven Woods* of 1904, most seem early. Not surprisingly, the next volume of Yeats's poems, *The Wild Swans at Coole* of 1919, is all in the later modern, or ironic, style. This is a highly subjective balance-sheet, admittedly, but it can be supported by closer analysis, and it reveals that *Responsibilities* is the first collection of Yeats's poetry to show a preponderance of the later, more modern and ironic, style over the earlier, more romantic and emotional, style.

To turn to his best in *Responsibilities*, there are at least a half dozen masterpieces of the dramatic lyric that he perfected: starting with "Pardon, Old Fathers," and going on to "September, 1913," "To a Friend Whose Work Has Come to Nothing," "The Cold Heaven," "The Magi," and "A Coat." Probably the best known of all is "September, 1913," yet for all the analysis and commentary that have been given to it, it still holds surprises if we look at it closely enough. Granted, the Hugh Lane controversy that provided the occasion for one of Yeats's most memorable poems is long over. Dublin now has a gallery to house the legacy of French impressionist paintings Hugh Lane left, and the Tate Gallery in London, which housed them for many years while Ireland was debating whether to provide a gallery for them, has relinquished the paintings to Dublin. Perhaps Yeats's shade is satisfied, so far as the poem had a social purpose, but the poem remains a moving, angry, lyrical expression of Yeats's ardent patriotism as well as his criticism, and as such it reminds us of the higher social function of art that has little to do with the controversy that provoked Yeats to write it. It is transitional between Yeats's romanticism and his modernism, holding up an earlier, idealistic Ireland against a later, more materialistic Ireland. It was Yeats's imaginary farewell to romantic Ireland, a country of heroic martyrs who fought the English again and again without success, while modern Ireland seems to rise up with dirty hands fumbling in the cash register. But the poem is not a farewell to Irish heroism; rather, it praises Ireland's nobler sons in order to shame its present citizens into being worthy of their heritage (just as he chides himself in "Pardon, Old Fathers"), and so the refrain has an opposite and ironic meaning: romantic Ireland is alive and well in Yeats's poem, not dead and gone. The highly quotable refrain is not simply a lament for lost heroism but an inducement to new heroism, and so Yeats is able to affirm his Irish patriotism by a negative affirmation. The ideals of courage and nobility and self-sacrifice that Yeats praises, by naming Irish martyrs he immortalized for the rest of the world, are there to remind readers everywhere, not merely in Dublin, of crassness and philistinism and to invoke self-criticism as an antidote. The poem is a memorial to John O'Leary, an elder Irish patriot whom Yeats knew well, and to others such as Edward Fitzgerald and Wolfe Tone, whom he could not know because they lived much earlier, and it celebrates their virtues as still potentially present in the Irish, despite their meanness in refusing to subscribe to a gallery to house French paintings. Thus Yeats was condemning short-sighted selfishness and praising long-suffering idealism at the same time, giving Ireland credit for a past that could redeem the present.

"To a Friend Whose Work Has Come to Nothing" is the companion poem to "September, 1913," with a complementary theme. It is less confrontation than consolation Yeats had in mind, because Lady Gregory, the aunt of Hugh Lane, was herself one of his heroines in the present generation of the Irish, a preserver rather than a desecrator of Irish idealism. She had been defeated in her effort to raise money for the gallery to house her nephew's collection of paintings, but Yeats portrays her as nobler in defeat than she might have been in triumph. He offers her a strategy, in fact, for making victory from failure. The consolation Yeats offers is a contrast between Lady Gregory's aristocratic virtues, "being honor bred," and the petty vices of her opponent, William Martin Murphy, whose popular newspapers denounced the Lane bequest, "Who, were it proved he lies, / Were neither shamed in his own / Nor in his neighbor's eyes," and so it presents an image of heroic action—or heroic self-restraint—that makes triumph out of defeat. Yet the strategy he advised for his friend, "Be secret and exult," was hardly possible when manifested as publicly as in his poem, and the irony of Lady Gregory's public performance of private virtue may have been appropriate to such a theatrical personality as she was, though picturing her "amid a place of stone," that is, in her manor at Coole Park, was a way of exposing her to the view of the world, both a tribute to her and an act of vengeance on her enemies. The poem is highly personal, intimate, and affectionate, yet it gives an impersonal image of stoic self-control in adversity, the sort of truly civilized behavior that he described later in *A Vision* as essential: "A civilization is a struggle to keep self-control, and in this it is like some great tragic person, some Niobe who must display an almost superhuman will or the cry will not touch our sympathy."[6]

Another example of Yeats's later style that is without question one of the great poems in *Responsibilities* is "The Cold Heaven." It is an accurate description of the winter climate and scenery of his native Ireland, but more than that, as a modern poem about the Irish landscape, it contrasts with "The Lake Isle of Innisfree," a romantic poem about the same landscape. The modern poem is harsh and forbidding in its imagery, as the romantic poem is green and beguiling. The poem is thrilling from beginning to end, and though its "rook-delighting heaven" (an ambiguous phrase that leaves the reader wondering whether heaven delights in rooks or rooks delight in heaven) is as sensuous as the "bee-loud glade" of "Innisfree," the emotion is opposite—harsh ecstasy, not luxurious peace. It is a wintry image of Ireland, as "Innisfree" is a summery image; the two poems are as complementary as their seasons. "The Cold Heaven" is full of that "quality of hard light" that Pound singled out for praise in "The Magi," and it shares some of that poem's visionary quality, too, without becoming prophetic. There is a rising tone of exaltation in it up to the stunning phrase "Riddled with light," and then a falling tone as the soul is freed from the body and "the ghost begins to quicken" for its purgatorial journey into death, where it will be "stricken / By the injustice of the skies for punishment." The poem ends, as so many of Yeats's greatest poems do, with an unanswered question that implies a mixture of doubt and belief: is punishment inevitable for the soul after death, because of "the hot blood of youth, of love crossed long ago"? It seems to say yes, but since the inquisitor is impersonal, "the injustice of the skies," it does not leave the feeling of eternal damnation but rather of an icy trial that the soul may suffer and endure. "The Cold Heaven," for all its harshness, is finally an exhilarating poem, for the landscape seems as much a desired condition of Yeats's soul in his later years as "Innisfree" did in his youth. It is reminiscent of an earlier poem, "The Coming of Wisdom with Time," which appeared in *The Green Helmet:*

> Though leaves are many, the root is one;
> Through all the lying days of my youth

---

6. William Butler Yeats, *A Vision,* 268.

> I swayed my leaves and flowers in the sun;
> Now I may wither into the truth.

It also brings to mind a passage in "Reveries over Childhood and Youth," the first section of Yeats's *Autobiography,* where he wrote:

> I had found again the windy light that moved me as a child. I persuaded myself that I had a passion for the dawn, and this passion, though mainly histrionic like a child's play, had moments of sincerity. Years afterward, when I had finished *The Wanderings of Oisin,* dissatisfied with its yellow and its dull green, with all that overcharged color inherited from the romantic movement, I deliberately reshaped my style, deliberately sought out an impression as of cold light and tumbling clouds.[7]

We may judge from this piece of self-criticism that "The Cold Heaven" was a poem Yeats himself regarded as the fulfillment of his effort to match craftsmanship with self-mastery in forging his later style. There is also a note of irony at the end of the poem, for in the final question it raises about the soul's destiny after death, there is the thought that if he is to be punished, yet left with the ecstasy of his vision, the punishment may be more purgative than punitive, and it is a constructive self-criticism he offers, not a self-condemnation, a refining and strengthening of his spirit, it would seem, for its last sojourn among the other shades.

So *Responsibilities* seems richer the more closely it is examined. It does not carry the poetic weight of the volumes that follow it, from *The Wild Swans at Coole* to *Last Poems,* but it is a transitional collection, with some poems that look back to an earlier style and more that point forward to the later style. What gives it special importance in the line of Yeats's whole development is the sense that the poet is becoming surer and surer of himself, more in command of his medium, the diction, the rhythm, the rhyme, the tone and symbol and theme. He was facing some of the controversies of his time with resolution, but was growing disillusioned with popular causes, Irish nationalism in particular, and was being drawn closer to those few who kept their heads above the crowd, like Lady Gregory, and to those he loved, like Maud Gonne and her daughter, Iseult. He was also developing an increasingly prophetic vision of the events that were changing the world for the worse: it is almost a surprise to realize that *Responsibilities* appeared on the eve of World War I and not during or after it. It begins with a prologue that apologizes to the poet's father for the seeming barrenness of his life and ends with a bitterly ironic image of himself

---

7. *The Autobiography of William Butler Yeats,* 48.

in the epilogue: "Notorious, till all my priceless things / Are but a post the passing dogs defile." One might suppose that Yeats was saying good-bye to his poetic career, with this hearty expression of self-contempt, but in fact he was only preparing himself for more ambitious efforts by humbling himself before the world—humbling, but not capitulating, since he had learned how to turn derision aside and "forgive even that wrong of wrongs," purging his conscience by mocking himself openly. *Purgative* may be the word most descriptive of *Responsibilities*, because Yeats was proving himself a stronger poet than he had ever been before, ascending by means of self-irony above adversity, whether public or private, coming fully into his own as the later Yeats.

Dying into a Dance: Theme and Symbol in *The Winding Stair*

"It looks as if I may have a spirited old age," Yeats wrote in a letter of 1919, when he was in his fifty-fifth year, and the works of the last two decades of his life give us ample proof of how well he understood himself. Gerontologists could marvel at the astonishing fecundity of Yeats's old age, and for lovers of his poetry, the creative burst of energy in his later years is cause for much satisfaction. Just think of his last twenty years: in 1919, *The Wild Swans at Coole* was published; in 1921, *Michael Robartes and the Dancer*; in 1925, *A Vision*; in 1928, *The Tower*; in 1933, *The Winding Stair and Other Poems*; in 1935, *A Full Moon in March*; and in 1939, when he died in January of his seventy-fifth year, *Last Poems and Two Plays*. It is the harvest of a lifetime; any single one of those volumes would have made him a major poet, yet they came as the culmination of a long career as poet and dramatist, capping an achievement already great enough to win him a Nobel Prize in 1923.

He might well have rested on his laurels, but as he said in his speech of acceptance in Sweden, a rejuvenation had been taking place in him over the years, such that when he was young, his Muse was old, but as he grew older, his Muse grew younger: "I am even persuaded that she is like those angels in Swedenborg's vision," he said, "and moves perpetually 'towards the day-spring of her youth.' "[8]

To understand the source of Yeats's imaginative power in old age would be to understand the secret of his genius, an insight beyond the reach of any reader, however psychic or psychoanalytic he might be, but when we look at the poetry of the later years, we can clearly see the emergence of regeneration as a major theme, and we can reasonably assume that this theme must somehow be linked to his remarkable capacity for self-regeneration as a poet. The focus of this theme of regeneration in Yeats's work is the

---

8. "The Bounty of Sweden," in *The Autobiography of William Butler Yeats*, 365.

collection *The Winding Stair,* where it is closely connected with the title image of the winding stair, potentially the most complex of all the major symbols in Yeats's poetry.

In his notes to *The Winding Stair,* Yeats spoke of his theme and his main symbol in explicit terms: "In this book and elsewhere," he says, "I have used towers, and one tower in particular, as symbols and have compared their winding stairs to the philosophical gyres." The particular tower is Thoor Ballylee in County Galway, he says, "where I have written most of my poems in recent years," though he notes that "A Dialogue of Self and Soul," one of the major poems, "was written in the spring of 1928 during a long illness, indeed finished the day before a Cannes doctor told me to stop writing. Then in the spring of 1929 life returned to me as an impression of the uncontrollable energy and daring of the great creators." This sense of coming back to life after being close to death is strongly felt in many of the poems of the volume, especially in "A Dialogue of Self and Soul," and we know from a letter he wrote earlier to his old friend Olivia Shakespear that the theme was in his mind even before he had found the right title for his poem: "I am writing a new tower poem, 'Sword and Tower,' which is a choice of rebirth rather than deliverance from birth. I make my Japanese sword and its silk covering my symbol of life." Since the theme of rebirth and the symbol of the winding stair are intertwined in it, there is no more trustworthy guide to the direction of Yeats's thought at this crucial juncture of his career than this poem. He had already written a number of poems about the tower in Galway, near Coole Park, which he had bought from Lady Gregory and restored as a summer home, and among them are some of his finest, "In Memory of Major Robert Gregory," "A Prayer for My Daughter," "Meditations in Time of Civil War," and the title poem of his collection of 1928, "The Tower," but in them the tower was the dominant symbol and the mood was often bitter—Yeats himself confessed, "Re-reading *The Tower* I was astonished at its bitterness, and long to live out of Ireland that I may find some new vintage. Yet that bitterness gave the book its power," he went on to admit, "and it is the best book I have written."[9]

In the poems after *The Tower* Yeats sought a new symbol and a new mood, and "A Dialogue of Self and Soul" was the first of his poems to stress the symbolic force of the winding stair within the tower, as well as the first to move from bitterness into joy, thus linking the symbol of the gyre with the theme of regeneration. Like so many of Yeats's later poems, it is a dramatic dialogue between opposite poles of his own personality; what he had earlier called the Self and the Mask become in this poem the Self and the Soul, and

9. Yeats to Olivia Shakespear, April 25, 1928, in *The Letters of William Butler Yeats,* ed. Alan Wade (New York: Macmillan, 1955), 742.

the metaphysical debate between them turns on the question of whether in old age death or life should be the main concern. The question is resolved in favor of life, which means that the Self is the surprising victor, not by a simple choice but by a process of purgation, or cleansing of conscience, which is so rigorous that it is as if the Self had been born again out of death. The relationship of the winding stair to the theme of regeneration is a dynamic one in which the upward and downward movements of consciousness between Self and Soul, life and death, give the poem an emotional and intellectual force equal to anything Yeats ever wrote.

"A Dialogue of Self and Soul" is a poem of inner conflict deliberately intensified to a point of maximum tension and then released; it is a poem of violent imagery—the dark tower of death looming above, the gleaming sword of life flashing below—but there is no bloodshed; instead, there is sweetness, laughter, and singing in the end, an exuberant outpouring of joy. The struggle of wills on the winding stair has ended in a new state of blessedness in which the Self has renounced bitterness and cast out remorse, is able to forgive its faults, be blest by everything, and look on everything as blest—even the blind man's ditch has become fecund in his eyes. The process of regeneration that takes place in this poem is not simply a victory of life over death, or Self over Soul, but the interaction between life and death, Self and Soul, producing a new resolution of internal conflicts and a new acceptance of the external world. Would it be too much to suggest that in this poem Yeats has achieved what in *A Vision* he said was the aim of his whole imaginative enterprise, namely, "to hold in a single thought reality and justice"?

If we can agree that there is a fulfillment of Yeats's vision in this poem, we should also be able to agree that the figure of the winding stair is central to it, and this figure is bound to lead us to the figure of the double cone or intersecting gyres that is central to his myth of human history and individual personality, for it is clear that Yeats intended the winding stair to be a concrete embodiment of a highly abstract concept; it is only one of many figures he used to portray the gyres, but it is the most frequent, most personal, and most familiar. He had published *A Vision* some years earlier, in 1925, and in it he detailed the multiple sources and meanings of the gyres, foreshadowing the figure of the winding stair in his poems. Thus, to understand what is intended in the symbol of the winding stair, we must necessarily look at what Yeats says about the gyres in *A Vision*.

Many readers of Yeats feel some uneasiness about entering into the more esoteric realms of his thought, outside the poetry, afraid they might be drawn unwittingly into a secret cult, and *A Vision* does speak in arcane language. However, as long as we know that our purpose is to clarify the poetry, we do not need to shrink from any pursuit that will deepen our appreciation of what poetry, by its very brevity, can only suggest. *A Vision* is esoteric, indeed, but one way to approach it is as a long and very elaborate footnote to the later poems of Yeats, much as we look at the notes that Eliot appended to *The Waste Land,* seeing it as valuable not for itself, but for what it helps us to understand in the later poems. Yeats, like Eliot, was well aware that he was writing in a rational and skeptical age, and that he had to try to make his work intelligible to readers not only better educated in the sciences than in the arts, but possibly indifferent to religious belief. So he put his own disclaimers into the introduction to *A Vision,* quoting his invisible instructors, who spoke to him through his wife, as saying, "We have come to bring you metaphors for poetry," and adding that the various geometrical and astronomical figures he used were meant to be metaphorical rather than actual, "stylistic arrangements of experience"[10] rather than real periods of history, a means of bringing order to his imaginative system. However obscure Yeats could be at times, he wished to avoid becoming what in his view Blake had often been, "a too literal realist of the imagination,"[11] and however heretical he could be, with his spiritualism and his mystical societies, he worked most of the time within the respectable tradition of Christian Platonism, or Renaissance humanism, which links classical thinkers such as Plato and Plotinus, Homer and Virgil, with medieval Christian thinkers such as Augustine, Aquinas, and Dante, and with later Christian mystics such as St. Theresa, St. John of the Cross, and Swedenborg. We must remember that Yeats's search for Unity of Being involved him in historical as well as psychic research, and that it is the intellectual complexity of his poetry, as much as the supernatural elements in it, that impels us to search outside it for meanings, and come back to it with, we hope, fuller understanding. So, with Yeats's own disclaimers in our minds, and with our feet firmly planted on the winding stair of his poetry, let us take a hard look at what he says in *A Vision* about the gyres.

In the opening section, called "The Great Wheel," Yeats quotes a passage from the pre-Socratic philosopher Empedocles, describing an imaginary vortex in time that contains Concord and Discord in equal measure, opposites that revolve with increasing and decreasing force, like twin stars in the heavens, and he gives his first diagram of a double cone to represent this image, but he does not pursue the reference further, because there is little more to be found of such figures in any Greek philosopher before Plato. He does, however, mention Heraclitus, who wrote that "the gods are mortals, men are immortals, each living in the others' death and dying in the others' life."[12] Thus Yeats

10. Yeats, *A Vision,* 8, 25.

11. Yeats, "William Blake and His Illustrations to the *Divine Comedy,*" in *Essays and Introductions,* 119.

12. Yeats, *A Vision,* 68, hereafter in this essay cited parenthetically in the text by page number alone.

came to associate the vortex of Concord and Discord in Empedocles with the death-in-life and life-in-death motif of Heraclitus.

"The first gyres clearly described by philosophy," Yeats goes on, "are those described in the *Timaeus* which are made by the circuits of 'the Other' (creators of all particular things), of the planets as they ascend or descend above or below the equator" (p. 68). He thus discovered a vortex in one of the Platonic dialogues, associated with the movement of the planets through the sky during the year, taking the shape of the twelve constellations, which in classical mythology form the zodiac, often pictured as a spiral ring or belt of stars rotating around the earth. From Empedocles and Plato, two classical Greek thinkers, then, Yeats managed to derive his gyres of time and space.

For his gyres of personality, human and superhuman, he turned to later, Christian thinkers, saying that Aquinas had described a circular movement of angels in their ascent and descent between God and man, a figure borrowed from Jacob's dream of angels going up and down a ladder, as recorded in Genesis 28:12: "And he dreamed, and behold a ladder set up on the earth, and the top of it reached to heaven; and behold the angels of God ascending and descending on it." In a note to this reference, Yeats says that a similar belief about the motion of spirits was held in the west of Ireland and that he had mentioned in his early book, *The Celtic Twilight,* in the essay "The Friends of the People of Faery," being told a folktale about a faery woman who could "swirl round on her feet" and "swirl up in the air," just "as if it was a winding stairs she went up, only far swifter" (p. 69). It would seem from this note that the winding stair image had come to Yeats first from Irish folklore, as a way of describing the motion of invisible spirits, long before he had encountered it in his reading or in his life, and if so, we can assume it went through a long gestation period before it was ready for his poetry. Yeats next speaks of a commentary by Macrobius on the Latin text of Cicero's "Dream of Scipio," where the soul in its journey from the heavens to the earth to be born, or "die into the body," follows a course from a sphere to a point—a course that would have the shape of a cone—and then returns after death to the star from which it came, exactly as described in Plato's *Timaeus.*

By far the most extensive account Yeats gives of the motions of souls or angels, however, he takes from the eighteenth-century Swedish philosopher and mystic Emanuel Swedenborg, whose influence on poets from Blake to Emerson to Baudelaire to Yeats was profound. He says that Swedenborg "speaks of gyres of spirits" in his *Spiritual Diary,* and, "In the *Principia,* a vast scientific work written before his mystical life, he describes a double cone. All physical reality, the universe as a whole, every solar system, every atom, is a double cone; where there are 'two poles one opposite to the other, these two poles have the form of cones'" (p. 69). There is no doubt that Yeats found in Swedenborg the images of the gyres that were most congenial to him, and with them a scientific mind (Swedenborg was a mining engineer before he became a theologian) that valued mathematics as much as poetry and believed that all human communication was necessarily symbolic and figurative rather than factual, and whose doctrine of the "correspondences" between physical and spiritual reality became the basis of the symbolist aesthetic. Yeats adds, "I am not concerned with his explanation of how these cones evolved from the point and the sphere, nor with his arguments to prove that they govern all the movements of the planets, for I think, as did Swedenborg in his mystical writings, that the forms of geometry can have but a symbolic relation to spaceless reality" (p. 69). Yeats took Swedenborg to be a scientific mystic who saw the spiral shape as the basic form of both matter and spirit, the active principle in the universe (how both Swedenborg and Yeats would have loved to hear of the much-later scientific discovery of the double-helix pattern of genes in every living cell!), who thought of poetry along with mathematics as the highest human expression, and who believed in the communication between men and angels, angels being human souls who enjoyed forever the divine harmony and love that souls in human bodies could only experience by analogy, or correspondences.

One of Swedenborg's most attractive beliefs, from Yeats's point of view, was that angels marry in heaven just as men and women do on earth, but that their marriages are harmonious and their intercourse, though sensually delightful, is without sin or lust, like the sexual pleasure Adam and Eve enjoyed before the Fall. In 1933, at the time he was completing the Crazy Jane poems that would go into *The Winding Stair,* he wrote Olivia Shakespear approvingly of "that saying of Swedenborg's that the sexual intercourse of the angels is a conflagration of the whole being" and asked her, "why not take Swedenborg literally and think we attain, in a partial contact, what the spirits know throughout their being? He somewhere describes two spirits meeting, and as they touch they become a single conflagration." We also know, from Yeats's reflections on his Nobel Prize, that he shared Swedenborg's belief that all angels are youthful men and women, there being neither infant nor elderly souls in heaven—and here again, Yeats had found a similar folk belief in Ireland, for as he said in an essay of 1914, "Swedenborg, Mediums, and the Desolate Places," Swedenborg's belief that men become angels "in the springtime of their life" is shared by country people in the west of Ireland who say that "to grow old in heaven is to grow young."[13]

The only other source for Yeats's figure of the gyres, according to his account in *A Vision,* was in the notes for a story by French novelist Gustave Flaubert, which was to have been called "La Spirale" but was never written. In it,

13. Yeats, *Explorations* (New York: Macmillan, 1962), 30–70.

Flaubert had planned to describe a man whose dreams grew in magnificence as his life grew more miserable, "the wreck of some love affair coinciding with his marriage to a dream princess."[14] But though there may be some parallel, as Yeats seems to have believed, between this unrealized story and the double cone of his vision, the reference is a slight one at best, hardly to be compared with the rich associations he found in Swedenborg and the pregnant suggestions he discovered in Empedocles, Plato, and Macrobius, as well as in Irish folklore.

What Yeats had found in these writers was a linking metaphor that mediated between the spirit and the flesh, the celestial and the terrestrial realms, and that thus gave him a means of representing metaphysical ideas by visible means. With a facility for finding correspondences that might have amazed even Swedenborg, Yeats was able in his poetry to project the gyres in innumerable metamorphoses, sometimes as a gyring motion, as in the whirling of the dancer or the circling flight of birds, sometimes in a natural shape like that of a seashell, sometimes as the winding sheet encasing a dead body, sometimes as winding hair or a skein of wool, sometimes simply as the abstract geometrical figure of a gyre, but most aptly and memorably as a winding stair, the stair of Thoor Ballylee, which was his home.

If we follow the turnings of the gyre through the collection that he called *The Winding Stair,* we find it appearing in various forms in at least a dozen poems, always prominent though never as dominant as in "A Dialogue of Self and Soul." In "Blood and the Moon" it is again used as a complementary symbol within the tower, this time, however, not as Self against Soul, but as the force of history against the ravages of time: the tower is the emblem of "a time / Half dead at the top," while the stair is a succession of great Irish writers Yeats chooses to call his "ancestors," whose thoughts inspire him now:

> I declare this tower is my symbol; I declare
> This winding, gyring, spiring treadmill of a stair is my
> ancestral stair;
> That Goldsmith and the Dean, Berkeley and Burke have
> traveled there.

Yeats pictures each of these eighteenth-century Irish writers as having imagined the Ireland of their time not "half dead at the top," but infused with an intellectual idealism and force that lifted it upward from earth toward heaven—first Goldsmith, by "deliberately sipping at the honey-pot of his mind,"

14. Yeats, *A Vision,* 70.

> And haughtier-headed Burke that proved the State a tree,
> That this unconquerable labyrinth of the birds, century
>   after century,
> Cast but dead leaves to mathematical equality;
> And God-appointed Berkeley that proved all things a
>   dream,
> That this pragmatical, preposterous pig of a world, its
>   farrow that so solid seem,
> Must vanish on the instant if the mind but change its
>   theme;

—and finally Swift, to whom Yeats gave the highest place of honor on the stair:

> *Saeva Indignatio* and the labourer's hire,
> The strength that gives our blood and state magnanimity
>   of its own desire;
> Everything that is not God consumed with intellectual
>   fire.

Throughout this complex and violent poem, Yeats has contrasted the purity of the "unclouded moon" in the sky with the impurity of the "blood-saturated ground" on which he stands, and it is the winding stair between them that gives him hope for a renewal of the idealism of Ireland's past. He imagines an "Odour of blood on the ancestral stair!" that will reinvigorate his time, when "every modern nation" is "like the tower, / Half dead at the top," and when "wisdom is the property of the dead" but "power" is the "property of the living," and he hopes that the wisdom of the dead writers he has named will give him, as a living writer, the power to purify his time like "the visage of the moon / When it has looked in glory from a cloud." "Blood and the Moon," which follows "A Dialogue of Self and Soul," thus transforms the winding stair image from a regenerator of the individual, in the first poem, to a regenerator of society, especially of Ireland, in the next poem, making the personal gyre symbol into a more inclusive symbol of renewal and rebirth.

Strangely enough, the winding stair itself does not appear again—it is as if in these two powerful poems at the beginning of the volume the symbolic resonance is established that will make the gyres rotate at the poet's will—but the gyre *does* appear: there are many other gyre images to be found in the poems that follow "A Dialogue of Self and Soul" and "Blood and the Moon." For instance, there is both the Heavenly Circuit and Berenice's Hair in the short poem called "Veronica's Napkin," astronomical figures that represent a circular constellation in the heavens and the whole cycle of constellations that form the zodiac, a sort of double vortex in itself, and there is also "the circuit of a needle's eye" in which God and his angels stand, undoubtedly Yeats's version of the kingdom of heaven—the needle's eye being the passage, as pictured in one of Christ's parables, through which a camel can go more easily than a rich man can enter heaven. Since Veronica's napkin was the legendary cloth that St. Veronica gave Christ while he was carrying his cross and on which Christ's image was imprinted, the poem places Christ and his cross—"a different pole"—at the center of one historical gyre, while Adam and the "Tent-pole of Eden" are placed at the center of an opposing gyre, the two together giving a vivid representation of the double vortex in a single short poem, embodying both the metaphysical and the physical patterns of the gyre—"symbolical glory of the earth and air!" What the poem seems to signify is that Christ's death reversed the movement of history, so that now, rather than entering into the kingdom of heaven through the Garden of Eden, man must enter it through the sacrifice of Christ: blood becomes a regenerative force as it was in "Blood and the Moon."

The next notable gyre images in *The Winding Stair* are to be found in the pair of beautiful poems written for Lady Gregory, "Coole Park, 1929" and "Coole Park and Ballylee, 1931." Both poems center on a human figure and a natural scene, "a woman's powerful character" that age has not destroyed and "gardens rich in memory glorified," but both poems use descriptions of the flight of birds as symbols of the journey of the human soul into death, and in both this flight follows a gyring or circling motion. The opening line of "Coole Park, 1929" brings the swallows in: "I meditate upon a swallow's flight"—and after naming Lady Gregory and some of her circle, Douglas Hyde, Lionel Johnson, "that meditative man, John Synge," and "those impetuous men, Shawe-Taylor and Hugh Lane," it brings the swallows back again, this time with human faces of departed spirits returning home, like swallows coming back north in the springtime:

> They came like swallows and like swallows went,
> And yet a woman's powerful character
> Could keep a swallow to its first intent;
> And half a dozen in formation there,
> That seemed to whirl upon a compass-point,
> Found certainty upon the dreaming air,
> The intellectual sweetness of those lines
> That cut through time or cross it withershins.

The swallows are a beguiling reincarnation of Lady Gregory's and Yeats's dead friends, and in their gyring motion they have temporarily been brought back from death into life, shaping a "certainty upon the dreaming air" that brings an intellectual sweetness with it to express what Lady Gregory's benevolent influence has accomplished. In "Coole Park and Ballylee, 1931," a similar feat is performed by a solitary swan, associated in this case with water, which represents "the generated soul." In his imagination, Yeats travels from Thoor Ballylee to Coole Park, moving with the water that flows from the stream beside his tower to the lake near Lady Gregory's house, and there he sees a swan fly up:

> At sudden thunder of the mounting swan
> I turned about and looked where branches break
> The glittering reaches of the flooded lake.
>
> Another emblem there! That stormy white
> But seems a concentration of the sky;
> And, like the soul, it sails into the sight
> And in the morning's gone, no man knows why;
> And is so lovely that it sets to right
> What knowledge or its lack had set awry,
> So arrogantly pure, a child might think
> It could be murdered with a spot of ink.

The swan has temporarily lifted his spirits with its flight and its beauty, and though he is painfully reminded of Lady Gregory's age and infirmity by the "Sound of a stick upon the floor, a sound / From somebody that toils from chair to chair," he returns to the swan again at the end of the poem very movingly, to convey the sense of Lady Gregory's spirit on its way toward death, still noble and graceful in its departure as in its life:

> We were the last romantics—chose for theme
> Traditional sanctity and loveliness;
> Whatever's written in what poets name
> The book of the people; whatever most can bless
> The mind of man or elevate a rhyme;
> But all is changed, that high horse riderless,
> Though mounted in that saddle Homer rode
> Where the swan drifts upon a darkening flood.

More and more, in this poem and those that follow, the gyres seem to be revolving away from life and toward death, for in "At Algeciras—A Meditation upon Death," Yeats uses the image of the seashell, "Not such as are in Newton's metaphor, / But actual shells of Rosses' level shore," to bring him to the thought of his own death as a journey into the unknown recesses of the ocean where the shell came from, and to

> Bid imagination run
> Much on the Great Questioner;
> What He can question, what if questioned I
> Can with a fitting confidence reply.

He does not answer the question in this poem, but in a further one, "Mohini Chatterjee," he does think of the soul's movement through many incarnations until it finds peace in another gyre image, the figure of the dancer:

> Old lovers yet may have
> All that time denied—
> Grave is heaped on grave
> That they be satisfied—
> Over the blackened earth
> The old troops parade,
> Birth is heaped on birth
> That such cannonade
> May thunder time away,
> Birth-hour and death-hour meet,
> Or, as great sages say,
> Men dance on deathless feet.

This poem, with its image of souls dancing in paradise, leads directly into "Byzantium," the best known of all the poems in *The Winding Stair*, where there is another fusion of the gyre image with the theme of regeneration, as in "A Dialogue of Self and Soul."

In fact, "Byzantium" is so loaded with gyre images that it deserves its place in the center of the volume. It has both a mummy and a dancer, and though it does not contain a winding stair, it does contain a winding path; for all its complexity, the poem is tightly unified, and one must read it in its entirety to feel the full effect of the interweaving of symbol and theme. We know from his letters that Yeats intended "Byzantium" as an answer to Sturge Moore's complaint that "Sailing to Byzantium" had been more about nature than about eternity, and in the later poem, he set out more determinedly than in any other poem to picture paradise as he imagined it, in form like the historical Byzantium, "as it is in the system towards the end of the first Christian millennium," Yeats noted as he began working on the poem in 1930. If his model was historical, his realization was clearly visionary, and it is the passage from the historical to the visionary that gives the poem its great power.

The first stanza of "Byzantium" presents a night scene in the city, a dream landscape magical in its mood of moonlit silence, and then, in the second stanza, the poem confronts the reader with the superhuman figure of a mummy that has been unwound into "an image, man or shade," which the poet addresses in language echoing Heraclitus: "I call it death-in-life and life-in-death." He then unwinds the winding path, and the gyre of mortality is superseded by the gyre of immortality as the miraculous cock "planted on the star-lit golden bough" crows "In glory of changeless metal" in the third stanza and ushers in the brilliantly lighted scene of the fourth stanza, where the "blood-begotten spirits come" to dance on the mosaic pavement, having left their mortality behind, "Dying into a dance" that repeats the winding path eternally, and so are reborn from death into immortal life. The fifth and final stanza is a dramatic image of souls riding to paradise on dolphins' backs and then being transformed into dancers themselves: heaven, in Yeats's vision, is a dynamic place, not a place of rest, and the theme of regeneration finds as much life in death as death in life, "those images that yet / Fresh images beget." With "Byzantium," Yeats had reached the upper regions of his gyres and had placed the whirling dancer at the top of the winding stair; in the following poems, with but few exceptions, he made his way down the stair again to the earth, from death back into life.

"Vacillation" is principally a poem of the downward gyre, although it contains a moment of visionary grace, when "my body of a sudden blazed," and "It seemed, so great my happiness, / That I was blessed and could bless." But this sudden rush of mystical ecstasy does not last, and as we know from a letter Yeats wrote to Olivia Shakespear, about the time he was writing the poem, "The swordsman (life) throughout repudiates the saint (death) but not without vacillation." It is a poem about life and death, but unlike "Byzantium," it is more about death in life than about life in death; its image of immortality is Frazer's golden bough, which "is half all glittering flame and half all green / Abounding foliage moistened with the dew," but instead of preparing for death as another kind of life, the soul in this poem wishes to "come / Proud, open-eyed and laughing to the tomb." There is a strong sense of the transience of life in its refrain "Let all things pass away," and in the dialogue between the soul and the heart, which echoes the earlier dialogue between the self and the soul, it is the heart that has the last word, or rather the last question: "What theme had Homer but original sin?" Homer becomes the poet's exemplar in the final section of "Vacillation," where he declines the Christian mysticism of Baron Friedrich von Hügel, with its ascetic denial of the senses, and chooses in preference Homer's belief in the interaction of gods and men:

> Homer is my example and his unchristened heart.
> The lion and the honeycomb, what has Scripture said?
> So get you gone, Von Hugel, though with blessings on your head.

For the most part, the poems that Yeats included in *The Winding Stair* as the final segment, entitled "Words for Music Perhaps," consisting of the Crazy Jane poems and the "Woman Young and Old" sequence, are also of the downward gyre, decidedly earthly in their imagery, even including the one heavenly poem called "The Delphic Oracle upon Plotinus," which is much more sensual than "Byzantium." Yeats told Shakespear that all the poems of "Words for Music Perhaps" came from opposition: "Sexual abstinence fed their fire—I was ill and yet full of desire."[15] It would be a mistake, however, to take these poems too literally—it is always a mistake to take Yeats's poems too literally—and we need to remember that other letter in which Yeats endorsed with enthusiasm Swedenborg's vision of the angels making love in heaven. The theme of regeneration is still primary in these poems, as in the earlier ones, and while much of the imagery is sexual, the gyres continue to appear in new guises. We find, for example, in "Crazy Jane Reproved," "the shell's elaborate whorl," and in "Crazy Jane and Jack the Journeyman" we find that "love is but a skein unwound / Between the dark and dawn"—a skein of wool that "bound us ghost to ghost"; we find many dancers: "Crazy Jane Grown Old Looks at the Dancers," "Those Dancing Days are Gone," "Come dance with me in Ireland," and "The Dancer at Cruachan and Cro-Patrick," and we find "Plato's spindle," a "winding sheet," and in "The Delphic Oracle upon Plotinus," the souls in paradise are "winding through the grove."

Gyres continue to appear frequently in these sometimes shockingly erotic poems, and there is one poem in particular in the "Woman Young and Old" sequence that could be said to sum up Yeats's deliberate connection in the later poems of sexual ecstasy with mystical ecstasy. It is called "Chosen," and in it, the first experience of sexual love between a woman and a man is equated with the union of souls in heaven, and the figure of the gyre is transformed from a spiraling zodiac into a cosmic sphere, an image that Yeats drew from his reading of Macrobius's *Commentary on Cicero's Dream of Scipio*, where it is said that when the Milky Way ("miraculous stream") intersects with the zodiac, the spiral pattern becomes a sphere, a symbol of perfect harmony. In a letter to Shakespear at about the time he was writing this poem, Yeats wrote, "One feels at moments as if one could with a touch convey a vision—that the mystic way and sexual love use the same means— opposed yet parallel existences." Thus we may believe that even in the more worldly poems of *The Winding Stair*, Yeats was using his gyres as stairways from earth to heaven and back again, while the regeneration that took place in his poetry at this time had as much to do with spiritual as with physical renewal. The secret of how Yeats was able to find such creative vitality in old

15. Yeats to Olivia Shakespear, August 17, 1933, in *Letters*, 814.

age remained his secret, and it may have been as mysterious a process to him as it is to his readers.

The mystery of regeneration in one of the finest of his shorter poems, "Stream and Sun at Glendalough," can serve as the poet's last word on the theme:

> What motion of the sun or stream
> Or eyelid shot the gleam
> That pierced my body through?
> What made me live like these that seem
> Self-born, born anew?

Yeats's characteristic answer to a question is another question, and in the continuing dialogue between Yeats and his readers, it is the unanswered question that makes the poetry linger unforgettably in our minds.

Last Poems: Learning Tragic Joy

There were two periods in his life when Yeats deliberately altered his way of writing poetry, and it will always be part of the fascination of reading him to wonder why he chose to do so. It is commonly agreed that the first significant change in Yeats's poetic style came in his middle years, when he was in his forties, and that the volume *Responsibilities* more than any other represents a growth in maturity of technique and of viewpoint, brought about by his own exacting self-criticism and by the effort, helped along by younger poet and friend Ezra Pound, "to go over my poetry and eliminate the abstract," that is, to make his expression more direct, truthful, terse, and realistic. In the process of changing his style, he also changed his age, remaking himself from an Irish romantic poet of the "Celtic twilight" into an international modern poet of what might be called the Western Apocalypse, the threat of the imminent collapse of civilization. No reader can doubt that the movement from early to middle Yeats, from *The Wind among the Reeds* to *Responsibilities,* is much more than a merely personal development, that in it we are following the course of history through a period of decline and fall, like that of the Roman Empire, and that Yeats's increasingly tragic view of the events in his own small country, notably the Easter Rising and the Civil War, mirror the barbarizing and brutalizing forces at work in the larger civilization.

Yeats was not just changing *with* the times, he was changing *against* them, championing traditional moral idealism, which he chose to think of as "aristocratic," in the face of what he looked on with horror as "the growing murderousness of the world," when "a conviction that the world was now but a bundle of fragments possessed me without ceasing." The middle poems of Yeats, from *The Wild Swans at Coole* through *The Winding Stair,* are clearly the work of a master who has learned how to see history as myth and whose art is both a confrontation with reality and a transcendence of it.

The second significant change in Yeats's poetic style came in his sixties, when he refused to remain "a sixty-year-old smiling, public man" and became instead the Wild Old Wicked Man of the *Last Poems.* His motives for this final metamorphosis were less historical than personal, and there is still a lively debate among critics about whether the change was for the better or the worse. Some would argue that the middle or later poems are the great achievement, the immortal part of his work, and that the very late poems represent a falling off, that he was overtaken by mortality in the last decade of his life. If the change from the early to the middle or later Yeats signifies a growth from youth to maturity, the change from the middle or later to the very late signifies to some readers a descent from maturity into senility, a decline rather than a fulfillment of his genius.

Most readers do find it easier to like the early and middle poems than the last poems, and there are good reasons for this natural preference. The melancholy voice and hypnotic rhythms of *Crossways, The Secret Rose,* and *The Wind among the Reeds,* beckoning us to an Irish hermitage somewhere green and misty, can be enchanting, and the stark imagery and prophetic utterances of *The Wild Swans at Coole, The Tower,* and *The Winding Stair,* inviting us to leave the worldly city and iron age we live in for the holy city and golden age of Byzantium, can be even more compelling. But the bawdy voices and drunken ranting of *Words for Music Perhaps, A Full Moon in March,* and *Last Poems* can be unsettling, making us fear that we are being led into intemperate old age and even madness, asking with Yeats, "Why Should Not Old Men Be Mad?" If the early Yeats charms us by posing as "The Man Who Dreamed of Faeryland," and the middle Yeats moves us by declaring that "A terrible beauty is born," what are we to make of the late Yeats, who defiantly proclaims that he is "a foolish, passionate man"? We may be willingly led from the youthful dreams of a unity of culture in a newly reawakened Ireland to the mature vision of a world in which "the blood-dimmed tide is loosed" and a "rough beast . . . / Slouches towards Bethlehem to be born," but having ascended the ladder of Yeats's imagination, we feel a little reluctant to descend it again and to lie down "where all the ladders start, / In the foul rag-and-bone shop of the heart."

Yet, unappealing as they may seem at first glance, such is the magic of Yeats's poetic style that we cannot hold back for long: the late poems became as seductive in their way as the earlier poems, and we begin to see that they are an inevitable part of his genius. The youthful reveries and mature visions have been transmuted into something else, a further revelation of truths about the human heart, which, as the prophet Jeremiah long ago declared, "is deceitful above all things, and desperately wicked: who can know it?" These dark words of Jeremiah echo through the late poems of Yeats, revealing much we would rather not know about "the fury and the mire of human veins," but also showing an astonishing amount of spiritual refreshment and delight, as in "The Gyres":

> Irrational streams of blood are staining earth;
> Empedocles has thrown all things about;
> Hector is dead and there's a light in Troy;
> We that look on but laugh in tragic joy.

Though this poem is directly related to *A Vision,* with its myth of history as a pattern of spirals moving upward and downward with the rise and fall of civilization, it depends less on myth than on the tone of the poet's voice. In fact, it is possible to say that all of Yeats's last poems depend less on his philosophical system than the middle poems do, and that they have a surprising strength: the personal vision of the poet has to a large extent replaced the historical vision. Thus, later in the same poem, "The Gyres," when he answers his own question—

> What matter though numb nightmare ride on top,
> And blood and mire the sensitive body stain? . . .
> What matter? Out of cavern comes a voice,
> And all it knows is that one word "Rejoice!"

—we feel that the cavern is not Plato's Cave of Shadows or Porphyry's Cave of Nymphs, but Yeats's own mind, and the voice is not that of Owen Aherne or Michael Robartes or Cuchulain, but the triumphant voice of Yeats himself, a poet old in years but still young in heart. We are bound to remember that when Yeats received the Nobel Prize in 1923, he looked at the design on the medal of a young poet with a lyre listening to his Muse, and reflected: "I was good-looking once like that young man, but my unpracticed verse was full of infirmity, my Muse old as it were; and now I am old and rheumatic, and nothing to look at, but my Muse is young. I am even persuaded that she is like those Angels in Swedenborg's vision, and moves perpetually 'towards the day-spring of her youth.' "[16]

Like all of his major themes, the final one of tragic joy was gathering force for a long time in Yeats before it found expression in his work, and it

---

16. "The Bounty of Sweden," in *The Autobiography of William Butler Yeats,* 365.

gains strength from all that preceded it. The American poet John Berryman even held that "Yeats's way was the ideal way. A long slow development, the work getting better, the character stronger, until the late great poems and world fame."[17] Yeats's achievement in the last poems is indeed a triumph of character and poetic skill: only a poet fully in possession of himself could have risked so much and come out unbowed. There is in many of them an air of reckless abandon, but he knows himself so well that he has no fear of scandal or ridicule, and what the poems of his last decade clearly contain, along with the wildness and passion, is an irrepressible gaiety that took him a lifetime to achieve. This gaiety appears in "The Apparitions":

> When a man grows old his joy
> Grows more deep day after day,
> His empty heart is full at length,
> But he has need of all that strength
> Because of the increasing night
> That opens her mystery and fright.
> *Fifteen apparitions have I seen;*
> *The worst a coat upon a coat-hanger*

The coat upon a coat-hanger is Yeats himself as an old man, and his condition would be merely pitiful but for the fact that his joy has grown deeper than his pity, and the bodily suffering of old age has become only one more of the pains of life, which, from his earliest years, Yeats had striven to overcome. "Indeed I remember little of childhood but its pain," he wrote in "Reveries over Childhood and Youth," the first section of his *Autobiography,* and he went on to declare: "I have grown happier with every year of life as though gradually conquering something in myself; for certainly my miseries were not made by others but were part of my own mind."[18] The tragic view of life, of nobility gained through suffering, was one that Yeats adopted early, as he tells us in the second section of his *Autobiography,* "The Trembling of the Veil":

> I am persuaded that our intellects at twenty contain all the truths we shall ever find, but as yet we do not know truths that belong to us from opinions caught up in casual irritation or momentary fantasy. As life goes on we discover that certain thoughts sustain us in defeat, or give us victory, whether over ourselves or others, and it is these thoughts, tested by passion, that we call convictions. Among subjective men (in all those, that is, who must spin a web out of their own bowels) the victory is an intellectual daily

17. John Berryman, quoted in *Poets in Their Youth,* by Eileen Simpson, 6.
18. *The Autobiography of William Butler Yeats,* 5.

re-creation of all that exterior fate snatches away, and so that fate's antithesis; while what I have called "the Mask" is an emotional antithesis to all that comes out of their internal nature. We begin to live when we have conceived life as tragedy.[19]

The tragic view was in Yeats's mind most of his life, but as a positive outlook rather than a negative one, a way of subduing the irrational forces within him. When he wrote, at the end of his life, "A General Introduction to My Work," he repeated this theme: "A poet writes always of his personal life, in his finest work out of its tragedy. . . . He is Lear, Romeo, Oedipus, Tiresias. . . . He is part of his own phantasmagoria, and we adore him because nature has grown intelligible, and by so doing part of our creative power."[20] We may say of Yeats that he conquered the pain within him by the power of his poetry, and that what we most respond to in his work is the heroic effort to transform personal suffering into impersonal art. He is an example, and a supreme one, of the redeeming force of art in life, and there is no better confirmation of that force than reading his *Collected Poems* through, since they confirm that he did indeed grow happier with every year of life. Here, the final poems have most to say about what the happiness meant, for they show him often at play, exhilarating in art and life in the face of death. "I thought my problem was to face death with gaiety," he wrote to Dorothy Wellesley a short while before he died; "now I have learnt that it is to face life."[21] What is surprising in the later poems is the discovery that Yeats was much happier in old age than he had been in childhood; he reversed the usual pattern in which childhood is the blissful and hopeful state of innocence, and old age is the state of gloominess and infirmity. He had recovered "radical innocence" in old age, as he says in "A Dialogue of Self and Soul":

> When such as I cast out remorse
> So great a sweetness flows into the breast,
> We must laugh and we must sing
> We are blest by everything,
> Everything we look upon is blest.

Tragic poet that he was, Yeats was also a poet of surpassing joy, and the two moods converged at the end. The increasing happiness of his late poems does not come from decreasing the pain, but from intensifying it; out of

---

19. Ibid., 127–28.

20. William Butler Yeats, *Essays and Introductions* (New York: Macmillan, 1961), 509.

21. *Letters on Poetry from W. B. Yeats to Dorothy Wellesley,* 149, hereafter in this essay cited parenthetically in the text by page number alone.

"Tragedy wrought to its uttermost," as he says in "Lapis Lazuli," comes "Gaiety transfiguring all that dread."

Yeats's last poems carry a paradoxical message, not of the serenity and peace of old age, but of the drama of a man who enters passionately into the strife of existence and finds in it "heroic ecstasy." They are by turns impudent, improvident, reckless, defiant—all the moods and themes are there from the earlier poetry, but they are expressed with a gusto that is often shocking: the latest poems are the liveliest, most exuberant, of all he wrote. Bacchus in his cups could not have been a more outrageous celebrator of life than Yeats in the poems of his last years, as in "The Spur":

> You think it horrible that lust and rage
> Should dance attention upon my old age;
> They were not such a plague when I was young;
> What else have I to spur me into song?

There is lust and rage in the late poems, plenty of it, but they, too, are redeemed by the gaiety and become purgative rather than corrosive. The laughter of Yeats rings through them, and it is Olympian laughter:

> Beautiful lofty things: O'Leary's noble head;
> My father upon the Abbey stage, before him a raging crowd:
> "This Land of Saints," and then as the applause died out,
> "Of plaster Saints;" his beautiful mischievous head thrown back.

The beautiful lofty things that Yeats memorializes are people he had known who were mostly dead by then, but he wrote of them as if they were still alive. Indeed, all the themes of the earlier poems are in the last poems, but they are seen in a different light and with a change of mood, for his view of them is both tragic and joyful.

Perhaps the best reason for reading the *Last Poems* is to see what a change of heart does to Yeats's familiar subjects, and as we compare them with all that has gone before, we find that for all their strangeness they are right, not a lesser art but worthy companions for the earlier poems. We read them together now—the early poems for their emotional power, of sorrow or pity or love; the middle poems for their intellectual power, their breadth of vision and historical sweep; and the last poems for their passion and humor, their zest and energy, their cleansing power of laughter and scorn, their nonchalance. In one of his most amusing letters to Wellesley—those letters that provide an illuminating prose context for all the final poems—Yeats held that "nonchalance is declared by Castiglione essential to all true courtiers—so it is to warty lads and poets." He has just written, he says, to

Laura Riding to complain that "her school," by which he means the younger generation of poets, is "too thoughtful, reasonable and truthful," and to chide her with the thought that "poets were good liars who never forgot that the Muses were women who liked the embrace of gay warty lads." Then in an aside, he adds, "I wonder if she knows that warts are considered by the Irish peasantry a sign of sexual power?" (p. 63). This intimate, unbuttoned Yeats, so willing to paint himself as a scandalous and unscrupulous old poet, a mocker of the seriousness of younger poets, is reflective of his superiority to all fashions in his final phase, his inclination to play the fool and the madman, if necessary, but never the wise elder statesman. We become captivated by the later poems of Yeats at the moment when we realize we are not just laughing at him but with him, which becomes easier as the poetry loses its strangeness and becomes familiar, as we are carried away by its buoyant vitality and disarming candor.

And what wealth and variety abound in the very late Yeats: of the 386 poems listed in the *Variorum Edition of the Poems of W. B. Yeats*, over 100 appeared in the 3 books of his final decade, *Words for Music Perhaps* (1932), *A Full Moon in March* (1935), and *Last Poems* (1939). In other words, more than one-fourth of Yeats's total output of poems were produced in the last ten years of his life, an indication of his immense fecundity in his late sixties and early seventies, as if the older he got, the more creative energy he possessed. In them there are major themes: old age, sexual passion, oracular images, politics, art, friendship, self-criticism, retrospective views and memories, prospective views and prophecies. None of these themes is new for Yeats, but his attitudes toward them are new and often startling, a departure from conventional views or even from his own earlier perspectives.

Take the theme of old age, first of all, since it is naturally the dominant theme in the late poems. No poet ever made more artistic capital out of old age than Yeats, early as well as late; he struggled with it all his life, but never capitulated to it. Growing old became as intense an experience for him as falling in love, and he found as much pain in the one as in the other; if he could and did make great poetry out of Maud Gonne's rejection of him, he could make equally great poetry out of the aging of his own body, "Decrepit age that has been tied to me / As to a dog's tail."

One of the finest of the poems on aging is "After Long Silence," addressed to an old friend, Olivia Shakespear, with whom he had once carried on a passionate love affair. The passions have cooled, but the love is miraculously stronger, intensified by the age of the lovers, who have given up the mating of the body for the deeper mating of the soul, making wisdom from the decay of flesh. The view of old age in this poem is not of a loss but of a gain, old love being wiser and better than young love, more harmonious and more satisfying.

If we turn from this distillation of the experience of old age to a poem written a little later, "A Prayer for Old Age" in *A Full Moon in March,* we may be surprised by what seems a remarkably different approach to the theme: "I pray," he says, "That I may seem, though I die old, / A foolish, passionate man." Here, Yeats appears to be renouncing wisdom for foolishness, thought for passion, and prays that he may live to write a more "lasting song" by thinking "in a marrow-bone"—that is, with his mind incarnate in the flesh, not rising above it. The second poem sounds as if it were meant to contradict the first, unless we recognize that to speak of bodily decrepitude as wisdom is itself to "think in a marrow-bone," since the image is one that compounds the flesh and the spirit, not separating but fusing them. Yeats seems to go still further in the direction of the fleshly passions in old age in "The Wild Old Wicked Man," the raciest of the poems in *Last Poems,* where the speaker frankly confesses that he is "mad about women" and asks God to permit him "not to die in the straw at home" nor to be taken by a bolt of lightning from "the old man in the skies,"

> But a coarse old man am I,
> I choose the second-best,
> I forget it all awhile
> Upon a woman's breast.

This poem is one of Yeats's most deliberately offensive, the sort of projection of senile lust that has turned some readers away from the later Yeats in embarrassment or disgust. But is it really so degrading after all? The old man is speaking of physical desire as a motive for living vigorously up to the moment of death, but he does not speak of consummation of that desire; rather, he speaks of a communication between man and woman that is only possible in age, not in youth:

> I have what no young man can have
> Because he loves too much.
> Words I have that can pierce the heart,
> But what can he do but touch?

If this late persona of Yeats is not saying the same thing that he did in "After Long Silence," he is surely saying something very like it: that sexual passion draws man and woman together, but that what they share is not mere fleshly pleasure but fleshly understanding, expressed in words more than embraces. The raciness of the poem makes it memorable, but the repeated refrain is far from racy: "*Daybreak and a candle's end*" speaks of the end of love, of the going out of the light, of the coming of dawn as the approach of death. It is a poem about old age that breaks all conventions by its lustiness but is finally a companionable and endearing work, full of the kind of purifying laughter that is one of the surest manifestations of tragic joy.

The Crazy Jane of *Words for Music Perhaps* is the female counterpart of the Wild Old Wicked Man, rowdily sensual and coarse, for whom "Love is like the lion's tooth" and "Fair and foul are near of kin." The theme of sexual passion is given full vent in the poems of Crazy Jane and her very worldly lover, Jack the Journeyman, "The solid man and the coxcomb." There is no doubt that Crazy Jane has enjoyed love in its most physical sense, but there is also no doubt that she is something more than a slave of passion, for

> "Love is all
> Unsatisfied
> That cannot take the whole
> Body and soul";
> *And that is what Jane said.*

In fact, Jane spends her time, when she is not in the arms of Jack, in disputation with the bishop, that starchy puritan who seeks to convert her to Christian asceticism, but in vain, for she knows something about love that she believes the bishop has left out of his doctrine unadvisedly—something that is truer than his teaching. The most widely known of the Crazy Jane poems is not so much about passion as about the union of flesh and spirit; it is less an erotic than a metaphysical poem, a distillation of Yeats's dialectic of contraries, the belief that truth comes from the unity of opposing forces in experience. "Crazy Jane Talks with the Bishop" involves many pairs of opposites—earth and heaven, fair and foul, grave and bed, lowliness and pride, love and sexuality, wholeness and division—and it is clear that Jane gladly embraces them all, whereas the bishop refuses to allow the claims of the flesh against the claims of the soul. It is Jane who has the last laugh, and though she appears foolish, the bishop is the one who is really fooled.

There are many other poems of sexual passion in Yeats's last volumes, notable among them "The Three Bushes," about the secret liaison between a lady, her chambermaid, and her lover, which Yeats wrote in collaboration with Dorothy Wellesley. We know from his letters to her that he regarded these sensual poems as complementary to his more mystical poems—that, in fact, he wrote them in bursts of inspiration that were interrupted by the inspiration of contrasting religious themes: "I dream of clear water, perhaps two or three times . . . then come erotic dreams. Then for weeks perhaps I write poetry with sex for theme. Then comes the reversal—it came when I was young with some dream or some vision between waking and sleeping with flame in it. Then I get a symbolism like that in my Byzantium poems with flame for theme" (p. 86). Yeats's poetry abounds in creative conflicts of this kind, and we may well believe that his late poems of sexual passion had as much to do with artistic fertility, and with the energy that drove his imagination, as with sexual fertility or the energy that may have come from his often-mentioned rejuvenating operation (called "the Steinach operation" to restore sexual potency) in his late sixties. We know from his letters to Wellesley that at the same time as he was relishing his exchanges with her on "The Three Bushes," so frankly sexual in imagery that even she was a little shocked, he was also working on "Lapis Lazuli," one of the most admired of all the *Last Poems*, which has as its theme art, not sexual passion.

Yeats had written earlier to tell Wellesley that he had received as a present a large piece of lapis lazuli carved "by some Chinese sculptor into the semblance of a mountain with temple, trees, paths, and an ascetic and pupil about to climb the mountain." He went on in the letter to develop the image on the stone into a theme for a poem: "ascetic, pupil, hard stone, eternal theme of the sensual east. The heroic cry in the midst of despair. But no, I am wrong, the east has its solutions always and therefore knows nothing of tragedy. It is we, not the east, that must raise the heroic cry" (p. 8). A year later, he wrote to say that he had just finished his poem "Lapis Lazuli" and thought it "almost the best I have made in recent years." It expands the scene carved on the stone into a defense of art in time of crisis; and it is Yeats's most eloquent expression of the major theme of his later poems, explicitly stated in another letter: "To me the supreme aim is an act of faith and reason to make one rejoice in the midst of tragedy" (p. 12). In the poem, he links Shakespeare's tragedies to the Chinese sculpture:

> All perform their tragic play,
> There struts Hamlet, there is Lear,
> That's Ophelia, that Cordelia;
> Yet they, should the last scene be there,
> The great stage curtain about to drop,
> Do not break up their lines to weep.
> They know that Hamlet and Lear are gay.

He brings in Greek sculpture as well as Chinese, speaking of the "handiwork of Callimachus, / who handled marble as if it were bronze," and says that though his work no longer survives, though it "stood but a day," "All things fall and are built again, / And those that build them again are gay." The poem ends with a lovingly detailed description of the scene carved on lapis lazuli, picturing the Chinese men climbing the mountain to the lookout, and concluding with the thrilling lines:

There, on the mountain and the sky,
On all the tragic scene they stare.
One asks for mournful melodies;
Accomplished fingers begin to play.
Their eyes mid many wrinkles, their eyes,
Their ancient, glittering eyes, are gay.

Old age was never more attractively presented than in this poem, where even the wrinkles seem to be smiling, and the equation of Shakespeare's tragic heroes with the Chinese philosophers in their landscape brings Western dramatic art and Eastern meditative art together in a superb reconciliation of opposites. Yeats proposed, at the end of *A Vision,* that "a wheel of the Great Year must be thought of as the marriage of symbolic Europe and symbolic Asia," and we can easily believe that Yeats conceived of "Lapis Lazuli" as a culminating piece, one of the keystones of his philosophy. The theme is gaiety at the end of life, as in the last act of a tragedy, or the mountaintop vista of old age: "Gaiety transfiguring all that dread."

None of the late poems surpasses "Lapis Lazuli" in the expression of tragic joy, but many of them bear it out in different ways. Certainly "The Municipal Gallery Revisited" must be cited as a comparably long and impressive poem, which combines the themes of friendship and retrospection, and touches on the related themes of art and politics as well. It is, like "The Circus Animals' Desertion," a summary of Yeats's whole career, since it recalls the controversy over the Hugh Lane gallery that figured so prominently in "September, 1913" and other poems of *Responsibilities* and introduces figures from the past in a way that recalls "In Memory of Major Robert Gregory." Walking through the gallery of portraits of Irish patriots he knew, Yeats is moved to exclaim:

"This is not," I say,
"The dead Ireland of my youth, but an Ireland
The poets have imagined, terrible and gay."

He thinks of how Irish Nationalism and literature have flourished together in his lifetime, and thinks especially of his cofounders of the Abbey Theatre, Lady Gregory and John Synge, and how they thought

All that we did, all that we said or sang
Must come from contact with the soil, from that
Contact everything Antaeus-like grew strong.
We three alone in modern times had brought
Everything down to that sole test again,
Dream of the noble and the beggar-man.

As he meditates on the portraits in the gallery, he sees that his own art has depended on the fortunate outcome of Irish history, troubled though it had been, on the emergence of a national literature and an independent nation, and above all, on strong personal friendships between those who brought into being "an Ireland the poets have imagined, terrible and gay," and this final thought leads him to the humane and deeply affecting concluding lines:

> You that would judge me, do not judge alone
> This book or that, come to this hallowed place
> Where my friends' portraits hang and look thereon;
> Ireland's history in their lineaments trace;
> Think where men's glory most begins and ends,
> And say my glory was I had such friends.

Readers of this poem might be led to wonder how a man who kept such high company and believed so fervently in the sacredness of friendship could have dreamed of the likes of Crazy Jane and the Wild Old Wicked Man, but they were part of his "contact with the soil," the other half of his "dream of the noble and the beggar-man." If we need to justify the coarseness and vulgarity of some of his later characters, we can view them as complementary to the Irish men and women he knew best, the Anglo-Irish gentry like himself who gave Ireland its rich new literary tradition. Heroic as the subjects of the portraits in "The Municipal Gallery Revisited" are, in Yeats's eyes, they too need the common people to draw on for their work, and they probably would not have shunned the lowly companions of Yeats's later poems any more than he did.

The late poems of rage can be balanced against the more lighthearted poems of joy, since there are enough of both to suggest another kind of creative conflict at work in Yeats's imagination. Among the poems of rage are the group of five political poems on Irish themes, "The Curse of Cromwell," "Roger Casement," "The Ghost of Roger Casement," "The O'Rahilly," and "Come Gather round Me, Parnellites," poems much more strident in mood than the middle poems of the Easter Rising and the Civil War. Yeats's Irish pugnacity could not be called one of his more winning traits, but it was as much a part of his natural character as his sexual frankness. He spoke of one of his Casement poems as a "ferocious ballad written to a popular tune," and fairly chortled when he wrote about it to his English friend Wellesley, "I shall not be happy until I hear that it is sung by Irish undergraduates at Oxford" (p. 107). His justification for such outright partisanship in the old quarrel between the Irish and the English was that "we may and sometimes must be indignant and speak it. Hate is a kind of 'passive suffering' but indignation is a kind of joy. . . . We that are joyous need not be afraid to denounce. . . .

Joy is the salvation of the soul" (p. 114). He compared his indignation to that of "our ancestor Swift," and said, "It is our Irish fight though it has nothing to do with this or that country" (p. 115). However partisan it may have been, Yeats's instinctive defense of Roger Casement, the Irish patriot condemned as an English traitor, resulted in lines that are likely to remain a part of the English language: *The ghost of Roger Casement / Is beating on the door.* Yeats's indignation was purgative, it seems, and what followed after the cleansing was joy.

Certainly there is much joy of the hearty laughing kind in the lighter late poems, such as "John Kinsella's Lament for Mrs. Mary Moore," with its refrain as whimsical in its regret for the passing of a prostitute as the other was indignant in its protest against the execution of a traitor: *What shall I do for pretty girls / Now my old bawd is dead?* This is the Wild Old Wicked Man in a lighter mood, an elegy that is a celebration of life and death, a happy sort of lament such as only Yeats could have written and then only in his later phase, when he could be lighthearted about death, the most serious of subjects.

"High Talk," I think, is also meant to be taken as wryly humorous, with its caricature of the poet, who must be Yeats himself, as "Malachi Stilt-Jack," who amuses children and frightens old women by his ungainly appearance, awkwardly clumping along on his fifteen-foot stilts, "Daddy-long-legs upon his timber toes." The poem is self-critical, surely, for Yeats is mocking his own high style, "all metaphor, Malachi, stilts and all." Yet the ending is more serious than comic, a nightmarish image of the poet striding alone on the seashore: "I, through the terrible novelty of light, stalk on, stalk on; / Those great sea-horses bare their teeth and laugh at the dawn." The figure of Yeats himself appears many times in the late poems, as in the earlier ones, but never more comically than in "High Talk," though the poem's final image rises above the comic to the heroic.

The most memorable late self-portraits are to be found in "The Circus Animals' Desertion" and "Under Ben Bulben," which are near each other at the close of the final volume of his poetry, and which leave us with a tragic and heroic view of the poet at the end of his life, surveying his career and preparing for his death. They sum up the lesson he has learned from a life dedicated to art and leave a challenge to Irish poets to come. Both poems are serious self-appraisals, yet both have their measure of humor, even of lightheartedness. There is in the very notion of the poet as a circus-trainer, whose imaginative creations are performing animals, a hint of the ridiculous, and in the desertion of the animals from their trainer there is the stuff of high comedy—how could a lion-tamer allow his beasts to slink away, without at least a crack of his whip? But we are left at the end of the poem with the poet desolate, his creations all vanished, plunged into the dark night of his imagination, "the foul rag-and-bone shop of the heart." The figure is tragic, but certainly not hopeless, because out of just such raw material of passion have come the heroic creatures he once made: they may come again, the poem implies, the work is not over yet.

The work is clearly over in "Under Ben Bulben," but the poet is confident it will go on making itself felt after he is gone. He sets up the standards that he has tried to follow and challenges Irish poets in generations to come to emulate the "Profane perfection of mankind" he offers, which is to be found in great artists of all ages—sculptors such as Phidias and Michelangelo, painters such as Calvert and Wilson, Blake and Claude, and poets such as—well, such as Yeats himself:

> Irish poets, learn your trade,
> Sing whatever is well made . . .
> Sing the peasantry, and then
> Hard-riding country gentlemen,
> The holiness of monks, and after
> Porter-drinkers' randy laughter;
> Sing the lords and ladies gay
> That were beaten into clay
> Through seven heroic centuries;
> Cast your mind on other days
> That we in coming times may be
> Still the indomitable Irishry.

Yeats's words are as unforgettable as any he wrote, but the sort of advice they offer would be the despair of any poet of lesser genius; his poem stands much more as a final piece of self-definition than as a creed for other poets. It is his farewell to life and art, as if he were Prospero breaking his staff and drowning his book, and it is as complex and contradictory, and as joyful, as Yeats himself:

> Know that when all words are said
> And a man is fighting mad,
> Something drops from eyes long blind,
> He completes his partial mind,
> For an instant stands at ease,
> Laughs aloud, his heart at peace.

From rage to laughter in a few lines of verse—what other poet could manage it, except the very greatest? And the defiant epitaph with which the poem ends, those words now carved in granite at Drumcliff, what is that but Yeats's last scornful laugh, the final cry of tragic joy from his lips?

> Cast a cold eye,
> On life, on death,
> Horseman, pass by.

This epitaph, though justly famous, seems too chilling and impersonal for Yeats, but then it is his Mask that is speaking, not his Self, and he would not have wanted anyone to like it; he wanted it to be daunting, but not self-pitying: it is perhaps the most unsentimental epitaph any poet ever wrote for himself. He wrote to Dorothy Wellesley that he expected to go "blaspheming" to the grave, and he was true to his word—no prayer for mercy for his soul, but a few words flung into the wind to defy death, as his ghost goes riding into the shades.

Yeats's theory of poetry and of life was one of creative conflict, whether of the Self and the Mask or of the intersecting gyres of history. In his youth, he had written idealistic poems of love; in old age, he wrote realistic poems of passion. Only by opposing himself, he believed, could greatness be attained, because it is "out of the quarrel with ourselves that we make poetry." Striving against himself brought vitality, mastery, wisdom, and made his work much more varied and interesting than it would have been had he been content with one personality, one style, one philosophical viewpoint all his life. In *A Vision,* he imagined civilization as a series of contrary forces: destruction and violence at the beginning and the end of an epoch, harmony and self-control, unity of culture, at the peak. There is a similar cycle of development in Yeats's own poetry, from early to middle to late, birth and maturity and death, then renewal and mastery and dissolution: his poetry not only evolved, it revolved. "Myself I must remake," he wrote in "An Acre of Grass," in *Last Poems,* and there is so much richness in each of his metamorphoses that, in the end, one does not think of choosing one of his styles, but of admiring a poet who constantly rose above himself and became his own critic, to reshape himself and his poetry so thoroughly that he became greater than the self he was born to be, and his poetry became greater than the age he was born into. "But I am not content," he continually said, and his discontent with himself was the secret of his achievement.

During his final illness with a weak heart and kidney trouble, in France, he worked feverishly on his poetry, correcting the "Death of Cuchulain" on the day of his own death, and changing the title of the poem that contained his epitaph from "His Convictions" to "Under Ben Bulben." He could never stop perfecting his work until the moment of his death, and his creative energy never flagged, as his very last poems testify. It was characteristic of him that, knowing his life was nearing an end, he mingled tragedy with joy in his last words: "I feel I am only beginning to understand how to write" (p. 194).

6

THREE ENGLISH IRONISTS
Hardy, Housman, and Owen

"Hardy the poet rates for us as decidedly the principal Voice of Irony among the poets of his age," John Crowe Ransom wrote in introducing a selection of Thomas Hardy's poems. He went on to argue that Hardy's irony was what made him modern, for in Ransom's view there had been a classical spirit and a romantic spirit in literature before, and they had prevailed successively until the late nineteenth century, when the ironic spirit took over. Ransom thought that Hardy was the premier example of the ironic spirit, because he was the first to articulate an essential conflict between natural law and moral law. The classical spirit, in Ransom's historical view of literature, had accepted natural law as fate, and had taken a tragic outlook on human destiny. The romantic spirit had taken the spirit of pity, or the moral law, as primary, and believed in the prevalence of goodwill in nature and in man. But the ironic spirit, which, according to Ransom, Hardy expressed more fully than any poet in the English tradition, recognized the gap between natural law, or fate, and moral law, or pity. Hardy, he thought, posed again and again in his poetry the conflict between natural determinism and human free will, dramatizing a struggle in which nature always has the upper hand, with death as its ultimate power over man. In Hardy's poetry, Ransom said, the typical situation is that "we are suspended irresolute in our choice between the universe of *ought to be* and the conflicting universe of *is*."[1]

Ransom was not the only poet who looked back on Hardy's work as marking a major shift in English poetic style: such diverse poets as Ezra Pound and W. H. Auden also viewed Hardy as an original master. Pound

---

1. John Crowe Ransom, introduction to *Selected Poems of Thomas Hardy*, xx.

praised Hardy often and in his *Guide to Kulchur* placed him with Homer and Dante in the highest class of poets in his personal Pantheon, attesting that

> No man can read Hardy's poems collected but that his own life, and forgotten moments of it, will come back to him, a flash here and an hour there. Have you a better test of true poetry? . . . No thoughtful writer can read this book of Hardy's without throwing his own work (in imagination) into the test-tube and hunting it for fustian, for the foolish word, for the word upholstered.[2]

Pound in other words thought of Hardy as a poet who was exceptionally truthful and exceptionally clear, who made other poets take a critical look at their poetry to see if it was as true to life as his.

Auden said he was especially lucky to have chosen Hardy as his first master when he began writing poetry, because Hardy was one of those poets who had crossed the dividing line between Victorian and modern, which Auden defined as lying between "poets for whom the ideas and hopes of liberal Christian humanism are still valid, and those for whom they are not."[3] On the testimony, then, of such diverse poets and critics as Ransom, Pound, and Auden—and despite Eliot's opinion in *After Strange Gods* that he was "demonic"—Hardy belongs in the first rank of modern poets in English.

Hardy's high achievement as a poet was long in coming, for he was not known as a poet until late in his career because of his early success as a novelist. For the first quarter of a century of his long literary career, Hardy was identified chiefly as a novelist, but when *Jude the Obscure* was published in 1895, the book was denounced from every pulpit in England for its frankness about sex and its fatalistic outlook, and Hardy turned to poetry exclusively for the last thirty years of his life. As he himself put it in the preface to the Wessex Edition of his *Novels and Poems* in 1912,

> Thus much for the novels. Turning now to the verse—to myself the more individual part of my literary fruitage—I would say that, unlike some of the fiction, nothing interfered with the writer's freedom in respect of its form or content. Several of the poems—indeed many—were produced before novel writing had been thought of as a pursuit; but few saw the light of day until the novels had been published.[4]

So, with the publication of *Wessex Poems* in 1898, Hardy became a poet rather than a novelist, and he was awarded the Order of Merit in 1910 for both his

---

2. Ezra Pound, *Guide to Kulchur*, 286–87.

3. W. H. Auden, introduction to vol. 5 of *Poets of the English Language*, xix.

4. Thomas Hardy, general preface to *Novels and Poems*, Wessex Edition, 1912, in *The Portable Thomas Hardy*, 697.

fiction and his poetry. It could be said that in his eighty-eight years, Hardy went from being a Victorian novelist to being a modern poet, because his novels for all their pessimism were traditional narratives of plot and character, while his poetry was as diversified in form as the work of any younger English poet. Using as his chief devices formal experiment and irony, Hardy created a body of work that rivals that of any major poet in the entire English tradition.

Hardy had started out life as a conventional Christian, teaching Sunday school in Dorset, where he grew up, and studying the restoration of historic English churches, but he underwent a profound change of belief when he read Darwin's *On the Origin of Species by Means of Natural Selection* in 1859, and the scientific or Higher Criticism of the Bible also led him to reject the prevailing liberal Christian humanism and to take up a position of skepticism and eventually fatalism. As early as 1866, when his poem "Hap" appeared, Hardy was thinking hard about God and wishing that "some vengeful god" might be in charge of the universe, rather than those huge impersonal forces the natural determinists were telling him about:

> Crass Casualty obstructs the sun and rain,
> And dicing Time for gladness casts a moan. . . .
> These purblind Doomsters had as readily strown
> Blisses about my pilgrimage as pain.

Even in his earliest poems, Hardy's irony reveals a clash between what his conscience told him he wanted to be true about the universe and what his reason increasingly told him was actually true. He held the hope for a time that poetry might somehow bridge the widening gulf between science and religion: "It may, indeed, be a forlorn hope, a mere dream, that of an alliance between religion, which must be retained unless the world is to perish, and complete rationality, which must come, unless also the world is to perish, by means of the interfusing effect of poetry."[5] But this hope proved vain, and the question of what Hardy finally came to believe remains a difficult one, for if in some of his poems a scientific determinism seems to prevail, in others a wistful hope lingers that poetry can somehow preserve belief in a benevolent God. Both of these seemingly contradictory views of human destiny, one obeying the natural law and the other obeying the moral law, are expressed by Hardy with his characteristic irony, thus leaving an ambivalence lingering in the reader's mind about what Hardy's own view of things really was. It may be best to see his poems as complementary, differing in viewpoint at different moments of his life, although irony is present with each new view and in every new poem.

---

5. "Apology" to *Late Lyrics and Earlier,* quoted in *The Portable Thomas Hardy,* 749.

Fatalism is strong in "The Convergence of the Twain (Lines on the loss of the *Titanic*)," a poem published soon after the great "unsinkable" ocean liner sank on its maiden voyage across the Atlantic in 1912. The poem places the event in clear perspective, showing the moral law at work in men as they build the ship that cannot sink and the natural law at work in nature as it constructs an iceberg that will sink it. The poem is beautifully constructed of three-line stanzas with triple rhymes, developed through a pattern of three main images: the ship at the bottom of the ocean after the event, the ship under construction before the event, and the iceberg forming to oppose it:

> And as the smart ship grew
> In stature, grace, and hue,
> In shadowy silent distance grew the Iceberg too.

The inevitable conflict between natural law and human will occurs when the ship meets the iceberg, and Hardy's poem comes to a crashing climax when

> the Spinner of the Years
> Said *"Now!"* And each one hears,
> And consummation comes, and jars two hemispheres.

As Hardy looks back at this event, soon after it happened, the forces of nature have once again prevailed over the ingenuity of man, and most of those aboard the once-majestic liner have drowned, but Hardy's irony underscores the lesson of human pride: in his view, there is justice in the sinking of the unsinkable ship, meaning that the moral law has operated along with the natural law in the disaster, though "no mortal eye could see / The intimate welding of their later history." Thus, "The Immanent Will that stirs and urges everything" has "Prepared a sinister mate / For her—so gaily great," and Hardy sees something more than blind chance at work when the ship and iceberg collide in a catastrophe that "jars two hemispheres." He has something like a Greek Fate ordering the tragic fall of man in this poem, the cause of which is his pride, and so, if natural law prevails over moral law as it always must, there is still justice in the universe, hard though it may be for man to bear.

But Hardy often wished for a kinder destiny for man and a kinder God than the Immanent Will to govern the universe, and in his poem "The Oxen" he expressed the wistful hope that the Christmas story might still be true. The folk belief that even the oxen kneel on Christmas Eve to honor the birth of Christ impels the speaker, despite his adult doubts, to follow a friend's invitation to visit the stable and there recover his childhood innocence, to wonder whether "I should go with him in the gloom, / Hoping it might be so." Hardy's attitude is still that of the doubter, not the believer, but his irony allows him a faint hope that the oxen know a Christian God exists even if men are no longer sure. The same faint hope is expressed in "The Darkling Thrush," where on a cold, bleak winter day he hears "An aged thrush, frail, gaunt, and small / In blast-beruffled plume" choosing "to fling his soul / Upon the growing gloom," and the speaker believes that the thrush may know more than he does about what controls the universe, ending one of Hardy's finest poems with the remote possibility

> That I could think there trembled through
>   His happy good-night air
> Some Blessed Hope, whereof he knew
>   And I was unaware.

Hardy's irony, then, could be tender as well as harsh, and if in one of his most ironic war poems, "Channel Firing," he could describe a ghostly dialogue between God and dead soldiers in their graves, ending with a fatal sound that implies, on the eve of World War I, that more soldiers are soon to go to their graves—

> Again the guns disturbed the hour,
> Roaring their readiness to avenge,
> As far inland as Stourton Tower,
> And Camelot, and starlit Stonehenge.

—then in another poem, "Afterwards," he could look beyond his own death and hope that his care for everything in nature would be remembered after he was gone, so that

> If I pass, during some nocturnal blackness, mothy and warm,
> When the hedgehog travels furtively over the lawn,
> One may say, "He strove that such innocent creatures
>   should come to no harm,
> But he could do little for them, and now he is gone."

In this late poem of Hardy's, it is as if he were trying to compensate for the loss of a loving God in the world by offering human sympathy in its place, slight and transitory though it might be.

Most characteristic of Hardy, perhaps, are his poems about Wessex, an archaic name for southwest England that goes back to the Anglo-Saxons, in which the familiar landscape he knew so well becomes the main subject, and he ascends "Wessex Heights" to mingle with the phantoms of the dead, to walk "Where men have never cared to haunt, nor women have walked with me," in the lonely freedom of the hills above the sea, of places with strange names like Ingpen Beacon and Wylls-Neck and Bulbarrow and Pilsdon Crest, where "ghosts then keep their distance; and I know some liberty." Hardy left his mark on the land as well as on the language; his poetry, with all its harshness and tenderness, its variety of moods and lyric forms, and above all its ever-present irony, continues to speak eloquently to readers who share his deep doubts as well as his slim hopes for the future of man. As he once explained his unique perspective on existence, "If there is any way of getting a melancholy satisfaction out of life it lies in dying, so to speak, before one is out of the flesh; by which I mean putting on the manners of ghosts, wandering in their haunts, and taking their view of surrounding things. To think of life as passing away is a sadness; to think of it as past is at least tolerable."[6] Hardy's poems about Wessex often have ghosts in them, especially the ghost of his first wife, Emma, "The Phantom Horsewoman" to whom he wrote a number of remarkable posthumous love poems, and his symbolic landscape is therefore a haunted place, though most of the ghosts that haunt it are friendly and as much at home there as Hardy himself was.

A. E. Housman's Shropshire is only a hundred miles from Hardy's Wessex on the map of England, but this county on the border of Wales is as distinct poetically from that other region on the English Channel as Robinson's New England town is from Frost's New England farm. The difference is not merely between a coastal landscape in Hardy and an agricultural landscape in Housman, but between a speaker who like Hardy himself broods over the dark hills and the sea, and an invented speaker, "a Shropshire lad," or farm boy, whom Housman made famous when his slender collection of poems came out anonymously under that title in 1896. It is also a difference of names for the land, which are as strange sounding in Housman's Shropshire as in Hardy's Wessex. No poem is more resonant with Shropshire names and the Shropshire landscape than "On Wenlock Edge," which gets its title from a rocky formation of wooded hills in the eastern part of Shropshire, near what was once the Roman camp of Viriconium or Uriconium, newly discovered in Housman's time and extensively excavated since. Its opening ballad quatrain—the stanza form Housman favored in most of his poetry—is replete with local names:

> On Wenlock Edge, the wood's in trouble;
>   His forest fleece the Wrekin heaves;

6. Ibid., 755.

> The gale, it plies the saplings double,
> And thick on Severn snow the leaves.

The Wrekin is a peak in the Wenlock Edge formation, and the Severn is one of the principal rivers of England, which flows south from the Welsh mountains to the Bristol Channel: what Housman is describing is a windy day in the Shropshire hills, when all nature seems disturbed and angry, a disquiet mirrored not only in the turbulent imagery but in the sounds of the words he chooses. There is in Housman's poetry, as there was in Hardy's, a stress on clashing consonants and jangling rhymes, forcing a cacophonous music of dissonant chords out of them to match the bitterness and the stoicism in the heart of man. Housman's Shropshire lad thinks that this weather has been endured by generations of men, ever since "Uricon the city stood," and as he looks at the troubled landscape, he reflects that it looked the same to the Roman two thousand years earlier: the human lot is to be always buffeted by nature until death comes, because "The tree of man was never quiet," and death looks, to him—as it often did to Housman—like a welcome relief from life, so that he ends with the ironically comforting thought that he will soon be as dead as the Roman:

> The gale, it plies the sapling double,
> It blows so hard, 'twill soon be gone:
> To-day the Roman and his trouble
> Are ashes under Uricon.

So the Shropshire lad appears to envy the Roman his release from anguish in death, and Housman often saw death as man's ironic reward at the end of life, as in his complimentary "To an Athlete Dying Young," probably his best-known poem, with its tribute to the runner who won his race in life and was a "Smart lad, to slip betimes away / From fields where glory does not stay," thus winning another race by dying young and going to his grave still honored, able to "set, before its echoes fade / The fleet foot on the sill of shade" and be admired by "the strengthless dead."

Such a view of life as best in death seemed excessively pessimistic to many of Housman's readers, popular though his poetry was, but Housman maintained that he was not a pessimist but a *pejorist,* making use of his classical scholarship by inventing a word for one who expects that "worse" (Latin *pejoris*) will come but not the "worst" (Latin *pessimus*). It was a small distinction but an important one for Housman, who gave as his final lecture at Cambridge in 1933, when he retired after a long, distinguished career as a classical scholar, "The Name and Nature of Poetry," in which he defined the peculiar pleasure that poetry gave him, as if it were the only consolation life offered. Housman said in his lecture, "I could no more define poetry than a terrier can define a rat," but he said he could recognize it by "the symptoms which it provokes," and elaborated:

> One of these symptoms was described in connection with another object by Eliphaz the Temanite [in the Book of Job]: "A spirit passed before my face: the hair of my flesh stood up." Experience has taught me, when I am shaving of a morning, to keep watch over my thoughts, because, if a line of poetry strays into my memory, my skin bristles so that the razor ceases to act. This particular symptom is accompanied by a shiver down the spine; there is another which consists in a constriction of the throat and a precipitation of water to the eyes; and there is a third which I can only describe by borrowing a phrase from one of Keats's last letters, where he says, speaking of Fanny Brawne, "everything that reminds me of her goes through my heart like a spear." The seat of this sensation is the pit of the stomach.[7]

Housman went on in his lecture to tell about how he composed poems on walks after lunch, when a pint of beer made inspiration "bubble up" from his stomach, and "there would flow into my mind, with sudden and unaccountable emotion, sometimes a line or two of verse, sometimes a whole stanza at once, accompanied, not preceded, by a vague notion of the poem which they were destined to form part of." The poetic process he described was wholly instinctual, and Housman said he never composed poetry except when "rather out of health," comparing his poetry to a "morbid secretion" like that of an oyster when it forms a pearl around a grain of sand that has sifted inside its shell. Thus poetry might give pleasure but it also gives pain, to the author as well as the reader, and as he put it in another poem, "I to my perils,"

> The thoughts of others
> Were light and fleeting,
> Of lovers' meeting
> Or luck, or fame.
> Mine were of trouble,
> And mine were steady,
> So I was ready
> When trouble came.

Housman wrote mostly short poems, but his longest poem was as classical as it was original, for though he called it "Hell Gate" and was clearly thinking

7. A. E. Housman, *Selected Prose,* 193.

of Homer and Virgil as well as Dante and Milton in composing it, he gave it what was for him an unexpectedly happy ending. In the poem, he pictures his speaker, like Aeneas in the Sibyl's Cave or Dante in the dark wood, following a downward path "through the sad uncoloured plain" to a walled city that is glowing with bonfires, accompanied by an unnamed "dark conductor" (just as Aeneas was guided by the Sibyl of Cumae and Dante by the shade of Virgil), who tells him as they arrive at the gate of the city: "You conjecture well: / Yonder is the gate of hell." He discovers that the sentries at the gate are the damned souls of men—unlike any earlier hell—but he recognizes one of them as a friend, as both Aeneas in Hades and Dante in the Inferno recognized friends they had known in life. On the drawbridge leading into hell, he sees the figures of Sin and Death, who are also present in Virgil's and Milton's hells, and he addresses Sin as a daughter of Satan, just as Milton did, but unlike the earlier poet he addresses her as if she were someone he had known:

> And the portress foul to see
> Lifted up her eyes on me
> Smiling, and I made reply:
> "Met again, my lass," said I.

He then recognizes the sentry by name as his friend Ned, who as the guardian of hell gate carries a musket. In a totally unprecedented act of defiance, Ned turns and fires at Satan, miraculously shooting him down:

> And the hollowness of hell
> Sounded as its master fell,
> And the mourning echo rolled
> Ruin through his kingdom old.
> Tyranny and terror flown
> Left a pair of friends alone,
> And beneath the nether sky
> All that stirred was he and I.

So the damned soul is saved by his friend's sudden and unexpected revolt, and both are rescued from hell. As they make their "backward way" toward life, the "everlasting fire" fades from his friend's body. When they look back at hell gate, all they see is that "the city, dusk and mute, / Slept, and there was no pursuit." Housman's modern version of the journey to hell and back implies that an escape is possible from eternal punishment through human love and loyalty, a theme that has a classical parallel in the myth of Orpheus and Eurydice, but with the difference that this time the living and dead souls can look back at hell without suffering the penalty Eurydice suffered of being taken back to hell, torn away once more from the arms of the desolate Orpheus, who had descended into hell to rescue her. In many of its lines and in its overall narrative, Housman's "Hell Gate" is ironic, because what happens at the end is unlike any classical parallel—unless it would be that of Dante, who is allowed to climb out of hell over Satan's frozen body at the end of the *Inferno,* with Virgil's shade beside him as his guide. Since Dante is drawn toward heaven by the love of Beatrice, who has sent Virgil to guide him, it may be said that the theme of love's providing the salvation from hell is echoed in Housman's poem, though not from a Christian perspective. The redeeming love of a friend is personal, not divine, in Housman's "Hell Gate," but his poem does have its overtones of Christian belief, and it proves that he was not always the *pejorist* he claimed to be in his poetry—notwithstanding Ezra Pound's witty parody "Mr. Housman's Message," with its mocking refrain: "Oh woe, woe, etc."

The modern movement in poetry emerged in the decade surrounding World War I, and of all the poets who wrote about the Great War, Wilfred Owen was the best. Paul Fussell, in *The Great War and Modern Memory,* makes a case for World War I as the watershed for modern poetry, arguing "that there seems to be one dominating form of modern understanding; that it is essentially ironic; and that it originates largely in the application of mind and memory to the events of the Great War."[8] Modern poetry was germinated well before the war, with the symbolist movement, but it could be said that the tone of ironic criticism that Baudelaire initiated long before the war came into fashion with the war. At any rate, Owen was a poet who experienced the war directly and who learned how to write ironically about it before he himself was killed in one of the last actions of the war. Owen was unwillingly involved in the mass slaughter of civilized men by other supposedly civilized men, a member of the appropriately named Artists' Rifles who served with honor (he was awarded a Military Cross for gallantry in 1918 just before his death) until he was wounded and sent to Craiglockart Hospital in Scotland to recover.

It was in 1917 at the hospital that Owen met other wounded officers who were also poets, notably Siegfried Sassoon and Robert Graves. Owen had written poetry before, but it was mostly mannered and late romantic—or Georgian, as the current group of poets were called in England. When he showed some of his poems to Sassoon and Graves in the hospital, they encouraged him to go on writing, and when he returned to the front he continued writing more of the same bitter and ironic poems about the war until he was killed in the Battle of the Somme, shortly before the Armistice

8. Paul Fussell, *The Great War and Modern Memory,* 35.

in November 1918. Owen's best poems were written in the last two years of his life, and he died at the age of only twenty-five, having published just four poems, but the rest of his poetry was edited by his friend Siegfried Sassoon and published posthumously in 1918, the same year Gerard Manley Hopkins's poetry was edited and published for the first time by his friend Robert Bridges. Owen's *Poems* were among many hundreds of collections of war poetry published immediately after the war, but his slim collection gradually became ranked as the outstanding war poetry of the century.

Owen had started out as a late romantic poet, a Georgian like Rupert Brooke and Edward Thomas, who were also killed in the war, and his poetry written in the period just before the war was part of a small body of fine but thin and nostalgic poetry of the prewar era. The war itself made him a poet. In the four years the war lasted, from 1914 to 1918, Owen matured from a youthful idealist to a bitterly ironic and disillusioned poet. He left behind a short preface to his poems, in which he attested that his poetry was not about heroes, but about "War and the pity of War. The Poetry is in the pity." He might have said that the poetry was in the irony rather than in the pity, for in a number of finely shaped short lyrics, he characterized the war experience as a sudden loss of idealism in the violence and mud of battle. His achievement as a poet included some innovative experiments with consonantal rhyme, and he used literary allusion effectively, one of his most memorable poems bearing the Latin title from an ode by Horace "Dulce et Decorum Est"—"it is sweet and fitting . . . to die for one's country." Owen deftly reserved the ending phrase of Horace to rhyme the Latin with the English word *glory:* "pro patria mori." Thus Owen, like Pound in *Mauberley,* wrote macaronic rhymes in two languages, and the two poets were also alike in reversing Horace's classical theme of glorious and patriotic sacrifice in war, treating it instead as a bloody and dehumanizing affair.

One of Owen's finest poems is called "Anthem for Doomed Youth," written while he was recuperating at Craiglockart and shown to Siegfried Sassoon in manuscript. It is in the form of an Elizabethan sonnet, with four quatrains and a couplet in iambic pentameter, but the rhymes are harshened with the sounds of guns and the meter is rugged and broken enough to sound almost like Hopkins's "sprung rhythm." The discordant, cacophonous music of "the rifles' rapid rattle" and the "wailing choirs of shells" is enhanced by the ironic metaphor of the title—the whole poem is like a funeral service set in the noise and clamor of battle. The analogy is maintained throughout: the funeral bells are the sounds of cannons and machine guns, the choirs the whining of shells over the heads of soldiers in the trenches, the candles the flickering lights in the eyes of the dying soldiers, and their deaths are like the closing of blinds in the houses where the soldiers are mourned by their families at home. Owen captured unforgettably the sense of outrage and indignation felt by the soldiers in war, whose idealism in joining the military service and fighting to defend their loved ones is crushed by the hellish mass slaughter of modern mechanized warfare, which leaves no opportunity for personal heroism and outweighs the satisfaction of feeling that they were fighting for a cause worth dying for. Owen's poetry, coming directly out of the frenzy of war, has an added poignancy that comes from the sense of personal loss of values and youthful idealism in the brutal violence of the "no-man's-land" of trench warfare. Owen's poems were authenticated by his own death on the battlefield, which made them all the more moving as an expression of the horror and pity of war.

In one of his longer poems, "Strange Meeting," Owen makes effective use of consonantal rhyme to embody a prophecy of his own death on the battlefield. Owen's classical learning, shown in other poems such as "Dulce et Decorum Est" and "Arms and the Boy" (an ironic allusion to Virgil's "Arms and the Man"), comes out again in the imagery of this poem, since it is his version of the journey of men's souls to hell, thus comparing with Housman's "Hell Gate" in its story if not in its ending. Owen's poem begins with the image of a soldier escaping from battle "Down some profound dull tunnel," which turns out to be the pathway to hell, though it is not at first clear to the man who is dreaming where he is, until one of the "sleepers" he sees along the way looks straight at him: "And by his smile, I knew that sullen hall, / By his dead smile I knew we stood in Hell." The speaker, who is a live soldier, then speaks with the dead soldier about why he is there and what he is experiencing in hell, and the words he hears are not reassuring:

> "Strange friend," I said, "here is no cause to mourn."
> "None," said that other, "save the undone years,
> The hopelessness. Whatever hope is yours
> Was my life also. . . ."

The dead soldier goes on to tell him how much he gave up in life of beauty and joy,

> "Which must die now. I mean the truth untold,
> The pity of war, the pity war distilled.
> Now men will go content with what we spoiled.
> Or, discontent, boil bloody, and be spilled.
> They will be swift with swiftness of the tigress,
> None will break ranks, though nations trek from progress."

The soldier paints a gloomy picture of the world of the living, with its senseless killing and its violent mob emotions, and though the soldier claims that he once had virtues and ideals, he regrets they were not sufficiently strong to keep him from fighting in the war himself and being killed:

> "Courage was mine, and I had mystery;
> Wisdom was mine, and I had mastery:
> To miss the march of this retreating world
> Into vain citadels that are not walled."

Finally, the dead soldier confronts the live soldier with the hardest fact of all, which comes with a shock:

> "I am the enemy you killed, my friend.
> I knew you in this dark; for so you frowned
> Yesterday through me as you jabbed and killed.
> I parried; but my hands were loath and cold.
> Let us sleep now. . . ."

As another poetic version of the journey to hell, Owen's "Strange Meeting" is original in its consonantal rhyming couplets and in its dialogue between two soldiers, one living and one dead, one responsible for the death of the other. It does not have the unexpectedly happy ending of Housman's "Hell Gate," but its more somber ending is a forecast of Owen's death on the battlefield, and in that respect it is the completion of his poetry, which was brief as was his life but which stands permanently as the deeply ironic criticism of war by one who fought and died in it, who felt remorse for the enemy he was forced to kill, and who saw war itself, even though it inspired his best poems, as a foretaste of hell.

7

THREE AMERICAN IRONISTS
Robinson, Frost, and Jeffers

The landscapes of modern poetry are American as well as English, and as Hardy, Housman, and Owen represent the realistic-ironic treatment of such varied settings as the south and west of England in Dorset and Shropshire, and the battlefields of World War I, so Robinson, Frost, and Jeffers represent the equally realistic-ironic treatment of such native American regions as New England, both the town and the farm, and the Pacific Coast.

Edwin Arlington Robinson was the first to show real artistry in portraying the distinctive characters and speech of a rural New England village, peopling his fictional "Tilbury Town" with recognizable personages such as the town banker, Bewick Finzer, the town butcher, Reuben Bright, the town drunkard, Miniver Cheevy, and many other citizens, most of them outcasts from the town and failures in their lives. Robinson as poet hovered on the edge of tragedy but never quite plunged over; he was "the prince of heart-breakers," as Robert Frost called him, and he spoke in a tone of ironic pathos perfectly suited to the individual failures he portrayed.

Robinson, born in a coastal town with the poetic name of Head Tide, Maine, grew up in the small inland town of Gardiner, which served later as the prototype of his Tilbury Town. He attended Harvard for two years but was not happy there and returned to Gardiner after his father's death and tried to make a living at a variety of occupations (even serving for a time as a slate stacker for the Holland Tunnel in New York), but he wanted to write poetry more than anything else, and he managed despite the state of his finances to publish his first collection of poems, *The Torrent and the Night Before,* at his own expense in 1896, and then in 1897 his second collection, *Children of the Night.* Darkness dominated both collections, and when a reviewer said that he found "the true fire" of poetry in Robinson's books but regretted that the author seemed to look at the world as "a prison house," Robinson replied indignantly: "The world is not a 'prison house,' but a kind of spiritual kindergarten where millions of bewildered infants are trying to spell God with the wrong blocks."

Robinson's poetry was so bleak in its outlook that he might never have succeeded as a poet except for the almost miraculous intervention of the president of the United States. A friend of his from Gardiner taught at Groton, a prep school where Theodore Roosevelt's son Kermit studied, and when the teacher introduced the pupil to Robinson's poetry, Kermit Roosevelt took it to his father in the White House. In 1905, when Robinson's fortunes were very low and he was sinking into the alcoholism that plagued him much of his life, he suddenly had an enthusiastic letter from President Roosevelt to ask what he could do for a poet whose work he admired. The result was that Robinson paid a visit to the White House and Roosevelt recommended him for a job in the New York customs house, a job that Robinson (like Hawthorne and Melville before him) found leisurely enough to allow him time to write. He wrote later to Kermit Roosevelt that Kermit's father had "fished me out of hell by the hair of my head."

Intellectually, Robinson inherited both the earlier New England puritanism and the later New England transcendentalism, and if he was constitutionally more in key with the puritans than with the transcendentalists—just as Emily Dickinson had been in her poetry—he took his influence more from abroad, from the naturalism of Émile Zola in France and the regionalism of Thomas Hardy in England, and from, even earlier, the eighteenth-century poetry of George Crabbe, who had written about small-town England as Robinson wrote about small-town New England. His sonnet to George Crabbe is so close to Robinson's own outlook that he may be said to have made Crabbe a latter-day citizen of Tilbury Town, for he pictures him as a lonely poet whose books gather dust on the shelf, but who nevertheless displays a "plain excellence and stubborn skill" that "fashion cannot kill," and so Robinson praises Crabbe for qualities he cultivated in his own poetry:

> Whether or not we read him, we can feel
> From time to time the vigor of his name
> Against us like a finger for the shame
> And emptiness of what our souls reveal
> In books that are as altars where we kneel
> To consecrate the flicker, not the flame.

While George Crabbe was a real poet for whom Robinson had great affinity, the other characters in Tilbury Town are fictional, but no less real. One of the best known of them is Richard Cory, the wealthiest man in town, whose wealth, instead of making him happy, only makes him envied by the townspeople and isolated from them. He is a success in their eyes but a failure in his own, as we judge from the fact that, despite his high position in the town, he commits suicide. The motive for his suicide remains a mystery, for Robinson portrays him only from the outside, from the view of those who admired him and "thought that he was everything / To make us wish that we were in his place." Since the reason for his death can never be fathomed, Richard Cory is one of Robinson's best-known but most enigmatic characters. No matter how many times they are read, the final lines of the poem "Richard Cory" never lose the shock of his sudden and unexpected end:

> And Richard Cory, one calm summer night,
> Went home and put a bullet through his head.

Was it his conspicuous wealth, his lonely existence without family or kin, or perhaps some secret crime he committed that led him to take his own life? We never know; what we are left with is the darkness inside his soul, which only grows more impenetrable as one reflects on it. Robinson keeps himself out of the poem, letting it be told by the people of the town, the "we" who are left to puzzle it out at the end. Despite having a name symbolic of a noble family— *Richard Cory* rhymes with *glory* and evokes the name of Richard Coeur de Lion—Cory's death leaves behind no other "king" in Tilbury Town.

Of all Robinson's many failures, perhaps the most sympathetic is old Eben Flood of "Mr. Flood's Party," because in his case the failure is from a weakness not of conscience but of flesh: old age has overwhelmed him and left him friendless, an unwilling exile, doomed to holding an ironic "party" with himself. His name is as symbolic as Richard Cory's, since pronouncing *Eben Flood* as if *Eben* is short for *Ebenezer* leads to the conclusion that while his fortunes may once have been at their flood, they are now at their ebb: "There was not much that was ahead of him." We see Mr. Flood pathetically alone, on a hillside looking down at the town where he was once happy, "Where friends of other days had honored him." Now he has only himself, and he has sought solace in drink, having carried along with him "The jug that he had gone so far to fill," from which he offers a toast to himself in the silence and darkness. Robinson ironically compares his Mr. Flood to two literary figures: Omar Khayyám, the Persian author of "The bird is on the wing" (Robinson quotes these words in "Mr. Flood's Party" from Edward FitzGerald's translation of the *Rubáiyát*: "the Bird of Time, has but a little while / To flutter, and the bird is on the wing"); and Roland, the medieval knight who in *The Song of Roland* blew his horn too late to bring reinforcements to the Christian troops of Charlemagne to save them from the attacking Moors. In the first case, Mr. Flood quotes Omar to say, not that he has little time to enjoy wine, women, and song as Omar did, but that he has little time to live, and in the second case, he catches Mr. Flood just as he is raising his jug to drink and says he is "Like Roland's ghost winding a silent horn." The allusions imply a doubly ironic contrast: Mr. Flood's drinking alone in old age shows neither the Persian poet's lighthearted hedonism nor the French knight's heroic martyrdom, but an ironic pathos at the end of life.

Later in the poem, Mr. Flood "lifted up his voice and sang" the familiar New Year's Eve drinking song "For Auld Lang Syne." Burns's Scottish words are nostalgic, but convivial, about "times long past," but they, too, have an ironic ring coming from Mr. Flood's lips, accented by the additional mockery of his slightly drunken condition, which is "Secure, with only two moons listening." There is a saving humor in this tipsy figure to relieve the pathos in Robinson's realistic portrait of the old man, who at the end is left with a bleak landscape around him and a lonely fate to contemplate, since

> there was nothing in the town below—
> Where strangers would have shut the many doors
> That many friends had opened long ago.

Eben Flood is the last of his generation in Tilbury Town, and Robinson's poem places him in the New England townscape as it dramatizes memorably, yet wryly, the pitiable state of extreme old age.

Robert Frost, a little younger than Robinson, came from a New England family, but was born in the Far West, in San Francisco, where his father had gone to be a newspaperman, and only after his father's early death did he return to his ancestral roots, first to Massachusetts and then to a New Hampshire farm owned by his uncle. There, in time, he was able to make fine poetry out of the farmer's life, the simplest kind of provincial existence, and to perfect the colloquial idiom of rural New England into a remarkably subtle poetic medium that seemed to come straight from the plain speech of New England farmers. In fashioning his poetic style Frost used the familiar English blank verse that Shakespeare and Milton and Wordsworth had used before him, but he transformed it into the laconic discourse of farmers working at their daily occupations, chopping wood or mowing hay or picking apples or mending stone walls. Frost was honest enough to confess that he "kept farm" for ten years mainly to listen to what people were saying in their isolated New England farm cottages, for as he confessed to a Boston critic early in his poetic career:

It would seem absurd to say it (and you mustn't quote me as saying it) but I suppose the fact is that my conscious interest in people was at first no more than an almost technical interest in their speech—in what I used to call their

sentence sounds—the sound of sense. Whatever these sounds are or aren't
(they are certainly not of the vowels or consonants of words nor even of the
words themselves but something the words are chiefly a kind of notation for
indicating and fastening to the printed page) whatever they are, I say, I began
to hang on them very young. I was under twenty when I deliberately put it
to myself one night after good conversation that there are moments when we
actually touch in talk what the best writing can only come near. The curse
of our book language is not so much that it keeps forever to the same set
phrases (though Heaven knows those are bad enough) but that it sounds
forever with the same reading tones. We must go out into the vernacular for
tones that haven't been brought to book. We must write with the ear on the
speaking voice. We must imagine the speaking voice.[1]

What Frost did with blank verse by "going out into the vernacular" of
New England farm speech was as radical in its way as the experiments of
the imagists with free verse, but it looked more like conventional poetic form,
with its lines of roughly regular length. Frost once remarked that he would "as
soon write free verse as play tennis with the net down," but he did write freely
within the limits of the traditional iambic pentameter line. As with Hopkins's
sprung-rhythm sonnets, whose lines contain deliberately increased numbers
of stresses, Frost emphasized in his blank verse the metrical variation possible
within each line, always using conversational speech as his guide. Many of
Frost's best poems are written in a flexible, colloquial blank verse, often in
the form of a dramatic dialogue, as in "The Death of the Hired Man," "Home
Burial," and "The Witch of Coos," or sometimes in dramatic monologues,
such as "Birches" or "Mending Wall," and sometimes in narratives that read
like short stories, as for instance the one that takes its title from Shakespeare's
Macbeth, "Out, Out—."

In "Out, Out—" the terse narrative in blank verse has many variant feet
within the lines, so that it almost seems as if there are no regular iambic
pentameter lines in the whole poem. The borderline between prose and poetry
is often hard to discern in Frost. Yet there are some fine effects that only a
skillful poet could manage, such as the alliteration of "*st*ove-length *st*icks
of wood, / Sweet-scented *st*uff" and the assonance of "But the h*a*nd! The
boy's first outcry was a rueful l*a*ugh, / As he swung toward them holding up
the h*a*nd / H*a*lf in appeal, but h*a*lf as if to keep / The life from spilling."
And certainly there is onomatopoeia in the repeated sound of the buzz saw,
which "snarled and rattled, snarled and rattled." One can also hear the fading
heartbeat of the boy, dying in the hospital, with "Little—less—nothing! and
that ended it."

1. Robert Frost, *Selected Letters*, 158–59.

Besides the colloquial accuracy of Frost's New England blank verse, there is the stark realism of his imagery and the faintly ironic tone that give the narrative a shocking force. "Out, Out—" opens with the noise of the buzz saw dropping sticks of wood about the length of a human arm, an ominous sound that foreshadows the cutting off of the boy's hand, just at the moment when his sister calls out, "Supper." Frost adds figurative irony to the matter-of-fact storytelling with "At the word, the saw, / As if to prove saws knew what supper meant, / Leaped out at the boy's hand." The boy's gesture of holding up his severed hand, "as if to keep the life from spilling" is especially chilling and pathetic, a futile attempt at self-preservation. But the ending is final in its tight-lipped naturalism: "No more to build on there. And they, since they / Were not the one dead, turned to their affairs." The fatalism of "Out, Out—" is tempered by the irony, conveying unmistakably the sense that nature is indifferent to man's sufferings, and that men must go on living in spite of individual deaths, but the life of the boy is so short as to exemplify its title, the phrase from a speech by Macbeth as he is nearing death, "Out, out brief candle!"

It is not nature's part to weep over death, as Frost also suggests in "The Need of Being Versed in Country Things," but it is part of being human, since nature goes right on with the process of life and death whatever happens, and only humans who are "versed in country things" are able, when the birds have left their nests in a decaying barn, "not to believe the phoebes wept." Frost's New England farmers are stoics who are disposed to suffer silently and uncomplainingly in their lonely lives—except for an occasional mother, like the one in "Home Burial," who cannot bear the loss of her son and leaves her husband because he is too stoical for her, or the compassionate wife in "The Death of the Hired Man," who tries to convince her husband that he should take in the wayward migrant worker who comes to his farm to die, but death takes him first, before the husband can make up his mind whether to take him in.

"The Death of the Hired Man" is one of Frost's finest dialogues, because it gives a sympathetic portrait of a homeless man, Silas, who dies alone at the end of the poem, but also because it gives a moving study of the farmer, Warren, and his wife, Mary, and so there are three characters in this little one-act play set on a remote New England farm, one of whom never speaks. Silas, the dying hired man of the title, is always offstage, but Warren and Mary talk about him from their different perspectives until the reader feels he knows Silas intimately at the moment of his death and can experience the loss Mary suffers when Warren returns to her with the news:

> "Warren?" she questioned.
> "Dead," was all he answered.

The ending is as final as that of "Out, out—" but the difference is in the manner of its telling, which is entirely dramatic in this poem, as it was thematic in the other. The last lines are in blank verse, as is the whole poem, but the variation from normal iambic pentameter is extreme: there is hardly a straight iambic foot anywhere in the line, and the break in the middle between the two speakers interrupts the flow even further.

The same departure from standard blank verse is to be seen in the opening line of the poem: "Mary sat musing on the lamp-flame at the table," where there are really only four main accents—"*Mary*," "*mu*sing," "*lamp*-flame" and "*table*"—instead of five, and none of the feet are strictly iambic (Frost once said there are only two kinds of feet possible in English, "strict iambic and loose iambic," and his were almost all of the "loose iambic" variety). That this line is followed by "Waiting for Warren" in the second line means that the sense of the first line spills over into the second, creating an additional variation in the meter as the poem begins. Considered from either end, then, Frost's realistic drama set on a New England farm is full of rhythmical variations, all of which are designed to emphasize the straightforward conversation of the participants, to make the poetry seem more like prose, and that is Frost's special achievement among American poets: he wrote poetry that was so close to prose and to the normal conversation of uneducated people that the reader must listen closely to know that he is reading a poem at all. Frost made good use of understatement along with irony to heighten his realism, and his skillful handling of tone and meter are never obvious but always subordinated to character and action, as in a play.

There is another feature of "The Death of the Hired Man" that escapes notice unless one is listening closely: the difference between husband and wife, who have clearly loved each other faithfully for a lifetime, but who have never reconciled their contrary viewpoints. The poem is about a man who dies alone, and Silas is the center of attention even though he is always offstage, but it is just as much about conjugal love, the affectionate understanding between a man and a woman who are forever different from each other in their human reactions. Frost puts into his very provincial setting a universal subject: the irreconcilable differences between the sexes, which love may overcome but cannot obliterate. Perhaps the most graphic illustration of the difference between male and female perspectives occurs in the middle of the poem, in the highly quotable (but still ironic and mystifying) definition of "home":

"Home," he mocked gently.

                              "Yes, what else but home?
It all depends on what you mean by home.
Of course, he's nothing to us, any more

> Than was the hound that came a stranger to us
> Out of the woods, worn out upon the trail."
>
> "Home is the place where, when you have to go there,
> They have to take you in."
>   "I should have called it
> Something you somehow haven't to deserve."

Since Warren and Mary have made a home together for many years, their contrasting definitions of it have become ingrained in their characters, as Frost himself once said in an interview:

> In *The Death of the Hired Man* that I wrote long, long ago, long before the New Deal, I put it two ways about home. One would be the manly way: "Home is the place where, when you have to go there, They have to take you in." That's the man's feeling about it. And then the wife says, "I should have called it / Something you somehow hadn't to deserve." That's the New Deal, the feminine way of it, the mother way. You don't have to deserve your mother's love. You have to deserve your father's. He's more particular.[2]

At the end, the wife can only entreat her husband to go in and speak to Silas, because her sympathy has gone out at once to the man who has worked on their farm many times without ever becoming a reliable worker, whereas her husband is still not willing to take Silas back into their home. Finally, neither has to decide, because Silas has died while they were discussing his fate, and nature has settled the issue between them once and for all. In this poem, as in many others he wrote, Frost showed that men and women will never be the same in their feelings, no matter how long they live together, and in some poems, notably "Home Burial," the differences grow worse rather than better, and the woman leaves her husband after their son's early death, though in "The Death of the Hired Man" the couple stay together despite their different responses to a man's death and even their different understanding of what "home" really is.

Frost wrote most of his best poems in the first two decades of the twentieth century, when the new movement in poetry was just getting under way, and though he went to England seeking recognition of his talent in 1912 and met Ezra Pound, he declined to join the imagists and write in the cosmopolitan international style of Pound and Eliot, preferring instead to take "the road less traveled by" and write in a regional American style. In his lifetime, however, Frost became a much more popular poet than either Pound or Eliot, earning

---

2. Frost, "The Art of Poetry II: Robert Frost," interview, 109.

by his realistic New England honesty the place of unofficial American poet laureate. This position was recognized in 1961 at the presidential inauguration of another New Englander, John Kennedy, when the eighty-six-year-old poet read "The Gift Outright" as a tribute to the whole country. Frost's agrarianism was a New England counterpart to the southern agrarianism of the Fugitives, and it ran deep in American life, embodying the Jeffersonian republicanism of the pioneer farmers who had first settled the country and of the later farmers who fought the British for their independence and won it: "Such as we were, we gave ourselves outright, / To the land vaguely realizing westward." Frost's agrarianism was instinctively regional, and it struck a responsive chord among most Americans, who could remember their roots in farming communities across the country, though their lives in the twentieth century were increasingly industrialized and urbanized.

Robinson Jeffers was the one poet of stature who made the Far West a symbolic region, specifically the California coast. Jeffers was born in Pittsburgh, but went west as a young man to college and eventually settled on the Monterey peninsula south of San Francisco. As Frost was born in San Francisco but made his home in New England, so Jeffers was born in the East but made his home in the West, both poets consciously choosing the setting they would symbolize in their poetry. It is the native American way of freedom, for Jeffers the westerner was even less an international poet than Frost the New Englander. He consciously turned his back on civilization and chose to live in a wild and unspoiled natural setting, more as a hunter and fisher than as a farmer. Jeffers, whose father was a professor of Hebrew at the University of Pittsburgh, grew up with a great admiration for the Old Testament and for classical Greek tragedy, and he deliberately chose to exile himself from the "perishing republic," as he called America, and to seek instead the solitude of the mountains and the sea, where he could cultivate permanent rather than temporary values and could shun the ephemeral issues of what he believed to be a corrupt and decadent society.

In his self-imposed exile in the Far West, Jeffers developed a poetic style and philosophy that had much in common with the naturalism of writers like Stephen Crane, Edwin Arlington Robinson, and Robert Frost, but with a harder edge that he did not shrink from calling "inhumanism." Jeffers saw man and nature pitted against each other, with nature always on the winning side, and he had the audacity to ally himself with nature against man, to assert in a series of short and long poems the superiority of nature: "the heart-breaking beauty will remain when there is no heart to break for it," he wrote in "Apology for Bad Dreams." Much influenced by reading Nietzsche as a young man, Jeffers took the view that Christian civilization had only succeeded in softening human beings, making them in Nietzsche's phrase "human, all too human," whereas Jeffers believed that choosing to live alone in nature could harden one to endure the worst life offered and to die in one's time with dignity. In an age of radical individualism, Jeffers was one of the most fiercely individualistic of all poets, and he filled his poetry so full of violence and barbaric cruelty—particularly the long narrative poems that made him famous, such as "Tamar" and "Roan Stallion"—that he was regarded by many in his lifetime as beyond the pale, a poet not merely of the frontier but of the primitive and the savage in man.

Yet in his avowed inhumanism, Jeffers reinvigorated primitive instincts and produced some highly original and lasting poems. His long free-verse lines, reminiscent of the poetry of Whitman and of the cadences of the King James translation of the Bible, were a distinctive contribution to the experiments with poetic form that were going on in his time, just as his philosophy of inhumanism was a significant departure from the views of many of his contemporaries. Jeffers's "boulders blunt as old bears' teeth" are as indigenously western as Frost's stone walls are indigenously New England, and he added to the symbolic landscape such features as the rocky cliffs, the wide Pacific ocean, and wild animals such as the swan, the pelican, the deer, and the seals, all part of his California-coast setting, "West of the West of things," where the land meets the sea and civilization reaches its last frontier. Jeffers could write a poem called "Oh, Lovely Rock" about the joy of being the hardest substance in nature, and when he visited Ireland he admired the rocky spectacle of the Giant's Causeway, which reminded him of the coast he knew so well. His most characteristic poems are about beasts of prey—the mountain lion, the eagle, and the shark, who live by killing other creatures for their food. One of his most memorable poems is "Hurt Hawks," where man the hunter encounters nature the hunter and offers the solace of death to the wounded red-tailed hawk.

"Hurt Hawks" shows great admiration and sympathy for the hawk as a strong wild creature who never yields even in misery to his baser instincts, will not be drawn to self-pity or dependency on others, will not suffer humiliation even when wounded, but will face pain and death without flinching. Jeffers sees the hawk, "intemperate and savage," as closer in spirit to what he calls "the wild God of the world" than are the "communal people," who band together in fear for self-protection. The speaker of the poem is a hunter with a rifle, who admits quite openly that "I'd sooner, except the penalties, kill a man than a hawk," displaying both contempt for man and admiration for a bird of prey. Jeffers's inhumanism in this poem would seem unbearable except that he does not simply condemn man but celebrates natural beauty and wildness, showing a compassion for the hawk that leads him to give it "the lead gift in the twilight," an ironic but fitting death for the proud creature who will never surrender "the old implacable arrogance" and who attains a natural immortality in death, for Jeffers goes beyond naturalism to supernaturalism at the end, portraying the hawk's soul soaring into the air and causing other birds to cry out at its passing. The ironic inhumanism of Robinson Jeffers is a western attitude, one that sorts well with the rugged wilderness of the California coast and places him as an individual poet at the extreme end of Western civilization.

For that civilization, which he had deliberately left behind, Jeffers shows little sympathy, but there are a few poems in which he describes his stance apart from it memorably. One of these is "Shine, Perishing Republic," the theme of which is complementary to Frost's patriotic inaugural poem, "The Gift Outright." It is enlightening to think of Frost in New England celebrating the emergent republic that started in the East, "in Massachusetts, in Virginia," and that went out to the "land vaguely realizing westward, / But still unstoried, artless, unenhanced, / Such as she was, such as she would become," and then to think of Jeffers, who presented the same republic as a volcano exploding and then hardening into petrified rock, or flaming out like a meteor, and who said approvingly that "meteors are not needed less than mountains: shine, perishing republic." Jeffers and Frost stand for strong regional differences among Americans, but even more definitely, for the contrasting responses of poets to agrarian New England and California's Last Frontier.

Although it was the sparsely populated coast that Jeffers preferred to live in and write about, he also portrayed his feeling about coastal cities (probably Los Angeles) in such a poem as "The Purse-Seine." This poem is about fishing, as other poems are about hunting, primitive actions of men that Jeffers admired more than their congregation into cities. In the poem, he describes the sardine-fishers going out at night in their boats to cast their huge seines for schools of fish, and he paints a thrillingly realistic picture of their prey caught in the net beneath the boat:

> I cannot tell you
> How beautiful the scene is, and a little terrible, then, when the crowded fish
> Know they are caught, and wildly beat from one wall to the
> other of their closing destiny the phosphorescent
> Water to a pool of flame. . . .

Jeffers transfers this scene to another setting, as he looks down from a mountaintop at night on a "wide city, the colored splendor, galaxies of light" and asks himself, "how could I help but recall the seine-net / Gathering the luminous fish?" The comparison of the people in the city to the sardines caught in the purse seine seems to him both beautiful and terrible, and he keeps his distance from them on his mountaintop, taking from the two spectacles the lesson that whether men prey on fish or on each other, the result is much the same: "surely one always knew that cultures decay, and life's end is death." The moral for Jeffers was simply that American and Western civilization was dying from its own rapacity, and that the right action to take in the midst of such decadence is to stand apart from it, like a southern Fugitive, or like one of Robinson's citizens of Tilbury Town or one of Frost's New England farmers.

All regional American poets, whether agrarian or inhumanist, have been staunch conservationists, but Robinson Jeffers was so identified with the cause of natural preservation that the Sierra Club collected his poetry into a book with photographs of the California coast and called it *Not Man Apart,* a phrase from one of Jeffers's most philosophical poems, "The Answer":

> Integrity is wholeness, the greatest beauty is
> Organic wholeness, the wholeness of life and things, the divine beauty of
>   the universe. Love that, not man
> Apart from that, or else you will share man's pitiful confusions, or drown
>   in despair when his days darken.

Robinson, Frost, and Jeffers are identified with the New England town, the New England farm, and the Pacific Coast, but their messages are much alike, for in the poetry of these three American ironists the regional symbolism expresses a consistently pessimistic outlook on American society, making naturalism or inhumanism preferable to any sort of sentimental humanism, and relieving the tragic situation of human beings by means of stark honesty and dark humor.

8

THE ORIGINAL IMAGIST
Ezra Pound

Ezra Pound and the Image

Hugh Selwyn Mauberley, Pound's ironic portrait of the artist, stands at the end of the imagist decade from 1910 to 1920, when literature in English became recognizably modern. "The age demanded an image / Of its accelerated grimace," he says in the second section of the poem, implying that the modern revolution in literary style came from two main impulses—focus on the image and defiance of the age, an age that was preoccupied in the second decade of the century, not with poetic movements but with the first world war. Modern literature thus had its beginning as a contradictory art, modern in form, antimodern in content, and so it would remain throughout its period of greatness. Virginia Woolf looked back in 1924, in her essay "Mr. Bennett and Mrs. Brown," and concluded that "in or about December, 1910, human character changed." We might not state it so dramatically in the last decade of the century, but surely we would agree that literary expression in English—if not human character itself—was radically altered between 1910 and 1920. Probably the best evidence is to be found in the poetry of Yeats, which underwent a visible metamorphosis during that period; whatever personal reasons there may have been for the change in Yeats's style, it brought him all the way from being a late romantic, mainly Irish poet to being an early modern, mainly international poet in a few short years, justifying the opinion of Pound in 1913 that Yeats was the only older poet writing in English whose work was worth serious study by younger poets.

Most of the poets and writers who would become Yeats's younger contemporaries emerged in the second decade, but Pound was as usual a jump ahead of the rest. In 1912, with *Ripostes,* his poetry struck a vein of real modernity.

Robert Frost's first books were published in London in 1913 and 1914, and in 1914 the *Egoist* began serializing Joyce's *Portrait of the Artist as a Young Man,* while introducing such new poets as H. D., William Carlos Williams, and Marianne Moore, and in 1915 *Poetry* magazine in Chicago published both T. S. Eliot's "Love Song of J. Alfred Prufrock" and Wallace Stevens's "Sunday Morning." When we recall that the first novels and poems of D. H. Lawrence, as well as the first novels of Virginia Woolf, also appeared in the second decade of the century, we can almost believe that modern literature rose like a phoenix from the ashes of the Great War. But that tempting metaphor is too simple, for the new style emerged well before the war, although it did not reach its apex until after the war, when Joyce's *Ulysses* and Eliot's *Waste Land* were published, in 1922. The second decade was a period of mutual inspiration for writers of widely different origins, partly coinciding with the war and being darkened by it, but not having the war as its main subject or cause.

The source of inspiration for the new literary era is mysterious, as it always is with the arts. Yeats would no doubt have attributed the source to the *Spiritus Mundi,* his phrase for primeval memory, but it might as well be attributed to the Spirit of the Age, the invisible Zeitgeist impelling very diverse writers to new forms of expression. It is not scientific to talk of Time-Spirits, though Ezra Pound in his early essay "The Serious Artist" (1913) did not shrink from comparing art and science: "The arts, literature, poesy, are a science, just as chemistry is a science. Their subject is man, mankind, and the individual." Pound maintained that the material of art, human nature, is a constant, as the material of science, physical nature, is a constant, but he believed just as firmly, as he put it in "Patria Mia" in 1913, in "the art of poetry, as a living art, an art changing and developing, always the same at root, never the same in appearance for two decades in succession." Whatever the underlying causes of modernism in literature may have been, for Pound, as instigator, they were rooted in human nature, which like all organic nature was in continual process of change, of creation and destruction, birth and death, and for him, the artist must be constantly striving to "MAKE IT NEW," that is, participating in a perpetual renaissance.

Pound had arrived in London in 1908, with *A Lume Spento,* his first volume of poems, already published at his own expense in Venice. If there were many other talented writers who contributed to the making of modern literary style, it was Pound who insisted most vehemently, "It is tremendously important that great poetry be written, it makes no jot of difference who writes it," and it was he who did most to encourage, cajole, badger, criticize, and act as literary agent for all the others. Between 1910 and 1920, Pound was at the center of the modern movement, almost *embodying* the Zeitgeist, it seemed, and it is hard to dispute the later judgment of Eliot in his introduction to *The Literary Essays of Ezra Pound* that "Mr. Pound is more responsible for the

20th Century revolution in poetry than any other individual." Pound's work as poet, critic, editor, and promoter of the new style was crucial to its initial period, the decade surrounding World War I, and what was most essential to his conception of the truly modern was a single word: *image.*

By the time Pound set it down in *Mauberley* that "The age demanded an image," he was ready to bid farewell to London and all that had been accomplished there in the twelve years since he had arrived from Venice, with a new renaissance in his mind. He joined Hulme's group, which he later named the School of Images, in 1909, and in 1912 he used the French spelling of "Les Imagistes" for the first time to designate the new poetic school. But after editing the first anthology, *Des Imagistes,* in 1914, he left the imagists to join the vorticists, and so moved beyond the short imagist poem that he, H. D., Aldington, Flint, and Hulme had fostered, but never deserted the imagist principles completely, because they were the credo of his modernism. *Mauberley* itself can, in fact, be seen as an imagist poem, built up out of successive concentrated images into a series of portraits of artists and their age—not the pure, static images he had begun with, but contrasting and ironic images that worked energetically upon and against each other. *Mauberley* is Pound's pivotal work, looking backward to imagism and forward to the *Cantos.* It is the same sort of critical self-portrait that Joyce made of his Stephen Dedalus and Eliot made of his J. Alfred Prufrock—an autobiographical persona criticizing aspects of the author's own personality, freeing him from certain limitations and allowing him to develop beyond them: beyond *Mauberley* are the *Cantos,* just as beyond Joyce's *Portrait* is *Ulysses* and beyond Eliot's "Prufrock" is *The Waste Land.*

But *Mauberley* casts its shadow backward more than forward, containing a capsule history of what might be called the imagist decade, during which Pound had helped to originate a poetic style focused on the image. This image was not all of one kind; it began as a brief, static, spatial, descriptive poem, then became more dynamic as it grew longer, and then more ironic and satirical as the images combined and clashed. One can see this development graphically illustrated in Pound's poetry, starting with the first imagist poems in *Ripostes* in 1912, then looking at the relatively pure Chinese images of *Cathay* in 1915 (which were not mere translations but original poems), followed by the satirical images of *Lustra* in 1915, then the mock-heroic images of "Homage to Sextus Propertius" in 1919 (also more Pound than Propertius), and culminating with *Hugh Selwyn Mauberley* in 1920.

The movement from static to kinetic to ironic images is the main progress of Pound's poetry, the ultimate phase being reached near the end of the imagist decade in the first cantos, where all three types of image are compounded in the *ideogram,* Pound's most complex image, a fusion of a number of short images into a larger whole in the manner of Chinese writing (but with word-images replacing picture-writing). Pound may have portrayed his fictional self, Mauberley, as "out of key with his time," but Pound himself, though at odds with his time, was always in touch with it even in opposing it, continually confronting the age with images that mirrored it critically. *Mauberley* includes, along with its sympathetic and satirical portraits of artists, some of the most telling images of World War I, tragic in their sense of disillusionment:

> There died a myriad,
> And of the best, among them,
> For an old bitch gone in the teeth,
> For a botched civilization,
>
> Charm, smiling at the good mouth,
> Quick eyes gone under earth's lid,
>
> For two gross of broken stature,
> For a few thousand battered books.

Imagism has often been slighted because as a movement it lasted barely a decade and produced only a handful of unforgettable poems, but in the work of Pound alone it produced a set of poetic ideas more responsible than any others for the radical change in English style that took place from 1910 to 1920, and it produced poems reflective of a continuing response to the age that was both creative and critical. Imagism proved in time to be much more than a passing artistic fad or stylistic novelty, unlike dadaism, futurism, or even surrealism, for as Stephen Spender has argued in *The Struggle of the Modern,* "The aims of the imagist movement in poetry provide the archetype of a modern creative procedure."[1] What Pound and the imagists together wrought was no less than a new definition of poetry—word-images in natural speech-rhythms—leading to changes in poetic technique and in fictional technique as well, for as Spender rightly suggested, "stream-of-consciousness" narration is really imagist prose, since it is the subjective portrayal of character through selection and association of images in the character's mind.

T. E. Hulme deserves credit for the initial emphasis on the image, for Hulme had formed the original School of Images in London in 1909, the year after Pound arrived on the scene, and Hulme first formulated, in his essay "Romanticism and Classicism" in 1910, the doctrine that "images in verse are not mere decoration, but the very essence of an intuitive language." Hulme, who had been a disciple of the philosopher Henri Bergson in Paris, was acquainted with the theory of creative evolution, was well versed in French

---

1. Stephen Spender, "The Seminal Image," in *The Struggle of the Modern,* 110.

symbolism and impressionism, and was the first to reach the conclusion that "the mystery of things is no longer perceived as action but as impression" and to declare in "A Lecture on Modern Poetry" in 1910 that modern art "no longer deals with heroic action, it has become definitely and finally introspective and deals with momentary phases in the poet's mind." But Hulme thought of himself as primarily a philosopher, using images as illustrations of ideas, while Pound was always primarily a poet, seeking theoretical justification for his practice, and it was Pound who produced, in "A Few Don'ts by an Imagist," in *Poetry,* March 1913, the best working definition of the essence of imagism: "An 'Image' is that which presents an intellectual and emotional complex in an instant of time." It was also Pound who showed in practice how far this definition could be carried into the making of short and then of longer poems. Pound emphasized how much concentration of intellect and emotion was possible in a poetic image, though it mirrored only a brief moment of experience. He took the image to be the poet's "primary pigment" and stressed the hardness, or concreteness, of sensory language, warning his fellow poets to "go in fear of abstractions." After all, his primary service to Yeats as his "private secretary" at Stone Cottage in 1913 and 1914 had been, in Yeats's own words, to "go over all my work with me to eliminate the abstract," and Pound convinced Yeats at that crucial period in his development that "the whole movement in poetry is toward pictures, sensuous images, away from rhetoric, from the abstract."[2] Besides concreteness, Pound stressed exactness of diction—the *mot juste* of Flaubert—and clarity, and urged poets "regarding rhythm: to compose in the sequence of the musical phrase, not in sequence of a metronome." Thus, along with the image emerged free verse, newly understood as an appropriate organic rhythm suited to the mood of the individual image.

Of course, Pound acknowledged in many ways his debt to French writers, in particular to the realistic prose style of Flaubert, Mauberley's "true Penelope"; to the lapidary poetic style of Théophile Gautier, in his *Émaux et camées;* and to Rémy de Gourmont's symbolist criticism. His favored spelling of *Imagistes,* which he capitalized, was a gesture of homage to the *symbolistes,* the first school of modern poets, whose best-known members were Baudelaire, Mallarmé, Verlaine, and Rimbaud. But Pound criticized the French symbolists as often as he praised them. The first principle of imagism was "direct treatment of the thing," clearly in contrast to Mallarmé's famous dictum that to name a thing was to take away half the pleasure of suggesting it, and while Verlaine had advised in his poem "The Art of Poetry" an "indefinite music," Pound spoke in favor of "an 'absolute rhythm,' a rhythm, that is, in poetry which corresponds exactly to the emotion or shade of emotion to be expressed." Pound wanted

2. Yeats, *Uncollected Prose,* vol. 2, 414.

the image to be a more definite and concrete expression than the symbol, and among French poets he praised the "hardness" of Laforgue and Corbière over the "softness" of others. Pound linked his belief in absolute rhythm to "a like belief in a sort of permanent metaphor, which is, as I understand it, 'symbolism' in its profounder sense."[3] In short, Pound's imagism was intended as a corrective to symbolism that would carry the latter toward a greater poetic realism, keeping the poet's vision always in touch with his senses, and holding firmly to the principle that truth should be visible in things, rather than invisible beyond them.

Pound's definition of the image is close to the core of modernism in literature in that it seeks to fuse symbolism with realism to make an expressive vehicle of numinous perception, where ordinary sensations become imbued with extraordinary supersensory power. If it has something in common with the symbol of the French poets, it has even more in common with other key terms that have been invested with meaning by modern writers of English. A direct line could be drawn from Hopkins's notion of "inscape" as "the soul of art," whereby "searching nature I touch self," which Hopkins thought equivalent to Duns Scotus's Latin word *haeccitas,* the "thisness" of things, through Joyce's idea of "epiphany," which he defined in *Stephen Hero* as the revelation of the "whatness" of a thing, the expression of a moment when "the soul of the commonest object seems to us radiant," through Pound's "image," to Eliot's "objective correlative," or "a set of objects, a chain of events which shall be the formula of that particular emotion, such that when the external facts, which must terminate in sensory experience, are given, the emotion is immediately evoked." What all these terms have in common is the belief in immanence, or incarnation, truth revealed through the visible world and expressed in exact, concrete language, close to the "Word made flesh" of Christian doctrine.

Each of these primary terms has become indispensable to the understanding of modern style, and if Pound's *image* has priority over *inscape, epiphany,* or the *objective correlative,* it is by virtue of being a term less specialized, more easily related to poetic language in all ages, given new significance for the modern age by becoming the whole expression, for as Pound put it, "The point of Imagisme is that it does not use images *as ornaments.* The image is itself the speech."[4] Pound's definition of the image was the culmination of a period of prolific experiment that had brought him through many trials and errors to the first crystallization of his own personal poetic style.

Pound was indeed the most protean of modern writers from the beginning to the end of his career, never ceasing to make new experiments in poetic

3. Ezra Pound, "Vorticism."
4. Ibid.

expression; his only real counterparts are in other arts, Picasso in painting, Stravinsky in music. At first he had imitated some of the masters of his youth—Browning, Rossetti, Swinburne, the early Yeats—and translated with growing originality from a number of foreign languages, seeking deliberately to enrich English with sounds and images from Provençal, Greek, Anglo-Saxon, Italian, Chinese, French, and German poetry. He was taking his example from the earlier European Renaissance, when writers were using ancient and modern languages to enrich each other, but in Pound's case, it was a one-man renaissance.

In his first critical book, *The Spirit of Romance,* published in London in 1910, when he was twenty-five years old, Pound began preparing the way for the new style that would emerge in 1912 with the imagists. Believing, as he said in his preface, that "all ages are contemporaneous," Pound defined poetry as an art of precision: "Poetry is a sort of inspired mathematics, which gives us equations, not for abstract figures, triangles, spheres and the like, but equations for the human emotions." As to what these emotions proceeded from, Pound said in a later chapter of his book that "for our basis in nature, we rest on the indisputable and very scientific fact that there are 'in the normal course of things,' certain times, a certain sort of moment more than another, when a man feels his immortality upon him." Pound then gave a capsule history of Western poetry, in which he put forward the view that the sense of immortality was first translated into the myths, where gods appeared in various forms to men—"speaking aesthetically, the myths are explications of mood," he said, and the Homeric epics of the *Iliad* and the *Odyssey* are the classical texts; then, as he saw it, in the medieval period, under the influence of Christianity, the myths were transformed into metaphors of love, with the beautiful, unattainable lady of the Provençal and Italian troubadours becoming an image of transcendent and perfect love, expressed most fully and satisfactorily in Dante's *Divine Comedy;* the next phase, for Pound, was to be the modern image. He did not say as much in *The Spirit of Romance,* because it was too early, but he implied it in the criticism that followed in the next few years, when imagism was more and more prominent in his thinking, and he explained it best in 1914, when he described the process by which he had composed his most famous imagist poem, "In a Station of the Metro":

Three years ago in Paris I got out of a "metro" train at La Concorde, and saw suddenly a beautiful face, and then another and another, and then a beautiful child's face, and then another beautiful woman, and I tried all that day to find words for what this had meant to me, and I could not find any words that seemed to me worthy, or as lovely as that sudden emotion. And that evening, as I went home along the Rue Raynouard, I was still trying,

and I found, suddenly, the expression. I do not mean that I found words,
but there came an equation . . . in little splotches of color.[5]

The words were slow in coming; Pound said that he first wrote a thirty-line
poem and destroyed it because it was a work of "second intensity," and then,
six months later, using the Japanese *haiku,* or three-line nature-image poem,
as a basic model, he wrote:

> The apparition of these faces in the crowd;
> Petals on a wet, black bough.

What Pound said he was attempting to make was a verbal equivalent for
a moment of revelation accompanied by intense emotion: "In a poem of
this sort one is trying to record the precise instant when a thing outward
and objective transforms itself, or darts into a thing inward and subjective."
Consciously or not, Pound here echoes the definition of sacrament in the
Catechism of the English Book of Common Prayer as "the outward and visible
sign of an inward and spiritual grace." Thus, Pound's description of an imagist
poem shows that it was an extension of religious symbolism, his modern
counterpart for the moments of inspired emotion that had once resulted in
Greek myths and medieval romances.

Of course, the image differs from myth and romance in being instanta-
neous, without story or sequence, seemingly independent of time and history.
If it succeeds, it must make up in intensity for what it lacks in duration.
Pound's "Metro" image consists of a single perception of beauty in the midst
of ugliness; what makes it modern is the combination of the city as setting
and the sense that it is a momentary experience, in the immediate present,
now. In defining *image* in 1913, Pound added, "It is the presentation of such
a 'complex' instantaneously which gives the sense of sudden liberation; that
sense of sudden growth, which we experience in the presence of the greatest
works of art."

Not everyone will agree that such an intense emotional effect is possible in a
poem as short as "In a Station of the Metro," but one can, by meditating upon
it (and such a short poem demands meditation from the reader) certainly see
that it contains a potential "equation for the emotions":

$$\frac{\text{faces}}{\text{crowd}} = \frac{\text{petals (beauty)}}{\text{bough (ugliness)}}$$

5. Ibid.

The faces and petals connote beauty, as the crowd and bough connote ugliness, and the emotion evoked is one of unexpected pleasure, of human beauty perceived in a sordid city scene. This brief image, with its contrast of light and darkness, foreshadows the constant motif of the *Cantos,* where light and dark images are repeated in so many different forms that they become the equivalents of heaven and hell: "In the gloom, the gold gathers the light about it" of the early Canto 17 contrasts with "First came the seen, then thus the palpable / Elysium, though it were in the halls of hell" in the later Canto 81.

Many of Pound's short imagist poems can be diagrammed in similar fashion, as equations for the emotions. Consider, for instance, the Chinese images in "Fan-Piece, for her Imperial Lord," which reads

> O fan of white silk,
>> clear as frost on the grass-blade,
> You also are laid aside.

The equation, or metaphor, that emerges makes the white silk fan the lady, the hand holding it the lord, and as the white frost coats the tender grass-blade, so the lord's love for his lady has cooled, and the "fan" has been discarded for another lady:

$$\frac{\text{fan}}{\text{(hand)}} = \frac{\text{grass-blade (lady)}}{\text{frost (lord)}}$$

The emotion implied in this image is that of sorrow in the loss of love, a contrast of warmth and coldness, as the metro image was a contrast of light and darkness.

From Pound's theory as well as his practice of the imagist poem, therefore, it is possible to extract the five constants that have become most characteristic of modern style ever since the second decade of the twentieth century:

1) Instantaneity (of Time)
2) Impersonality (of Viewpoint)
3) Intensity (of Feeling)
4) Irregularity, or Asymmetry (of Form)
5) Immanence, or Incarnation (of Truth, Reality, Being)

These qualities, inherent in the simple imagist poem, were transmitted to the longer and more complex poems of the age, not only the *Cantos,* but also *The Waste Land, The Bridge,* and *Paterson,* and to the more successful experimental novels, particularly *Ulysses, Mrs. Dalloway,* and *The Sound and the Fury,* which are in essence extended imagist poems. Thus, to the extent that the imagist poem is a microcosm of the more striking features of modern literary works of greater length and complexity, it is possible to identify imagism with modernism.

It was certainly the image that Pound most sought in the contemporary writers he admired during the shaping decade of modernism, the imagist decade of 1910–1920: he included Joyce's poem "I Hear an Army Charging" in his anthology *Des Imagistes* in 1914, he praised Yeats for "The Magi" and other poems of the imagist type, and eventually he edited the manuscript Eliot sent him of *The Waste Land* to remove all that was not image from the poem. Yeats responded by praising Pound for "The Return," a poem that he commended when he read it aloud, at the *Poetry* banquet in his honor in Chicago in 1914, as "the most beautiful poem that has been written in the free form, one of the few in which I find a real organic rhythm."[6] We may take this poem as an excellent example of Pound's development from the static or spatial image to the dynamic or kinetic image. It records a visionary experience rather than a sensory experience, but Pound had maintained all along that an image could be subjective in origin if it were expressed concretely. What distinguishes this poem from the shorter imagist poems is not merely its length, but also its distinctive free-verse rhythm, a musical cadence of the sort that a two- or three-line poem cannot exhibit to any notable degree.

"The Return" may be subjective and visionary in origin, but the image in it is concrete and dynamic. It depicts the return of the gods to earth, like hunters coming back from a chase. Its effectiveness depends upon the coordination of rhythm and imagery, the agreement of the falling trochaic and dactylic feet with the troubled and hesitant motion of the gods and their hounds, returning exhausted, it seems, from the hunt, like ghostly figures in a snowy landscape, yet carrying with them the sense of bravery and prowess, of being "Wing'd with Awe" and "Inviolable," virtues still visible even in defeat. The words *silver* and *pallid* give the image the quality of an etching or line-drawing, a sort of brief "Twilight of the Gods," like Wagner's *Götterdämmerung* sketched in gray and white. What is clear about the poem even at a first reading is its fineness of imagery and its suavity of music, its elegant visual and verbal harmony; what is indefinite about it is the context of the experience in which the gods appear to return. Pound says "See" and invites us to follow his vision where it leads, irrespective of when or why it appeared to him. Much of Pound's poetry has a similar obscurity about it, of seeming detached and isolated from time; but this, too, may be seen as his imagist principle at work: it is the moment of vision or perception crystallized and "liberated" from time, extracted from the flux or continuity of experience that surrounds it. Given the image, out of

6. Yeats, *Uncollected Prose*, vol. 2, 414.

the poet's experience, we are expected to supply the context out of our own experience. In the case of "The Return," we need not be at a loss for long: the image of heroic defeat is a tragic one, compelling admiration and sympathy, an image of lost grandeur out of the past, recovered momentarily through the poet's evocation, which preserves it in memory for all time.

Yeats provided his own context for "The Return" when he printed it at the end of the preface he called "A Packet for Ezra Pound" in his later edition of *A Vision,* where it served as a symbol of the cyclical motions of his gyres of world history and individual personality. In presenting it, he said, "You will hate these generalities, Ezra, which are themselves, it may be, of the past— the abstract sky—yet you have written 'The Return,' and though you but announce in it some change of style, perhaps, in book and picture it gives me better words than my own."[7] Pound himself provided a further context for the poem when he wrote, in one of the very last cantos, near the end of his immensely prolific, controversial, and personally tragic life:

> The Gods have not returned. "They have never left us."
>   They have not returned.
>   (Canto 113)

The strength of the poetic image, as Pound conceived it, is that, being independent of time, it can endure through time, gathering meaning as it goes, and we may judge from the example of Pound's work that the very limitations of the imagist poem, its isolation and detachment, can become a strength: the image, because it is free from time, is potentially applicable at any moment of time.

Pound said early in his career, "It is better to produce one Image in a lifetime than to produce voluminous works."[8] What the age demanded was an image plastic, quick, ephemeral, consumable, like a "prose kinema" or motion picture; what Pound gave the age were images brief, quickly taken in, but concentrated and intense, so that whether they are static, dynamic, or even ironic, they persist in the mind and at their best endure like solid marble. Imagism is a name for a technique that became distinctively modern and for a belief that in the rapid motion and flux of modern existence it is still possible to experience "moments of immortality," even visionary moments when "the gods return." Through the immediacy and intensity of a single image, or a set of images placed together in dynamic relation, beauty may be revealed as immanent, incarnate, present now as always. Pound's response to his age

---

7. Yeats, *A Vision,* 29.
8. Pound, "A Retrospect," in *The Literary Essays of Ezra Pound,* 4.

was a criticism of it, but much of his poetry now seems to transcend the age he both opposed and reflected; thanks to his lifelong struggle against the dominant and destructive materialism of his age, we have not just "a mould in plaster / Made with no loss of time," but a large body of poetry that is "assuredly, alabaster / [And] the 'sculpture' of rhyme."

The Image in the *Cantos*

> Le Paradis n'est pas artificiel
>   but spezzato apparently
>   it exists only in fragments . . .
>
> and that certain images be formed in the mind
>   to remain there
>   to remain there, resurgent ΕΙΚΟΝΕΣ
>   (Canto 74)

While the necessary work of explicating the *Cantos* goes on, rendering them word by word a little more intelligible, let us confront, for a moment, the probability that all attempts to grasp them as a continuous whole, a sequential long poem unified by theme or logical pattern, are doomed to fail, and that the sincerest efforts to explain every last allusion and personal reference in Pound's vast and bewildering opus will also fail. What then? The failure, if it occurs finally, will not be due to lack of dedication, ingenuity, or erudition on the part of the legion of interpreters who have already proved themselves as patient, learned, and resourceful an audience as any great poet could wish for, but will be due to the nature of the work itself and to the fragmentary character of the age in which it was written. It will still be true that no poet, no artist in any medium, will have embodied the spirit of the age, in all its heroic and tragic aspects, more fully than Pound, and the *Cantos* will remain his masterwork. It mirrors better than anything else he wrote the world-encompassing vision that dared to bring the diverse histories, religions, cultures, and languages of mankind into creative relation with each other, in the hope of sparking a new renaissance as splendid as that of the Greeks or the Italians. It mirrors also the shattered recognition of the collapse of that vision in the destructiveness of two world wars, the last of which left the poet himself diminished to a tiny speck of animate matter amid the ruins:

> As a lone ant from a broken ant-hill
> from the wreckage of Europe, ego scriptor.
>   (Canto 76)

If the *Cantos* do prove too much to explicate completely, we may still ask which are the most moving, the early cantos, in which the great scope of Pound's imagination is displayed, and Odysseus and Dionysus, Sigismondo da Malatesta and Confucius are drawn into company with the poet in search of a "live tradition" linking past and present; or the late cantos, which show the depths of the poet's humiliation inside the prison cage at Pisa or the insane asylum at Washington, where he is forced to his knees at last:

> That I lost my center
> > fighting the world.
> The dreams clash
> > and are shattered—
> > > (Canto 117)

If there is a single unifying motif in the *Cantos,* it is the figure of Pound as tragic hero, plunging from the heights to the depths, unwittingly bringing about his own fall—a fall more terrible because it was not foreseen by the poet but thrust on him by history, and more pitiable because he is forced in the process to recognize the cause of it, his own pride, vanity, hubris. The *Cantos* present an unplanned tragedy enacted in 117 episodes, a tragedy that must be read in all its concrete complexity.

But can one read the *Cantos* as tragedy—this immense, gripping, baffling, overwhelming set of poems with a single title? Pound himself most often spoke of it as an epic, or "poem containing history," a definition that in his practice justified a great deal of tedious summarizing and quoting of historical documents, especially in those long, dry middle cantos devoted to Chinese and American history. But at their best the *Cantos* do not contain history so much as images—images of the natural world and its creatures, of men and women, past and present, of gods and goddesses and other mythical personages. Seen this way, the *Cantos* may be called an imagist epic, its 815 pages (in the latest edition) the longest imagist poem on record—longer even than *The Waste Land,* which Pound called "the longest 19 pages in the English langwidge" when he returned the manuscript to Eliot (much reduced by his red pencil), and longer than *The Bridge,* which Hart Crane intended as an answer to *The Waste Land,* and longer than *Paterson,* which William Carlos Williams intended as a native American version of the *Cantos.* Of course, not all of the cantos can be called imagist, since some contain few images and none are imagist throughout, though some come close. But since the cantos often sparkle with memorable images, like a string of jewels threaded through the poem, and since the imagist poem as Pound conceived it was the form most fitting to express the age, the *Cantos* can be taken as a culminating work of modern poetry, the richest and densest and most inclusive set of images any poet succeeded in constructing.

So, if the *Cantos* can be read as an epic, or as a set of dramatic lyrics, or as a long philosophical poem, what is most distinctive about them is their imagist content:

> As the young lizard extends his leopard spots
>   along the grass-blade seeking the green midge half an ant-size
> and the Serpentine will look just the same
> and the gulls be as neat on the pond
> and the sunken garden unchanged
> and God knows what else is left of our London
>   my London, your London
> and if her green elegance
>   remains on this side of my rain ditch
>   puss lizard will lunch on some other T-bone
>
> sunset grand couturier.
>   (Canto 80)

These images do not cohere, but they stand out, separate from each other, as the mind that contemplates them passes from observation to memory to prophecy and back to observation, in a flow of free association without logical connection or thematic unity. Each is simply the register of a vital intelligence intent on experience, giving shape to each passing moment with words that bestow color, pattern, visual delight, humor, fading majesty. The lizard, the Serpentine Pond, and the sunset are arbitrarily chosen out of the flux of appearances and made into images by a persistently humane, curious, and accurate perception. As Paul Valéry maintained, "A work of art should always teach us that we have not seen what we have seen," or, as Paul Klee insisted, "The artist does not reproduce the visible. He makes visible." The *Cantos* repeatedly make us see the world with finer discrimination, more appreciatively, as if we were learning to use our eyes for the first time: such is the power of the image as Pound practiced it.

If seeing Pound's tremendously complex poem as a set of images is a deliberately naive reading, it may be justified as a way of establishing that Pound's purpose in writing the *Cantos* was not so much meaning as seeing, or, as he put it early in his career, "The image is itself the speech." Pound put forward this principle long before he started writing the *Cantos,* at the time when he was most engaged with other poets in reforming English poetry by writing short, concentrated images in free verse. When that effort succeeded and imagism became a movement, Pound left it to turn his attention to longer poems, but his art remained consistent with his early principles. The major poems of his middle period—"Near Perigord," "Homage to Sextus Propertius," and *Hugh Selwyn Mauberley*—build images into personae, giving some of the pictorial quality of Chinese ideograms to English poetry and making words form pictures by the increasing use of concrete nouns and verbs. He further modified the image and the persona by the use of irony, so that the visual and personal became critical as well. Pound showed, even before he undertook the *Cantos* as a sustained poem, that the poetic image could be not merely descriptive but characterizing and self-mocking. Yet it was still the image, not the statement, that mattered most to Pound.

By the time he began writing his long poem in earnest, he had mastered a complex verbal instrument involving multilingual allusion, irony, and personification, but still centering on the image as what he called his "primary pigment." He had not changed his initial definition—"An 'Image' is that which presents an intellectual and emotional complex in an instant of time"—he had simply increased the intellectual-emotional potentialities within the image, allowing it to incorporate the past as well as the present. The difference between an early imagist touchstone such as "In a Station of the Metro" and a canto is not as great as it might seem: it is the difference between a short, simple, descriptive image and a long, complex, dynamic-ironic image, or set of images, both being the perception of what Pound called "moments of metamorphosis," when a sensible transformation takes place in experience.

The *Cantos* at their best extend the imagist poem indefinitely but retain its five chief virtues: instantaneity, intensity, irregularity, impersonality, and immanence. They also retain its chief faults of isolation and detachment, which translate into fragmentation and discontinuity. When Pound is brought to confess in a late canto, "I cannot make it cohere," it is more than just a personal confession: he is confronting the failure of any modern artist to bring order out of the chaos of a collapsing civilization; Yeats had confessed to this in "The Second Coming": "The center cannot hold / Mere anarchy is loosed upon the world," and Eliot also confessed to it in *The Waste Land:* "These fragments I have shored against my ruin." Imagism, the technique of presenting experience as moments of illumination in an otherwise dark time, invented and promoted by Pound as the artist's response to a disintegrating culture, accounts for some of the highest achievements of modern literature, while at the same time it demonstrates the artist's failure to bring about through his imagination a new cultural unity in a hoped-for renaissance. The *Cantos* remain the most ambitious effort to unify world culture by the power of a single imagination, but the very technique Pound used was fragmentary, and the result was a magnificent ruined tower that had the grandeur as well as the essential gaiety of tragedy:

The scientists are in terror
    and the European mind stops
Wyndham Lewis chose blindness
    rather than have his mind stop.
Night under wind mid garofani,
    the petals are almost still
Mozart, Linnaeus, Sulmona,
When one's friends hate each other
    how can there be peace in the world?
Their asperities diverted me in my green time.
A blown husk that is finished
    but the light sings eternal
a pale flare over marshes
    when the salt hay whispers to tide's change

Time, space,
    neither life nor death is the answer.
And of man seeking good,
    doing evil.
In meiner Heimat
    where the dead walked
        and the living were made of cardboard.
    (Canto 115)

If the images in the *Cantos* make us see more keenly, they make us see that the nature of our time is tragic, with men isolated from each other, more dead than alive, perceiving truths only in flashes. Pound differed from his fellow men in "Being more live than they, more full of flames and voices" (Canto 7), and his major poem describes the age we live in as well as anything written.

But only our age? Pound believed that images are the essence of great poetry in all ages, and his early translations from classical Greek and Chinese poetry are imagist poems in their own way, making Sappho and Li Po imagist poets by extension, and the images in the *Cantos* are replete with antiquity, more often drawn from the past than from the present. Considering that a large part of Pound's achievement was the renewal of past moments in the present, "To have gathered from the air a live tradition / or from a fine old eye the unconquered flame," and that one of his earliest statements in *The Spirit of Romance* was that "all ages are contemporaneous," we cannot assume that Pound conceived of the modern age as necessarily more tragic than ages before it. The burden of all the non-imagist discourse in the *Cantos* is directed at the causes of the decay of civilizations after their peak—why China declined after Confucius and Li Po, why Greece declined after Homer and Sophocles, why Italy declined after Dante and Cavalcanti and Botticelli and Duccio, why America declined after Jefferson and Adams—and he believed the main cause was materialism, which he called usury, but whether or not we agree with his diagnosis, the fact is that all civilizations must decline, and they must because the great artists, leaders, and thinkers must die, and so we mourn with Pound the passing of his generation of great writers:

> Lordly men are to earth o'ergiven
> these the companions:
> Fordie that wrote of giants
> and William who dreamed of nobility
> and Jim the comedian singing:
> "Blarrney castle me darlin'
> you're nothing now but a StOWne"
> (Canto 74)

Add to this inevitable loss of greatness in every age the parallels that Pound continually draws between the heroes of the past and those of the present, and we have the emergent sense that what is great in human nature, like what is beautiful in nature as a whole, is in the process of continual death and birth, that the metamorphosis so essential to Pound's philosophy is itself tragic, since to "MAKE IT NEW," something must grow old and die, and the something is what is most precious: individual life, personal existence. One cannot read Pound's elegy to "these the companions," Ford Madox Ford, William Butler Yeats, and James Joyce, who were the renovators of literature in his time, without being reminded of the prophecy in Canto 1, where Tiresias says to Odysseus, in Pound's American renewal of Andreas Divus's Latin renewal of Homer's Greek:

> Odysseus
> Shalt return through spiteful Neptune, over dark seas,
> Lose all companions.

Could Pound have foreseen how closely his career would parallel that of Odysseus, that he too would outlive all his peers, or is the fulfillment of Tiresias's prophecy in Pound's later canto purely fortuitous? It is a measure of Pound's genius that we cannot be sure the striking coincidence of myth and reality in his poem is mere accident; it seems possible that even the mythical descent into hell with which the *Cantos* begin was a subconscious preparation for Pound's real descent into a living hell at the end of World War II. Unforeseen or not, the parallel holds, and the later images are powerfully reinforced and given new meaning by the earlier ones.

So, if the images in the *Cantos* do not cohere, they do coincide, and in their coincidence is the "live tradition" that links past with present in a constant metamorphosis of things and of men, reincarnations of the most beautiful and the best, as well as of, alas, the ugliest and the worst. If the recurrent images in the *Cantos* convince us that change is tragic because it brings age and death to all that is worth preserving, they also convince us that change is renewal, bringing the greatness and the beauty back to life again:

> till the shrine be again white with marble
> till the stone eyes look again seaward
> > the wind is part of the process
> > the rain is part of the process
> (Canto 74)

Perhaps even the vituperative prose, the bigotry and wrongheadedness that are part of the *Cantos* are also "part of the process," since the images shine forth all the more resplendently out of the hell of avarice and filth, the fascism and anti-Semitism, that flows around them, just as Sigismondo's Tempio, with its delicate carvings by Agostino di Duccio and its fine paintings by Piero della Francesca, shines more brilliantly for its violent and scandalous patron, who built his artistic monument on a murderous career. We might prefer to read an abridged edition of the *Cantos,* stripped down to their essential images by the same merciless red pencil that its author once exercised on *The Waste Land,* but we have to cope instead with a huge, unfinished set of poems in which the best is mixed with the worst—and in which, perforce, the best gains by contrast with the worst. As the prophecy of Odysseus's journey is echoed in the later career of Pound, who despite struggles does outlive "all companions," so the regenerative process seems to operate in the poem to bring images of light and love out of the darkness of hatred and profanity that surrounds them, as "In the gloom, the gold gathers the light about it" (Canto 17).

Yet Pound also sets down beyond forgetting that "What thou lovest well remains / the rest is dross," and if we apply his rule to the *Cantos,* then each reader is free to make his own personal anthology from the poems that Pound took more than half a century to produce. There is much that survives any selection, and most of what survives will undoubtedly be the images—not whole cantos but passages of cantos, sometimes only a few lines, sometimes a dozen or more, that "carve the trace in the mind" of something experienced and precisely described with the hand of a master.

Looking at my own well-marked copy of the *Cantos,* which has survived almost half a century of reading, I find many lines underscored, some in the first thirty cantos, more in *The Pisan Cantos,* and many in the late *Drafts and*

Fragments of Cantos CX–CXVI, along with scattered cantos that endure in memory in their entirety, such as Canto 13, the Confucian canto; Canto 45, the Usura canto; and Canto 49, the Seven Lakes canto, so that altogether there are more than a hundred pages of perdurable poetry in them, such as one would not hesitate to call major and irreplaceable. Looking still more closely, I find I have marked four major groups of images in the *Cantos:*

1. Observations of the present—either personal:

> We also made ghostly visits, and the stair
> That knew us, found us again on the turn of it,
> Knocking at empty rooms, seeking for buried beauty.
> (Canto 7)

—or artistic:

> Gold fades in the gloom,
> Under the blue-black roof, Placidia's
> (Canto 21)

—or natural:

> And Brother Wasp is building a very neat house
> of four rooms, one shaped like a squat indian bottle.
> (Canto 83)

2. Re-creations of past experience—either historical:

> Tching prayed on the mountain and
> wrote MAKE IT NEW
> on his bath tub
> (Canto 53)

—or literary:

> Ear, ear for the sea-surge, murmur of old men's voices:
> "Let her go back to the ships,
> Back among Grecian faces"
> (Canto 2)

3. Personifications—either of heroes:

> Kung walked
> by the dynastic temple

> into the cedar grove
> (Canto 13)

—or of gods:

> And in thy mind beauty, O Artemis,
>   as of mountain lakes in the dawn,
> Foam and silk are thy fingers
> (Canto 110)

4. Visions, fleeting glimpses of paradise:

> Thus the light rains, thus pours, *e lo soleils plovil*
> The liquid and rushing crystal
>   beneath the knees of the gods.
> Ply over ply, thin glitter of water;
> Brook film bearing white petals.
> (Canto 4)

> The light has entered the cave. Io! Io!
> The light has gone down into the cave,
> Splendor on splendor!
> (Canto 47)

Reflecting on my personal choice of images in the *Cantos,* the most frequent and persistent in my mind seem to be the visionary ones, though the visionary often proceed from the natural, and the reader learns to wait for them to appear with a sense of suspense, as if for a climax. Many of the dominant images are of eyes or of light, as if the visual and the visionary were connected in Pound's imagination: "First came the seen, then thus the palpable / Elysium," he attests, and adds, "though it were in the halls of hell." For Pound, seeing was believing, in the most literal sense of those verbs, and the poetic image was his form of sacrament, a means of affirming that, as he put it in a late canto,

> The Gods have not returned. "They have never left us."
>   They have not returned.
> Cloud's processional and the air moves with their living.
> (Canto 113)

Thus, although the images of the *Cantos* are fragmentary and the poet cannot, by his own admission, make them cohere, so that his role must be a tragic one, writing in a secular, materialistic age that lacks any unifying belief, still he is able to remind himself at the end, with a measure of the humor or *hilaritas* that never deserted Pound in his darkest hours:

> But about that terzo
> > third heaven
> > > that Venere,
> again is all "paradiso"
> > a nice quiet paradise
> > > over the shambles,
> and some climbing
> > before the take-off,
> to "see again,"
> the verb is "see," not "walk on"
> i.e. it coheres all right
> > > even if my notes do not cohere.
> > > (Canto 117)

To ask again the question we began with: If the *Cantos* remain incomprehensible in their totality, after all attempts to annotate them have been made, what then? Will we give up reading them, or treat them as a curious experiment with language, an unreadable but quotable monument like *Finnegans Wake*, challenging but impenetrable? No reader who has been through the *Cantos* once, and has seen with Pound's eyes the images of beauty, heroism, and visionary exaltation that appear again and again, can doubt the magnitude of the achievement, no matter how dim his understanding of the exact sense of the poem as a whole. Pound murmurs near the end, "I tried to make a paradiso terrestre," and he did make an earthly paradise through the images in his poem; though they come and go, "The clock ticks, the vision fades," still the words are there on the page to remind us that this paradise is not artificial, it is real. The cumulative effect of the visual images in the poem is so irresistible that each reader in the end becomes a witness who testifies, like Acoetes in Canto 2:

> I have seen what I have seen. . . .
> "He has a god in him,
> > though I do not know which god."

Beyond Baedeker: The *Cantos* as Ultimate Guidebook

Pound's *Cantos* contain some of the century's finest poetry: they are a collection of superbly lyrical images to delight both the eye and the ear; they are also a means of exploring the heights and depths of human experience, and they do compare, finally, with the cantos of Dante's *Divine Comedy,* Pound's chief model. They are, furthermore, his poetic "guide to culture," much superior to his prose work of that name, transporting us through space as well as time to places we might find on a map or in a history book, but could not truly see or visit without his expert guidance, and also to other places that are not on any map or in any history book, places of the mind to which his poem alone can take us.

Pound spoke of his poem as an epic, which it is, and he defined an epic, in his *ABC of Reading,* as "a poem including history," which it does, but the history is primarily artistic and cultural, rather than political, social, military—or even, despite his fervent desire to make it so, economic. It is not a series of facts or events, but a succession of moments of civilization when artists and writers created the kind of "news that stays news" that Pound called literature and so marked an epoch by their cultural achievements. The low moments are Pound's hell, or as he explained in a 1927 letter to his father—frankly admitting he was "afraid the whole damn poem is rather obscure"—they are the moments when "Live man goes down into world of Dead," descending into hell as Homer and Dante had before him. But if at first, as Eliot complained about the early hell cantos, "Mr. Pound's Hell, for all its horrors, is a perfectly comfortable one for the modern mind to contemplate, and disturbing to no one's complacency: it is a Hell for the *other people,* the people we read about in newspapers, not for oneself and one's friends,"[9] later his hell becomes distinctly uncomfortable to contemplate, and Pound found himself to be the chief resident of that later hell, when, starting with the Italian cantos, he became trapped in the hostilities of World War II, then imprisoned in the iron cage at Pisa, and afterwards confined in the "Hell Hole" at St. Elizabeths Hospital. The high moments are Pound's heaven, his "moments of metamorphosis" or "bust through from quotidien [*sic*] into 'divine or permanent world,' Gods, etc.," where great art has been created before and can be created again. The true measure of Pound's genius came late in his career, in conditions of extreme adversity, as H. D. testified in her *End to Torment: A Memoir of Ezra Pound,* where she reflected on their parallel creative lives, which had begun with the imagists in London early in the century, and marveled, "There is a reserve of dynamic or daemonic power from which we may all draw. He lay on the floor of the iron cage and wrote *The Pisan Cantos.*"[10]

9. Pound to his father, Homer Pound, April 11, 1927, in *The Letters of Ezra Pound, 1907–1941,* 210; Eliot, *After Strange Gods: A Primer of Modern Heresy,* 47.
10. Hilda Doolittle, *End to Torment: A Memoir of Ezra Pound,* 44.

If we approach the *Cantos,* then, as the ultimate guidebook, and let our-selves be taken far beyond the Baedeker level of guidebooks, we may discover in it some of the continuity that it otherwise seems to lack, for Pound's mental journey through space and time and memory constitutes, I am more and more convinced, the thread that connects Canto 1 with the final drafts and fragments of Canto 117, a principal source for whatever unity the *Cantos* contain.

It is certainly no accident that the *Cantos* start in the middle of Homer's *Odyssey:* we know it was Pound's deliberate choice to begin with a descent into hell, or the world of the dead, for him both a modern journey and an ancient one, and to begin at the beginning, with Homer as his guide to the classical origins of Western civilization. Later, he would repeat this journey to hell with Dante as his guide, arriving thereby at the climactic point of Western Christian civilization, which from Pound's viewpoint was not limited to the medieval world: as early as *The Spirit of Romance,* in 1910, he insisted that "Dante conceived the real Hell, Purgatory, and Paradise as states, not places." His other major guides were Ovid, from whom he drew his counter-theme of metamorphosis, or godly and heavenly visions, and Confucius, whose Eastern idealism formed the basis of a classical Chinese civilization containing neither hell nor heaven, but mirroring what Pound's Western civilization had lacked, at least after the Renaissance: an orderly and hierarchical society governed by a philosopher-prince who gave due honor to the arts. And for a fifth guide, to the more modern territories of Western civilization, I would argue that he chose, more than any other, his fellow countryman Henry James, the American expatriate writer who had been a "passionate pilgrim" to Europe long before Pound arrived. Homer, Ovid, and Dante were to Pound the greatest poets in world literature, as he repeatedly affirmed both in his essays and in his poetry; Confucius was the greatest philosopher, because, as he says in *Guide to Kulchur,* "Kung's insistence on the ODES lifts him above all occidental philosophers"; and Henry James was the greatest prose artist, as we know from his early tributes to James as well as from key passages in the *Cantos.*

To see Henry James as Pound's principal travel guide to modern Europe, we must remember that, as he explained in a letter of 1922, he wrote *Hugh Selwyn Mauberley* as "an attempt to condense the James novel," and in *Guide to Kulchur* he did not shrink from comparing James to Homer, speaking of "the quite H. Jamesian precisions of the *Odyssey.*" We hear his first faint echo of James in the longer poem as early as Canto 2, for when Pound says of Helen of Troy, "She moves like a goddess," he is recalling Homer's description of her in the *Iliad,* but he may also be paraphrasing James's description, in his *Italian Hours,* of a woman in a Venetian painting, "She walks a goddess." Pound at any rate left no doubt that by Canto 7 he was summoning up the ghost of James to guide him, because there he gives us an unforgettable sketch of his own meeting with the elder American expatriate writer soon after Pound arrived in London in 1908:

> And the great domed head, *con gli occhi onesti e tardi*
> Moves before me, phantom with weighted motion,
> *Grave incessu*, drinking the tone of things,
> And the old voice lifts itself
> weaving an endless sentence.

The association of James's eyes, *con gli occhi onesti e tardi* [with eyes honest and slow], with the eyes of Homer, Ovid, and other classical poets described by Dante in his Limbo, the First Circle of the *Inferno, con occhi tardi e gravi* [with eyes slow and grave], places James at once among the most honored of Pound's guides, and the Latin phrase *grave incessu*, or "solemn walk," is an echo of Virgil's *vera incessu*, the "walk of a true [goddess]," which Aeneas utters when he recognizes his mother, Venus—an oblique reference that also places James alongside Dante's trusted guide, Virgil. What is remarkable in the changes that Pound made in both Dante and Virgil is that he drew the word *gravi* from the Italian and placed it in the Latin as *grave*, thus altering his sources significantly so that James acquires "honest" rather than "grave" eyes in his portrait, and his walk becomes "grave" rather than "true." Pound would have known that the phrase from Virgil correctly reads *Vera incessu patuit dea* [By her gait the true goddess is made known], describing the movement of Venus when Aeneas recognizes her as his mother in disguise (*Aeneid* 1:145), because Pound must have borrowed it consciously from a well-known story by James, "The Figure in the Carpet," where it is used to verify the elusive theme of a writer whose works are mystifying:

> "But how does he know?"
> "Know it's the real thing? Oh I'm sure that when you see it you do know.
> *Vera incessu patuit dea!*"[11]

James quite deftly implies that "the figure in the carpet" will be seen as clearly as the figure of the goddess by those who have eyes. Thus in his first clear description of Henry James, Pound was paying tribute to James paying tribute to Virgil—a kind of double allusion that honored both writers at once—and was at the same time aligning himself in subtlety with James, since neither Pound nor James easily displayed "the figure in the carpet" in his work—if

11. Henry James, *In the Cage and Other Tales* (New York: Doubleday Anchor, 1958), 155.

indeed it ever was there, since in James's story it is never found. But if his first sketch of James is in a profoundly serious mood, Pound sketches him again with a lighter touch, in the much later Canto 74, which opens *The Pisan Cantos:*

> Mr James shielding himself with Mrs Hawkesby
> as it were a bowl shielding itself with a walking stick
> as he maneuvered his way toward the door

Here James is remembered as the shy and reclusive artist, using his housekeeper at Lamb House, Rye, to shield himself from a too inquisitive public, and a little further on, in Canto 79, Pound adds an affectionate touch to the humor of his portrait of James:

> her holding dear H. J.
> (Mr. James, Henry) literally by the button-hole . . .
> in those so consecrated surroundings
> (a garden in the Temple, no less)
>
> and saying, *for once,* the right thing
> namely: "Cher maître"
> to his checquered waistcoat, the Princess Bariatinsky,
> as the fish-tails said to Odysseus, ἐνὶ Τροίη

This sketch of James, at a garden party in London, being accorded the French accolade of "dear master" by a princess, whom Pound compares to one of the Sirens ("fish-tails") singing to Odysseus, shows the virtue of "hilarity" that Pound celebrates throughout the *Cantos,* a hilarity nowhere more refined than in these skillful descriptions of his fellow American writer.

Pound shared the virtue of humor with James more than with Homer, Ovid, Dante, or Confucius, and there was another significant quality he shared with James—the American sense of Europe as homeland. Homer, Ovid, and Dante were Europeans by birth, but James and Pound were Europeans by adoption, which meant, as James explained in one of his travel essays about England: "An American, of course, with his fondness for antiquity, his relish for picturesqueness, his 'emotional' attitude at historic shrines, takes Oxford much more seriously than its sometimes unwilling familiars can be expected to do."[12] Pound, like James, took Europe more seriously than Europeans did, which meant that he perceived in it a decadence and decline from the Europe of Homer, Ovid, and Dante, which was sadly in need of being salvaged and

---

12. Henry James, *The Art of Travel,* 163.

renewed before it was permanently lost: the earlier poets had heroically raised human culture to the highest possible level of perfection, and as latecomers and adopted sons, James and Pound each in his way sought to preserve and rejuvenate European culture by their very American literary pilgrimages. When Pound quotes James again in Canto 87 of *Section: Rock-Drill*, it is to question the condition of European civilization in modern times:

> Or as Henry again: "we have, in a manner of speaking,
> > arrived.
> Got to,["] I think he says "got to, all got to."

Pound had quoted the same Jamesean phrase ("where in a manner of speaking etc. we have got to") in his *Guide to Kulchur* (p. 84), and had followed it with a typically Jamesean justification for the extreme refinement of his characters: "H. J.'s excuse for some of his characters was that 'if they didn't exist and if no counterparts existed we, still, ought for the honour of the race to pretend that they existed." Pound echoes this apology in his final brief mention of Henry James, in Canto 101 of *Thrones*: " 'Should,' said H. J., 'for humanity's credit / feign their existence.' "

So James was Pound's guide intermittently and in various guises, from Canto 2 to Canto 101, but of course Pound went much further afield than James did in his pilgrimages, taking in classical Chinese culture as well as European, using Confucius as his guide to a world not only beyond a Baedeker guide but beyond the Western civilization of Europe and America. Pound's Orient was more ideal than real; he made Confucian China an Eastern equivalent of Homeric Greece and a counterbalance to what he regarded as the excessive abstractness of Western thought. In practice, Pound came to equate what he called the Chinese *ideogram* with what he called the Greek *paideuma*—a complex cultural whole by which world civilization could be measured. In *Guide to Kulchur* he explained that "the term Paideuma" means "the tangle or complex of the inrooted ideas of any period," whereas "the ideogramic method consists of presenting one facet and then another until at some point one gets . . . a just revelation irrespective of newness or oldness." Pound added, "The writer's aim, at least this writer's aim, is revelation."

In the *Cantos*, which constitute his poetic "guide to culture," Pound's methods are *not* those of any of his admired guides, for they were storytellers and philosophers, while he was neither a storyteller nor a philosopher, but an imagist who fashioned personae and ideograms out of language, a maker of memorable but discontinuous sketches and scenes that form a mosaic of images in the mind of the reader, a complex set of revelations. If we take the *Cantos* as our ultimate guidebook, then, we cannot expect to read them as a connected chronological story nor as a set of logical propositions, but we

can read them as a disjunctive succession of images that allow us to travel
not only in space but also in time, through inspired descriptions that may
become revelations, the way Pound must have meant for us to read his poem,
since, to quote his *Guide to Kulchur* again, "We do NOT know the past in
chronological sequence . . . but what we know we know by ripples and spirals
eddying out from us and from our own time."

If Pound does take us far beyond a Baedeker in his mental travels, he would
undoubtedly have agreed with the judgment of Henry James, a connoisseur
of world travel who looked at every landscape with an artist's eye, "that Italy
is really so much the most beautiful country in the world, taking all things
together," because it is "thick somehow to the imagination . . . thick with the
sense of history and the very taste of time."[13] There are no limits to the
horizons of the *Cantos,* but Pound indulged himself most often in what James
called "the luxury of loving Italy," and when we look at the poem carefully
for its settings, we can see that, of the 117 cantos, over one-third are partly or
wholly located in Italy. The choice of Italy as a principal setting for his "forty-
year epic" was as natural as the choice of Homer's *Odyssey* as his starting-
point, for when Pound left his native United States in 1908, he went straight to
Venice like a homing pigeon. When he was allowed to choose his home once
again in 1958, on his release from St. Elizabeths Hospital, he made a beeline
back to Italy, first settling in the Castle Brunnenburg, where his daughter,
Mary, lived; then taking his wife, Dorothy, back to Rapallo, where he had
lived for many years before the war; and finally returning home to Venice
with his mistress, Olga Rudge (Mary's mother), where he chose to stay most
of the time until his death there in 1972. If Italy is Pound's home country
in the *Cantos,* Venice is his home city, and it is appropriate that he should
be buried there and with nothing more than his name on the stone, for his
poetry contains all the epitaphs he will ever need.

Pound evokes Venice in his first image of Italy in Canto 3, the Venice of
1908 into which he came as a penurious American youth of twenty-three:

> I sat on the Dogana's steps
> For the gondolas cost too much, that year,
> And there were not "those girls," there was one face,
> And the Buccentoro twenty yards off, howling "Stretti",
> And the lit cross-beams, that year, in the Morosini,
> And peacocks in Koré's house, or there may have been.

This initial image of Venice is realistic, given Pound's circumstances, because
only from a distance could he watch the gondolas and hear the gondoliers

---

13. Henry James, *Henry James on Italy: Selections from "Italian Hours,"* 219.

singing a Neapolitan love song (the "Stretti" they howled meant "in close embrace"), but it is not nearly so alluring as the image of Venice in Canto 17, which is descriptively as rich as any passage in the *Cantos:*

> Marble trunks out of stillness,
> On past the palazzi,
>   in the stillness,
> The light now, not of the sun.
>   · Chrysoprase,
> And the water green clear, and blue clear

Pound seems able in this passage to hire a gondola to take him along the Venetian canals, where his keen powers of observation match the exact word of his early imagism—"Chrysoprase" being a greenish stone the color of the Venetian lagoon—and the effect is a revelation of the beauty of Venice. But there is further realism at the beginning of Canto 26, where he is again the naive American registering his first impressions of the city built from the sea:

> And
>   I came here in my young youth
>   and lay there under the crocodile.
>   By the column, looking East on the Friday,
> And I said: Tomorrow I will lie on the South Side
> And the day after, south west.
> And at night they sang in the gondolas
> And in the barche with lanthorns;
> The prows rose silver on silver
>   taking light in the darkness.

Thus, throughout the *Cantos,* Pound seems to balance realistic memories of Venice with more inspired descriptions, reflecting briefly in Canto 76 that

> the Canal Grande has lasted at least until our time
>   even if Florian's has been refurbished
> and shops in the Piazza kept up by
>   artificial respiration

while in the same canto he recalls with obvious delight

> the jewel box, Santa Maria Dei Miracoli,
> Dei Greci, San Giorgio, the place of skulls
>   in the Carpaccio

> and in the font to the right as you enter
>   are all the gold domes of San Marco

These tender recollections of the many churches of Venice temper Pound's often strident railing against Christianity, and though he wonders in Canto 83, while he is in the prison camp at Pisa, "Will I ever see the Guidecca again?" he answers his own question, in the opening lines of Canto 110, as he starts the final section, *Drafts and Fragments,* with a concise and enchanting image of the Byzantine church of the Madonna, Santa Maria Assunta, on the island of Torcello in the Venetian lagoon:

> Thy quiet house
> The crozier's curve runs in the wall,
> The harl, feather-white, as a dolphin on sea-brink

Thus Pound's descriptions of Venice, his home city in Italy, together form a visual guide that is unsurpassed by that of any other locale in the *Cantos,* although he captured many arresting images of other Italian places, including Rapallo, another seaside city where he lived for many years and where he observed the ritual launching of votive lights at night—"in the pale night the small lamps drift seaward"; Verona, with its Roman arena; Ravenna, with its Byzantine mosaics and tomb of Dante; Siracusa, with its miraculous fountain; Taormina, with its "high cliff and azure beneath it"; Terracina, where he hoped to see the shrine of Aphrodite restored "till the stone eyes look again seaward"; and of course Rimini, with its Tempio, which Sigismondo da Malatesta built to honor his mistress, Ixotta, commissioning the Florentine master Piero della Francesca to paint his portrait and the Renaissance sculptor Agostino di Duccio to carve a marble portrait of Cythera in her "moon-barge." Nor is Pisa neglected, for though Pound's life there was painful, he responded with an artist's sensibility to one of Italy's most picturesque places, noticing in Canto 74 "the smell of mint under the tent flaps / especially after the rain / and a white ox on the road toward Pisa / as if facing the tower" and finding in Canto 77 that "The Pisan clouds are undoubtedly various and splendid as any I have seen" and again in Canto 79 marveling at the "Moon, cloud, tower, a patch of the battistero all of a whiteness."

If Venice and Italy are home country to Pound in the *Cantos,* Greece was the country of his imagination, the place he most often evoked after Italy, but a place he had read about in Homer, not a place where he lived. We see that distinction in the very first canto, which is about Greece but is drawn from Homer, with Andreas Divus's Latin version of the *Odyssey* as intermediary and the Anglo-Saxon meter of *The Seafarer* for sea-rhythm—three removes from the actuality of Greece, yet still quite convincingly physical in its opening image of sailors embarking on the Mediterranean:

> And then went down to the ship,
> Set keel to breakers, forth on the godly sea, and
> We set up mast and sail on that swart ship,
> Bore sheep aboard her, and our bodies also,
> Heavy with weeping, and winds from sternward
> Bore us out onward with bellying canvas,
> Circe's this craft, the trim-coifed goddess.

The evocation of the Greek sea continues in the second canto, with place-names that specify the locale:

> And by Scios,
>   to left of the Naxos passage,
> Naviform rock overgrown,
>   algae cling to its edge,
> There is a wine-red glow in the shallows,
>   a tin flash in the sun-dazzle.

Pound wanted to begin his epic in the Eastern Mediterranean, at the dawn of Western civilization, and he did so beautifully with the help of Homer. His other evocations of Greece are more Dionysian, more from Ovid's *Metamorphoses* than from Homer's *Odyssey*, for Pound believed in those dark fertility rites, the Eleusinian mysteries, and attempted to re-create them often, especially in cantos 17, 39, and 47, by describing orgiastic celebrations of natural and sexual fertility:

> Dark shoulders have stirred the lightning
> A girl's arms have nested the fire,
> Not I but the handmaid kindled
>   Cantat sic nupta [Thus sings the bride]
> I have eaten the flame.
>   (Canto 39)

and again:

> By prong have I entered these hills:
> That the grass grow from my body,
> That I hear the roots speaking together,
> The air is new on my leaf,
> The forked boughs shake with the wind.
>   (Canto 47)

Pound's Greece was a compound of Homer's sea voyages and Ovid's metamorphoses of the gods, not a real place like Italy, but even so, his evocations of the world of classical Greece are powerful, and they do put the reader in touch with a classical *paideuma* that blends mythical visions of ghostly spirits and godly presences with real actions such as sailing and plowing and making love, affirming Pound's vigorous polytheistic paganism, which he expressed staunchly in his *Guide to Kulchur:* "I assert that the gods exist."

Kung and Eleusis were the poles of Pound's later philosophy, as he expressed in the phrase "Between KUNG and ELEUSIS"—his China being every bit as literary and mythical as his Greece. The reader encounters his China first in Canto 13, where he quotes the Analects of Confucius, or Kung, whom he personifies as a witty sage who maintains that "When the prince has gathered about him / All the savants and artists, his riches will be fully employed" and who teaches filial piety as the root of social order and never speaks of life after death, but dwells instead on human self-control—"mastering thyself"—and on natural beauty:

> And Kung said "Without character you will
> be unable to play on that instrument
> Or to execute the music fit for the Odes.
> The blossoms of the apricot
> blow from the east to the west,
> And I have tried to keep them from falling."

The benevolent figure of Confucius dominates this early canto, as his thought dominates the later Chinese cantos, including the long sequence of Chinese-history cantos, 52–61, which are drawn from the writings of Confucius—except, that is, for a few occasional flashes, notably the brief appearance of Emperor Tching Tang, whose chief accomplishment in Pound's eyes was that he "wrote MAKE IT NEW / on his bath tub." Far finer than the Chinese-history cantos in evoking China as a geographical place is Canto 49, the Seven Lakes canto, which poetically embodies the Confucian philosophy of self-control, the need for inner order in nature and in man, by its descriptions of eight painted scenes and poems, beginning with

> Rain; empty river; a voyage,
> Fire from frozen cloud, heavy rain in the twilight
> Under the cabin roof was one lantern.
> The reeds are heavy; bent;
> and the bamboos speak as if weeping.

This Chinese scene is so peaceful in its rich, dark colors that it is reminiscent of Pound's earlier Chinese translation, *Cathay,* whose beauty had prompted Eliot to call Pound "the inventor of Chinese poetry for our time." Canto 49 is singular among the cantos in this respect, for though Pound often used Chinese ideograms, or picture-writing, in his later cantos, to the bafflement of most Western readers, he never evoked the ideogram of classical Chinese culture more fully or more distinctively than in this set of imagist scenes, which ends metaphysically with "The fourth; the dimension of stillness. / And the power over wild beasts."

Wherever Pound may be at the end of Canto 49, he is certainly beyond China, beyond Baedeker, beyond any earthly realm we could ever hope to visit, in a fourth dimension that is not physical at all, but metaphysical, a "dimension of stillness" where he feels some mysterious "power over wild beasts." All we can be sure of is that he is far away from Confucius and seems to be evoking Orphic rather than Eleusinian mysteries, for it was the poet and musician Orpheus who in Greek legend had the power to charm even wild beasts with his singing. Orpheus also made a trip to the world of the dead and back, as Dante and Pound imagined for themselves. To enter this realm beyond the visible world, Pound had to leave behind the Italian, the Greek, and the Chinese scenes that make up more than half of the *Cantos;* he had to leave behind as well the other countries he described more briefly, including his native United States—not the contemporary, but the historical United States, during the revolutionary period, when Adams and Jefferson as Founding Fathers presided over the birth of a new nation; England, where he lived during the imagist decade, when his poetic career began, memorialized in the *Cantos* by keenly personal anecdotes of Yeats and Eliot and Hulme and Ford Madox Ford and Henri Gaudier-Brzeska and other writer and artist friends; Provence, part of the real France where he once walked in the steps of the troubadours and recited their songs; and even Spain and Germany. Pound also leaves behind his discoveries, described in the very late cantos of *Section: Rock-Drill,* of ancient Egypt, which he discovered by means of hieroglyphs sent to him by his son-in-law, Boris de Rachewiltz, and of even more ancient Sumeria, which he discovered by means of pictographs gleaned from his reading of works by "Alfalfa Bill" Murray, the governor of Oklahoma who led him to the pre-Egyptian cartoons unearthed by L. A. Waddell, a Scottish archaeologist who investigated the Aryan roots of language. It may be said of Pound that all his travels were in search of origins, and it is no wonder that they led him beyond earthly bounds into regions of the imagination where only the greatest visionary poets could guide him. Like Dante, Pound became one of their company, joining Homer and Ovid and Virgil, Dante's chief guide, by entering, in some of the most memorable passages in the *Cantos,* into "The fourth; the dimension of stillness."

These visionary passages begin with the world of the dead, out of Homer, in Canto 1 and the metamorphosis of Dionysus, out of Ovid, in Canto 2 and resume with the hell cantos (out of Dante), 14 through 16. These early cantos about hell are notable for the vivid imagery of the disembodied spirits Odysseus encounters on his descent into hell in Canto 1, such as that of Elpenor, his shipmate, "a man of no fortune and with a name to come," and that of Tiresias, the seer who prophesies that he (Pound as well as Odysseus) will "lose all companions" on his journey home, and, in Canto 2, for the shapes of grapevines and dolphins and panthers, "void air taking pelt," that Dionysus creates by "god-sleight" aboard Acoetes' ship, and, in cantos 14 through 16, for the murky, excretory filth that engulfs the victims of Pound's wrath, filth that he connects with bloody trench scenes from the battlefields of World War I.

It is in Canto 36 that we get Pound's first extended description of heaven, which he evokes by translating the medieval Italian Ballata of Guido Caval-canti, Dante's contemporary whom Pound places in his Pantheon of great poets, into English words full of the imagery of love and light:

> Where memory liveth,
>   it takes its state
> Formed like a diafan from light on shade . . .
>
> Willing man look into that forméd trace in his mind . . .
>
> But taken in the white light that is allness . . .
>
> From him alone mercy proceedeth.

We might already be in Dante's *Paradiso* in this canto, but Pound differs from his Italian guide in moving between hell and heaven not consecutively but alternately, and there is much hell to get through before Pound reaches heaven again after this taste of it in Canto 36.

In particular, the Italian cantos and the Pisan cantos are full of hellish visions that he mixes with the realistic imagery of World War II in Italy and the American prison camp at Pisa. The Italian cantos, 72 and 73, were for a long time not printed in their proper position in the numerical sequence of the *Cantos* because they were lost, but they belong there, just before the Pisan cantos, because they are the most Dantesque: not only were they written entirely in Italian, the language of Dante's poem, but Pound, like Dante, seems to be undergoing the torments of the damned in them, when he encounters the dead spirits first of Marinetti, the founder of futurism, who in Canto 72 bizarrely begs Pound to let him use his mortal body to go on fighting for Italy, and then of Cavalcanti, whom Pound dramatically resurrects to ride on horseback out of the medieval hell and decry the destruction of Sigismondo's Rimini by the Allied troops, who were moving northward in Italy when Pound wrote these cantos in 1943–1944. Appropriately, at the end of Canto

73, Cavalcanti's troubled spirit ascends to the *terzo cielo*, the third heaven of Venus, goddess of Love, Pound's favorite among the circles of Dante's paradise and a fitting rest for the soul of the Italian love-poet, who there joins Sordello's mistress, Cunizza, among the blessed. These two long-lost Italian cantos provide a needed dramatic transition between the very prosy cantos of Chinese and American history that precede them and the highly poetic Pisan cantos that follow them, which open with the stunning line "The enormous tragedy of the dream in the peasant's bent shoulders," then go on to describe the lynching of Mussolini and his mistress by the mob at Milano in a gruesome finale of World War II in Italy.

The Pisan Cantos, cantos 74–84, are by general agreement the climax of the poem, containing more quotable lines than any other sequence, and in them Pound is constantly in a hellish setting but often in the heavenly places of his imagination. What had distinguished Canto 45, the Usura canto, from all the earlier cantos distinguishes *The Pisan Cantos* as well, for in them Pound deplores the effects of materialism on human culture while at the same time praising the highest achievements of artists who shaped that culture. "With usura," he laments in Canto 45, "no picture is made to endure nor to live with / but it is made to sell and sell quickly," making it plain that the pursuit of money is not enough to inspire great artists, yet the architects of San Zeno and Saint Trophime and Saint Hilaire, like the painters Fra Angelico and Mantegna and others Pound mentions in his Pantheon of Italian and Flemish and French artists, did make handsome and durable buildings and frescoes, and they can still be admired even in a materialistic, usurious age such as the twentieth century. He repeats this theme of art-in-spite-of-usury or heaven-in-the-midst-of-hell throughout the *Cantos*, but it is especially dominant in *The Pisan Cantos*, where Pound wonders, in Canto 74, in a reprise of Canto 45,

> I don't know how humanity stands it
>   with a painted paradise at the end of it
>   without a painted paradise at the end of it

Clearly, Pound knows he is in hell, since he can see the ominous Torre del Fame, or Tower of Hunger of Count Ugolino, from his caged tent in the prison camp at Pisa, and he can recognize it as the setting for one of the most memorable passages of Dante's *Inferno*, canto 33, where Dante is nearing the bottom of hell and perceives to his horror the gnawing figure of Ugolino, the starving man who cannibalized his own children. But despite his consciousness of a living hell, Pound also proves himself capable of heavenly visions, whether they are reminiscent of the mythical Dionysian transformations of Canto 2, "O lynx, my love, my lovely lynx / Keep watch over my wine pot," or of his real memory of Yeats muttering "Sligo in heaven" as he looked out at the sea at Rapallo, or of his expression of his own belief that "What thou lovest well remains" despite all the "dross" and his certainty that "First came the seen, then thus the palpable / Elysium, though it were in the halls of hell."

Pound's ability to sink to the lowest hell and rise to the highest heaven by the power of his imagination is what above all keeps us reading the *Cantos,* as it kept him producing them, despite the iron cage at Pisa and the "Hell Hole" at St. Elizabeths, from which he arises memorably in Canto 90 of *Section: Rock-Drill,*

> from under the rubble heap
> > m'elevasti
> out of Erebus, the deep-lying
> > from the wind under the earth,
> > m'elevasti
> from the dulled air and the dust,
> > m'elevasti
> by the great flight
> > m'elevasti

If *The Pisan Cantos* are the climax, the final *Drafts and Fragments* are the fitting conclusion of the poem, and in them, as in cantos 45 and 81, Pound followed the sage advice his friend Wyndham Lewis offered in a letter drafted in 1948 for Pound at St. Elizabeths: "You are in a chaos. Why not face the fact and sing the chaos, songbird that you are?"[14] In the late cantos, we hear most often Pound's voice still singing bravely out of the chaos of his life:

> The hells move in cycles,
> > No man can see his own end.
> The Gods have not returned. "They have never left us."

These lines, among the last and finest in the poem, confirm in Canto 113 that Pound never in his worst days lost his power of language or vision, and they also confirm, for any reader who works his way through to them, that Pound's work as a whole is a magnificent and irreplaceable guidebook to as wide a range of human culture as has ever been assimilated by a single writer, taking us far beyond Baedeker, to regions where only great poets such as Homer and Ovid and Dante can take us, even as far as

14. Wyndham Lewis to Ezra Pound, May 1948, *Pound/Lewis: The Letters of Ezra Pound and Wyndham Lewis,* ed. Timothy Materer, 247.

                    that terzo
                    third heaven,
                        that Venere,
        again is all "paradiso"
                    a nice quiet paradise
                        over the shambles

In that "third heaven" of love, where we know from Canto 73 Pound would have placed Guido Cavalcanti, and to which no doubt he himself hoped to ascend, "it coheres all right / even if my notes do not cohere"—Pound's final admission in Canto 116 that he had erred mightily in his life and in his poem, but "To confess wrong without losing rightness," as Pound does at the end, means that the reader can "excuse his [Dante's] hell / and my paradiso."

9

An English Imagist
D. H. Lawrence

D. H. Lawrence would have been a poet of distinction without an imagist movement, but he became a modern poet, and a major one, by becoming an imagist, and in time he attained greater distinction than any of the other English poets who helped found the imagist movement. T. E. Hulme, F. S. Flint, and Richard Aldington were all imagists before Lawrence was, and yet their poetry remains something of a curiosity, seldom read or anthologized today despite its merit, while Lawrence's poetry has been second only to his fiction as the work of a writer of genius. Certainly Lawrence's poetry is as original as his novels and stories, if not quite as scandalous, and it may be that when Lawrence's reputation as the "priest of love" no longer generates the emotion it once did, his reputation as a poet may equal or even surpass his reputation as a novelist. It can already be said that of all English writers only Thomas Hardy rivals Lawrence as both a poet and novelist of the first rank.

If the audience for Lawrence the poet ever equals the audience for Lawrence the novelist, then Lawrence the imagist will be seen as central. For it is clear enough that the early poetry of Lawrence, as good as it was, was not as strikingly original as the later poetry, and it was not until Amy Lowell persuaded Lawrence to join the imagists in 1915 that his poetry showed its fullest individuality. His earlier "rhyming poems," as he liked to call them, were largely narrative and dramatic, sometimes making effective use of Midlands dialect, while the later "unrhyming poems" were largely descriptive—short free-verse lyrics of the imagist type.

In fact, it was Lawrence who most enthusiastically promoted free verse as the key to the new poetry (though the manifesto printed in each new edition of *Some Imagist Poets* demurred, "We do not insist upon 'free verse' as the only method of writing poetry"), and it was Lawrence above all the imagists who defined "free verse" in his own distinctive way as "poetry of the instant": "There is poetry of this immediate present, instant poetry, as well as poetry of the infinite past and infinite future."[1] Lawrence felt an attractive force drawing him to the imagists in 1915, when he might well have gone on with his established patterns of rhythm and rhyme, being content with the sort of realistic storytelling that distinguished such early poems as "Love on the Farm" or the dialect humor and drama of "Whether or Not." But Lawrence could not remain traditional in either poetry or prose; he was a literary pioneer who sought to explore new territories of the mind, and his revolutionary impulse meant that he must join the imagists in experimenting with verse technique. As he explained in the passage quoted earlier, introducing his *New Poems* in 1918, after the last edition of *Some Imagist Poets* had appeared:

> Such is the rare new poetry. One realm we have never conquered: the pure present. One great mystery of time is terra incognita to us: the immediate instant. The most superb mystery we have hardly recognised: the immediate, instant self. The quick of all time is the instant. The quick of all the universe, of all creation, is the incarnate, carnal self. Poetry gave us the clue: free verse.

So Lawrence became a theorist as well as a practitioner of imagism in his later career, and no poet benefited from the movement more than he did, since the concentration, concreteness, and musicality of the imagist poem was the sort of shaping force that he needed for his immense imaginative energy, a force that the earlier pioneering work of Whitman alone could not provide (though Lawrence praised Whitman more highly than Pound).

Lawrence caught the spirit of imagism in mid-career, and it gave him a fresh burst of inspiration for his poetry, even a new identity as a poet. More than any other writer, Lawrence proved the value of imagism for poets who joined it later in their careers, since he did not contribute to forming imagism but intuitively understood its principles and knew how to adapt them to his own practice. To look at a complete collection of his poetry, vast as it is in scope, is to be struck by the number of short free-verse lyrics he wrote, beginning as early as "Brooding Grief" in 1913, though he placed that poem among what he would call his rhyming poems:

> A yellow leaf, from the darkness
> Hops like a frog before me;
> Why should I start and stand still?

1. D. H. Lawrence, "Poetry of the Present," introduction to the American Edition of *New Poems* (1918), reprinted in *The Complete Poems of D. H. Lawrence*, 181–86.

> I was watching the woman that bore me
> Stretched in the brindled darkness
> Of the sick-room, rigid with will
> To die: and the quick leaf tore me
> Back to this rainy swill
> Of leaves and lamps and the city street mingled before me.

We know that this poem came directly from Lawrence's own experience, because he wrote it in about 1913 and there is a similar passage near the end of his autobiographical novel, *Sons and Lovers,* published in 1913, in which the narrator, Paul Morel, an artist like Lawrence, watches as his mother slowly dies in their house in the Midlands mining town where he grew up, and thinks of her as he walks along the street: "Suddenly a piece of paper started near his feet and blew along down the pavement. He stood still, rigid, with clenched fists, a flame of agony going over him. And he saw again the sick-room, his mother, her eyes. Unconsciously he had been with her, in her company. The swift hop of the paper reminded him she was gone."[2]

Lawrence's novel and his life provide a context for the poem, and yet the poetic expression is more universal than is possible in either autobiography or fiction. The poem is about the experience of grief, the death of a very close relative, "the woman who bore me," but objectified through the image of the leaf hopping along the pavement and reminding the speaker of the death he has been witnessing in his mother's room: it is as if the detached leaf has become the departed human life, and its mingling with the "rainy swill / Of leaves and lamps and the city street" becomes a naturalistic merging of death with life in a darkly brooding scene. Lawrence in a few lines—rhyming in no regular pattern, with no regular meter—has encapsulated the feelings associated with his mother's death, and by shaping it into a poem, he has given the human suffering of grief a wider appeal than the novel evokes by its detailed narrative-descriptive account of the same death. To compare this early imagist poem by Lawrence with the same episode in his fiction is to see how his poetry at its best could distill words into briefer and more memorable expression than his prose.

This poem's appearance in 1913 shows that Lawrence was writing poems of the imagist type before he joined the movement, and indeed his readiness to accept Amy Lowell's invitation to be one of the six English and American poets in *Some Imagist Poets* must have stemmed from his awareness that some of his poems were already well suited to the imagist theory. He wrote many more, however, in an ever-freer verse, and with a sense of self-fulfillment,

---

2. D. H. Lawrence, *Sons and Lovers,* 480.

for this new "poetry of the instant" was for Lawrence a realization of his own peculiar genius and at the same time a participation in the poetic movement of most consequence around him, which gave him the satisfaction of fulfilling his own ambitions in the company of other poets who, like him, sought a visible change in the form of English verse.

A little later in the imagist decade, the second decade of the twentieth century, Lawrence would write one of his most effective imagist poems about another kind of autobiographical experience, the one that, after his mother's death, was perhaps the most important to his emotional development: his love for Frieda Richtofen, a married woman, and their scandalous elopement from England, leaving behind her husband and children. In "On the Balcony," Lawrence presents a scene of sensual attraction that is also a scene of strife between two lovers in a series of visual images that mirror their feelings indirectly. The implied narrative in this largely descriptive poem is that a man and woman, sensually aware of each other's presence—"your naked feet in their sandals"—stand on a balcony looking out on a mountain and river above and below them (the setting is probably the Bavarian Alps near Munich, where Lawrence and Richtofen lived for a time), and as they watch a storm above them in the sky and wheat harvesters in the field below them near the "pale-green glacier river," they see a boat pass along the river as the "thunder roars," and then the boat disappears from sight.

The implied emotional drama running through these images is of lovers who are strongly attracted to each other physically, yet torn by their feelings of conscious separateness, so that they must repeat to themselves as if in affirmation of their love, "But still we have each other!" yet at the same time ask as if in unavoidable but final parting, "what have we but each other?" The implied ending of their love story is that they will have to part eventually; the brief statement that "The boat has gone" seems to be their recognition that their love will not last, and that having experienced both the pleasure and the pain of being together they must divide into separate selves ultimately. Though Lawrence wrote often and passionately about his relations with Richtofen in shockingly frank descriptions of lovemaking, he nowhere expressed more effectively than in this short imagist poem the human conflict between the lovers, who desired a complete and harmonious union that would be a form of mystical identity, but who realized that such total empathy is not possible between human beings and so ended their love/hate, attraction/repulsion, pleasure/pain relationship as separate selves who must go their own way and die their own deaths, as in time they did.

Lawrence was a painter as well as a poet, and though his visual art never matched his verbal art, his keen eye often looked at the world as a spectacle, and his observations were sometimes those of a painter who takes visual satisfaction in what he sees, not merely a lover who looks for erotic pleasure in the world around him. One of his finest imagist poems is a nude study of a woman, in which his visual delight in the shape and texture of the woman's body exceeds any physical attraction it may have for him. The poem, called "Gloire de Dijon," is as voluptuous in its imagery as a Renoir nude, and more voluptuous than any of Lawrence's own paintings of nude women, because it is without any coarseness or vulgarity, a pure visual rendering of the light falling on the surfaces of the woman's body as it might fall on ripe fruit in a still life. There is of course the male point of view that chooses the woman's naked body for its subject, but like a classical Greek sculptor or a French impressionist painter, Lawrence maintains the aesthetic distance that allows him to admire the female physique with his eyes, in its perfection of form and texture, its golden contours, without seeking to embrace it with his arms. The metaphorical comparison with a flower, and specifically with a cultivated species of yellow rose that carries the poetic French name "Glory of Dijon," a flower named for the capital of Burgundy, serves to make this nude portrait all the more an aesthetic rather than an erotic object: indeed, the woman becomes a symbol of natural fertility like the flower, and a symbol of natural beauty as well. In this short poem Lawrence sums up his appreciation of nature's regenerative and creative power, which the "rain-disheveled petals" heighten by their suggestion of spring showers, and treats feminine beauty aesthetically, not just erotically.

Lawrence felt an attraction to the animal and vegetable world almost as strong as the attraction between the sexes, and he wrote a number of excellent poems about "Birds, Beasts, and Flowers" that characterize such diverse species as elephants, tortoises, snakes, and hummingbirds, as well as roses and gentians, in unforgettable visual sketches. Lawrence was ultimately a religious poet—or, as T. S. Eliot once said in criticism of him, he tried as a writer to fulfill the second commandment of Christ, "Thou shalt love thy neighbor as thyself," without fulfilling the first commandment, "Thou shalt love the Lord thy God with all thy heart, and with all thy mind, and with all thy soul." Lawrence's religious belief may have been what Eliot called in *After Strange Gods* a form of "modern heresy," yet it was sincere in its pursuit of a spiritual, not merely a physical, union between man and woman or man and animal. "Swan" is a striking animal poem of the imagist type in which Lawrence's religious quest is apparent. The figure of the swan in this poem is never a simple natural creature but is at first an original physical force of nature, elemental in its energy as an atom, endowed with a "happy energy" that seems to have unbounded power from the beginning of time, awesome to men but not threatening to them—until, that is, it becomes a domineering masculine presence among women and "we men are put out" by the godlike apparition of "the vast white bird." For his shocking final description of the swan, which suddenly "stamps his black marsh feet on their white and marshy flesh," Lawrence draws on the Greek myth of Leda and the Swan to make the bird an incarnation of Zeus, the king of the gods, visiting himself on a mortal woman in the shape of a swan and raping her to produce divine offspring (which in the myth were the male twins Castor and Pollux and the female twins Helen and Clytemnestra).

Thus, in his "Swan," Lawrence rewrote a Greek myth as Yeats did in "Leda and the Swan," but with the difference that he imaged it as a godlike natural force that inspires both happiness and fear in men, while Yeats symbolized it as an intrusion of divine power into human history, causing tragedy to occur among men in the Trojan War but initiating a whole cycle of classical civilization as well. Lawrence the imagist compares with Yeats the symbolist in the brevity of his poetic retelling of a central Greek myth, but contrasts with him in his highly effective use of free verse—Yeats used the traditional sonnet form with equal skill; the difference between them sums up the difference between imagism and symbolism as poetic movements, "The natural object is always the perfect symbol," as Pound put it, and Lawrence's swan begins in the realm of nature for all its supernatural energy, while Yeats's swan is a god in the shape of a bird from the beginning when he descends on Leda with "A sudden blow, the great wings beating still." Lawrence's swan is like his "Snake" and his "Hummingbird," natural creatures with godlike power, viewed as better than human beings because more instinctual, to be worshiped rather than destroyed by men, who should venerate the created universe and replace human aggressiveness with natural awe, allowing both man and nature to survive.

The force of nature that Lawrence found most to be feared was death, yet Lawrence, who courted death for most of his forty-five years, made up his mind at the end to accept death as a release into nature, rather than as annihilation. He was fascinated by the Etruscan passage tombs or "cities of death" he discovered in Italy, where "the journey to oblivion" was treated as a transition to a happier state, and he wrote about readying his "Ship of Death" as if it were, like Noah's ark, a survival vessel for transporting the soul from life into death. "The Ship of Death" is Lawrence's most memorable image of the death-journey, but a shorter, more definitely imagist poem about death is "November by the Sea." The experience of death in this fine late poem is sublimated into a winter sunset image, in which the whole physical ordeal is resolved into a beautiful description of the end of a year and the end of a day. Lawrence gave the sunset new meaning while at the same time he gave new meaning to death: both are seen as natural processes that are inevitable, but not merely sad and painful, since they mix darkness and light, motion and rest, age and youth. The sun becomes an agent of light and life which must endure the darkness of night and death, but which appears to seek the transformation rather than to resist it, and which changes its light-giving power as it descends, becoming "a few gold rays" and then "thickening down to red" and finally disappearing into the sea, which "wins" this race with the sun, as "the dark winter" takes over the year at the "winter solstice," or shortest day. The soul of man is compared to this "great gold sun" in its decline into death, "setting fierce and undaunted . . . behind the sounding sea between my ribs," losing the "race" of life, yet with a final image of light that seems still to shine in the darkness, "my sun, and the great gold sun." The image is of death as a beautiful ending to life, or it may be seen as a stage in the cyclical process that will bring the soul back to life, just as the dying sun is reborn every day. Lawrence's view of death was ambivalent, both in this poem and in the more famous "Ship of Death," but he continued to hold the belief in immortality shared by both Greeks and Christians over the centuries of Western civilization, and he found a way of transmitting it at the end of his own life, in "November by the Sea," that at least redeems death from its grimness and at best transforms it into a natural resurrection of the soul.

Imagist poems were not all that Lawrence wrote, certainly, but they form an impressive part of his work and are as representative in theme, subject, and style as any of his poems. He needed the discipline of a controlled free verse, which the imagists taught him, and it was he who embodied it superbly in the "poetry of the instant" that he believed to be the essence of modern poetry, agreeing with Pound's famous definition of the image as "an intellectual and emotional complex in an instant of time." His religious quest was for a finite moment of eternity, and he felt he had found it in the imagist practice of free verse that became his own characteristic practice; if he did not see such a moment as Eliot did, as a form of Incarnation, of the Word made flesh, Lawrence nevertheless believed that "the quick of all time is the instant," and that by free verse he could express a mystical union of "the soul and the mind and the body surging at once, nothing left out. They speak all together."[3] Though a latecomer to imagism, Lawrence embraced its theory, gave further distinction to its experiments, and produced some of its classic poems, thus becoming the most important of the English imagists who took part in this originally Anglo-American poetic movement.

3. Lawrence, *Complete Poems*, 181–86.

10

Further Imagists
H. D., Williams, Moore, Cummings, and MacLeish

Imagism as a theory of poetry replaced symbolism in the early twentieth century by changing the direction of metaphor, the basic poetic figure of speech. Symbolism expressed the subjective reality of external objects; imagism reversed the emphasis and stressed the objective reality of subjective thoughts. The symbolist poet started with a mental awareness or inner perception and moved outward to the realm of objects, while the imagist poet started with an awareness of objective reality and moved inside, or as Pound said of his two-line touchstone of imagism, "In a Station of the Metro," "In a poem of this sort one is trying to record the precise instant when a thing outward and objective transforms itself, or darts into a thing inward and subjective."[1] The first rule of imagism, according to Pound, was "direct treatment of the thing, whether subjective or objective," an attempt to resolve the subject/object duality implicit in symbolism into a new subject/object unity. "The image is itself the speech," Pound insisted. The second rule of verbal economy, or brevity, and the third rule of free verse, or organic rhythm, were meant to be part of this new unity of subject with object in the imagist poem. Imagism as a theory meant that spontaneity and immediacy were essential to poetry, that all the familiar formulas of meter and rhyme must be abandoned and the poet must make a new start from his own experience.

As a school of poetry, imagism started in London and spread through the English-speaking world by means of little magazines such as *Poetry* and the *Little Review* in Chicago, *Others* in New York, and the *Egoist* in London. In time, almost all poets writing English were affected by it, but the center of activity moved from London to the United States. The cause was championed

1. Pound, "Vorticism," 467.

by American Amy Lowell, who took over from Pound as leader of the imagists after he edited the first anthology, *Des Imagistes,* in 1914. Lowell edited the three anthologies of *Some Imagist Poets* published in Boston in 1915, 1916, and 1917, inducing John Gould Fletcher and D. H. Lawrence to join her and three of the original imagists, Hilda Doolittle (H. D.), Richard Aldington, and F. S. Flint. Since three were American (Lowell, Fletcher, and H. D.) and three were English (Lawrence, Aldington, and Flint), the "Amygists," as Pound nicknamed them, continued to be an Anglo-American group, just as they had been ever since the first School of Images founded by T. E. Hulme in March 1909 was joined in April by Pound.

But the leading imagists tended to be Americans, and the influence of the short, concrete, free-verse poem was more strongly felt in the United States, where the literary tradition was short, than it was in England, where the literary tradition was long. With the major exception of D. H. Lawrence, the poets who identified themselves as imagists were Americans attracted to the new movement in poetry and eager to shape individual styles of their own. Though Englishman T. E. Hulme was the inventor of imagism in theory, an American, Ezra Pound, became its leader in practice. And Pound conferred the title of the first imagist on H. D., who was an American and a close friend, to whom he had once been romantically attached.

H. D., who showed Pound in London in 1912 what he would call the first imagist poems, was always the most instinctive imagist; her style and form seemed to suit the movement from the moment it was born. That moment was in October 1912 at the British Museum tearoom in the heart of London, where, according to her own account, H. D. showed Pound the manuscript of "Hermes of the Ways" and a few other poems she had recently written in the manner of the classical Greek lyric, and Pound, after editing them, scrawled "H. D. Imagiste" at the bottom of the manuscript and sent it off to Harriet Monroe in Chicago to be published in her new magazine, *Poetry,* in January 1913.[2] The birth of imagism was as impetuous as its history was brief: the movement, strictly speaking, lasted only through the imagist decade, roughly the second decade of the twentieth century (it could be dated from as early as Christmas 1908, when Hulme's "Autumn" was published in London, to as late as 1917, when the last anthology of *Some Imagist Poets* was published in Boston). But H. D. was exceptional: she was the one poet whose natural style was so close to the original principles of the imagist poem that it never really needed to change.

She began with the aim of translating lyrics from the classical Greek anthology into current English, and in her autobiographical novel *Bid Me*

---

2. See Hilda Doolittle, *End to Torment: A Memoir of Ezra Pound,* 18.

to Live, her writer-heroine says her ambition is to spend her life writing just one Greek chorus; it is no wonder her poetry has a strongly Greek flavor throughout. Her first imagist poems all had Greek titles, such as "Hermes of the Ways" and "Priapus" and "Oread," and what Pound liked so much about them, what he called their "hardness" and "clarity," came, in his opinion, from their being "straight talk, straight as the Greek." One of her early imagist poems is called "Epigram (After the Greek)":

> The golden one is gone from the banquets;
> She, beloved of Atimetus,
> The swallow, the bright Homonoea;
> Gone the dear chatterer.

The Greek names are obscure and seemingly without allusion, just a male name, Atimetus, and a female name, Homonoea, which together imply a classical setting for this brief elegy, and no more. The description of the young girl who is now dead is terse; merely the phrases "golden one," "swallow," and "dear chatterer" impart a sense of her character, her beauty and innocence and lightness now "gone from the banquets." What H. D. captured in her short lyric is the image of a girl, once loved for the brightness and delicacy of her presence, now mourned in passing: the elegiac tone is understated but unmistakable, like an epitaph for the tomb of an unknown lady.

Many of H. D.'s poems have a similarly feminine subject, though the treatment is rather masculine in its harshness of attitude and coldness of speech, derived no doubt from her cultivation of a lapidary Greek style in English. Thus the early "Oread" gets its name from the mountain nymph of Greek mythology, though the poem is about a human encounter with the sea:

> Whirl up, sea—
> whirl your pointed pines,
> splash your great pines
> on our rocks,
> hurl your green over us,
> cover us with your pools of fir.

The scene is a rocky coast somewhere, with evergreens growing near the water, and it portrays an imagined clash between a human figure and the ocean, natural beauty and violence coming together as the waves mount up and cover the speaker—yet the Oread appears to welcome such destructive action by the water, not to shrink from it. In his *Autobiography,* William Carlos Williams portrays H. D. as a woman he and Pound both fell in love with but found reckless and vulnerable. He reports that on one occasion she stood outside and invited the rain to beat on her during a violent thunderstorm, and on another occasion, when they were at the beach together near Point Pleasant, New Jersey, there was an incident that sounds very much like the situation of "Oread":

> Hilda had come down just before my arrival and, getting into her bathing clothes, had gone to the shore after the others. They all saw it. There had been a storm and the breakers were heavy, pounding in with overpowering force. But Hilda was entranced. I suppose she wasn't used to the ocean anyhow and didn't realize what she was about. For without thought or caution she went to meet the waves, walked right into them. I suppose she could swim, I don't know, but in she went and the first wave knocked her flat, the second rolled her into the undertow, and if Bob Lamberton hadn't been powerful and there, it might have been worse. They dragged her out unconscious, resuscitated her, and had just taken her up to the house.[3]

It would seem, then, that in writing her poem about a mountain nymph, H. D. was combining her own reckless temperament with the imagined audacity of a mythical Greek spirit, and the result was distinctively her own creation, yet redolent of classical paganism.

Most evident in H. D.'s brand of imagism is a peculiar mixture of pleasure and pain, as if all beauty were tragic to her sensibility. Perhaps her most characteristic imagist poem re-creates Helen of Troy, the most beautiful woman in Greek mythology, whose abduction from her husband, Menelaus, by the Trojan prince Paris started the Trojan War. H. D.'s "Helen" seems a remote ideal like the Greek heroine, yet the view of her is as much from the inside as from the outside; she is seen as a woman who suffers for her beauty and is forced to endure the hostile glances of those who blame her for causing the war between the Greeks and the Trojans. "All Greece hates / the still eyes in the white face," H. D. begins her description of Helen, and she goes on to intensify the hostility of those who fought for her, adding that "All Greece reviles / the wan face when she smiles," and ending with the image of "God's daughter, born of love" (Zeus had raped Leda, a mortal woman, to conceive Helen) being loved only in death by the Greeks, who "could love indeed the maid / only if she were laid / white ash amid funereal cypresses." The cold perfection of H. D.'s portrait of Helen is at once attractive and forbidding: she is "born of love" and yet she is hated, and the Greeks who fight to recapture her from the Trojans wish that she were dead. Indeed, there is a deathlike pallor on her already, perceptible in her white skin, wan smile, and cool feet, and the final stroke

---

3. *The Autobiography of William Carlos Williams,* 69–70.

of H. D.'s sketch portrays her body consumed on a funeral pyre into "white ash amid funereal cypresses." Though H. D. has in recent years been claimed as a feminist, her true originality was better described by René Taupin, who said, "Her poetry is extremely feminine, but is lacking in sensuousness."[4] Her imagism objectifies female beauty, making it aesthetically pleasing and acutely painful at the same time; her poems are like delicate roses with sharp thorns.

William Carlos Williams was almost as instinctive an imagist as H. D., as Pound certainly recognized, but Williams took longer to discover free verse, as his early poems demonstrate, and he moved back and forth from poetry to prose, much as Pound was also doing at the time, so that if Williams was not among the very first imagists, he was nevertheless part of the movement from its inception and became one of the best of the imagist poets in the course of his career. Of all the English and American imagists, only Williams in New Jersey wrote their poetic tribute, "Aux Imagistes," using the French spelling that Pound preferred and sending it to London to be published in the *Egoist* in 1914, the year he was included by Pound in the first imagist anthology, *Des Imagistes*. Williams valued the recognition, as he showed in his poetic tribute: "I have never been so exalted / As I am now by you."[5] Then, in July 1916, Williams edited an issue of *Others* in New York that was replete with imagists both old and new: Ezra Pound, Amy Lowell, John Gould Fletcher, Carl Sandburg, Wallace Stevens, Marianne Moore, and Williams himself. So Williams became a promoter of the imagists in America, and along with Amy Lowell he was an effective advocate of the new movement. Moreover, Williams went on practicing imagism for the rest of his career, and his last collection before his death, *Pictures from Brueghel*, published in 1962, was among his best and most characteristically imagist productions.

Williams seemed almost scornful of beauty in his kind of imagism: he was looking for vitality and utility in the world around him, applying the American test of pragmatism to his experience, thinking of a poem as "a machine made of words" rather than as a thing of beauty. Wallace Stevens called Williams's poems "rubbings of reality" and said, "The anti-poetic is his spirit's cure. He needs it as a naked man needs shelter or an animal needs salt."[6] To Williams, who counted himself one of them, imagist poets were "frost bitten blossoms" that might bear bitter fruit, but as unsentimental realists they could be trusted to tell the truth no matter what the cost. His poems smack of honesty, above all other qualities, a deliberate honesty cultivated by his choice of words, which were few and usually concrete. There is no better example

4. René Taupin, *Influence of French Symbolism*, 141.
5. Reprinted in William Pratt, ed., *The Imagist Poem*, 78.
6. Stevens, *Opus Posthumous*, 255.

of Williams's imagism than the very short and simple line drawing of "The Locust Tree in Flower":

> Among
> of
> green
>
> stiff
> old
> bright
>
> broken
> branch
> come
>
> white
> sweet
> May
> again

Each word is a line: free verse is carried to an extreme of brevity in this poem, and it works. The blossoming of the gnarled limbs of the locust tree into white flowers in May is conveyed as successfully as if the tree were made of words. The whole poem is ungrammatical and unfinished: "Among / of / green" is nonsense at the beginning, yet it makes sense of the natural process by which naked branches unfold into white flowers, and there is no period at the end, but there is a sense that the process will go on again and again, season after season. The colors of spring are green and white, contrasting in their vitality, as is also true of the oldness and brightness, the brokenness and sweetness of the locust tree in flower. Williams suggests by his image of spring that what is vital in nature can break through the coldest and hardest surfaces to renew life in the world, and he counts on its endless recurrence.

There is a similar confidence in the equally brief portrait Williams gives of star and sun in "El Hombre," its Spanish title suggesting that "The Man" is a good name for either star or sun:

> It's a strange courage
> you give me, ancient star:
>
> Shine alone in the sunrise
> toward which you lend no part!

Williams manages to draw from a simple juxtaposition of sunrise and star the meaning that nature has room for lesser and greater lights in the heavens, and may have as much room in the human sphere as well. What he celebrates in this poem is the virtue of courage, exemplified in the shining of a star after the sun has risen, which from the human viewpoint signifies the persistence of will even when its results are unseen, so that something as small as a human being does have a place in the universe, however insignificant it may be. The analogy is apt in Williams's case, since as an imagist he felt that a poem could be small and yet significant, and as a poet he could feel that his star might go on shining even when another poet (perhaps his friend Ezra Pound?) shone more brilliantly. Four lines are enough to make the image clear, and Williams takes his "strange courage" straight from the example of nature and applies it to himself, as a poet who wrote small but durable poems, encouraged by the imagist movement to do so.

Williams's own favorite among all his poems was "The Red Wheelbarrow," a perfect instance of imagism: direct, brief, free verse. Yet it remains puzzling to many readers, because like all good imagist poems it has concreteness without abstraction, and abstraction is for many readers necessary to tell them what a poem means. Williams resists explanation; he wants the poetic image to speak for itself and hopes that the reader who reflects on it long enough may see the point.

What is the point? First of all, that a red wheelbarrow is one of the most elementary human tools: it is the ultimate in simplicity and usefulness. When he sees it wet with spring rain and near a flock of white chickens, it makes him think of natural fertility as well. He asserts at the beginning that "so much depends / upon" something as unassuming as a red wheelbarrow, asking the reader to make the connection between man and nature, which supports life, since this simple tool is essential to agriculture and human beings know instinctively, whether they live in cities or on farms, that cultivating nature is necessary to their survival. Out of the elementary colors of red and white comes the image of a wheelbarrow that links man to nature, and if we add the organic rhythm of free verse, as Williams deftly does, we have the perfection of the imagist poem: a two-beat, one-beat "meter" through four brief "stanzas" that are as fixed in their way as a sonnet, yet apparently as spontaneous and easy as life. Williams was a master imagist, as his own favorite poem demonstrates: in a few words he could imply a whole philosophy of life but at the same time leave the reader the challenge of figuring it out for himself and so give him a share of the poet's satisfaction in the outcome.

Williams's longer poems, especially the best of them, *Paterson* and *Of Asphodel, That Greeny Flower,* are extensions of imagism, because they link images in free-verse patterns to, in *Paterson,* the personality of an American city, and, in *Asphodel,* his lifelong love for his wife. Williams would maintain throughout his career, as he put it once in a letter to Pound, that "there is nothing for it but to go on with a complex quantitative music and to further accuracy of the image," and his final book of poems, *Pictures from Brueghel,* returned to the short imagist poem as an instinctive form that he never really deserted.

Marianne Moore, though she was a student at Bryn Mawr when H. D. was there, did not meet H. D. then, nor did she meet Pound or Williams, other Philadelphia imagists, until after she made her name as a poet. Yet she was publishing her first poems in the *Egoist* and *Poetry* soon after imagism got its start in their pages, and she had a natural affinity for the sort of experiments with free verse that imagism encouraged. Her own poetry was so odd that, as she herself said, it had to be classified as poetry because there was no other category in which to put it, and in time she became the chief representative of what Pound, echoing Ford Madox Ford, called "the prose tradition in poetry." She was, in other words, not so much a lyricist as a witty realist, whose powers of observation were exceptional, whose breadth of reading was prodigious, and who could mix fantasy and fact with the precision of organic rhythm required by free verse.

"I notice a word here and there and then I match them up," Moore said disarmingly once of her poetic technique, adding, "my writing is, if not a cabinet of fossils, a kind of collection of flies in amber." She disavowed her connection with imagism, although she admitted that it was the Aldingtons (Richard and H. D., when they were married and editing the *Egoist*) who first encouraged her to publish her poems, and T. S. Eliot would say in introducing her *Selected Poems* for his publishing house, Faber and Faber, that "she had taken to heart the repeated reminder of Mr. Pound: poetry must be at least as well written as prose." So if Moore was never a member of any of the imagist groups, she was nonetheless instinctively imagist in her care for words, as well as in her keen observation of the natural world and in her sense that free verse meant simply that "the rhythm is the person."

One of her best early poems appeared in the *Egoist* in May 1916 with the unlikely title "You are like the realistic product of an idealistic search for gold at the foot of the rainbow," which was later happily shortened to "To a Chameleon":

> Hid by the august foliage and fruit
>> of the grape-vine
>>> twine
>>>> your anatomy
>>>>> round the pruned and polished stem,
>>>>>> Chameleon.
>>>>>> Fire laid upon
>>>>> an emerald as long as
>>>> the Dark King's massy
>> one,

> could not snap the spectrum up for food
>   as you have done.

The shape of this poem obviously contributes something to its meaning and indicates that Moore's experiments with free verse led her to arrange words in a visual pattern with something like the shape of her subject, so that here the sinuous winding of the words down the page follows the slender body of the lizard, if the reader connects the subject with the poetic form. She leads in that direction by the descriptive image of the chameleon twining its body around "the pruned and polished stem" of a grapevine. She also captures the chameleon's special ability to change its color to match its surroundings, by starting with "fire," which is red, then mentioning "emerald," which is green, and saying that the chameleon contains both, but even more, that it can "snap the spectrum up for food," meaning that it has the whole array of colors at its command. Finally, she brings a mythical allusion into her image of the chameleon, mixing the imaginary with the real, when she speaks of "the Dark King," who must be Pluto, the king of the underworld in Greek mythology, keeper of all precious stones, who has at hand an emerald as long and "massy" as a chameleon, but she maintains that no inorganic mineral could imitate the living animal's capacity for change. Thus in shape, in imagery, and in allusion, Moore has made a chameleon out of words, a remarkable achievement for such a short poem, clearly an imagist classic.

An even earlier poem of Moore's was "To a Steam Roller," which appeared in the *Egoist* in 1915 and which must have amazed the readers of that day as much as Eliot's "Love Song of J. Alfred Prufrock" amazed the readers of *Poetry* the same year. It is a poem in which something man-made and ugly becomes an object of admiration and even humor because of the poet's deft choice of words. The shape of "To a Steam Roller" is original, but it is not a visual representation of the machine. Rather, it is Moore's special adaptation of free verse to the syllable count, in the manner of French poetry, so that each of her three stanzas is formed of four lines, the first of which has five syllables, the second and third twelve syllables, and the last line fifteen syllables. Why? There is probably no answer except that she liked to control her free verse by forcing herself to count the syllables, giving each poem a new and disciplined form. At any rate, she practiced syllabic verse so often that it became identified with her, and since no modern poet shows greater diversity of form than Marianne Moore, it apparently worked for her as a stimulus for originality. As to the images of "To a Steam Roller," which are even more important than the verse shape, there are really two: the image of the steamroller as a huge monster that enforces uniformity by its relentless crushing down of every particle into a homogeneous mass and the image of the butterflies, which are suddenly introduced, coming out of nowhere but the poet's imagination, to achieve a complementary visual effect. The butterflies, in their delicacy, lightness, brilliant colors, and evanescent flitting through the air, are in every respect the opposites of the steamroller, in its heavy, lumbering, dull, monotonous flattening of the earth. In a witty mockery of the steamroller, the poet suggests that "to question the congruence of the complement is vain, if it exists," leaving the reader with the distinct impression that steamrollers and butterflies belong to the same world and are therefore equally worthy of the poet's attention. Even the abstract language in this poem, which includes an explanation of what individual taste is not—"impersonal judgment in aesthetic matters [is] a metaphysical impossibility"—fits the image of the steamroller as a machine made by man to force an unnatural conformity on nature and adds to the wry humor of the treatment. Indeed the poem is as witty as it is imagist, a demonstration that the poetic imagination can take any subject it pleases and transform it into a verbal miracle. Whether or not she admitted the influence, Moore first schooled herself in the imagist doctrines of realism, brevity, and singularity of form, and then gave herself free rein to write any kind of poem, long or short, with only one commandment in mind: never repeat yourself. She never did.

E. E. Cummings (or, as he preferred it, e. e. cummings) and Archibald MacLeish were of the second generation of imagists, and they extended the movement into the 1920s, Cummings by a radical individualism that made him the most outspoken exponent of modernism in poetry, and MacLeish by his summing up of the imagist principles and practice in a single poem, "Ars Poetica," which embodies imagism at its best. It was Cummings who more than any other imagist carried the movement's experiments with form to the very limits of freedom: as Lionel Trilling once said, Cummings set free all the parts of speech, even articles and conjunctions. Such a "liberation" was highly American, and Cummings is still the poet who was freest of all the writers of free verse. If Cummings sometimes went too far in his experiments, he started with imagism, and he maintained that Ezra Pound was "the true trailblazer of our epoch, the Einstein of modern poetry."

Cummings, slightly younger than Pound and the first imagists, took their experimentation with form to its logical extreme, and in so doing created his own kind of originality. Though few of his poems are strictly imagist, most of them followed the lead of Pound and others toward maximum individuality of form, and he made use of the typewriter with a vengeance, breaking words down into letters or placing punctuation marks where they did not belong. His conception of free verse was one of almost total freedom in the use of words, consistent with the philosophy he articulated in his "so-called novel," *The Enormous Room,* early in his career, and in *i: six nonlectures,* talks that he gave at Harvard, his alma mater, late in his career, that "so far as I am concerned, poetry and every other art was and is and forever will be strictly and distinctly a question of individuality."[7] There is in Cummings's work an extension of the imagist experiments to the limit of artistic license, making his poetry both instructive and ingenious.

One of his best poems of the imagist type goes by the abstract title "Impression V," but might be called by the more concrete title "Sunset":

> stinging
> gold swarms
> upon the spires
> silver
>
>   chants the litanies the
> great bells are ringing with rose
> the lewd fat bells
>   and a tall
>
> wind
> is dragging
> the
> sea
>
> with
>
> dream
>
> -S

The form of this poem calls attention to itself, as often happens in Cummings's poems, yet in this case the form contributes to the meaning every bit as much as it does in Marianne Moore's "To a Chameleon" or in Williams's "Red Wheelbarrow." What the spacing out of words and even of letters over the page adds to the image of the sunset is a grouping of major visual effects into three main components: first the gold color of the setting sun falling on silver spires in a city, then the ringing of huge bells in a tower, and finally the motion of the wind as it stirs the water of the nearby sea. The reader pictures an ancient city by the sea, quite possibly Venice, as the setting of the poem and sees the sun's rays like a hive of bees descending on it, then hears the church bells ringing out an evensong, which is reverent in mood and yet sensuous in the sounds made by "the lewd fat bells," and then both sees and feels the movement of the wind over the water, as Cummings breaks the last phrase down into single words and a final consonant "-S." What is happening to the tone of the poem at the end is arresting: there is a sleepy motion at

---

7. Cummings, *i: six nonlectures*, 24.

work in the wind and the sea that leads into the night and the dreams that will follow the sunset, beyond the visible, audible, sensible world. Certainly Pound's definition of an image as "an intellectual and emotional complex in an instant of time" is fulfilled in this poem, which has a metaphysical effect in its passage from the outer world of the senses into the inner world of dreams.

Cummings wrote few poems as compact as this early "Impression V" or as close to the imagist mode, but quite late in his career, in 95 *Poems* in 1958, Cummings published what may be the shortest of all imagist poems, with no title but the number "1":

l(a

le
af
fa

ll

s)
one
l

iness

Of course this poem can hardly be read aloud: it is a poem more for the eye than for the ear, with its interruption of the key word *loneliness* by the fragmented image "a leaf falls," yet there is a method in Cummings's madness. He is bringing together by means of his peculiar typographical arrangement on the page the concreteness of a familiar autumn sight, a leaf falling from a tree, and the thematic mood of loneliness connecting nature and man in a seasonal bond. There are only four words in this poem, and even spread out by letters there are only nine lines, making it an even shorter imagist work than Pound's celebrated "In a Station of the Metro" (which has fourteen words, not including the title) or Williams's "The Locust Tree in Flower" (which has thirteen words exclusive of the title). Thus it is an imagist tour de force, winning the contest for brevity against any other contender, and it is also proof that a poem can be experimental to the extreme and yet be a meaningful expression of authentic experience, universal in its import. There are many autumn poems in many languages, but no poem captures the sadness of the fall season, when nature is visibly dying, more concisely than this one. It is also an ultimate expression of Cummings's philosophy of individualism, since the falling leaf and the mood of loneliness connote a final separation of every individual from the world of the living by each one's inevitable death, a theme that is even broader than the season because it can occur at any time of life. In E. E. Cummings, then, imagism reached its apogee of originality and individuality, beyond which it would be impossible to go.

Archibald MacLeish, who like Cummings arrived on the poetic scene after the first imagists had created the new movement, nevertheless can be credited with the poetic summing up of imagism in his "Ars Poetica" in 1926, written well after the imagist decade had ended. It is inconceivable that such a poem could have been written without imagism, because the technique as well as the philosophy of MacLeish's most famous poem is imagist. It consists of a sequence of images that are discrete but that at the same time express and exemplify the imagist principles and practice of poetry.

The Latin title is borrowed from Horace, who wrote a prose treatise in the first century A.D., the Silver Age of Rome, called "Art of Poetry," advising poets among other things to be brief and to make their poems lasting. MacLeish wanted to link the classical with the modern in his poetic "treatise," as a way of implying that the standards of good poetry are timeless, that they do not change in essence though actual poems change from age to age and language to language. His succession of opening images are all about the enduring of poetry through time, as concrete as "globed fruit" or ancient coins or stone ledges, and as inspiring to see as a flight of birds or the moon rising in the sky. The statements are not only concrete but paradoxical, for it is impossible that poems should be "mute" or "Dumb" or "Silent" or "wordless," which would mean that there was no communication in them at all; rather, what MacLeish is stating in his succession of paradoxical images is that the substance of poetry may be physical but the meaning of poetry is metaphysical: poems are not about the world of sensible objects as much as they are about invisible realities, and so the universal emotions of grief and love can be expressed in words that convey the experience in all its concreteness, yet the words reach into the visionary realm beyond experience, toward which all true images point. The final paradox, that "A poem should not mean but be," is pure impossibility, but the poet insists it is nevertheless valid, because beyond the meaning of any poem is the being that it points to, which is ageless and permanent, a divine essence or spiritual reality behind all appearances. MacLeish's modern "Art of Poetry" is a fulfillment of the three rules of imagism (be direct, be brief, and use free verse), of Pound's definition of the image, and at the same time of Horace's Latin statement on poetry, that good poetry is one proof that there is a permanence in human experience that does not change but endures through time.

Imagism spawned a number of classic short poems by a number of different poets, enabling them to write with a characteristic modern style and yet with great individuality, so that no two imagist poems are alike, finally, nor can any two imagist poets be confused with each other, even though the ideal imagist poem is impersonal. Short as they are, the best imagist poems are among the finest poems of the century, and though imagism only accounts for part of the work of poets as diverse as H. D. and Williams and Moore and Cummings and MacLeish, it is the original shaping element that made them all modern to start with.

11

Two American Symbolists
Wallace Stevens and Hart Crane

"Modern reality is the reality of decreation," Wallace Stevens wrote, "in which our revelations are not the revelations of belief, but the precious portents of our own powers."[1] Stevens was using the word *decreation,* which had been coined by the French philosopher Simone Weil, in a new sense. Weil had identified decreation with all "human reality," for she was a Christian Jew who believed the only true creator is God, and man at best is a "co-creator," that is, "We participate in the creation of the world by decreating ourselves."[2] Weil invented the word *decreation* to mean all man's efforts—not merely his artistic efforts—to participate actively in God's creation from the beginning of time, and these efforts necessarily involved self-sacrifice, a recognition on man's part that he was more creature than creator. But Stevens found in Weil's word a new understanding of what the modern artist does, and it was he who applied the word *decreation* specifically to modern art, arguing that the creative powers formerly attributed to God must now be assumed by man, since "in an age in which disbelief is profoundly prevalent or, if not disbelief, indifference to questions of belief, poetry and painting, and the arts in general, are, in their measure, a compensation for what has been lost."[3]

More than any other modern poet, Wallace Stevens believed art could compensate for the loss of religious belief, and he maintained that the role of the artist had to become that of the priest, because "the poet is the priest of

---

1. Wallace Stevens, "The Relations between Poetry and Painting," in *The Necessary Angel: Essays on Reality and the Imagination,* 175.
2. Simone Weil, "Decreation," 80.
3. Stevens, *Necessary Angel,* 171.

the invisible."[4] Stevens drew upon religion to make poetry, using the religious term *decreation* to define the act of imagination by which art is made from life, and taking the role of poet himself "as a role of the utmost seriousness," since he assumed that in the modern age "it is for the poet to supply the satisfactions of belief."

He knew it was paradoxical to hold that, when priests could no longer claim the authority they once derived from religious faith, poets might claim it for their art. He never shunned paradox, however, and he maintained that aesthetics could take the place of religion if only it were more widely accepted: "Religion is dependent on faith. But aesthetics is independent of faith. The relative positions of the two might be reversed. It is possible to establish aesthetics in the individual mind as immeasurably a greater thing than religion. Its present state is the result of the difficulty of establishing it except in the individual mind."[5] For those who believe with Stevens that poetry can take the place of faith, he is the greatest of modern poets, but even he was aware that the very individuality of art is a deterrent to its becoming as universal among human beings as religion once was. He certainly did not mean for the poet to become an evangelist; rather, he wanted him to be a revealer of reality, *reality* meaning for Stevens an invisible realm beyond the senses, just as it had meant for the French symbolists. In one of his essays, he quoted approvingly the celebrated pronouncement of Rimbaud, "It is necessary to be a seer, to make oneself a seer. The poet makes himself a seer by a long, immense and reasoned unruliness of the senses."[6] And in another essay he quoted Baudelaire approvingly, from his poem "La Vie antérieure" ["The Former Life"], in which the French poet wrote movingly of what Stevens called "one's inherited store of poetic subjects," which come from the ages of shared religious belief that formed the basis of poetic symbolism. Stevens went on to affirm that for him, as for Rimbaud and Baudelaire, "there is inherent in the words *the revelation of reality* a suggestion that there is a reality of or within or beneath the surface of reality. There are many such realities through which poets constantly pass to and fro, without noticing the imaginary lines that divide one from the other."[7] Indeed, Stevens had so much in common with the aesthetics of the French symbolists that he became an American symbolist himself, often using French words and phrases in his poetry as well as in his prose, going so far as to state that "French and English constitute a single language." He even, late in life, wrote a tribute to Baudelaire in the form of a long poem with a French title, "Esthétique

4. Stevens, *Opus Posthumous*, 169.
5. Stevens, "Adagia," in *Opus Posthumous*, 166.
6. Stevens, "The Irrational Element in Poetry," in *Opus Posthumous*, 227.
7. Stevens, "Two or Three Ideas," in *Opus Posthumous*, 213.

du Mal" ["Aesthetic of Evil"], which is in many respects a summing-up of Stevens's own artistic credo.

The fifteen sections of Stevens's "Esthétique du Mal," as we know from his letters, were composed in 1944, when Stevens was sixty-five years old, in response to a letter he read in John Crowe Ransom's *Kenyon Review,* which raised, in the context of World War II, the question of the relation between poetry and pain.[8] A month after he read the letter, Stevens sent his long poem to Ransom, implying that he had been reflecting much longer on the question, probably most of his life, since the poem has the ring of a mature meditation on the problem of reconciling art and evil. Even more probably, the poem had its origin in Stevens's reading of Baudelaire's collected poems, and he intended his "Esthétique du Mal" to be an American equivalent of *Les Fleurs du mal:* if Baudelaire dared to make all his poems "flowers of evil," Stevens could dare to go a step beyond him, making an "aesthetic of evil" out of a single poem.

Stevens's meditation on poetry and pain begins with the declaration that "Pain is human," and in the imagined setting of Naples, he reflects on the destruction of Pompeii by volcanic eruption, which leads him to see that pain exists only in human consciousness, not in nature:

> Except for us, Vesuvius might consume
> In solid fire the utmost earth and know
> No pain

He goes on to reflect that Christ had been "A too, too human god, self-pity's kin," who had suffered for mankind and thereby made man less able to endure pain, but now that hell has "disappeared, / As if pain, no longer satanic mimicry, / Could be borne," man should face pain as part of his experience, and like Baudelaire (abbreviated to "B.") make his flowers, or poems, out of evil—not, he insists, a sentimental "Livre de toutes sortes de fleurs d'après nature" ["Book of All Sorts of Flowers after Nature"], but a book of "transparent sounds" that will tell him that

> The genius of misfortune
> Is not a sentimentalist. He is
> That evil, that evil in the self, from which
> In desperate hallow, rugged gesture, fault
> Falls out on everything: the genius of
> The mind, which is our being, wrong and wrong,

8. See *The Letters of Wallace Stevens,* 468–69.

The genius of the body, which is our world,
Spent in the false engagements of the mind.

Thus man's mind can right the wrongs that life contains, and Stevens posits that though "The death of Satan was a tragedy / For the imagination," now "the phantoms are gone and the shaken realist / First sees reality," and it is possible to understand that good can come from evil, even when "Life is a bitter aspic," for "Natives of poverty, children of malheur, / The gaiety of language is our seigneur." In other words, human beings may be poor and unfortunate, but "our lord" (that is, the poet) draws on "the gaiety of language" to make poetry out of the misery of existence. If we understand that each life is "a fragmentary tragedy / Within the universal whole," it is possible that "a man, / Reclining, eased of desire, establishes / The visible" and "calls it good, / The ultimate good." If "The greatest poverty is not to live / In a physical world," Stevens concludes his "Aesthetic of Evil" by saying

The adventurer
In humanity has not conceived of a race
Completely physical in a physical world.
The green corn gleams and the metaphysicals
Lie sprawling in majors of the August heat,
The rotund emotions, paradise unknown.

So the reality Stevens would fashion out of poetry is one in which the evil of existence becomes the good of art, and individual human pain and tragedy is resolved in works of imagination that the poet, "The adventurer in humanity," makes by transforming physical pain into a metaphysical "paradise unknown." Thus Stevens wished to replace religion with aesthetics by following the example of the French symbolists, although the result would be apparent only to those who read and understood his poem, leaving still the admitted "difficulty of establishing it except in the individual mind."

If Stevens became an American symbolist by rewriting Baudelaire's theory of art expressed in "Esthétique du Mal," he also became a "musician of silence" in his poetry as Mallarmé and Valéry had done before him, translating words into musical sounds that could reach deeply into human feelings. Perhaps Stevens's greatest virtuoso piece as a musician of translating silence into language is the early "Peter Quince at the Clavier," a sonata in words. The four sections of this poem are like the movements of a symphony or a piano sonata, and it could almost be said that the music *is* the meaning. The strange title suggests that the whole poem is being played on a piano by someone named Peter Quince, a fictitious character who was the director of the play-within-a-play of Shakespeare's comedy *A Midsummer Night's Dream*, but here he stands for the poet himself. The "subject" of the poem is another literary allusion, the Apocryphal book *The History of Susanna* in the Bible, but the story of Susanna and the Elders becomes a metaphor for the love that the poet-pianist is expressing for the unnamed woman in "blue-shadowed silk" who stands beside him.

Stevens's musical poem, then, is really a love poem, spoken by a man to a woman, "here in this room, desiring you," a man who insists that his fingers on the keys are not making mere music but "Music is feeling then, not sound," a statement that is the theme of the first section of the poem, which may be regarded as the moderato movement of the sonata. In it, the suggested story of Susanna and the Elders is told as analogy: the beauty of Susanna and her terror at the peeping "red-eyed elders" who watch her bathing is translated into music through words. The poem opens with the man, whose fictional counterpart is Peter Quince, expressing his feelings on the piano to a beautiful woman, whose fictional counterpart is Susanna, and the rest of the poem is the story of Susanna. Since the story tells of feminine beauty betrayed by men who tried to possess and violate it, and who suffer death as punishment for their treachery, the poem is about the transience of human life contrasted with the "immortality" of love, beauty, music, and poetry.

The first section ends with the introduction of Susanna and the hidden desire of the elders, who are represented by musical instruments that play "witching chords" that make "their thin blood / Pulse pizzacati of Hosanna." The second section offers an abrupt change, both in tone and in form, for while the first section has steadily mounted to a climax, through rhyming iambic tetrameter lines, the second shifts to a languorous mood, with free-verse rhythm and occasional rhymes, mirroring Susanna's sensuous enjoyment of her bath. This section may be called the adagio, or slow, movement of the sonata, which is luxurious in its portrayal of the beauty and pleasure of the woman bathing. Then comes another abrupt change, signaled by other musical instruments—"A cymbal clashed, and roaring horns"—to describe the leering elders as they look lustfully at Susanna naked in her bath, and quickly a third, allegro movement of the sonata follows, in dactylic tetrameter couplets that mimic the embarrassment of Susanna, her anguish at being seen naked by men, and the swift flight of her "attendant Byzantines," or maids, accompanied "with the noise of tambourines." The final section then returns to the moderato of the opening section, with a philosophic calm in its movement, the theme restated in iambic tetrameter couplets, not only the earlier theme that "Music is feeling" but the new theme that "the body's beauty lives"—and goes on living in the re-creation of Susanna's beauty by the poet, in a musical coda that plays "on the clear viol of her memory / And makes a constant sacrament of praise."

Thus, if Stevens in one poem could, like the French symbolists, make a theory of art in the form of a poem, he could in another make a musical sonata or symphony in the form of a poem. Stevens, for all his playfulness and virtuosity, was a thoroughly serious poet, a "connoisseur of chaos" with a strong sense of the poet's responsibility, capable of sarcastically addressing to "a high-toned old Christian woman" his most fervent belief, that "Poetry is the supreme fiction, Madame."

Stevens's first major poem, "Sunday Morning," appeared in *Poetry* magazine in 1915, the year that Eliot's "Love Song of J. Alfred Prufrock" appeared in the same magazine, but Stevens was several years older than Eliot when he began to acquire a reputation as a poet. From 1915 until 1955, the year he died, Stevens produced a body of poetry that rivaled Eliot's and Pound's in its solidity and unity. "Sunday Morning" is a series of eight blank-verse stanzas presenting an alternative to Christian worship ("paganism," Stevens would later call it) in the form of a woman's meditation on nature, in which she concludes paradoxically that "Death is the mother of beauty, mystical" and accepts the fact that beauty arises from death in the changing seasons and the reproductive power of living beings, all of which must, like the pigeons, "sink, / Downward to darkness, on extended wings." "Notes towards a Supreme Fiction" extends the definition of poetry begun in "A High-Toned Old Christian Woman" by a long soliloquy with three blank-verse sections that develop the dicta that "It Must Be Abstract," "It Must Change," and "It Must Give Pleasure." For forty years Stevens wrestled with the question of what poetry is, never doubting that it was the most important human creation (or "decreation"), since it is "the imagination pressing back against the pressure of reality." But perhaps his most complete definition of poetry came in "The Idea of Order at Key West," published in his second book, *Ideas of Order,* in the 1930s.

"She sang beyond the genius of the sea," he says eloquently as the poem opens, and the sea in this poem represents the changing, organic universe, nature in all its seething vitality, observed in the semitropical setting of the Florida Keys, an island chain stretching into the Caribbean. The singer is a woman, as in "Sunday Morning," but this woman is not meditating; she is transforming the sea into a poem by her song, changing inchoate natural form into order, a rational human tongue giving shape to the spirit of things. She is "the single artificer" and the "maker" whose "rage for order" gives meaning to the "words of the sea." The speaker of the poem and his interlocutor, Ramon Fernandez (typically, Stevens dismissed the name as an arbitrary choice when asked, though it was the real name of a Mexican philosopher and critic who published essays in French that Stevens must have read), represent the human audience for the poet's song, who find a mystery they can appreciate but cannot explain in the woman's singing, which has "Mastered the night and portioned out the sea." Stevens's poem posits a human order temporarily superimposed upon an ever-changing universe, but in the end all order seems to dissolve again in images of "fragrant portals, dimly-starred" (the heavenly gates, it seems) and the mystery of "our origins, / In ghostlier demarcations, keener sounds" (some kind of spiritual rebirth in another world, or heaven). Though Stevens gestures toward invisible realities, his honesty tells him that the order created by the human imagination can only be a temporary order, however "supreme" he may have hoped his "fictions" could be, and thus the poet or singer is ultimately a tragic figure, "the snow man" who, in the poem of that name, "nothing himself, / Beholds the nothing that is not there and the nothing that is," and who in another poem names himself as "the man with a blue guitar," of whom he can say, "Things as they are / Are changed upon the blue guitar," and one of whose last poems is "Farewell without a Guitar," signifying that death is a form of natural change that includes the human order and that cannot be transcended.

In saying that "modern reality is the reality of decreation," then, Stevens was making a poet's assertion that belief in a divine order may be superseded by belief in a human order, and he was willing to argue that "it is as if in a study of modern man we predicated the greatness of poetry as the final measure of his stature, as if his willingness to believe beyond belief was what had made him modern and was always certain to keep him so."[9] But if we look upon "The Idea of Order at Key West" as Stevens's fullest expression of his poetic philosophy, it both projects the poet's heroic role and sees his tragic limitations: the singing ends, the singer vanishes, and the credo becomes an elegy.

Wallace Stevens may be seen as the American poet who strove most ambitiously to create an imaginative human order to replace the lost belief in a superhuman order, but great as his achievement is, his "supreme fiction" remains a huge abstraction more than a new reality. He asserted confidently that "God and the imagination are one," but God is missing from the poem he wrote called "The American Sublime":

> And the sublime comes down
> To the spirit itself,
>
> The spirit and space,
> The empty spirit
> In vacant space.

9. Stevens, "A Collect of Philosophy," in *Opus Posthumous*, 202.

At its highest reaches, Stevens's American symbolism is a symbolism of space, a counterpart to Yeats's Irish symbolism, which is a symbolism of place.

Hart Crane was an equally ambitious American symbolist who tried to create a new supreme fiction quite different from that of Wallace Stevens by transferring the lost belief in God to something much more concrete: the Brooklyn Bridge. *The Bridge* was Crane's major effort at producing a counterstatement to Eliot's *Waste Land,* which he viewed as a brilliant poem with a devastatingly negative message about modern man. Crane felt that if he seized on a man-made artifice, the Brooklyn Bridge—"the most superb piece of construction in the modern world," he called it—he could thereby give concrete expression to American life, "our constructive future, our unique identity, in which is included also our scientific hopes and achievements of the future." So impressive were certain sections of the poem that they were published by Eliot himself in the *Criterion* and by Marianne Moore in the *Dial*—two of the most respected editors and literary magazines of the twenties. But as a whole, the poem proved disappointing to Crane, a fragmentary masterpiece, a magnificent failure, and Crane himself became so disillusioned before he had finished his epic that he confessed in a letter, "The bridge as a symbol today has no significance beyond an economical approach to shorter hours, quicker lunches, behaviourism and toothpicks."[10] In short, Crane came to realize that a technological marvel could only be a utilitarian, not an aesthetic, work; it was an obsolescent machine that would last only as long as it proved useful. As Crane put it when speaking about another of his poems, "I was really building a bridge between so-called classic experience and many divergent realities of our seething, confused cosmos of today, which has no formulated mythology yet for classic poetic reference or for religious exploitation."[11] If Stevens's supreme fiction suffers from excessive abstraction, it was at least less transitory than Crane's materialistic symbol of the bridge, which could not be transformed by even the most inspired poetic idealism into a permanent image of human aspiration.

Thus, although *The Bridge* remains Crane's central work, it survives in sections rather than as a whole, and his reputation as a major poet depends less on the attempted epic, which really succeeds only in the first section, "Proem: To Brooklyn Bridge," with its startling religious imagery of the bridge as a "harp and altar of the fury fused," that might "by Thy curveship lend a myth to God," than on his shorter poems, especially the early "Voyages," six lyrics on a related theme of man's journey into the unknown vastness

---

10. Hart Crane to Waldo Frank, June 20, 1926, in *The Letters of Hart Crane, 1916–1932,* 261.

11. Hart Crane, "General Aims and Theories," in *The Complete Poems and Selected Letters and Prose of Hart Crane,* 217.

of the sea, his poems about the Caribbean, which include "Hurricane" and "Key West," his tribute to Charlie Chaplin's comic tramp—a metaphor for the poet—in "Chaplinesque," and his last poem, "The Broken Tower." Of them all, it is "The Broken Tower" that remains Crane's most fully realized American symbol.

"The Broken Tower" was published posthumously in 1932, soon after Crane had committed suicide, plunging to his death from an ocean liner on his way back from Mexico to the United States. He had written the poem in a burst of inspiration following an early morning visit to the Spanish baroque cathedral of Taxco, a mountain village in Mexico, where he had climbed the bell tower and rung the bells. From this simple experience Crane fashioned a poem that best symbolizes his ideal of a human order arising out of the ruins of Christian faith, a faith that he, like Stevens, took to be no longer recoverable, because in his view, "the great mythologies of the past (including the Church) are deprived of enough facade to even launch good raillery against."[12]

The poem opens with images of Crane's actual experience of ringing the bells in the cathedral tower at dawn, but soon rises to a more visionary level, where the poet as bell ringer feels the tower of religion to be broken, the bells jangling, and he himself as poet ringing out "broken intervals" of sound. The world itself is seen to be "broken," that is, disintegrated, lacking in unity and order, and the poet has entered it to "trace the visionary company of love," which he sees as a worthy calling but one that he is not sure he is capable of fulfilling:

> My word I poured. But was it cognate, scored
> Of that tribunal monarch of the earth
> Whose thigh embronzes earth, strikes crystal Word
> In wounds pledged once to hope—cleft to despair?

In short, the poet doubts whether he has been divinely inspired, and whether his uttered words can carry anything like the former authority of Holy Scripture, the Word of God. He receives no answer to his question, and so his doubt about his own effectuality as a prophet is unresolved, but suddenly his thought turns to a human love, which he now believes to be the real inspiration for his poetry, and he builds for the woman he loves (a real woman, Peggy Cowley, the writer Malcolm Cowley's wife, with whom Crane had fallen in love in Mexico) a new tower of words—"a tower that is not stone"—to replace the broken tower of Christian faith, hope, and love. In this inner tower of love, constructed by the poet, is the peace he seeks, a harmony of heaven and earth.

---

12. Crane, *Complete Poems and Selected Letters*, 218.

The commodious, tall decorum of that sky
Unseals her earth, and lifts love in its shower.

Crane hoped that his poetry might become a new expression of hope, and Allen Tate said of him that "he had an instinctive mastery of the fused metaphor of Symbolism,"[13] which meant that Crane's poetry was often dense with meaning and could be as cryptic as any French symbolist poem in its condensed imagery. He once had to explain to an editor that the phrase "adagios of islands" in the second and best known of the "Voyages" was poetic shorthand for the image of a boat cruising slowly through clustered islands, a meaning that was not easily deduced, and certainly the final aggregate images of the poem are powerful and at the same time mystifying, profound, and memorable, like much French symbolist poetry:

> Bind us in time, O Seasons clear, and awe.
> O minstrel galleons of Carib fire,
> Bequeath us to no earthly shore until
> Is answered in the vortex of our grave
> The seal's wide spindrift gaze towards paradise.

The poet is praying to the elements—the seasons and the stars (the "minstrel galleons of Carib fire" are the stars above the Caribbean Sea, perceived as wandering lighted Spanish ships)—to let him stay forever afloat on the ocean, the goddess of his voyage, until his death comes by drowning "in the vortex of our grave" (a prophetic image of Crane's own death later in the Caribbean), and he is transported to the imagined heaven toward which the seal, adrift on a floe of ice, perhaps, seems to be pointing with its upward-looking eyes. All these whirling words are difficult to decipher, and yet Crane believed in a "logic of metaphor" which according to him "antedates our so-called pure logic, and which is the genetic basis of all speech," and he thought that every good poem added a dimension to consciousness that would not exist without it: "It is as though a poem gave the reader as he left it a single, new *word*, never before spoken and impossible to actually enunciate, but self-evident as an active principle in the reader's consciousness henceforward."[14] The "words" that Crane's poetry added to the language are quite different from those Stevens's poetry added, as different as his worship of nature as goddess was from Stevens's worship of the imagination as God, or as Crane's imagery of the sea as the body of a woman ("Mark how her turning

---

13. Allen Tate, "Hart Crane," in *Essays of Four Decades* (Chicago: Swallow Press, 1959), 310.
14. Crane, *Complete Poems and Selected Letters,* 221.

shoulders wind the hours") is from Stevens's imagery of the sea "Like a body wholly body, fluttering / Its empty sleeves," and yet both of these American symbolists contributed greatly to the richness of English as a poetic language. And both finally took a tragic view of man, whether as poet or common individual, who dies in the act of ordering or loving the universe, hearing "the dark voice of the sea" in Stevens's poem beckon him beyond all human ordering to the "fragrant portals, dimly-starred" where there are "ghostlier demarcations, keener sounds," or abandoning himself in Crane's poem to the vast immeasurable expanse of the sea, "this great wink of eternity / Of rimless floods, unfettered leewardings." If neither Stevens nor Crane wholly succeeded in their high but unrealizable ambition of making their poetry into a new religion, their American symbolism often did succeed within more human bounds, achieving the sort of "decreation" that Simone Weil believed men are capable of, their best poems penetrating deeply into the mystery of things and leaving permanent proofs of the imaginative power of words.

12

A Transatlantic Ironist
T. S. Eliot

Eliot at Oxford: From Philosopher to Poet and Critic

Though T. S. Eliot rose in less than a decade to a position of literary dominance, he was a long time deciding what he wanted to be. He was twenty-six
when he moved to Oxford in the fall of 1914, just after World War I had erupted
in Europe, and his main interest was philosophy, which he had been studying
assiduously for many years, at Harvard, Paris, and Marburg. He seems to have
had every intention of completing his doctoral thesis in philosophy within a
year, returning to Harvard to defend it, and then embarking on an academic
career as a philosopher in the United States. After all, it was what he was
expected to do: he had received a Sheldon Traveling Fellowship from Harvard
to support him while he wrote his dissertation on the English philosopher F.
H. Bradley; he had been admitted to Merton College, Oxford, where Bradley
himself was a Fellow; and he had as his tutor Harold Joachim, who was both
an expert on the philosophy of Aristotle and the leading exponent of Bradley's
philosophy. Furthermore, his parents in St. Louis, Henry Ware Eliot and
Charlotte Champe Stearns Eliot, were wholly in sympathy with his ambition
to become a philosophy professor at an American university, and their moral
as well as financial support was crucial to Eliot, their seventh, youngest, and
most promising child. But during his year at Oxford, Eliot changed his career
ambitions for good, so that instead of becoming a perhaps distinguished
but predictably conventional professor of philosophy at Harvard—or at Yale,
like his friend Brand Blanshard, a fellow American philosophy student at
Oxford[1]—he became a poet and critic of such originality and distinction that
he helped bring about a twentieth-century revolution in English literary style.

---

1. See Brand Blanshard, "Eliot at Oxford."

The evidence of his writing suggests a gradual but decisive change during the period of nine months between two crucial events in his life—meeting Ezra Pound in London in September 1914 and marrying Vivienne Haigh-Wood in London in June 1915. He spent most of the intervening period at Oxford, and though he eventually chose London as the place where he would settle for the rest of his life, Oxford was the place where his mind and his career changed.

The critical importance of the Oxford year is confirmed in biographies of Eliot by Peter Ackroyd and Lyndall Gordon, but most tellingly by Richard Ellmann, the authoritative biographer of Yeats and Joyce and Wilde, who never got around to writing a complete account of Eliot's life, but wrote a concise account for the 1981 edition of *The Dictionary of National Biography*. Since Ellmann was an American literary scholar who himself became an Oxford don, his view of Eliot's Oxford year is especially pertinent:

> The year 1914–15 proved to be pivotal for Eliot. He came to three interrelated decisions. The first was to give up the appearance of the philosopher for the reality of the poet, though he equivocated a little about this by continuing to write reviews for philosophical journals for some time thereafter. The second was to marry, and the third to settle in England, the war notwithstanding.[2]

Ellmann thought it was not any direct influence at Oxford that provided the stimulus for change, but Eliot's meeting with Ezra Pound in London before going to Oxford, since it was Pound who encouraged Eliot to marry, to settle in England, and to become a poet rather than a philosopher, and since Pound also succeeded—where Eliot himself had failed—in getting some of Eliot's poems published. Ellmann's opinion is supported by Eliot's own testimony that "my meeting with Ezra Pound changed my life. He was enthusiastic about my poems, and gave me such praise and encouragement as I had long since ceased to hope for. I was happier in England, even in wartime, than I had been in America: Pound urged me to stay . . . and encouraged me to write verse again."[3] Besides the influence of Pound, Eliot's marriage to Vivienne Haigh-Wood, an Englishwoman, helped keep him firmly planted in England, against his parents' strong wish that he come back home. The choice of expatriation was painful, leading to a permanent rift in his relations with his mother and father that Eliot as a dutiful youngest son could never really justify; it probably remained a scar on his conscience the rest of his life, though his decision to expatriate himself seems as much in character now as the choice of a literary over a philosophical career.

2. Richard Ellmann, "T. S. Eliot," *The Dictionary of National Biography, 1961–1970*, 326.
3. Quoted in Valerie Eliot's introduction to *The Letters of T. S. Eliot, Volume I, 1898–1922*, xvii.

Just as essential to his career, however, was what was going on in his mind, and the letters, poems, and essays he wrote suggest that philosophy was becoming less and less attractive to him, and poetry and literary criticism more and more attractive. The letters are particularly instructive about the change in Eliot's thinking during the decisive year he spent at Oxford from the fall of 1914 to the summer of 1915. One of his first letters from Merton College, at the end of September 1914, to his old Harvard friend Conrad Aiken, expresses elation that "Pound has been *on n'est pas plus aimable* [kindness itself] and is going to print 'Prufrock' in *Poetry* and pay me for it," but Eliot was nevertheless disheartened, because "the devil of it is that I have done nothing good since J. A[lfred] P[rufrock] and writhe in impotence," and in his next letter to Aiken in mid-November, Eliot said somewhat bitterly of Oxford, "Only the most matter of fact people could write verse here, I assure you." By February of 1915, however, Eliot was writing to Pound to say that he had read Pound's article on vorticism (in the *Fortnightly Review*) and found it reassuring:

> I distrust and detest Aesthetics, when it cuts loose from the Object, and vapours into the void, but you have not done that. The closer one keeps to the Artist's discussion of his technique the better, I think, and the only kind of art worth talking about is the art one happens to like. There can be no contemplative or easychair aesthetics, I think; only the aesthetics of the person who is about to do something. I was fearful lest you should hitch it up to Bergson or James or some philosopher, and was relieved to find that Vorticism was not a philosophy.[4]

Pound's aesthetic theories made an immediate appeal to Eliot because they were something different from his academic study of philosophy, which he deprecated as "contemplative or easychair aesthetics," and he saw Pound as a poet who put his theories into practice. That Pound was also a discerning judge of other people's poetry, we have the expert witness of Conrad Aiken, a promoter of Eliot's poetry since his Harvard days. Aiken had been trying for years to help Eliot find a publisher for his poems, but when Aiken showed them to Pound, he immediately recognized their merit and saw to it that they were published; as Aiken later explained, "the real clincher turned out to be 'the Love Song of J. Alfred Prufrock' ":

> This I had shown to every conceivable editor in England with no luck whatever. Harold Monro, at the Poetry Bookshop, which I had taken to

4. Eliot to Conrad Aiken, September 30, 1914, November 16, 1914, and Eliot to Pound, February 1915, *Letters of T. S. Eliot,* 58, 68, 86–87.

frequenting and where Brooke had introduced me, at a "poetry squash," to
Flint, Aldington, Hodgson and others, rejected Eliot's poem for *Poetry and
Drama* as "crazy." He similarly dismissed "La Figlia che Piange," which Eliot
had sent me in a letter and which I showed to Monro at a party—I think
he suspected it was a covert way of getting him to read a poem of my own.
He was very rude about it, as only Monro could be, and as I was to remind
him many years later, when we became very close friends and were together
members of the *Criterion* circle. And so, defeated everywhere by the English
publishers, I naturally turned to Pound, who saw instantly that the poem
was a work of genius, said that he would transmit it to Harriet Monroe for
Poetry—no doubt *commanding* her to print it—and history was made.[5]

Pound, by the time he met Eliot, had already edited the first imagist anthology, *Des Imagistes;* otherwise he would undoubtedly have included Eliot's
"Preludes" in it, but he did include five Eliot poems in *The Catholic Anthology,*
which he edited in 1915: along with the earlier "Prufrock" and "Portrait of a
Lady," and a prose poem called "Hysteria," Pound chose two poems written by
Eliot at Oxford: "The *Boston Evening Transcript*" and "Miss Helen Slingsby"
(later called "Aunt Helen"). So Eliot's Oxford year was not totally barren
poetically; he also wrote a third Boston poem there called "Cousin Nancy"
as well as putting the finishing touches on a short London imagist poem
called "Morning at the Window." Pound, who as a foreign correspondent for
Poetry got "The Love Song of J. Alfred Prufrock" published in 1915 after a
long wrangle with Harriet Monroe, was able through his other editorial roles
to publish more Eliot poems in the *Egoist* as well as in the *Little Review,* and
in 1917 to induce the Egoist Press (financed by Pound himself) to print Eliot's
first book of poems, under the title *Prufrock and Other Observations.*

If, when Eliot went to Oxford in the fall of 1914, he thought of himself as
primarily a philosopher, at least by 1917 Pound had convinced him to think of
himself as primarily a poet, and Eliot must have been grateful for this change
in his profession, although in June of 1915, when he suddenly married Vivienne
Haigh-Wood after a whirlwind courtship (he had met her only two months
earlier at Oxford), he listed himself on the marriage license in London as "of
no occupation." At that signal moment, having encouraged Eliot to marry and
settle in London and become a poet rather than a philosopher, Pound even
went so far as to write a letter to Eliot's father on Eliot's request, in which he
tried to persuade the St. Louis brick manufacturer that his son had a singular
talent for poetry and "if a man is doing the fine thing and the rare thing,
London is the only possible place for him to exist." And Pound made a pledge
to Eliot's father that "I am very much interested in T. S. E.'s work and that if

5. Conrad Aiken, "Ezra Pound: 1914," 4–5.

(or when) he comes back to London I shall continue to use such influence, as I have, in his behalf to get his work recognized."[6] Pound was as good as his word, and through him Eliot became a published poet soon after he left Oxford, but what he did during the year he was at Oxford prepared him for the literary career on which he was about to embark.

The poems Eliot first showed to Pound, which he had written before arriving in England, were proof enough of his mastery: no more classic works of modern poetry exist than "The Love Song of J. Alfred Prufrock," "Preludes," and "Portrait of a Lady." But the few poems he wrote at Oxford, though slight in themselves, were the further proof he needed that he could follow Pound's advice and go on writing new poems, even in unfavorable circumstances. His Boston poems and "Morning at the Window" are minor Eliot, perhaps, but they are important links between the earlier poems and the later Sweeney poems he would write in London before 1920. The Oxford poems, as they might be called, are not set in Oxford, but in Boston and London. They are deft descriptive sketches of city life with a satirical and ironic tone, and they are valuable because they were composed during his Oxford year, when his letters from Merton College give a rather dismal picture of his response to the academic setting: "In Oxford I have the feeling that I am not quite alive—that my body is walking about with a bit of my brain inside it, and nothing else," he wrote, and more emphatically, "Oxford is very pretty, but I don't like to be dead" (p. 74).

The image of Boston that Eliot gives in "The *Boston Evening Transcript*," "Aunt Helen," and "Cousin Nancy" is of a provincial capital where the leading families rule, those Boston Brahmins or blue bloods of which Eliot's own family were prominent members (Charles W. Eliot, a distant cousin, was president of Harvard when Eliot entered in 1906). All the portraits seem to be of relatives—from Cousin Harriet, to whom the speaker brings the *Boston Evening Transcript* as if it were a sort of divine tablet, to Aunt Helen, who "lived in a small house near a fashionable square," to Cousin Nancy (whose last name is Ellicott—very nearly Eliot), who shocks her kinswomen by her "wild" behavior—"Miss Nancy Ellicott smoked / And danced all the modern dances." All the women seem strong-willed enough to exert authority over the men and intellectually superior, too, because they keep on their shelves the books (and probably the busts) of Arnold and Emerson, "Matthew and Waldo, guardians of the faith," whose combined moral and literary influence prevails in the family, as might have been the case in most educated families of the late Victorian period, when Arnold and Emerson, though lapsed Christians,

---

6. Ezra Pound to Henry Ware Eliot, June 28, 1915, *Letters of T. S. Eliot*, 102, hereafter in this essay cited parenthetically in the text by page number alone.

were regarded as semidivine writers by many English and American readers. But Eliot calls these icons "The army of unalterable law," thereby slipping in an ironic allusion to a demonic figure, the "Lucifer in Starlight" of George Meredith's sonnet, implying that the seemingly benevolent poets are also potentially malevolent influences. Taken together, Eliot's three Boston poems make a subtle critique of the narrowness of the New England capital and its female tyrants, and even of the authors they most admired, and since Eliot had himself escaped the family clutches by going to England, these poems may be seen in retrospect as a formal farewell to his family past and to the American provincial scene. If we regard them as expressive of his own rebellion against family influence, at the very moment when he was deciding to expatriate himself for good, we may see these three short poems as something more than a set of memorable descriptive pieces about Boston: they are an irreverent family portrait gallery hung like a set of trophies on Eliot's Oxford wall.

"Morning at the Window," on the other hand, is as much an imagist poem as any Eliot would write, a brief nine lines of free verse that form an impersonal yet depressing sketch of London, indeed of the very street near Russell Square where Eliot lived at the time he met Pound, as we know from his letter of September 8, 1914, to his brother Henry Ware Eliot Jr. The letter describes the view from his window at 28 Bedford Place in unseasonably hot weather, including "a dreadful old woman, her skirt trailing on the street," who is singing as "the housemaid resumes her conversation at the area gate" (p. 55). Eliot's poem begins with the image of "the damp souls of housemaids / Sprouting despondently at area gates," and ends with the image of an "aimless smile" torn from "a passer-by with muddy skirts." What this short poem shows is that Eliot could extend his imagist scenes of Boston in the earlier "Preludes" to London in "Morning at the Window," with the same despondent mood prevailing, a continuation of his realistic yet ironic cityscapes that had their apotheosis eventually in *The Waste Land.*

What was happening poetically in Eliot's mind during his Oxford year is well mirrored in these poems, but what was happening critically and philosophically to his thinking at the same time was more complicated and harder to fathom. It is to be found not only in the letters, but also in the reviews he was writing for philosophical journals and in the dissertation he was writing on Bradley—drier works than the poems, certainly, yet containing further clues to his decision to become a poet rather than a philosopher.

The letters tell us that when he first settled there, Eliot preferred Oxford to Harvard, finding indeed that "I like it quite well enough to wish that I had come here earlier and spent two or three years," partly because he enjoyed the walks around Oxford—"I think that the English countryside is more beautiful than the French"—but mainly because "I have begun to entertain the highest respect for English methods of teaching in addition to the disapproval for our own" (pp. 61, 65). Eliot was glad he had chosen Harold Joachim as his tutor, he wrote, because "J. is perhaps the best lecturer here. He sticks pretty close to the text" (p. 67). And Eliot was still speaking of himself that fall as a philosophy teacher, not as a poet, for he said in the same letter of November 9, 1914, to his philosophy professor, J. H. Woods, at Harvard: "For anyone who is going to teach the Oxford discipline is admirable. It has impressed upon my mind the value of two things: the value of personal instruction in small classes and individually, and the careful study of original texts in the original tongue—in contrast to the synoptic course" (p. 68). Eliot was reading Aristotle in Greek with Harold Joachim and finding it difficult to master the *Posterior Analytics,* but possible with the help of Joachim and an English commentary, and the intellectual rigor of this study, which went beyond any challenge he had encountered at Harvard, would stand him in good stead for the remainder of his life, not as an academic philosopher but as a practicing poet and critic.

For outdoor exercise at Oxford, besides walking, Eliot also enjoyed "rowing violently upon the river in a four oar" (p. 68), and because of his earlier training in crew racing at Harvard, he was chosen the stroke of a crew that won a race with another boat, for which he was awarded a pewter mug inscribed with the names of the victorious crew of the Merton College Junior Fours. When he lost the mug in a later move, he regretted the loss as the only proof of his athletic prowess. However, another member of the crew, James H. St. John, an American Rhodes scholar in history from Iowa, kept his mug with Eliot's name on it and later remembered the thrill of winning it in 1914: "Eliot 'stroked' us to a victory over the other four, even without counting the handicap; and each of us received a small pewter mug, with the arms of Merton College and the names of the crew engraved on it. I really believe that Eliot was sort of a 'spark-plug' in our victory."[7]

While Eliot's letters from Merton College show that he liked both the mental and physical discipline he found at Oxford, they also make it clear that he never had the pleasure of meeting F. H. Bradley in person, because Bradley was a recluse in poor health, and by February of 1915 he was writing to Conrad Aiken to lament, "Oxford I do not enjoy: the food and climate are execrable," and to admit frankly that

> The great need is to know one's own mind, and I don't know that: whether
> I want to get married, and have a family, and live in America all my life,

---

7. James H. St. John, "Some Reminiscences of T. S. Eliot," *Miami Dimensions* magazine (Oxford, Ohio, 1965), 4. St. John became an associate dean of the College of Arts and Science at Miami University in Oxford, Ohio, and donated his cup, inscribed with the names of the team members and "Merton College Junior Fours, 1914"—probably the only one now in existence—to the Dorothy R. Altman Poetry Reading Room of the King Library, where it is on permanent display.

and compromise and conceal my opinions and forfeit my independence for the sake of my children's future; or save my money and retire at fifty to a table on the boulevard, regarding the world placidly through the fumes of an aperitif at 5 p.m.—How thin either life seems![8]

So in spite of his preference for London over Oxford and Pound's encouragement, Eliot was still trying to decide in the winter of 1915 what he would do with his life, but he was feeling more and more discontent with the academic atmosphere and growing disillusioned about his philosophical pursuits, as he confessed in a letter of January 6, 1915, to Norbert Wiener, a Harvard classmate and later a famous mathematician who was then studying with Bertrand Russell at Cambridge. Eliot said he was beginning to make up his mind "to avoid philosophy and devote oneself to *real* art or *real* science. (For philosophy is an unloved guest in either company.)" And he was disparaging about his own efforts to overcome what he called his "relativism" by finishing his dissertation on Bradley:

> I took a piece of fairly technical philosophy for my thesis, and my relativism made me see so many sides to questions that I became hopelessly involved, and wrote a thesis perfectly unintelligible to anyone but myself; and so I wished to rewrite it. It's about Bradley's theory of judgment, and I think the second version will be entirely destructive. . . . —no definition of judgment, that is, is formally either right or wrong; and it simply is a waste of time to define judgment at all. (p. 81)

Near the end of his life, Eliot would see his dissertation in print for the first time; though he had sent a completed copy to Harvard in 1916, and it was accepted, he never returned there to defend his thesis and so never obtained the doctoral degree he had earned. In his 1964 preface to *Knowledge and Experience in the Philosophy of F. H. Bradley,* Eliot said his essay had become unintelligible even to himself: "Forty-six years after my academic philosophizing came to an end, I find myself unable to think in the terminology of this essay. Indeed, I do not pretend to understand it."[9] Eliot's frankness both at the time he was writing his dissertation and at the end of his distinguished literary career shows that he made his choice of a literary rather than a philosophical career wisely, and though he may have exaggerated the unreadability of his work on Bradley, it remains a curiosity among his writings, being far less interesting than either his poetry or his critical prose, because it is much more abstract.

8. Eliot to Aiken, *Letters of T. S. Eliot,* 88.
9. Eliot, *Knowledge and Experience in the Philosophy of F. H. Bradley,* 10.

In a review in the *New Statesman,* which Eliot wrote in 1916, the year after he left Oxford, Eliot set down most clearly the reasons for his deciding not to be an academic philosopher in the United States and for his choosing instead the literary profession in London:

> Mr. Leacock has exposed some of the essential faults of American education, some of the reasons for the insolvency of American literature. He draws a truthful picture of the American graduate student, the prospective Doctor of Philosophy: his specialisation in knowledge, his expansion in ignorance, his laborious dullness, his years of labour and his crowning achievement—the Thesis. . . . This labour is fatal to the development of intellectual powers. It crushes originality, it kills style. Few, very few of these "original contributions" are well written or even readable.[10]

We may guess that Eliot grew tired of his dissertation long before he finished it, and certainly he took little credit for it in his later years; nevertheless, his time at Oxford was not wasted, and Eliot bore witness to the end of his life that he remained in debt to both his tutor, Joachim, and his author, Bradley, at Oxford, for when he consented to having his dissertation on Bradley printed in 1964, he said in his preface, "To Harold Joachim I owe a great deal: the discipline of a close study of the Greek text of the *Posterior Analytics,* and, through his criticism of my weekly papers, an understanding of what I wanted to say and of how to say it." Practically speaking, his Oxford tutor showed Eliot how to improve his skills of reading and writing, and so his thought was clarified by the academic training he received at Merton College, even if his pursuits at the time were excessively dry and abstract. But his debt to Bradley was even greater, for if Eliot acknowledged that he could no longer understand the language of his dissertation, he still maintained that "my own prose style was formed on that of Bradley," and he was struck at the end of his life by "how little it has changed all these years."[11] He must have meant that for him Bradley was an exponent as much of style as of ideas; in other words, Eliot had gone to Oxford not merely to study philosophy but to absorb as much as he could of Bradley's mind, by studying his work in proximity to his person, though he was never to meet the English philosopher and would later write, "Except to the other fellows of Merton College, Oxford—and he is rarely there—he is personally hardly known."[12]

10. Eliot, unsigned review of *Essays and Literary Studies,* by Stephen Leacock, 404.
11. Eliot, *Knowledge and Experience,* 9, 11.
12. Eliot, "A Prediction in Regard to Three English Authors, Writers Who, though Masters of Thought, Are Likewise Masters of Art," *Vanity Fair* (February 1924): 29.

Eliot in leaving Oxford and Bradley behind in 1915, then, was not placing himself outside the sphere of the philosopher's influence, for he wrote admiringly about Bradley well after he had been recognized in London both as poet and critic. In 1924, he placed Bradley in the high company of Henry James and James Frazer as three "writers who, though masters of thought, are likewise masters of art," and praised him as "wholly and solely a philosopher" (in contrast to Bertrand Russell, who had been one of Eliot's philosophy teachers at Harvard), attesting for himself that

> Once you accept his theory of the nature of the judgment, and it is as plausible a theory as any, you are led by his arid and highly sensitive eloquence (no English philosopher has ever written finer English) to something which, according to your temperament, will be resignation or despair—the bewildered despair of wondering why you ever wanted anything, and what it was that you wanted, since this philosophy seems to give you everything that you ask and yet to render it not worth wanting.[13]

In his fuller essay on Bradley in 1927, Eliot would again praise him for his style as much as for his ideas and would make it even clearer why he could admire a writer who seemed impossibly abstract, as Bradley did to many readers, and who as a thinker seemed the ultimate skeptic. He spoke of Bradley's manner as being "a curious blend of humility and irony" and went on to characterize his style in ways that sound reminiscent of Eliot himself:

> And many readers, having in mind Bradley's polemical irony and his obvious zest in using it, his habit of discomfiting an opponent with a sudden profession of ignorance, of inability to understand, or of incapacity for abstruse thought, have concluded that this is all a mere pose—and even a somewhat unscrupulous one. But deeper study of Bradley's mind convinces us that the modesty is real, and his irony the weapon of a modest and highly sensitive man.[14]

Anyone who wants to understand why Bradley so fascinated the young Eliot as to draw him all the way to Oxford and then to become the principal model for Eliot's mature prose style—one of the most masterful styles in modern English—should reflect on this description. The philosopher's zest for irony and his frequent profession of ignorance carried over to Eliot the critic, and link both Bradley and Eliot to Socrates, whose most effective weapon

---

13. Ibid., 98.
14. Eliot, "Francis Herbert Bradley," in T. S. Eliot, *Selected Essays*, 394–95.

throughout the Platonic dialogues is the ironic profession of ignorance: indeed, Eliot praised Bradley with the paradoxical statement that "scepticism and disillusion are a useful equipment for religious understanding," and said approvingly that "the tendency of his labours is to bring British philosophy closer to the Greek tradition."[15]

When we read Eliot, then, we are reading Bradley through his eyes, because Eliot employed Bradley's English version of Socratic irony consistently in his writing. To compare passages from *Appearance and Reality*—which Eliot regarded as Bradley's *Metaphysics* and which he immortalized with a direct quotation in one of the longer notes to *The Waste Land*—with passages from Eliot's early critical essays is to see just how closely the younger writer stuck to the older writer's example, though he was applying his mind to concrete works of literature while Bradley had applied his mind to abstract thought. Thus Bradley, in chapter 33 of *Appearance and Reality*, entitled "Body and Soul" (the source of the passage Eliot used in the notes to *The Waste Land*), wrote that it is the nature of the self to pass beyond itself and that "self-sacrifice is also a form of self-realization," and this sentiment is echoed in Eliot's famous and equally paradoxical pronouncement in "Tradition and the Individual Talent" (1919), "The progress of an artist is a continual self-sacrifice, a continual extinction of personality." And again, Bradley wrote in his introduction to *Appearance and Reality*, "I certainly do not suppose it would be good for everyone to study metaphysics . . . but there is no other certain way of protecting ourselves against dogmatic superstition," while Eliot wrote in "The Metaphysical Poets" (1921), "It is not a permanent necessity that poets should be interested in philosophy, or in any other subject. We can only say that it appears likely that poets in our civilization, as it exists at present, must be *difficult*."[16]

To say that Eliot was a disciple of Bradley throughout his life would be stretching the influence further than Eliot himself would have wished (he said that he came nearer to being a disciple of Henri Bergson, whose lectures he attended in Paris in 1910), but we can say that Eliot picked up from Bradley some characteristic features of style, notably an ironic self-deprecation, which he brought to a higher degree of perfection in his prose, just as he picked up from Laforgue certain bitingly ironic turns of phrase that he raised to higher perfection in his poetry. We can also say that Eliot found Bradley's skeptical idealism an attractive philosophy when he was young and used it effectively to support his image of the "prison of self" in *The Waste Land*, placing near the end of his poem, as a gloss on "each in his prison, thinking of the key," a note

---

15. Ibid., 404.

16. F. H. Bradley, *Appearance and Reality*, 369; Eliot, *Selected Essays*, 7; Bradley, *Appearance and Reality*, 4; Eliot, *Selected Essays*, 248.

from Bradley's *Appearance and Reality* beside a note from Dante's *Inferno*, thus equating Bradley's argument that the self is limited to appearance, or the world of physical sensation, and is excluded from reality, or the realm of the Absolute, with Dante's fearsome image of a soul in torment in the lowest circle of hell, where Count Ugolino starves in a tower with his sons, imprisoned and unable to escape a horrifying death. Later, however, Eliot used Bradley more positively, since in *Four Quartets* the word *reality* is used as Bradley used it, to mean the realm of the Absolute, his abstract term for God, notably in the memorable line of "Burnt Norton," "Human kind / Cannot bear very much reality." Hence we may conclude that Bradley was a continued influence on Eliot's poetic ideas as well as on his prose style throughout his career.

Eliot did not regard Bradley as the ultimate philosopher, however; that was an accolade he reserved for Aristotle, because Aristotle had become what Eliot would call "the perfect critic." It was at Oxford, while studying the philosophy of F. H. Bradley under Harold Joachim, that Eliot acquired his lasting respect for Aristotle. His essay "The Perfect Critic" appeared in his first book of criticism, *The Sacred Wood*, published in 1920. In it he credits Aristotle with being a greater critic than Coleridge, whom Eliot calls "the greatest of English critics, and in a sense the last," because Coleridge was "philosophic" in the derogatory sense of using metaphysical abstractions, whereas Aristotle was "primarily a man of not only remarkable but universal intelligence," who could apply his thought to any subject impersonally and who knew instinctively that "there is no method except to be very intelligent." Thus in Eliot's view Aristotle provided the only true example of the perfect critic, "for everything that Aristotle says illuminates the literature which is the occasion for saying it."

Eliot defined in this early essay better than anywhere else his own critical ideal: "The end of the enjoyment of poetry is a pure contemplation from which all the accidents of personal emotion are removed," and it is evident that such a contemplative state led Eliot, even that early in his career, beyond literature and philosophy toward religion, where he recognized already, long before his conversion from Unitarianism to Anglo-Catholic Christianity, that "without a labour which is largely a labour of intelligence, we are unable to attain that stage of vision *amor intellectualis Dei* [the intellectual love of God]." Thus Bradley led Eliot toward Aristotle, and Aristotle led him toward an analytic yet visionary reading of literature that was ultimately Christian. At the end of his landmark essay "Tradition and the Individual Talent" in 1919, Eliot quoted Aristotle in Greek:

ὁ δὲ νοῦς ἴσως θειότερόν τι χαὶ ἀπαθές ἐστιν
[but mind is doubtless something more divine and is impassive]
(Aristotle, *De Anima*, 1.4.408b.29)

And Eliot used this sentence, which he must have discovered at Oxford, to say that his remarks about the relation between the literary tradition and the individual artist would have to "halt at the frontier of metaphysics or mysticism," as Eliot himself would have halted at the time. Eliot was an admitted skeptic and relativist as a young man, who willingly followed Bradley up to a certain point in his thinking because Bradley too halted at the frontier of what he called the Absolute. But later Eliot would carry both his poetry and his criticism beyond the frontier of metaphysics and mysticism, into the realm of invisible realities that faith alone could penetrate, where Dante was the supreme poet, in Eliot's view, and mystics such as St. John of the Cross were his guides toward those moments of Incarnation that are the poet's quest in *Four Quartets*. Bradley's philosophy had led Eliot further toward religious belief than he had anticipated by showing him that the "self" was elusive and always reached beyond itself, and that "our common everyday knowledge is on the whole true as far as it goes, but that we do not know how far it does go," that is to say, Eliot saw that empiricism pursued to the limit, as Bradley relentlessly pursued it, might find itself confronting a world beyond the senses, the world of the Absolute, or Reality.

Thus in the year 1914–1915 Eliot discovered the poet in himself with the help of Pound and the critic in himself with the help of Bradley and Aristotle, and he could leave the philosopher in himself behind at Oxford while taking up the dual roles of poet and critic in London, finding, as he wrote at the end of his essay on Aristotle, that "the two directions of sensibility are complementary; and as sensibility is rare, unpopular, and desirable, it is to be expected that the critic and the creative artist should frequently be the same person." They were the same person in Eliot, even more than in Pound or Yeats among the major poets of the century, and his philosophical training made the critic in him work always closely with the creator, whether he was writing poetry or prose.

On July 10, 1915, Eliot wrote to J. H. Woods at Harvard, asking him to withdraw his application for renewal of his traveling fellowship, and explaining, "My reason for resigning is that I wish now to remain in London and engage in literary work. This may perhaps seem a sanguinary choice and is admittedly a great risk." He mentioned that all he had was "an initial literary capital of eight guineas from *Poetry* in Chicago," but he had a new wife and the encouragement of Pound to bolster him. As he settled firmly into the literary profession in London, he wrote to his brother Henry on July 2, 1915, "I feel more alive than I ever have before."[17]

17. *Letters of T. S. Eliot,* 109, 105.

Myth and Anti-Myth: The Strange Fertility of *The Waste Land*

> What are the roots that clutch, what branches grow
> Out of this stony rubbish? Son of man,
> You cannot say, or guess, for you know only
> A heap of broken images, where the sun beats,
> And the dead tree gives no shelter, the cricket no relief,
> And the dry stone no sound of water.
> (*The Waste Land*, 1.19–24)

These lines sound like a litany for a dead civilization; they express a condition of doubt and disbelief so deep that the only affirmation possible is one of imminent catastrophe. It does not lessen their impact that they were written early in the century, in the period after World War I, for the sense of crisis is still present, and the disillusionment they express has been repeated many times since, meaning that we have not yet found a way out of the Waste Land, which is still the central symbol of Western civilization for the whole twentieth century. Our age has been haunted by a nightmarish vision from which it seems impossible to wake up; visions of a final Apocalypse are as familiar in the twentieth century as visions of unspoiled Nature were in the nineteenth century.

Eliot's lines can still cause readers to shudder, despite the fact that the dark prophecies they contain of the collapse of civilization have not come to pass. We are still living in one of the most violent centuries of human history: the second world war brought us nearer to the brink of universal catastrophe than the first, and the unprecedented nuclear explosions that ended it still threaten us with a third world war and the possibility of a real apocalypse. The powerful death wish of Western civilization has been expressed in some of the greatest works of modern art and literature, and yet the end has not come. Is it only a matter of time until we destroy civilization finally, or is that probability only symbolic? Symbols have the power to move us most when their source is most mysterious, and it is possible that we have not yet understood the masterpieces of our age fully enough: in particular, we do not know whether their prophecies are more of fact than of myth, whether they are predictions of the immediate future or connections with the remote past.

If civilization as we know it does survive into another century, and if people continue reading these lines of poetry, they may read them less as prophecies than as myths, proof that great works of literature may not merely describe the present condition of men but link the living with the dead, reawakening our collective memory of the precariousness of the human situation, not only now but throughout history. Then the true meaning of works as darkly eloquent as

"Sunday Morning," "The Second Coming," *Hugh Selwyn Mauberley,* and *The Waste Land* may be clearer, as bearing witness to supernatural events outside of time that may affect human lives inside time. Prophecies tell us miracles may occur; myths tell us they have occurred.

The question at the heart of modern literature is whether, given the suicidal tendencies of civilization, belief in supernatural events is still possible, that is, whether there is some lingering sense that things have happened before the beginning of time and things will happen after the end of time, subjecting us to a supratemporal destiny that is the source of myth. Yeats asked in his essay "The Symbolism of Poetry" as early as 1900: "How can the arts overcome the slow dying of men's hearts that we call the progress of the world, and lay their hands upon men's heart-strings again, without becoming the garment of religion as in old times?" And he answered his question a few years later in an essay called "Discoveries": "All symbolic art should arise out of a real belief, and that it cannot do so in this age proves that this age is a road and not a resting-place for the imaginative arts."[18] But Yeats was not discouraged, and he went on to write some of the most impressive symbolic works of the century and to fit them into an overarching visionary system that dared, as in the poem "Byzantium," to "hail the superhuman / I call it death-in-life and life-in-death." And Pound spoke just as openly in his early essays of some invisible reality discernible to the human imagination, saying in 1910 in *The Spirit of Romance:* "I believe in a sort of permanent basis in humanity, that is to say, I believe that Greek myth arose when someone having passed through delightful psychic experience tried to communicate it to others and found it necessary to screen himself from persecution. Speaking aesthetically, the myths are explications of mood."[19] Both Yeats and Pound worked from symbolism toward myth in their poetry, from a personal to an impersonal or superpersonal level of experience, and both succeeded in giving new meaning to old myths—the traditional role poets have played in Western culture—but not in a traditional way, since they made highly unconventional uses of myth.

Myth, in the sense we understand it in modern literature, is not an explanation of natural phenomena, as it was for primitive people, or a credible narrative of supernatural and natural happenings, as it was for the Greeks. Myth in the modern sense is a psychic image of subconscious wishes or fears that recall similar emotions felt by people in the past, out of either history or legend, and so it gives us the sense of participating in the continuity of human experience; it connects a time when people did believe in supernatural realities—call them ghosts, fairies, or gods—with a time when people no

18. Yeats, *Essays and Introductions,* 162–63, 294.
19. Ezra Pound, *The Spirit of Romance,* 92.

longer consciously believe in them, yet somehow cannot understand their deepest feelings without them. The apocalyptic visions of twentieth-century literature are descriptions of the present in the light of the past, and for that reason, they are prophecies not simply of the end of our particular civilization, but of the end of all civilization, fusing moments of human destiny together as a sequence of tragedies: the Fall of Troy, the Fall of Rome, the Waste Land of medieval romance, the Second Coming of Christ.

Though Yeats and Pound helped people understand the modern sense of myth, it was Eliot who probably defined it most fully for our age when he wrote his essay "*Ulysses*, Order, and Myth" in 1923, in response to Joyce's *Ulysses*, which he recognized as a new and highly effective literary use of myth:

> In using the myth, in manipulating a continuous parallel between contemporaneity and antiquity, Mr. Joyce is pursuing a method which others must pursue after him. They will not be imitators, any more than the scientist who uses the discoveries of Einstein in pursuing his own, independent investigations. It is simply a way of controlling, of ordering, of giving a shape and a significance to the immense panorama of futility and anarchy which is contemporary history. It is a method already adumbrated by Mr. Yeats, and of the need for which I believe Mr. Yeats to have been the first contemporary to be conscious. It is a method for which the horoscope is auspicious. Psychology (such as it is, whether our reaction to it be comic or serious), ethnology, and *The Golden Bough* have concurred to make possible what was impossible even a few years ago. Instead of narrative method, we may now use the mythical method. It is, I seriously believe, a step toward making the modern world possible for art.[20]

What Eliot spoke of as "the mythical method" was really an adaptation of myth to a scientific and skeptical age. Eliot mentions science favorably in his definition of myth, citing psychology, ethnology, and anthropology (*The Golden Bough*, by James Frazer) as bases for myth and comparing Joyce with Einstein, a theoretical physicist, as the discoverer of a method by which artists of the present can order their experience through myth. Unlike Pound and Yeats, Eliot emphasized the rational choice of the artist, needing no validation of belief but presenting modern experience in juxtaposition with earlier myths, classical or Christian, as a technique that in itself would be enough to convince the reader of the truth embodied in his fiction, leaving it to him to make as much or as little of the connection between myth and reality as he might. Eliot did not ask readers to believe in myth, but to see its relevance to events or images the novelist or poet might choose even now to project.

---

20. T. S. Eliot, "*Ulysses*, Order, and Myth," in *Selected Prose of T. S. Eliot*, 177–78.

Eliot's definition helps to explain better than any other how modern writers have made effective use of myth. Joyce in his novel does not ask the reader to believe in the heroic exploits of Ulysses, but to assume that they are somehow remotely connected with the story of Leopold Bloom, the wandering Irish Jew, in his rambles about the city of Dublin on one particular day, June 16, 1904, meeting Stephen Dedalus, a young Irish artist, and returning home to his wife, Molly Bloom, a singer. Joyce's narrative is so full of naturalistic details that it can be followed on a map of Dublin, while the parallel with Ulysses' journey back from the Trojan War and across the eastern Mediterranean to his native island of Ithaca, where his wife, Penelope, and his son, Telemachus, wait for him, is never explicitly stated, except by means of the title, leaving the reader to see as much of the analogy as he can make out—which may be nothing at all if he has never read Homer's *Odyssey*, or may be a point-by-point correspondence of every episode if he knows the original Greek epic thoroughly and if he has the patience to follow it through Joyce's subjective stream-of-consciousness narration. It is the sort of parallel that requires a highly ingenious writer to construct and a highly ingenious reader to follow, yet the myth is there, and, as Eliot insisted, it does give a deeper meaning to the novel.

Similarly, Yeats does not ask us to believe that each of the poems in his huge *Collected Poems* has an appointed place on the gyres of history elaborated in *A Vision*, but there is no doubt that the parallels exist for those who know both the poems and the vision and that they add a dimension of meaning to the individual poems as well as to the whole collection, at any rate for readers who find such fascination in Yeats's poetry that they want to understand it as fully as possible. Eliot gave Yeats credit for discovering the new mythical method even before Joyce, and even before he wrote *A Vision*, and so we know that what he was speaking about was an emergent pattern in Yeats's work rather than a completed system. Though Yeats had once insisted that artistic symbolism required the support of religious belief, by the time he introduced *A Vision* to the world, he had changed his tactics—if not his mind—so that he left the question of his own belief open to doubt:

> Some will ask whether I believe in the actual existence of my circuits of the sun and moon. . . . to such a question I can only answer that if sometimes, overwhelmed by miracle as all men must be when in the midst of it, I have taken such periods literally, my reason has soon recovered; and now that the system stands out clearly in my imagination I regard them as stylistic arrangements of experience comparable to the cubes in the drawings of Wyndham Lewis and to the ovoids in the sculpture on Brancusi. They have helped me to hold in a single thought reality and justice.[21]

21. Yeats, *A Vision*, 24–25.

Yeats used other arts, rather than sciences, in explaining his mythological figures, but the same skepticism was present in his mind as in Eliot's regarding the credibility of the myths he used.

For Pound in the *Cantos,* there is a still different use of mythical parallels to thread through his sequence of 117 poems and to provide the disparate fragments with a semblance of unity. Chiefly, Pound used Homer's *Odyssey,* Ovid's *Metamorphoses,* and Dante's *Divine Comedy* as his mythical sources, beginning with Ulysses' descent into hell, where he summons the spirits of the dead to guide him on his journey; continuing with the metamorphoses of Dionysus out of Ovid, where a young boy captured as a slave on a boat bound for Naxos suddenly becomes a god and transforms the ship into grapevines and the crew into dolphins; and eventually entering Dante's hell and moving among the usurers and sodomites on his way toward an envisioned purgatory and paradise. Pound left the question of his belief in these myths as open as Yeats did, writing in his *Guide to Kulchur,* "I assert that the gods exist," but admitting, "That anyone 'believes' now seems doubtful," and ostensibly settling for a latter-day Christian humanism by saying, "I believe in the benign influence of *litterae humaniores.*"[22] Some of the *Cantos* show Pound's fascination with Greek religion, especially the Eleusinian mysteries, with their initiatory ceremonies uniting sexual and vegetal rites, and the Dionysian orgies or frenzied dances of women. And it is late in the *Cantos* that he admits "The gods have not returned" (Canto 113). There are many myths active in Pound's poem, but he leaves it very much to the reader to guess whether there are real gods in them, just as did Joyce and Yeats.

Eliot, in his famous notes to *The Waste Land,* linked his poem directly to two works of anthropology, Frazer's *Golden Bough* and Jessie L. Weston's *From Ritual to Romance,* suggesting that "any reader familiar with these works will immediately recognize in the poem certain references to vegetation ceremonies." He does not mention myth at all; he mentions primitive religious rites, and so far as he uses myth in the poem itself, it is much more implicit than explicit. We are not asked to believe that the legend of the Holy Grail is true, but only that many of its elements—the Fisher King, the Chapel Perilous, the Waste Land of the title—are visibly present in the modern city, which is described realistically but by means of fragmentary scenes and snatches of conversation rather than by a continuous narrative. In short, the myths that are involved in the major works of modern literature are not offered as true in themselves, but as providing glimpses of meaning and order amidst the relatively meaningless chaos of modern existence, calling to mind resemblances between a fragmented present and a remote but orderly past, a past still relevant, containing a unifying belief in a supernatural divinity, with

22. Pound, *Guide to Kulchur,* 302.

real gods and heroes—conspicuously absent in the modern city that is the Waste Land of Eliot's poem.

The resemblances are not so much similarities as incongruities, sharp contrasts between present and past. If the original use of myths was to entertain audiences and at the same time instruct them in the basic articles of their religion, the modern use is to startle and shock the audience into an awareness of radical discontinuity with the past. To see Ulysses drinking in a Dublin pub, or the Fisher King sitting on the Thames embankment, is to experience a jarring conjunction of myth and reality, which causes the reader not so much to believe in its probability as to be aware of its improbability. The "mythic method" Eliot praised in Joyce's novel has strangely disquieting effects, creating discords more often than harmonies. In fact, so far as myths enter into the modern imagination, they are like the metaphysical conceits of Donne or Herbert or Marvell, which Samuel Johnson described as "two ideas yoked together by violence." Metaphysical imagery does reappear in modern poetry, along with the ironic use of myth. It is absurd to think that Homer's many-minded Greek hero Ulysses might be transformed into a Jewish advertising agent moving about the streets of Dublin, and yet that is just what Joyce forces on the reader of his novel; it is equally absurd to suppose that the Holy Grail might suddenly be seen in the streets of London, yet that is the quest that Eliot invites his reader to undertake. The real Ulysses and the true Grail never appear in Joyce's novel or in Eliot's poem; they are only implied as ironic contrasts to the characters and situations described, which are for the most part petty and sordid scenes of city life, hardly the stuff of epic or romance. The amount of mythical material actually used by Eliot and Joyce is slight: a reader could hardly reconstruct the events of the *Odyssey* or *Le Morte d'Arthur* from *Ulysses* or *The Waste Land;* he must know them from outside the works, from other sources or from footnotes. The most concrete use of myth in either the novel or the poem is to be found in their titles; the rest is left to the reader's knowledge and imagination.

If his title is the only explicit reference to the myth, then we must ask whether Eliot's "mythical method" is not really an "anti-mythical method," and whether "making the modern world possible for art" is not really making it seem more improbable than ever? Improbable it may be, but the most impressive modern uses of myth, whether by Joyce, Yeats, Eliot, or Pound, are as much anti-myth as myth, so ironic in their contrast of the mythical and the real as to imply that supernatural events of any kind can only be seen in direct opposition to the monotony and triviality, the constant boredom, the purely material satisfactions, of daily life in the modern city.

Yet whether we call them myth or anti-myth, these works have given and still give interpretations of experience that help to make sense of it, as only the greatest works of art can do. By presenting the worst possibilities of civilization, forcing on us images of violence and degradation so extreme as to make us believe that the end of the world must be near, they cause us to weigh our destiny on a cosmic scale, to see with Eliot "fear in a handful of dust" in *The Waste Land* or to be conducted by J. Alfred Prufrock through

> Streets that follow like a tedious argument
> Of insidious intent
> To lead us to an overwhelming question.

The question is never asked, only implied, and the answer, if there is one, is to be found in the continuing relevance of myths that seem so buried in our collective memories that they are like the dead struggling to be reborn. We may agree with Pound that "The gods have not returned" and yet at the same time agree with his afterthought that "They have never left us"; or, to put it another way, certain masterworks of modern literature make us feel that the ancient myths that seem so contrary to our experience may still communicate meanings that are vital to us, that would otherwise be lost. In an age of irony such as ours, it may be said that only the unbelievable can be believed.

Of all the anti-myths of the twentieth century, none has had a more pervasive influence than *The Waste Land*—perhaps the greatest irony of all, for how can a poem about sterility have proved so fertile? It has been analyzed and explicated over and over, and yet it remains an enigma; its obscurity has only enhanced its fame; it continues to be a most improbable masterpiece; yet somehow we cannot get beyond it or out of it. We know that it was not so much composed in a rational way as thrown together out of many incongruous pieces. Eliot spoke of the original manuscript as "a sprawling chaotic poem" and confessed that he gave it to Pound for editing because he did not know how to do the job himself. When Pound returned it, the poem had been reduced to half its length, to "the form in which it now appears," Eliot attested. He not only accepted Pound's many excisions, but later said, when the original manuscript was lost, that if it ever turned up again it would be proof of "Pound's critical genius." The mysterious disappearance of the manuscript added another twist to the labyrinth of the poem, and when it did finally come to light after Eliot's death, it made good Eliot's claim that Pound had contributed significantly to the finished poem, since it was clear that every line red-penciled by Pound was well abandoned: few critics have suggested that any of the omitted lines should be restored. What remained was a curious collaboration of poet and editor, which Pound with characteristic humor celebrated in sardonic verses when he returned the final version of the manuscript:

> These are the poems of Eliot
> By the Uranian Muse begot;
> A Man their mother was,
> A Muse their Sire.

How did the printed Infancies result
From Nuptials thus doubly difficult

If you must needs enquire
Know diligent Reader
that on each Occasion
Ezra performed the Caesarean Operation.[23]

We might almost think, with all we now know about the strange origin of the poem—Eliot's nervous breakdown, his wife's hysteria, his need for editorial help from Pound—that *The Waste Land* not only uses myth but is itself a mythical creation: surely no great poem has ever seemed as mysteriously fated as this one.

When the original manuscript was published in 1971, some mysteries were cleared up, but others emerged for the first time, since it was discovered that Eliot's original title for the poem had been "He Do the Police in Different Voices," an unlikely allusion to an unlikely source, *Our Mutual Friend*, Charles Dickens's mid-Victorian novel about London. *The Waste Land* depends for much of its meaning on its title, yet the title was the poet's last inspiration rather than his first. Eliot never really explained his title, even in the notes he added after the poem simultaneously appeared in October 1922 in the *Dial* in New York and in the *Criterion*, Eliot's own magazine, in London; when he published the poem as a book, he let it be known for the first time that the title came from a scholarly study of medieval versions of the Grail legend, Jessie L. Weston's *From Ritual to Romance*, rather than from a literary source such as Malory's medieval English narrative, *Le Morte d'Arthur*. Eliot must have been seeking a more explicit connection with the Grail myth, and in view of the fact that the Weston book was new at the time Eliot was working on his poem, it can be surmised that he found the right title for the completed poem in a book he happened to read while he was trying to put the various parts of the poem together, meaning that it was a fortuitous event like the composition and editing of the poem, the result more of creative coincidence than of a deliberate plan. Once he did find the right title, however, the rest of the poem seemed to fall into place around it, as Pound was quick to sense when he cut the poem down to fit the title, bringing order into the chaos by removing many lines irrelevant to the underlying myth of the Holy Grail.

This myth was itself originally a series of connected tales rather than a single story, and it had been written down in French and German as well as in English during the Middle Ages, when Christian belief was at its strongest

23. *Letters of Ezra Pound, 1907–1941*, 170.

throughout Europe. It included many adventures of the Knights of the Round Table, such as battles and love affairs, but centered on the quest for the chalice in which Christ's blood was supposed to have been caught at the crucifixion— not so much a quest for the chalice itself as for a vision of the Holy Grail, which only a knight of pure heart and absolute faith could ever hope to see. In the various versions of the myth, only three knights had such a vision, Sir Galahad, Sir Perceval, and Sir Bors, and it came to them in the midst of a desolate country where the crops had been withered by a long drought and the king had suffered a wound that made him impotent along with all the other human beings in his kingdom. The renewal of life in the Waste Land of the medieval romances depends on the vision of the Holy Grail, after the knight has visited the king and gone to pray for his restoration to health. In the original Grail legends, the knight enters the Chapel Perilous, prays for the renewal of life, and is granted the vision of the Holy Grail; he then returns to touch the wound of the king with his lance, whereupon the king's wound is healed and the land and the people become fertile again.

From all this nexus of stories, Eliot chose the one about the Waste Land for his theme, led in that direction by Weston, who believed it was the center of the Grail legends, but led even more by his own intuition that the modern world had become a place of sterility and living death. Seizing on the element of the Grail legend that had the greatest contemporary relevance, he applied it to the poems he had composed over a period of about three years, accepting as he made his choice the strong argument Weston made in her book:

> The misfortunes of the land have been treated rather as an accident, than as an essential, of the Grail story, entirely subordinate in interest to the *dramatis personae* of the tale, or the objects, Lance and Grail, round which the action revolves. As a matter of fact I believe that the "Waste Land" is really the very heart of our problem; a rightful appreciation of its position and significance will place us in possession of the clue which will lead us safely through the most bewildering mazes of the fully developed tale.[24]

What the anthropologist meant by calling the Waste Land the heart of the Grail legends was of course different from what the poet meant: to her, it put the seasonal vegetation rites ahead of the Christian sacraments in the evolution of the legends into courtly romances, while to him, it put the symbol of nature violated and made sterile by man, the modern city as Waste Land, at the center of his poem.

We have only to think of what Tennyson did with the Grail legends in *The Idylls of the King* to appreciate the difference between that romantic

---

24. Jessie L. Weston, *From Ritual to Romance*, 63–64.

treatment of myth and the modern treatment of myth in *The Waste Land.*
Tennyson's poem concentrated on the characters and actions in an idealized
pastoral setting; it was a faithful retelling of the main episodes of *Le Morte
d'Arthur,* presented as historical narrative and expressed in traditional English
blank verse. Eliot's poem is a series of fragmentary passages, in a mixture of
free verse, blank verse, and rhyming quatrains, which never retells the story,
mentions none of the kings or queens or knights or ladies, and contains
no vision of the Holy Grail. Indeed, Eliot's use of the Grail myth is more
remarkable for what it leaves out than for what it includes; once he has
mentioned the myth in his title, he makes it almost invisible in his poem:
no poet ever made more effective use of ironic symbolism than did Eliot in
The Waste Land.

And that is just the point of the poem, for the change from romanticism
to modernism can be summed up in the contrast between Tennyson's epic
and Eliot's epic. Eliot transforms Tennyson's ideal nature into naturalism and
his moral purity into moral perversity, and he infuses all the symbolism
with irony. Readers of Tennyson's poem are transported into a realm of
fantasy where nature and man are better than they really are, a nostalgic
dream of medieval chivalry, while readers of Eliot's poem are transported
into a fallen realm of nature sterilized and man made impotent, a hellish
artificial landscape where people live among "a heap of broken images" and
contemplate "the broken fingernails of dirty hands." Tennyson beguiled his
readers with a dream world drawn from Arthurian romance, quite in contrast
to real life in Victorian England, while Eliot shocked his readers into seeing
the world of the modern city at its worst, implying that it is more like the
Waste Land of the Grail legend than like the court of King Arthur at Camelot.
Eliot used the same body of myth, but in a way opposite to Tennyson's: he
made it an ironic symbol for his anti-mythical epic. Eliot is the revolutionary
traditionalist violently transforming his sources in order to force them into
contact with contemporary experience.

In *The Waste Land,* we see the modern city as it is, nature desecrated by
man, but what we do not see is as important as what we see: the mythical
possibility of rebirth and regeneration. This land that is now laid waste,
"breeding lilacs out of the dead land," was once fertile soil; these people
now isolated from each other, "each in his prison, thinking of the key," were
once capable of loving and of being loved. The Fisher King sits fishing "with
the arid land behind me," and the Chapel Perilous is empty, "only the wind's
home," making a vision of the Holy Grail—by which the land and people
could be restored to vitality—unthinkable, because there is no one pure
enough of heart and strong enough of faith to see this missing symbol of
immortality. *The Waste Land* ends, as it begins, in desolation; the quester
never sees the Grail, the life-giving rain never falls on the parched landscape,

and the overwhelming question remains in the reader's mind: is the Grail invisible because it never existed, or only because we have lost the power to see it? The poem never answers the question, but it leaves a lingering doubt. The myth is left incomplete as the poem is; its fragmentary form forces us to look for a hidden unity, and its incompleteness creates a desire for completeness. Every reader thus may see in the poem a mirror of his own state of mind: it is a poem of doubt, and also a poem of belief; the reader is left to draw his own conclusions about whether the Waste Land will ever be fertile again—as readers have been doing for most of this century. If there is any way out of this anti-mythical Waste Land, each reader must find it for himself—accounting, perhaps, for the poem's persistent appeal, since we can hear it, as people once heard the Oracle of Delphi or the Voice of the Thunder in the Hindu Upanishad, as a highly prophetic enigma, the meaning of which escapes us.

In an age of doubt, skepticism, and disbelief, Eliot's anti-mythical poem may be the only means of communicating belief, because it depends not on the reader's prior belief but on his willingness to see connections with myth that are the foundation of belief; if myths are relevant to our experience, even ironically, then the possibility of a transcendent order of reality is not wholly lost. I. A. Richards, one of the first critics to respond sympathetically to the poem, said that it represents "the complete separation between his poetry and *all* beliefs," but Eliot responded to this compliment by saying, "I cannot see that poetry can ever be separated from something which I should call belief," allowing as he did for the possibility that "doubt and uncertainty are merely a variety of belief." It may be that the poem that seemed to be about the end of belief and of civilization itself will turn out to be about the beginning of both: an ancient myth about physical and spiritual rebirth resuscitated, extended forward in time to touch and quicken what Eliot termed "the living death of modern material civilization."[25] We see only the negative side of the myth that Eliot wanted us to see; the positive side remains hidden, but perhaps not permanently so.

Largely because of its negativism, its devastating criticism of the urban industrial civilization we inhabit, *The Waste Land* has proved to be the most durable and influential poem of the twentieth century. And we may well ask ourselves: if the poem has its basis in myth, and the criticism of modern civilization it voices is true, then how can the myth be false? We may ask further, if the poem can be negatively relevant for so long, can it also become positively relevant, that is, can anti-myth become myth? The poem continues to leave those questions in the reader's mind, as Eliot may have meant for it

---

25. T. S. Eliot, "A Note on Poetry and Belief," 16; Eliot, *After Strange Gods,* 65.

to do: the reader of *The Waste Land* himself becomes a quester for the Grail, and Eliot's irony does its work, leaving an unseen vision to haunt us with the hope of an unfulfilled prophecy, for if it ever were fulfilled, the world would no longer be a Waste Land, and some new myth would have to take its place.

To Doubt Yet Be Devout: The Lesson of the Later Eliot

Radical skepticism and withering cynicism leading toward total despair were the immediate messages of *The Waste Land*, when it appeared simultaneously in the *Dial* in New York and in the *Criterion* in London in 1922. As a result of the shock waves it produced, Eliot became an international literary celebrity almost overnight and might easily have gone on writing poems full of disillusionment and pessimism for the rest of his career. *The Waste Land* was his most "popular" poem, in the sense that it was known to readers everywhere because of the scandal it created, and though few professed to understand it, the impact of the poem reached far beyond those few, just as Einstein's Theory of Relativity was known far beyond the circle of those who understood it. The notoriety of *The Waste Land* was greater than its readership, and having created the sort of sensation writers dream of, Eliot might have been tempted to go on writing poetic sequels, but he did not. Except for "The Hollow Men" in 1925 and *Sweeney Agonistes* in 1927 Eliot refused to follow the path of least resistance that *The Waste Land* had created and chose instead to write poetry of a very different kind, as radical in its way as *The Waste Land* had been.

Rather than separating poetry from belief, as I. A. Richards had credited him with achieving in *The Waste Land*, Eliot reversed himself: starting with "Journey of the Magi" in 1927 and *Ash Wednesday* in 1930, and culminating in the *Four Quartets* from 1935 to 1942, Eliot reunited poetry and belief, restoring the traditional link between them to become, in the latter half of his career, the major Christian poet of the century. It was a dramatic turnaround, which left many of his intellectual admirers speechless, feeling betrayed by a poet who in his early career had seemed to mirror the loss of all civilized values and then in his later career expressed the possibility, however remote, of the renewal of traditional, orthodox Christian faith.

If Milton set himself the task, as he said in *Paradise Lost*, "to justify God's ways to man," Eliot may be said to have set himself the opposite task, to justify man's ways to God. The ways of man are the ways of sinners and doubters, rather than of firm believers, and Eliot's poetry is eloquent in its expression of doubt, more hesitant in its expression of belief. In Puritan seventeenth-century England, Milton could assume a community of belief in God, making the poet's task welcome and widely appreciated, whereas Eliot's task in twentieth-century England and America, a time of general agnosticism, was lonely and thankless for the most part, since to accomplish it meant, as he put it, "to recover the sense of religious fear, so that it may be overcome by religious hope."[26] For Eliot, belief must be tested constantly against unbelief to determine whether it is strong enough to survive without a supporting community of believers.

It did survive, and Eliot arguably became the Milton of the twentieth century, but his Christianity and his poetry passed through several stages of trial, with three principal poems as their focus: *The Waste Land, Ash Wednesday,* and *Four Quartets.* Each of the three major poems is distinctive in form, mood, and meaning; all three are as unique as any poems written in an age of radical experiment, and each new form expressed a new phase in Eliot's spiritual evolution.

Eliot wrote *The Waste Land* in the dramatic-impersonal form, *Ash Wednesday* in liturgical-personal form, and *Four Quartets* in musical-philosophical form. He expressed the attitude of doubt in the first poem, of prayer in the second, and of vision in the third, which shows how remarkable was his metamorphosis from doubter to believer and demonstrates visibly that Eliot's faith, like his art, was never static but always dynamic, mirroring his constant struggle between soul and body, self and world, the human and the divine, with no certainty about the outcome. Though there seems to be a line of progress from *The Waste Land* to *Ash Wednesday* to *Four Quartets* that is analogous to the stages of hell, purgatory, and paradise in Dante's *Divine Comedy,* there is no direct allegorical parallel, since Eliot's poems are not symmetrical like Dante's masterpiece, but appear fragmentary and disorderly, as incoherent as nightmares or dreams, yet expressing a coherence of inner intuition, a spiritual quest for divine revelation, for meaning in the midst of meaninglessness and for order in the midst of disorder.

The Grail symbolism is implied in *The Waste Land,* where the quester is an unidentified voice among many voices, who searches in vain for some valid belief but finds it nowhere, and ends with the unanswered question "Shall I at least set my lands in order?" to which the tangle of multilingual quotations at the end suggests a negative answer or none at all. Though the Voice of the Thunder speaks in the final section of the poem, as it did in the Hindu Upanishad long ago, lack of any common belief in God renders the speech unintelligible; there is no knight of pure heart and unwavering faith to see the vision of the Holy Grail in the Chapel Perilous, and life in the Waste Land continues to be more intolerable than death, April remains the cruelest month, and personal belief seems an uncertain hope.

But in *Ash Wednesday* the quester, now identified as "I," begins a painful effort to divest himself of the love of worldly things in order to prepare himself

---

26. Eliot, *The Idea of a Christian Society,* 62.

to respond to a higher love. He prays for peace, asking that God "Teach us to care [for spiritual satisfactions] and not to care [for physical pleasures]," and experiences momentary joy in the garden where "the fountain sprang up and the bird sang down," but this joy is transient, and at the end of the poem he is still drawn toward the world, where "the lost heart stiffens and rejoices / In the lost lilac and the lost sea voices," and he is still a praying sinner on his knees who entreats God to "Suffer me not to be separated / And let my cry come unto Thee."

Finally, in *Four Quartets* the quester (still "I") is rewarded by a few unaccountable moments of vision of the Incarnation, symbolized as experiences of timelessness, "the moment in the rose garden," rather than as direct encounters with God. Indeed, all of Eliot's religious expression is of a passive and receptive character, rather than of an assertive and resolute character: man does not penetrate into the divine realm by the power of his vision, as Dante or Milton did, but if he is persistent and patient enough, then "reality," or "the still point of the turning world," may open to his sight. Eliot's pilgrim's progress through his major poems shows how a highly intelligent and skeptical mind of the twentieth century may achieve a profound spiritual awakening against the prevailing tendency of his time toward disbelief and so afford proof of the revitalizing effect of religion on poetry and of poetry on religion, expressing the continued capacity of human beings for Christian faith, which is to say for humility as the spiritual attitude essential to salvation: "The only wisdom we can hope to acquire / Is the wisdom of humility: humility is endless."

Eliot's progress from an early philosophical skepticism to a later poetic faith began with his New England family background (though two generations removed to St. Louis, where he grew up) and his Harvard education, both of which influenced his mind and conscience profoundly and which together help to account for the notable continuity in Eliot's thought, despite the distance between his initial attitude of relativism and his final attitude of reverence. Eliot's grandfather, William Greenleaf Eliot, was a pillar of New England society who became a pillar of St. Louis society: as a minister, he founded the First Unitarian Church, and as an educator, he helped found two preparatory schools, Smith Academy for boys and the Mary Institute for girls, and a university that was first called Eliot Seminary but became Washington University. Eliot absorbed the family religion, saying later, "I was brought up as a Unitarian of the New England variety," which meant that he thought of himself as "outside the Christian Fold,"[27] because he believed in God the

27. Eliot, letter to an Anglican nun, December 6, 1932, printed in *Poets at Prayer*, by Sister Mary James Power (New York: Sheed and Ward, 1938).

Father without God the Son or God the Holy Ghost. The family religion was less a matter of faith than a combination of reason and morality, as Eliot remembered it: "I was brought up in an environment of that intellectual and puritanical rationalism which is found in the novels of George Eliot— an author greatly admired in my family, though her choice of a pseudonym was deplored."[28] Such an extreme Protestantism led Eliot as a young man to reject Christianity altogether, and as he later confessed, "for many years I was without any definite religious faith."[29]

During his decade of serious philosophical study, Eliot went from one philosopher to another—Bertrand Russell, Henri Bergson, F. H. Bradley— in his search for ultimate truth, but never found it, and poetry became his alternative faith, a synthesis of the aestheticism of Ezra Pound and the symbolism of the French poets. But in mid-career, Eliot took up Christianity— "One may become a Christian partly by pursuing skepticism to the utmost limit," he said later,[30] and again, "The conversion to Christianity is apt to be due, I think, to a latent dissatisfaction with all secular philosophy, becoming, perhaps, with apparent suddenness, explicit and coherent"[31]—and so, according to his account, "in 1927 I was baptized and confirmed into the Church of England; and I am associated with what is called the Catholic movement in that church."[32] Eliot's later Trinitarian orthodoxy stunned the audience of intellectuals who had been attracted to his earlier poetry of radical skepticism, but it was a total belief in the Word made flesh: "I take for granted that Christian revelation is the only full revelation, and that the fullness of Christian revelation resides in the essential fact of the Incarnation, in relation to which all Christian revelation is to be understood."[33]

Eliot's later Anglo-Catholic orthodoxy was a return to his ancestral faith: just as his Puritan ancestor Andrew Eliot of East Coker, Somerset, had fled Anglo-Catholic England in the early seventeenth century to practice his faith freely in New England, so Eliot fled from Unitarian New England in the early twentieth century to Anglo-Catholic England, and eventually embraced the faith of his forefathers, thus bringing a cycle of family belief to completion.

But in between his Unitarianism and his Anglo-Catholicism, Eliot gravitated toward philosophy and poetry, which served him as substitute faiths during the period when he thought of himself as a "relativist," that is, between 1906, when he entered Harvard, and 1927, when he entered the Anglican

28. Eliot, "Sermon Preached in Magdalene College Chapel, Cambridge, 7 March 1948."
29. Eliot, letter to an Anglican nun, December 6, 1932, in *Poets at Prayer,* 126.
30. Eliot, "Sermon Preached," 6.
31. Eliot, essay 1 in *Revelation,* 13.
32. Eliot, letter to an Anglican nun, December 6, 1932, in *Poets at Prayer.*
33. Eliot, essay 1 in *Revelation,* 2.

church. His receptivity to ideas and his tolerance of contrary beliefs were characteristic of the Unitarian broad-mindedness in which he was raised, as well as the scientific temper that prevailed at Harvard. Eliot was drawn to Harvard because it was the main arena of what he later called "the active first decade or first twelve years of the century," when there was an extremely lively climate of thought: "Then appeared the most important writings of Mr. Russell and M. Bergson, the vogue of William James was at its height, and the New Realists in America were dusting the arena under the imperial and slightly amused gaze of Mr. Santayana."[34] In this free market of ideas at Harvard, led by an imposing array of thinkers, Eliot must have felt that philosophy offered the most challenging field of intellectual development, and he gravitated toward Bertrand Russell, the English mathematician turned philosopher, though his temperament was probably nearer that of William James, the American philosopher-psychologist. Although Eliot came to admire James's brother, the novelist Henry James, even more than William James, he wrote sympathetically about William James after he left Harvard, saying that he embodied "the union of sceptical and destructive habits of mind with positive enthusiasm for freedom in philosophy and thought," and that "he hated oppression in any form; the oppression of dogmatic theology was remote from him, who lived in the atmosphere of Unitarian Harvard; but the oppression of idealistic philosophy and the oppression of scientific materialism were very real to him. Many of James's ideas may be due rather to his antipathy to other people's narrow convictions than to convictions of his own."[35]

Although Eliot could not share William James's characteristically American geniality and optimism, and never had James as a teacher at Harvard, he was well aware of his influence. In particular, Eliot would have known James's celebrated lectures of 1901–1902, *The Varieties of Religious Experience: A Study of Human Nature.* These lectures, read now, contain illuminating insights into Eliot's later spiritual growth: James clearly favored individual emotions over abstract reasoning, despite his reputation as a professional philosopher and psychologist. James pointed out in his lectures "the gap between the thirteenth and twentieth centuries," as Eliot would do later, and even dared to praise "the value of saintliness" in an age of worldliness, saying of Saint Teresa, the Spanish mystic, that our age would judge "that saintliness of character may yield almost worthless fruits," while "the spirit of her age, far from rebuking her, exalted her as superhuman." James quoted not only Saint Teresa but also Saint John of the Cross, who would become one of Eliot's chief spiritual guides

---

34. Eliot, "New Philosophers," unsigned review, 296.
35. Eliot, "William James on Immortality," unsigned essay, 547.

in his later poetry, saying with approval, "The lives of saints are a history of successive renunciations."[36]

Eliot adopted a surprisingly similar view of saintliness much later on, and he no doubt would have agreed with William James's statement in his lecture "Mysticism" that "personal religious experience has its root and centre in mystical states of consciousness." James observed that mystical states suffer from *ineffability* and *transiency* and depend on the *passivity* of the individual will, and he anticipates Eliot in admitting that "my own constitution shuts me out from their enjoyment almost entirely, and I can speak of them only at second hand." Thus James regarded mysticism as the highest state of religious consciousness, as Eliot would later, despite the fact that for James as for Eliot, and as for the figure in Eliot's poem "A Song for Simeon," there was "Not for me the martyrdom, the ecstasy of thought and prayer, / Not for me the ultimate vision," and Eliot could only hope in *Four Quartets* for those "moments of incarnation" that could not be sustained because, as he put it, "Human kind / Cannot bear very much reality."

William James was a skeptical and scientific philosopher whose influence was dominant at Harvard when Eliot was an undergraduate, but he understood how skepticism might lead from philosophy to poetry, as it did for Eliot. In his lecture "Philosophy" at the end of *The Varieties of Religious Experience*, James noted that all religious experience is emotional and "essentially private and individualistic," stemming from a deep source of being, whereas "philosophic and theological formulas are secondary products." James recognized that "our responsible concern is with our private destiny, after all." Thus in James's view, as in Eliot's later on, religion can never be superseded by science because "religion, occupying herself with personal destinies and keeping thus in contact with the only absolute realities which we know, must necessarily play an eternal part in human history." James spoke in ways that Eliot would later echo of "that unsharable feeling which each one of us has of the pinch of his individual destiny," which "may be disparaged for its egotism, may be sneered at as unscientific, but it is the one thing that fills up the measure of our concrete actuality."[37]

Science and philosophy, as James summed them up earlier and as Eliot would come to see them, were impersonal in their treatment of individuals, while religion and poetry dealt with the individual human being as primary material, and though Eliot would espouse an "impersonal" theory of poetry, it was only as a relative emphasis in a scientific age, for Eliot knew that poetry, like religion, is essentially personal and private, and only becomes public when

36. William James, *The Varieties of Religious Experience*, 270, 271.
37. Ibid., 329, 379, 377.

it is shared as attempted—but never wholly successful—communication with others. Eliot, however, in his later conversion to Anglo-Catholicism, took up a position of religious orthodoxy that James with his religious pluralism could never have embraced. For Eliot, it was the very individual and emotional side of human nature, which religion and poetry included but science and philosophy excluded, that was in need of control, and he affirmed that "the difficult discipline is the discipline and training of emotion; this the modern world has great need of; so great need that it hardly understands what the word means; and this I have found is only attainable through dogmatic religion."[38]

However far Eliot may have gone in the direction of religious orthodoxy, if we understand his conversion to Anglo-Catholic Christianity as another example of the many "varieties of religious experience" that William James once catalogued, it is easier to understand how Eliot could move from an extreme skepticism through philosophy and poetry to religious affirmation, since James provided for such a range of possibilities in human experience—though not specifically by a single human being. What James of course could never have foreseen was the example of Eliot, with his enormous range of religious emotions from doubt and disbelief to fervent prayer and deep faith, nor his expression of it in masterpieces of poetry. Eliot provides the signal instance of a major poet whose feelings ran from deep despair to devout worship, and whose poetry expresses the depths, as well as the heights, of a more extreme variety of religious experience than was dreamed of in William James's philosophy. The early poems, from "The Love Song of J. Alfred Prufrock" through "The Hollow Men," express radical skepticism and disbelief, mirroring the poet's long descent into doubt, which reaches its nadir in *The Waste Land*. The later poems, from "Journey of the Magi" through "Little Gidding," express a regenerate faith that can endure the "dark night of the soul" or *via negativa* of Christian mystics such as St. John of the Cross and can ascend gradually but tentatively to the mystical vision of a Christian poet such as Dante, where "the fire and the rose are one."

If we look closely at this progress from negation to affirmation in Eliot's later poems, we see that his Ariel poems, especially "Journey of the Magi" and "A Song for Simeon," approach Christian faith from the perspective of those who discover it late in life, as he did. The Magus who retells the familiar biblical story of the Epiphany, of the coming of wise men from the East to witness and worship the Christ child at Bethlehem, is one who saw the divine light but did not understand it. He is still asking, at the end of his life, "were we led all that way for / Birth or Death?" He is sure that he has been

---

38. Eliot, "Religion without Humanism," in *Humanism and America: Essays on the Outlook of Modern Civilization*, ed. Norman Foerster.

given some revelation but is unsure what it means, so that in the end he can only say ambiguously, as though asking both for the release of death and for the revelation of Christ to come again, "I should be glad of another death." Together with the naturalistic details of the journey that Eliot interpolates into the biblical account—"the camels galled, sore-footed, refractory," and "the camel men cursing and grumbling," and especially "the villages dirty and charging high prices"—he has made the Magi's journey a return to the roots of Christian belief for himself, as well as for anyone who, like him, might experience a latter-day conversion, and yet might wonder if it is a real rebirth in the midst of what is still a Waste Land.

In the figure of Simeon, the old priest in the Jewish temple who is allowed to see the Christ child once before his death, Eliot expresses a longing for death by "one who has eighty years and no tomorrow," and who prays that before death comes he will be granted the peace of God through the sight of "the Infant, the still unspeaking and unspoken Word," after which, with the *Nunc dimittis* at the end of the Christian mass, he prays, "Let thy servant depart, / Having seen thy salvation." Taken together, "Journey of the Magi" and "A Song for Simeon" were Eliot's poetic reincarnation of the Persian and Jewish priests of "the old dispensation" who greeted the birth of Christ with mingled resignation and joy, because in their way they were unprepared for the new religion, just as, Eliot implies, the modern human being is unprepared for true belief and must approach it as one who is discovering it anew, breaking through the familiar formulaic language to the unfamiliar and frightening reality of God revealing himself in human form for the first and only time in history. The mood of both Ariel poems is an ironic blend of weariness and hopefulness, a resigned rejoicing.

Ash Wednesday is a different and much more extended expression of religious consciousness. It is in fact Eliot's most definitely Christian poem, because it is like an extended prayer, given on the day of repentance in the yearly calendar of Christian observance. Ash Wednesday marks the first day of Lent, the period of fasting and self-denial that culminates in Easter Sunday, and for devout believers it is a time of mortification of the flesh in preparation for the Passion and Resurrection, a deliberate reenactment of Christ's forty days of fasting in the wilderness before he began his formal ministry. It requires saintly self-renunciation, which, as William James saw as early as 1900, is quite out of place in modern civilization: asceticism is painful, and our advanced civilization seeks to avoid pain in every possible way, or, as Eliot put it sarcastically in an early review, "Certain saints found the following of Christ very hard, but modern methods have facilitated everything."[39] So

---

39. Eliot, review of *Conscience and Christ: Six Lectures on Christian Ethics*, by Hastings Rashdall.

what Eliot expressed fervently in the six sections of *Ash Wednesday* is the need to take the Lenten season seriously, to put on an unfamiliar hair shirt and accept a severe discipline of the feelings, to turn away from the world and turn toward God. The language he chose to use is directly derived from liturgy, specifically from the Book of Common Prayer, composed by Thomas Cranmer in the sixteenth century, when, following the Reformation led by Martin Luther and John Calvin, the Anglican Church was created out of the larger Catholic Church. Just as Eliot had sought the roots of biblical faith in his ironic retelling of certain familiar narratives from the gospels, so he sought the roots of Anglican faith in dramatizing the familiar phrases of the English liturgy, emphasizing by the language of the Ash Wednesday service the turning away from worldly things to things of the spirit.

Ash Wednesday is a long and complex poem, and like all of Eliot's poetry, it is hard to paraphrase, but the essential movement can be outlined in fairly few words. From an opening section in which the speaker strives to reject earthly pleasure and ambition ("I pray that I may forget / These matters that with myself I too much discuss / Too much explain"), he moves in the second section to a symbolic death and dismemberment by "three white leopards" (counterparts of the three beasts who confront Dante at the beginning of the Inferno) and offers a prayer to the Virgin Mary as intercessor between man and God, "The single Rose / Is now the Garden / Where all loves end," and then, in the third section, begins the ascent of the soul up the purgatorial stairs, still attracted despite himself to worldly desires ("Blown hair is sweet, brown hair over the mouth blown / Lilac and brown hair"), confessing in the *Non sum dignus,* "Lord, I am not worthy / but speak the word only." The fourth section of the poem presents the figure of a mysterious and beautiful woman, who is not the Virgin Mary but is "Going in white and blue, in Mary's colour" in the Garden of Eden, or earthly paradise (which Dante places at the top of his Mount Purgatory), and he hears a voice that repeats the theme from St. Paul's Epistle to the Ephesians, "Redeem the time," and knows that it means a new understanding of "the word unheard, unspoken," which is the Incarnation of Christ, the Word made flesh. Section 4 is the climax of the poem in its affirmation of Christian spiritual beauty and peace. But section 5 returns to the condition of hopelessness in which "the lost word is lost" and there is a "desert in the garden," while the sixth and final section expresses a mood of weary resignation to the fact that the speaker's prayer has not been answered, that "Although I do not hope to turn again" to the world, I do so in spite of myself—"though I do not wish to wish these things / From the wide window towards the granite shore / The white sails still fly seaward"—and all that is left for the repentant sinner is to pray with Dante in his vision of paradise, "Our peace in His will," and to plead with God in private, "Suffer me not to be separated / And let my cry come unto Thee."

Four Quartets is even harder to paraphrase than *Ash Wednesday,* simply because it is longer and more diverse. Eliot originally thought of calling it "The Kensington Quartets," because he was living in West London at the time he composed the four long poems that make up the sequence, but the poem is not about London except in passing. The only specific references to Kensington, according to Valerie Eliot, are the Gloucester Road Underground Station in part 3 of "Burnt Norton," "a place of disaffection" where there are "strained time-ridden faces" and "Men and bits of paper" are "whirled by the cold wind / That blows before and after time," as they ride on the railway under the city, and the Cromwell Road in part 2 of "Little Gidding," where Eliot "trod the pavement in a dead patrol" as an air-raid warden during the London blitz in the early 1940s. But the main places of the poem are far from London: the country house called Burnt Norton in the Cotswolds near Chipping Campden, which Eliot visited in 1934 just before writing the first of the poems that he eventually collected into *Four Quartets;* the Somerset village of East Coker from which his ancestor, Andrew Eliot, a simple cordwainer or shoemaker, had left for New England in the seventeenth century; the rocks on the Massachusetts coast near Gloucester called the Dry Salvages, one of the first landmarks the early Pilgrims might have seen when they crossed the Atlantic; and the Ferrar family church in Huntingdonshire called Little Gidding, where King Charles I took refuge from Cromwell's Puritans in the mid–seventeenth century before his execution, and to which Eliot himself made a pilgrimage before finishing his poem in 1942. These three English places and one American place are the main settings for each of the "quartets," rather than London, where Eliot lived from 1915 until his death in 1965, as would have been reflected in "The Kensington Quartets," and so Eliot's title *Four Quartets* reflects the poem's musical form rather than its setting.

Just as he had called his earlier group of four imagist poems "Preludes," emphasizing their brief musical form, like a set of short piano pieces, so he called his last group of four long poems after the string quartets he often listened to, in particular the brooding, dissonant late quartets of Beethoven, one of which—the Quartet in A Minor, Opus No. 132—has five movements rather than the usual three or four movements of the sonata form, and each of Eliot's poetic quartets has five movements.

Four Quartets was Eliot's final masterpiece, a work that so keen a judge as John Crowe Ransom thought "may well come to be for us the poem of the century."[40] It is a culminating work for Eliot, certainly, for in it the private vision that had first looked at the world and despaired, then turned from the world to penitence and prayer, at last sought and found release from it "at the

---

40. John Crowe Ransom, "The Poems of T. S. Eliot: A Perspective," 16.

still point of the turning world." The release is momentary but undeniable. The whole poem is a spiritual pilgrimage toward the highest possible end: mystical union with God. But though it ends with Dante's vision of God in the *Paradiso,* where "the fire and the rose are one"—the blinding light of the sun at the center of the celestial rose—and though Eliot said of Dante near the end of his life, "I still, after forty years, regard his poetry as the most persistent and deepest influence on my own verse,"[41] to him, Dante's vision was the "higher dream," while Eliot felt that for himself and his age only the "lower dream" was possible. In other words, Eliot in his poem expressed a mystical yearning for invisible truth that remained partial and intermittent, a few brief moments of revelation, rather than emulating the sort of sustained and transcendent vision of unseen realities that Dante achieved in the *Divine Comedy.*

Given that distinction, the *Four Quartets* may be said to constitute the nearest approach a modern poet has made to the realm of Christian revelation. The subject of the poem is no less momentous, although Eliot's method of developing it is not by an allegorical dream of heaven, which was the method of Dante. It is rather by a realistic description of earth, at times and places where human experience has reached beyond itself, where:

> Sudden in a shaft of sunlight
> Even while the dust moves
> There rises the hidden laughter
> Of children in the foliage
> Quick now, here, now, always—
> Ridiculous the waste sad time
> Stretching before and after.

It is with these lines that "Burnt Norton" ends. They state as well as any passage the recurrent theme of the whole poem: divine revelation, or what Eliot calls "reality," is a "pattern of timeless moments," but these moments occur infrequently and unpredictably in any given life. The greater part of life is a "waste sad time," and each person must subsist on brief moments of ecstasy, for "Human kind / Cannot bear very much reality." Only the saint may hope to arrive at "the point of intersection of the timeless with time," which can be reached if at all only by self-sacrifice. The ordinary man or woman (including the poet himself) must accept a momentary experience of timelessness or immortality:

> For most of us, there is only the unattended
> Moment, the moment in and out of time,

---

41. Eliot, "What Dante Means to Me," 106.

The distraction fit, lost in a shaft of sunlight,
The wild thyme unseen, or the winter lightning
Or the waterfall, or music heard so deeply
That it is not heard at all, but you are the music
While the music lasts. These are only hints and guesses,
Hints followed by guesses; and the rest
Is prayer, observance, discipline, thought and action.
The hint half guessed, the gift half understood, is Incarnation.

These moments may be shared, in a community like that Eliot described at length in *The Idea of a Christian Society,* but such a community of firm believers is an ideal, not a reality, in the modern world, and so Eliot returns to a past shrine at Little Gidding, where the Ferrar family established for a time a close-knit Christian community to which even the king might come for refuge.

But the *Four Quartets* are not a communal poem; in fact, they remain the most personal and private of all Eliot's major poems, in spite of the hopefulness of their closing lines, which allude to the final vision of Dante's *Divine Comedy,* in Eliot's view the greatest of all poems:

> And all shall be well and
> All manner of thing shall be well
> When the tongues of flame are in-folded
> Into the crowned knot of fire
> And the fire and the rose are one.

What emerges from Eliot's final masterpiece is the sense that real religious experience in our time, if it is even possible in a secular age, is an acutely individual affair, expressible only in terms far removed from common understanding. The speaker of the *Four Quartets* is no less isolated than the speaker (the disembodied voice) of *The Waste Land,* and the belief he expresses in the face of doubt is as lonely and difficult as the earlier speaker's despair. The world remains largely what it has been after the poem ends, more Waste Land than Promised Land; only the speaker himself has changed, and it is an open question whether he is not more isolated in his later affirmation of belief than he was in his earlier expression of despair. Eliot may have resolved the doubt of his early poems into the devout faith of his later poems, but to doubt was public, a widely shared feeling in the twentieth century, whereas to be devout was to be alone with oneself—and perhaps, if the prayer of his later poetry was heard, with God.

13

The Fugitives
Southern Poets and the Theme of Alienation

Individualism, which is characteristic of modern art and literature, has had two major effects: innovation and alienation. Innovation, the radical experimentation with form that many think of as essentially "modern," stems from the desire for complete originality, not only for every artist but for every work: Picasso in painting, Stravinsky in music, and Pound in poetry have been the most prolific innovators, because they treated their medium of color, sound, or language as infinitely plastic, yielding up a new form for every mood of the artist in every moment of his life. Alienation, the other pole of artistic individualism, is the complement of innovation in which the artist finds himself totally alone, creating meaning from within himself since he can find objective meaning in the world only through his own subjective experience. The mythical hero of alienation is Narcissus, whose self-love killed him. Complete individualism may lead to self-destruction, and suicide or madness is the price many modern artists have been forced to pay. Innovation and alienation both spring from acute self-consciousness, and the modern artist has had to be, as if in self-defense, ironic as well as tragic in his style. Every modern artist has been in some sense Wallace Stevens's "connoisseur of chaos," forced by the general collapse of religious belief to impose some personal order and meaning on his existence, picking up whatever fragments of meaning and beauty might still lie glittering in the Waste Land of Western civilization.

Innovation and alienation have been active principles in many modern artistic movements—impressionism, symbolism, realism, naturalism, cubism, surrealism—but in modern American poetry two groups have mattered most: the imagists and the Fugitives. The imagists were an international school that flourished in London in the second decade of the century, while the Fugitives were a regional group centered in Nashville in the third decade of the century. They were complementary in many ways, but chiefly, the imagists stood for innovation in form while the Fugitives stood for alienation as theme. It was the imagists who taught poets how to write in single moments of revelation, brief instants of heightened perception in which an image emerges and is recorded in words, expressing an insight into the human condition. They shared the common belief that reality exists in isolated moments of intense feeling and that language is most communicative when it is terse and concrete, registering an instant when the visual becomes visionary. The Fugitives started, not from experimenting with words, attempting "to squeeze the water out of poems," as Ezra Pound once described the imagist program, but from gathering to discuss philosophy, history, and literature. It was only after years of discussion that they began to exchange the poems they were writing. They chose the name "Fugitives" without really understanding what it meant, knowing only that it reflected an attitude, not a technique. Allen Tate later defined the meaning of Fugitive as "quite simply the Poet—the Wanderer, even the Wandering Jew, the outcast, the man who carries the secret wisdom of the world." As the imagists developed their technique through the poems they wrote, so the Fugitives developed their theme through their poems, expressing alienation in a way that was common to their poetry yet peculiar to each member of the group.

The Fugitives were southerners by accident of birth, which gave them the distinction of being Americans with a past, but a guilty past. What they remembered was the defeat of the South in the Civil War, and it was a tragic memory. They perceived that this memory set them apart, yet gave them a common identity, for as Tate wrote in his *Memoirs and Opinions*, "One must entertain the paradox that the South has enjoyed a longer period of identity in defeat than it might have been able to preserve in victory." Thus, to be southern was to be cut off from the rest of America, which did not have to live with such a painful memory, and from the modern world in general, with its material advantages. So some of the Fugitives' alienation came from their regional history of failure and their sense of backwardness in their society, but it also came from their modernity, which, however reluctant, made them American as well as southern. Their identity was complex, and it was compounded by internal conflict; as Tate expressed it, it was the consciousness of growing up at the turn of the century in "a new world so different from the old that I would never understand it, but would be both of it and opposed to it the rest of my life."[1]

To understand why the Fugitives had a firmer grasp on the modern theme of alienation than any other group of modern poets, it is necessary to take

---

1. Allen Tate, *Memoirs and Opinions, 1926–1974*, 37, 17.

account of the conflict they experienced within themselves, between a world still rooted in the feudal agrarian society of the antebellum South, remembered long after its defeat, and the urban industrial society of the North, which was the world they recognized to be dominant around them, a materialistic civilization producing money, machines, and power, but few values or models to live by. As Tate put it in his *Memoirs and Opinions,* "This old order, in which the good could not be salvaged from the bad, was replaced by a new order which was in many ways worse than the old. . . . The cynical materialism of the new order brought to the South the American standard of living, but it also brought about a society similar to that which Matthew Arnold saw in the North in the eighties and called vigorous and uninteresting."[2] It was the fate of the Fugitive poets to be both southern and modern, but they felt out of touch with both, hence their heightened sense of alienation, leading them to write poems that were ambivalent, complex, and ironic.

Thus the poetry of the Fugitives was doubly alienated, from the past as well as from the present, and the shadow of alienation seemed to grow longer and darker over time, in the works of the four principal Fugitive poets, John Crowe Ransom, Donald Davidson, Allen Tate, and Robert Penn Warren, as well as in the work of the one important woman Fugitive, Laura Riding, who was not a southerner like the others but was a talented poet who shared their sense of intellectual alienation.

In Ransom's poetry, the distance separating speaker from subject is maintained with such delicacy that the reader may be hardly aware of it, until jarred by a sudden word that seems out of place—such as *vexed* in "Bells for John Whiteside's Daughter" or *transmogrified* in "Janet Waking," words that are connected with death but that seem to interfere with the generally sympathetic tone of the speaker in confronting the death of a little girl, in the first poem, or of a little girl's pet hen, in the second poem. Ransom writes about old-fashioned ways with often archaic words and with a general manner of courtly politeness, speaking of "ladies" and "gentlemen" as if they still existed, but there is always a hint of mockery in his voice, as when he stresses that his farmers are "*antique* harvesters" (my emphasis) or writes a poem to "Philomela" that evokes the whole tradition of nightingale poems from the Greeks to the Romans to the Germans to the French to the English, yet mocks each of them slyly in turn, and then mocks himself, as he tries valiantly to reinvigorate the myth of Philomela, and then, with a final ironic touch, produces a new nightingale poem himself.

Davidson's alienation was of a more serious kind than Ransom's all along, because he felt a greater need to identify himself with a specific regional past,

---

2. Ibid., 151.

not the plantation South but the pioneer South, with its natural grandeur of woods, rivers, and mountains. Davidson was more sympathetic with the democratic pioneer settler than with the aristocratic planter, and in his poetry it is the land even more than the people that arouse his sympathy. "Sanctuary," one of his finest poems, describes the wilderness lovingly, as a refuge of man from man, where there are "sweet springs of mountain water" and "thick beds of balsam," and where the native American Indians have left their mark. But in the end of this poem about "the secret refuge of our race," Davidson shows his awareness of the inevitable encroachment of human civilization on the wilderness, and in a series of poignant final images, he describes the vanishing of nature as if it will inevitably follow the native Indian into extinction. The alienation of man from nature, in spite of the speaker's imaginative sympathy with it and momentary peace within it, is the more moving because of the sense of inevitability, the tragic sense that man cannot prevent nature from being spoiled by his own hand. Davidson's irony is not as witty or detached as Ransom's, but is sorrowful and resigned, expressing a deeper shade of alienation than that of the older poet.

For Allen Tate, it was the historical tradition that was the most important, and he stubbornly resisted his alienation from it, though in the end it seems as unavoidable as Davidson's alienation from nature. Tate found some poetic consolation in the parallel he drew between the Trojan War and the American Civil War: the Trojans had been defeated by the Greeks but lived on to found the new city of Rome and a new civilization, implying that there might be some hope for the survival of the South after its defeat by the North. But alas, in the two companion poems he wrote about the decline of Western civilization, "The Mediterranean" and "Aeneas in Washington," Tate showed his sympathy for Aeneas and his Trojans, leaving their city in flames and wandering for a long time in exile before founding a new city to the west, but showed little hope for the "landless wanderers" who "cracked the hemispheres with careless hand," that is, the American settlers in the New World, who reached only a "tired land / Where tasseling corn, grapes sweeter than the muscadine, / Rot on the vine." Nor is there hope in the new capital of Washington, where Aeneas and his men, "Stuck in the mire," wonder about their newfound Troy and "what we had built her for." The poet's attempted identity with past greatness, artistic, mythical, or historical, and his connection with the literary tradition by which he consciously links himself to Virgil, is only partially successful, leading him eventually to further alienation.

In his most famous poem, "Ode to the Confederate Dead," Tate pays his tribute to the historical South, those kinsmen who had fought bravely to defend their land and had been honorably defeated, but in so doing he does not draw closer to them; rather, he finds himself farther from them after meditating on their graves, for the heroic failure has been translated into the "verdurous anonymity" of death, and the speaker feels conscious of his own morbidity in trying to memorialize them. He is trapped more than ever in his mind, with "mute speculation, the patient curse / that stones the eyes," and subconsciously thinks of the image of the jaguar leaping "For his own image in a jungle pool, his victim"—Narcissus come to life in an image of suicide, as the speaker tries but fails to find objective reality in the past. The end of Tate's "Ode" is as complete an image of isolation as can be found in modern poetry, as the speaker leaves the Confederate cemetery behind him, with its "shut gate and . . . decomposing wall" and thinks of his own death in the shape of a "gentle serpent, green in the mulberry bush, . . . Sentinel of the grave who counts us all!"

Tate's alienation is even more final and desolate than Davidson's, and though Tate wrote somewhat more hopeful poems later, the "Ode" still stands at the center of his work, like Eliot's *Waste Land,* a masterpiece that could not be transcended and that dominates his achievement as a poet. For Warren, who was the youngest of the major Fugitives, the alienation is seen most often between man and man, as in one of his earliest poems, "To a Face in a Crowd," which appeared in the *Fugitive* magazine in the mid-1920s, expressing the loneliness of the individual in an urban mass society, where all that remains of the rural community of the South is the memory of defeat:

> We are the children of an ancient band
> Broken between the mountains and the sea.

What is left of human brotherhood now is only an anonymous face in a lonely crowd:

> Your face is blown, an apparition, past.
> Renounce the night as I, and we must meet
> As weary nomads in this desert at last,
> Borne in the lost procession of these feet.

Warren wrote most sensitively about the separation of man from man, a separation so absolute that it gives rise to a pervasive sense of guilt from a nameless crime that has never been committed, an Original Sin that pursues each man in spite of his desperate attempt to escape it. In Warren's poetry, especially in the definitive "Eleven Poems on the Same Theme," which appeared in 1942, the name Fugitive attained its most conscious expression as the alienation of the individual from his fellow men. The fullest treatment of the theme is the long narrative poem "The Ballad of Billie Potts," where a frontier highwayman in western Kentucky is cast off by his parents and returns later to be murdered by them—a parable of the prodigal son in reverse, since Billie receives an ironic and tragic welcome from his father and mother, who do not discover his identity until they have killed him.

To these four major Fugitives, Laura Riding adds another dimension as the only woman Fugitive; the group helped her achieve early recognition, which grew to be international by the time she published her final collection, *The Poems of Laura Riding*, in 1938. But by then her association with Robert Graves, who became acquainted with her through their joint appearance in the *Fugitive*, overshadowed her poetic reputation, and her public renunciation of poetry undermined her later literary career. Yet when she was first published in the *Fugitive*, the editors quickly nominated her for a prize and accepted her as one of them, calling her "a new figure in American poetry," and she responded to their encouragement. Riding would later call *poetry* "a lying word," but her Fugitive period was her best, and her discovery as a poet by the Fugitives led to the later fame and controversy surrounding her. What matters is that her special combination of femininity and audacity incorporated the Fugitive theme of intellectual alienation; in fact, she could be called the most alienated of all the Fugitives, since she recognized herself as an outsider from the beginning. When she sent her first—and arguably her best—poem, "Dimensions," to be published in the *Fugitive* in 1923, she was already expressing the sense that she could be "measured" only "by myself." She held consistently to that highly individualistic view in all her best poems, many of which the Fugitives chose to publish in their magazine, indicating their approval of her viewpoint as well as her poetic talent. She came eventually to see herself as cut off from the world by her poetry and so to distrust the very talent she had for writing it, but she deserved the praise she won from the Fugitives in the 1920s, despite all the disclaimers she would later make about poetry in general and about her own poetry in particular.

Thus the Fugitives, each in his or her distinctive way, gave expression to alienation as a persistent theme, exploring it individually in a series of memorable poems that trace the alienation of man variously from his traditions, from nature, and from human fellowship. This alienation from the world is linked in certain key Fugitive poems to a religious alienation, the separation of man from God. In such poems as Ransom's "Antique Harvesters," Davidson's "Lee in the Mountains," Tate's "Seasons of the Soul," Warren's "Bearded Oaks," and Riding's "Dimensions," though they are not ostensibly religious poems, the speaker points to a condition in which man is isolated by the loss of faith in a divinely ordered creation and the loss of a transcendent redemptive love. Tate, looking back on all his poetry, said that "its main theme is man suffering from unbelief."

If the Fugitives seem to be original but minor poets with a definite regional identity, together they formed a major movement that gave full expression to the principal theme of their age, placing man as an isolated and alienated figure opposed to the urban, industrialized mass society dominant in the twentieth century, and their poetry articulates explicitly what other modern poets implicitly assumed about the condition of man. They matter individually, but they matter even more collectively, since there is a coherence that drew them all into touch with each other when they started writing poetry and that gives significance to their poetry as a whole, making the sum of Fugitive poetry greater than its parts and forming a composite poetic figure out of a diversity of viewpoints and a variety of styles: the Fugitive they created became in time the embodiment of the modern poet.

14

JOHN CROWE RANSOM, ELUSIVE IRONIST

Writing an editorial for the *Fugitive* in the mid-1920s, John Crowe Ransom summed up his philosophy, calling irony "the rarest of the states of mind, because it is the most inclusive; the whole mind has been active in arriving at it, both creation and criticism, both poetry and science." To Ransom, irony took the fullest measure of man, and he employed it with great subtlety and refinement throughout his career in a body of poetry that is among the chief ornaments of the age. The oldest of the Fugitives—he had published his early *Poems about God* before they began publishing their magazine—Ransom came nearest to expressing the traditional values of southern society, so much so that some of his poems seem almost to belong to another age, an age more dignified, polite, and gracious than his own. His "Bells for John Whiteside's Daughter" and "Janet Waking" have a classic simplicity that makes them as fine as any poems ever written about children, yet even in these portraits of innocence, there is the jarring word that shakes the reader's confidence: we are "vexed" at the "brown study" of John Whiteside's daughter, and it is a "transmogrifying bee" that kills Janet's pet hen. The detachment of the poet is felt as keenly as his sympathy, just at the crucial moment when the feeling is deepest, leaving the reader to wonder what he really thinks. A doubleness of meaning pervades all of Ransom's poetry, until one begins to believe that "The Equilibrists" may be his most characteristic poem, a memorable elegy for lovers who can never make up their minds between heaven and hell, honor and pleasure, and who die still undecided, in "their torture of equilibrium." Ransom's irony is most obvious in the early "Amphibious Crocodile," a delightful caricature of the American abroad, but it appears with great subtlety in the companion poem "Philomela," which stands as Ransom's "Ars Poetica."

"Philomela" borrows its title from Matthew Arnold, but it differs at least as much from Arnold's poem about the nightingale as Arnold's poem differs from Keats's more famous "Ode to a Nightingale." Ransom opens by obliquely recalling, through names, the Greek myth of Philomela, who was brutally raped by her brother-in-law Tereus; he cut out her tongue to insure her silence, but she cleverly wove the story of her rape into a tapestry for her sister, Procne, Tereus's wife. Then in revenge Philomela and Procne killed Tereus and Procne's son Itylus and served the flesh to his father—"your improbable tale," as Ransom wryly calls it, "Is recited in the classic numbers of the nightingale," because in death Philomela becomes a nightingale, singing sweetly of her sorrow, while Procne is transformed into a swallow, and Tereus into a hawk. The first stanza of Ransom's eight-stanza poem ends by regretting that modern poets, especially American, cannot emulate the nightingale's song, because "It goes not liquidly for us."

Nevertheless, Ransom continues, there have been nightingale songs from Greek through Latin through German through French to English, and each has had its validity: the Latin poet Ovid "duly apostrophized" the nightingale, the Teutons (Germans) also sang like the nightingale, even though they were "swilled and gravid" (that is, drunk and heavy), and the French cleverly "gallicized" the bird, but "never was she baptized"—no nightingale was ever converted to Christianity—and the English, in embodying the nightingale's song, had to deal with "The untranslatable refrain" that was originally pagan. Neither did the nightingale ever cross the Atlantic, Ransom adds: "Not to these shores she came! this other Thrace / Environ barbarous to the royal Attic," for the bird could not sing a "democratic" song "in a cloudless boundless public place / To an inordinate race." And so he, as an American poet who could not hear the nightingale at home, crossed the Atlantic to study at Oxford (a rare autobiographical reference to Ransom's years as a Rhodes scholar), and even then, though he went to Bagley Wood, where Arnold once heard it, and listened dutifully, he could not seem to hear the nightingale sing properly, because "My ears are called capacious but they failed me," and instead, "Her classics registered a little flat!" Formally, but with tongue in cheek, he addresses the nightingale at the end of his poem as "Philomela, Philomela, lover of song," being forced to lament that "I am in despair if we may make us worthy," for he recognizes that he is one of the barbarians from America, "A bantering breed sophistical and swarthy," not able to equal the great poets of the past who have written nightingale songs in every European language, for

> Unto more beautiful, persistently more young,
> Thy fabulous provinces belong.

The poem is full of ironies about the scandalous origins of the nightingale's song and the difficulty of capturing it in words, but the final irony is left for the reader to decipher: Ransom has lamented that he cannot write a new nightingale poem, yet in his ironic way he, an American poet, has added one more distinctive nightingale song to the long European tradition.

It was one of the original French symbolists, Paul Valéry, who held that a poem is never finished, it is abandoned, and John Crowe Ransom was one of the least abandoning of modern poets, but it must be admitted that he sometimes husbanded his creations too long for their own good. "Bells for John Whiteside's Daughter" is a rare exception, for it is one of his best poems, and Ransom said that not a line of it was ever changed, from its first appearance in the *Fugitive* magazine until its last appearance in his *Selected Poems*. On the other hand, fine poems such as "Here Lies a Lady," "Conrad at Twilight," and "Prelude to an Evening" should have been abandoned at an early age, instead of being kept around to accumulate the strained diction and even downright doggerel of their final published versions in Ransom's *Selected Poems* of 1969. It would have been better for Ransom's high reputation as a poet-critic if he had put the later "Lady," "Conrad" (unhappily retitled "Master's in the Garden Again"), and "Prelude" to rest with the early *Poems about God*, which he had the good sense to abandon soon after publication. We might wish to preserve the prose justifications Ransom wrote for these later versions as valuable pieces of self-criticism,[1] but we would not be losing much in the way of poetry if we quietly disposed of the later versions of poems he himself refused to abandon. That Ransom did have doubts about the later versions is clear, since he printed each of them in his last *Selected Poems* beside an earlier version, leaving it to his readers to decide which is better. And while Ransom came to prefer the later version, his readers are free to follow D. H. Lawrence's perennially sound principle "Trust the tale, not the teller," which in Ransom's case means "Trust the poem, not the poet" and continue to regard the earlier "Lady," "Conrad," and "Prelude" as the classic texts.[2]

It is the same with Ransom as with certain other modern poets who were tireless tinkerers: we are forced to choose the versions we prefer from the rather mixed bag of the poet's own selections. What reader, if given the choice, would not favor the earlier and longer versions of Marianne Moore's "Poetry" or W. H. Auden's "September 1, 1939" and "In Memory of W. B. Yeats" over the later, truncated versions that Moore and Auden preferred? There are certain early poems of Yeats, too, which he fired in the crucible of his later style to make them more painful and less pleasing, which are better read in the earlier collections of his poetry. It seems that Ransom, like Yeats and Moore and Auden, wanted his poems to change along with the poet and match their language to his changing views, but while his motives for revision may be

---

1. The prose statements appear in the section "Sixteen Poems in Eight Pairings" in *Selected Poems* (1969), 3d ed., rev. and enl., 107–59.

2. See the earlier *Selected Poems* (New York: Alfred A. Knopf, 1945).

understandable, it is better on the whole for a poet to write later poems to suit later moods than to rewrite earlier poems to express later and perhaps alien sympathies.

Trust the poem, not the poet, means that we should try to preserve each poem at its best, and recognize that the poet is a more protean being than his works. In the celebrated case of Yeats, it has long meant that readers must take account of two different poetic styles, the early Yeats and the later Yeats, and concede (at any rate, outside of Ireland) that the later Yeats is the better poet, a modern poet, realistic, ironic, tragic, while the early Yeats is a romantic poet, mystical and lyrical, to be loved but not entirely trusted when he dreamed of an Irish fairyland set apart from the world. What it means for Ransom is that we recognize what might be called a middle Ransom, better than either the early or the late, who wrote best for an audience of fellow poets during his mainly Fugitive period of the 1920s, and who was otherwise a first-rate critic and theorist of poetry but less than a first-rate poet. Ransom himself, when justifying his later revisions in his final *Selected Poems* of 1969, gave the most plausible explanation of why his middle years were best for the composition of poetry: "During the *Fugitive* days of my fourth decade I was at great pains to suppress my feelings in what I wrote. I was both sensitive and sentimental as a boy; and I did not like that boyishness in my adult poems. My friends seemed to think that I managed it."[3] By his friends, he meant Donald Davidson, Allen Tate, Robert Penn Warren, and other fellow poets of the Fugitive group in Nashville, under whose sympathetic but always critical gaze Ransom perfected his mature style, which was erudite, ambiguous, restrained, ironic. It is the style of a master, and though Ransom seemed to regret later that he had "suppressed" his feelings in his mature poems, it was surely by holding his natural sentimentality in check that he made the style what it was. In his middle years, Ransom was capable of expressing deep feeling in subtle and refined ways. Earlier, in the *Poems about God,* and much later, in the "B" versions of *Selected Poems,* 1969, he was a more frank sentimentalist, and a lesser poetic craftsman.[4]

Reading his work as a whole, we can see that all of his best poems were written during the two decades between 1920 and 1940, and that what he did poetically before and after those decades is largely irrelevant to his achievement as a poet. His classic poems began with the publication of "Dead Boy" in the *New York Evening Post* in 1920[5] and ended with the publication

3. *Selected Poems* (1969), 146.

4. These "B" versions appear in the section "Sixteen Poems in Eight Pairings" in *Selected Poems* (1969).

5. First published as part of a three-sonnet sequence entitled "Sonnets of a Selfish Lover" on February 24, March 1, and March 6, 1920; then published in the *Sewanee Review* (April 1924) as "The Dead Boy"; it first appeared with the title "Dead Boy" in *Two Gentlemen in Bonds* (1927).

of "Address to the Scholars of New England" in 1939 in the first issue of the *Kenyon Review,* which Ransom founded after he had left Vanderbilt for Kenyon. To be even more specific about his poetic oeuvre, we can say that Ransom wrote about thirty poems, give or take a few (as sympathetic a critic as Randall Jarrell would have taken away all but a dozen), for which readers are lastingly grateful, and that of these, at least twenty were published during the four brief years of the *Fugitive* magazine, from 1922 to 1925, although not always in the magazine itself. If any proof were needed of the salutary influence that the Fugitive association had on Ransom's poetry, here it is. Before 1920, there were the *Poems about God,* which brought him recognition but were quickly forgotten once his Fugitive poems appeared. After 1925, Ransom added only a handful of poems that were equal to his best. But he went on revising many of the earlier poems, sometimes to their benefit, more often to their detriment. Beyond simplifying two of his titles from their earliest publication—fortunately, "An American Addresses Philomela" became simply "Philomela" and "History of Two Simple Lovers" became "The Equilibrists"— he did not make any really important changes in most of his poems before 1945, when the first *Selected Poems* confirmed his stature as a poet of distinct originality and surpassing skill. It is this volume to which the majority of readers will continue to return for the definitive versions of his best poems.

By 1963, however, when the second *Selected Poems* appeared, Ransom had begun altering some of his early poems almost beyond recognition, a process that was carried to extremes in the third and final *Selected Poems* in 1969. By then, he had convinced himself that he had written two different and satisfactory versions of eight of his poems (including one he exhumed from *Poems about God*), and so he printed them side by side, with accompanying explanations that tell us more about the poet's intentions than about his accomplishments. The social essays of the agrarian period and the literary essays of the Kenyon period added to Ransom's full stature as a man of letters; there is no reason to regret that the poems of the Fugitive period came first rather than last.

Readers have as much right to select their favorite version of a poem as the poet has to publish it in more than one version. There can even be added fascination, when reading a poet we admire, in comparing the various printed forms of his poems with each other, to see which is best. Such exercises of taste are an inescapable part of the pleasure of reading Emily Dickinson, now that we have so many variant wordings of her poems, and in some cases it is difficult to decide whether there *is* a best version: sometimes, all her choices seem good ones. With Ransom, the earliest version is usually the best, giving us at least a basic criterion of judgment, and making the first *Selected Poems* in 1945 the source of most of his classic texts. If someday there is a variorum edition of Ransom's poetry, it will give us multiple revisions of many poems, and each reader will have the pleasure of comparing alternate versions and deciding whether he agrees with the editor's choice or not. It is predictable that some readers will disagree with any editor's selection of a standard text, just as they have disagreed with texts for Emily Dickinson's poems offered by successive editors, from Thomas Wentworth Higginson to Thomas H. Johnson. It is equally predictable that Ransom's best poems will survive both his own revisions and the choices of his editors, exactly as Emily Dickinson's poems have survived and even prospered through their many editions—none of which had the benefit of her own editorial choices, as those of Ransom did, for better or for worse.

Having argued for reader's choice over author's preference, where more than one version of a Ransom poem exists, let me provide a major exception to my general rule that Ransom's poems are best in their earliest versions or after slight revisions. There is certainly convincing evidence that when Ransom revised a poem substantially, he usually ruined it. Such is the case with "Conrad at Twilight" and "Prelude to an Evening," cited earlier, and with other "A" and "B" versions published in the *Selected Poems* of 1969. The major exception is a poem entitled "The Vanity of the Bright Young Men," which appeared neither in the first (1945) nor in the last (1969) *Selected Poems*, but only in the second *Selected Poems*, published in 1963. This poem began its public career in 1924 as "Tom, Tom, the Piper's Son" and ended it in 1969 as "The Vanity of the Bright Boys." It was revised many times between 1924 and 1969, and it reached its highest state of perfection, in my opinion, in 1965, in *The Fugitive Poets: Modern Southern Poetry in Perspective* (a revised edition came out in 1991). In this single instance, I would argue, a Ransom poem became better in a later, much revised version (though not the last version), as can be verified by a careful study of the variants.

"The Vanity of the Bright Young Men" is in its many metamorphoses a poem about a young intellectual who sees himself as set apart from others (the Fugitive theme of alienation) by his sense of a high destiny, as yet mysterious and unrealized, which will lead him through the green world of nature clad in melancholy black until his wished-for coronation as the "Heir Anointed" in a throne room imagined to await him when he is finally recognized as the prince he really is. In every version, however, the young man is seen as egotistical, unaware that he is fantasizing about himself, and so Ransom's irony pervades the entire series of poems, though it is more subtle in the earlier and middle versions than in the last version, and they are therefore better poems.

There are altogether fourteen published versions of this one poem, more than for any other single poem by Ransom. Twelve of these versions appeared in other volumes, but two of them were sent to me by Ransom while I was editing *The Fugitive Poets*. I used the one I thought best, and only discovered later that it was indeed the best of all the versions of the poem Ransom offered for print.[6] True, in the majority of cases, only slight adjustments in wording were made by Ransom, and so there are really only three major forms of the poem, each with a different title; the principal choice is thus between the early "Tom, Tom, the Piper's Son" (four versions), the middle "The Vanity of the Bright Young Men" (nine versions, including one incomplete variant titled "The Vanity of the Male"), or a single version of "The Vanity of the Bright Boys," Ransom's last attempt at revision before he finally abandoned the poem. Thus there was a metamorphosis in three different forms of one Ransom poem, taking place over a period of forty-five years, from its first appearance in 1924 until its last mutation in 1969. I will concentrate on only the two best versions here to prove my point that the 1965 poem is the best.

The first version of the poem was oddly called "Tom, Tom, the Piper's Son."[7] The four published versions of "Tom" are almost identical, and Ransom was pleased enough to reprint the first version as version "A" in his final *Selected Poems* with the comment, "It is not too bad a poem for publication."[8] One might almost agree with Randall Jarrell, a hanging judge where poetry was concerned, that "Tom" is one of the dozen best of all Ransom's poems, except for some lingering doubts about the puzzling nursery-rhyme title, which is perhaps the weakest element in the poem. Ransom effectively used borrowings from children's books in some of his best poems—the talking geese of "Bells for John Whiteside's Daughter" and the "forgetful kingdom of death" in "Janet Waking" are prime examples—but the allusion to the pig-stealing Tom of the nursery rhyme in this poem about a serious and self-centered young man is slightly off-key. Either the title is too light or the poem is too heavy; in any case, the poem remains arresting, but puzzling, as Ransom chose to preserve it for its first thirty years. The chief puzzle it contains is why the surly Tom would ever imagine himself as a royal prince, even a "changeling" one, when his only accomplishment seems to be selling his "wares"—a fact that led Ransom to disparage the poem in *Selected Poems,* 1969, because, as he put it dryly, "Tom seems to characterize himself as a Fuller Brush Man, or some other kind of door-to-door salesman." Granted that all young men have delusions of grandeur, giving the poem a valid psychological basis, there is still something ludicrous about a salesman who envisions himself as the heir to a throne, as Tom seems to do. We may also agree with Ransom's later criticism of the meter of "Tom," when he says, "Musically, the short two-foot line which follows the long pentameter above it gives us something of a jolt." In his later revisions, the short lines are lengthened to three feet, making the rhythm more fluid. But when Ransom says that he came to "detest" the poem

6. For complete texts of all fourteen versions, see my essay "The Metamorphosis of a Poem."
7. *Fugitive* 3 (August 1924): 100–101; reprinted as version "A" in *Selected Poems* (1969), 130–31.
8. *Selected Poems* (1969), 131.

because of its "hateful ending" that is "without any resolution of Tom's final despair," readers will find it hard to agree. In fact, the ending,

> And duly appeared I at the very clock-throb appointed
> In the litten room,
> Nor was hailed with that love that leaps to the Heir Anointed:
> "Hush, hush, he is come!"

is the strongest part of the poem, because it mounts to an imagined kingly climax that the hero clearly desires, though he is not sure he is worthy of the honor he seeks: to be crowned as the "Heir Anointed." The mixture of ambition and insecurity in Tom is what makes the poem memorable, in spite of flaws in the title and the meter, and the character of the hero is appealing, even if his motives are somewhat obscure. He dreams of success, but feels himself a failure, and the ending is not "hateful," but appropriate to a young man who both loves and loathes himself.

The second metamorphosis appears in a variety of versions, since Ransom allowed two editors—Miller Williams[9] and me—to see unpublished typescripts of the poem. This confidentiality on Ransom's part has given us evidence of how many times he was willing to rework a poem before it appeared in print. There are only two published versions of "The Vanity of the Bright Young Men," one in his *Selected Poems* of 1963 and the other in *The Fugitive Poets* of 1965; the remaining seven versions must be regarded as working drafts. The chronology of the nine versions is not entirely certain, since the draft Ransom sent me first in the summer of 1964 is more like the third metamorphosis into "The Vanity of the Bright Boys" (1969) than is the version he sent me a little later (the one I chose to print in my anthology). His first typescript bore a note that "The Vanity of the Bright Young Men" was "an old piece I've tinkered with lately," a fact that I already knew from the newly titled version that had appeared in the *Selected Poems* of 1963. It was a few weeks later in 1964 that I received, unsolicited, a second typescript, with a note at the top saying, "Final text—if you still like it." I did like it, much more in the second version than in the first, though I realized that it was closer to the version that had appeared in *Selected Poems* of 1963. I cannot explain why, after he had written a two-line ending that made the outcome less ironic, he decided to return to the terser, more ironic climax of the earlier version, nor did Ransom offer me any explanation, but I was grateful for the afterthought that brought me "The Vanity of the Bright Young Men."[10]

9. See Miller Williams, *The Poetry of John Crowe Ransom*, 81–83.

10. Printed in William Pratt, ed., *The Fugitive Poets: Modern Southern Poetry in Perspective,* both editions (1965, pp. 51–52; 1991, pp. 6–7).

Initially, the most striking of all the changes in this second version is the title, which transforms the obliquely sardonic "Tom, Tom, the Piper's Son" into the explicitly critical "The Vanity of the Bright Young Men." The gain in intelligibility is considerable, for what had seemed a vaguely autobiographical, private poem has become a publicly satirical one: the young man is representative of all male intellectual vanity, and his imagined ascendancy to the throne has become a wish-fulfillment fantasy portraying, in the manner of a parable, the sin of intellectual pride. The poem in its new form becomes a perfect complement to "Blue Girls" (retitled "The Vanity of the Blue Girls" in *The Fugitive Poets*, according to Ransom's instruction, so that the two poems would make a pair) and stands as a classic moral tale in verse. Boys are traditionally expected to be intelligent, as girls are expected to be beautiful, and Ransom evidently wanted the poem to reflect the dangers of male intellectual vanity, the risk of arrogance and alienation, as he had earlier shown the transience of feminine beauty. I think Ransom must have come to believe that "Tom, Tom, the Piper's Son" was too limited, too personal in its appeal, and wished to give the poem the sort of universality of theme that "Blue Girls" displayed from its first publication. To my mind, he succeeded, and "The Vanity of the Bright Young Men," especially in its 1965 version, is a better poem than any version of the earlier "Tom, Tom, the Piper's Son."

There is more to be admired than the change of title, for the identification of the now unnamed hero as a young scholar makes him a more understandable figure than Tom the traveling salesman. To see the hero as "A familiar only to books" and "Going alone to assembly" immediately calls up the image of a college boy, even of a bookworm, and thus gives the appropriate setting to what has become a little drama of intellectual pride. If we could not see why Tom the Piper's Son should have imagined himself as the king's son, we can easily see why the Bright Young Man should dream of such a high destiny: he has been reading books rather than selling wares. And one of the vicarious pleasures of reading, whether in literature or in history, is imagining oneself as the conquering hero, ruler, or king. Ransom has established a psychological motive for the pride of his young man, who now bears some resemblance to Stephen Dedalus in Joyce's *Portrait of the Artist as a Young Man*. Like Joyce, Ransom manages to envelop his hero in dramatic irony, so that we can see him both envied and mocked, in his assumption of a high destiny. He is a more sympathetic hero than the earlier Tom, who seemed unaccountably sullen because there was no apparent source for his pride.

Not only the tone surrounding the hero, but the rhythmic movement of the poem is improved in its second metamorphosis. All versions of "Vanity" (except the transitional "Vanity of the Male") have three-stress short lines, an audible gain over the two-stress lines of "Tom." The best version has an increased frequency of present participles, giving both metrical symmetry and rhetorical parallelism to the poem. There is an internal rhyming effect in "minding," "liking," "going," "pushing," "glaring," "brushing," "walking," "wasting," "passing," and "translating" that carries the poem smoothly along with a mounting anticipation, almost to the end, to be succeeded in the resolution of the final two stanzas by the past-tense verbs "towered," "marched," "showed," and "appointed," to the climactic "Unhailed," which greets the hero as he imagines himself entering the throne room as the "Heir Anointed." That this crescendo effect is deliberate in this version is borne out by a marginal comment in Ransom's penciled scrawl on the typescript he sent me: "I want adjective or participial phrases all the way in this long 9-stanza sentence, with the main clause beginning only in St. 8." The combined rhythmical and rhetorical progression enhances the overall unity of the poem to an impressive degree, I think, and makes of it an almost seamless garment up to the awesome (yet faintly ironic) exclamation in the last line: "Hush, O hush, he is come!" Ransom is at his best, always, when a powerful feeling is capped by a chilling irony, and here the climactic hush and the "bell's last throb" are deftly undercut by the pointed negative of "Unhailed." The effect here is like that of the "primly propped" body of the once vivacious little girl at the end of "Bells for John Whiteside's Daughter" and the "clack" of the kites' beaks over the "red vitals" of the stout heart of "Captain Carpenter": in many of Ransom's best poems, the forces of nature exert their dominion over the vitality of men with a tragic finality.

In short, "The Vanity of the Bright Young Men," especially in the version published in 1965, is I think one of Ransom's minor triumphs. Coupled with "Blue Girls," it makes a poetic fable of a young man proudly but precariously waiting to be acclaimed a hero, but with his promise as yet unfulfilled. It is a sympathetic, albeit ironic, character study with universal implications, fit to be in the select company of Ransom's finest poems. What a pity that Ransom kept working at the poem, until he had provided it with the snappier title and the falsely happy ending of "The Vanity of the Bright Boys," which suffers in comparison with either the youthful "Tom, Tom, the Piper's Son" or the more mature "The Vanity of the Bright Young Men."

It would be kinder not to dwell too much on the obvious faults of this third and final version of the poem, which is embarrassing to any serious admirer of Ransom's poetic skill, but it is instructive to examine them. The phrase "bright boys" makes the title both sarcastic and slangy, and changes the hero of the poem into a child and the tone into one of condescension, reinforced by the too cute "sweet babe royal" of the sixth stanza. Shifting the first-person speaker to a third-person observer was a mistake in a poem that depends so much on identification of the reader with the central figure: all the other thirteen versions of the poem are in the first person, and why Ransom should have wished to put his hero at a distance in the final version is hard to understand. He breaks two of the quatrains into couplets, weakening the rhythm of the poem without gaining any special dramatic effect, and his equating of "vegetary operations" with "shrubbery" is pedantic humor, hardly the subtle sort of erudition that he carried off in the "pernoctated" of "Philomela" or the "transmogrifying" of "Janet Waking." All of these changes are for the worse, but the final two stanzas and the "Envoi" are disastrous: they plunge the poem into a bathos that Ransom in his Fugitive days would have rejected outright.

L'ENVOI

Dawn, you've purpled a politic Prince,
He's done no running and peeking since
Thrones are trash, and Kings are dumb;
Say, would he rather his kingdom come?

The excuse he gives in his prose commentary is that his hero's "wish is gratified not nullified," but if the hero's wish is granted in this happy ending, what "vanity" is left for him to admit? He has become a schoolboy hero: not the deluded dreamer, but one whose dreams have come true. Tom the Piper's Son has been transformed at the last moment into Jack the Giant Killer. Though Ransom admitted in his commentary that the last version of this most-revised of his poems is "heavy with sentiments and byplays," he apparently did not recognize that the finely tuned moral irony had been lost and that the rhetorical and rhythmical climax was dissipated in a round of boyish applause.

While it is to be regretted that Ransom did not abandon his poem in the midst of its second metamorphosis, when it was nearest perfection, we must be grateful for the pleasure and instruction he left behind in the many drafts and printed revisions of a single short poem. His sharing of the trials and errors of his poetic workshop leaves us with a remarkable case history in the art (and the artifice) of revision, almost a whole anthology of a single poem. That the poem is, in its highest metamorphosis, one of Ransom's best makes the study of its successive versions all the more rewarding. In the various stages of revision, not excluding the last one, Ransom winningly displayed his talents as a poet, a critic, and a teacher; perhaps it was the teacher in him that prevailed, when he elected to make public all the effort a given poem had exacted from him, willingly leaving it to his readers to judge when, or whether, he had succeeded or failed. Or perhaps he was still in doubt himself about which of the versions of the poem he liked best; given his reserved and skeptical turn of mind, it is quite possible that even fourteen ways of looking at a poem were not enough to satisfy him, and that after forty-five years of trying he never finished the poem—as Valéry would say, he simply abandoned it.

For the most part, though, Ransom's gentle, elusive irony did not rise and fall but persisted steadily throughout his career, extending from poem to poem at his best, and eventually placing him alongside his venerated masters, Thomas Hardy and Edwin Arlington Robinson, as a somewhat more learned and subtle ironist, whose poetry reflects a deliberate, humorous understatement that is one of the ultimate refinements of modern poetic style. If he was a southern agrarian who embodied in his poetry "the aesthetics of regionalism," as he liked to call it, he was even more characteristically a moral dualist, aware of human fallibility but sympathetic to failure as the normal human condition. To read him is to perceive behind the studiously polite mask of the "gentleman in a dustcoat" the discerning gaze of the "antique harvester," reminding the reader of the frightening omnipresence of death:

> For we are nothing; and if one talk of death—
> Why, the ribs of the earth subsist frail as a breath
> If but God wearieth.

15

Donald Davidson's Tennessee and Allen Tate's Kentucky

The Fugitives were a regional group of poets, but they always insisted that regionalism was not their aim; indeed, they opposed a conscious regionalism, but came to realize that an unconscious regionalism was part of their background. They might well have agreed with Thomas Hardy that "a certain provincialism of feeling is invaluable. It is of the essence of individuality."[1] Though most of them came from the American South, and indeed from just two states, Tennessee and Kentucky, they were aware of much broader perspectives, for they were acquainted with the world tradition of literature from their education in classical preparatory schools in the South, where Greek and especially Latin were still taught as basic languages. This education in ancient languages was furthered at Vanderbilt University, where before World War I classical literature was still at the center of higher education, and in the cases of John Crowe Ransom and Robert Penn Warren was continued by advanced study as Rhodes scholars at Oxford. Thus, the regional identity that brought the Fugitives together was not a conscious part of their intellectual heritage at first, and it only became so after long discussion had convinced them that they were southerners as well as classicists in their poetry. When they wrote as Fugitives in the 1920s, they were writing as modernists as well, and so to their southernness and classicism was added their modernism— an unusual mixture of ingredients, but one that guaranteed individuality for their poetry.

The Fugitives were a large group of poets, numbering sixteen in all, though only five of them kept writing poetry long enough to achieve national

---

1. "Hardy Talks to Himself," in *The Portable Thomas Hardy,* 752.

and international reputations (and of those, Laura Riding was an anomaly, being neither southern nor classical, though distinctly modern). The oldest and youngest members of the group, Ransom and Warren, and the two middle members, Donald Davidson and Allen Tate, together spanned almost a generation, Ransom having been born in 1888, Davidson in 1892, Tate in 1899, and Warren in 1905. Of the four, the senior pair, Ransom and Davidson, were from Tennessee, and the junior pair, Tate and Warren, were from Kentucky. It was important to their sense of regional identity that they all came from small towns in the South, where the marks of individual character were most strongly defined, Ransom from Pulaski and Davidson from Campbellsville, Tennessee, both on the Deep South border with Georgia and Alabama, and Tate from Winchester and Warren from Guthrie, Kentucky, both in the Border South or Blue Grass region of central Kentucky.

These four major Fugitives did not often write about their home territory of Tennessee and Kentucky, but simply assumed it as part of their makeup, though the farming communities from which they had come later made them agrarians as well as Fugitives. Their home was the rural South, but they were cosmopolitan in their outlook through education and travel, and in time they became as sophisticated a group of poets and critics as the French symbolists and the Anglo-American imagists had been before them, though Nashville was hardly the metropolis that Paris and London were. It was the peculiar combination of the provincial and the cosmopolitan that made them distinctive from the first and that kept them so to the end, as southerners, classicists, and modernists all at once.

Their southernness gave them long memories, or what Nathaniel Hawthorne called "a home feeling for the past," which was often apparent in their poetry, nowhere more than in the poems they wrote about the American Civil War, the historical watershed between the present and the past to most southerners. Davidson's "Lee in the Mountains" and Tate's "Ode to the Confederate Dead" are centerpieces of Fugitive poetry because they are written from a broad southern perspective on the Civil War and pit the past against the present with distinctive irony.

Tate's "Ode" may be called the greatest of the Fugitive poems, but it is also a southern Waste Land, since it pictures a modern southerner in the act of trying to memorialize the past heroism of his countrymen, fallen on the various battlefields of the Civil War—Shiloh (in Tennessee), Antietam (in Maryland), Malvern Hill, and Bull Run (both in Virginia)—but finding he is so cut off from them, so trapped in his own self-consciousness, that he is like a living dead man among the ruins of a buried civilization. The speaker in Tate's poem is truly a Fugitive, separated from the past generations of his region by a barrier of time and from his contemporaries by an introspective loneliness, an existential alienation so complete that it leads him to contemplate suicide.

The personal heroism of the Confederate soldiers, dying for a cause in which they believed, however doomed it might have been, is no longer possible, and an alternative of purposive action in the present seems equally untenable. Though the setting of the poem is regional and the perspective is historical, the theme is modern and international, for as Davidson perceptively wrote to Tate after seeing an early manuscript version of the "Ode" in 1927, "Your *Elegy* is not for the Confederate dead, but for your own dead emotion."[2]

The allusions in the poem are classical as well as historical. Zeno and Parmenides were Greek philosophers who maintained that reality is unchanging, and that change and motion are only illusions; Zeno's celebrated paradoxes of Achilles' endless pursuit of the hare and of the arrow's unending flight toward a target were offered as proofs that real motion could not occur in infinitely divisible space. "Stonewall" is the well-known nickname of the Confederate general Thomas Jackson, whose accidental death from a wound inflicted by one of his own soldiers was felt by many to doom the Confederacy to defeat, and the battles in Tennessee, Maryland, and Virginia were all decisive in that defeat, marked today by extensive cemeteries of the kind where the speaker of the poem is standing—though he never says which cemetery it is.

In Tate's southern apocalypse, the graves of the Confederate dead are symbols of a past culture that can be remembered but not recovered, and the cemetery is the symbol of an empty present in which the individual is isolated from his fellow men, engaged in an endless soliloquy among the dead. The traditional social order to which the Confederate soldiers belonged, rooted in a particular region and held together by family loyalty and common religious belief, is no more, and nature itself seems to partake of the deadness of the past in the autumn season, with the bleak weather wearing away the tombstones and their marble angels. In his meditation, the speaker imagines himself to be in a dark void of space, as if at the bottom of the sea, where the flying leaves—natural symbols of death associated with the dead soldiers—are a constant reminder of mortality, forming a refrain that is repeated with slight changes several times in the poem:

> Seeing, seeing only the leaves
> Flying, plunge and expire

In the second main section, the speaker attempts to reenact in his mind the heroism of the soldiers; he imagines them waiting to charge the enemy in a furious motion of animal energy, but a motion that does not really produce

2. Donald Davidson to Allen Tate, *The Literary Correspondence of Donald Davidson and Allen Tate*, 186.

change, merely a human sacrifice that hastens the inevitability of death. As he recalls the familiar names from the Civil War, the famous general and the major battlefields, he realizes how brief their moment was, and he wishes time could stop but knows it cannot: he sees himself as already dead, "a mummy, in time." The hound bitch calls up another image of death, and then the third principal section of the poem begins, with the reflection that death has transformed the soldiers' bodies into elements of earth and sea, and the speaker has a frightening, surrealistic vision of their bones beneath the ground, spectres that seem to beckon him toward the grave, where the spiders weave their webs and the screech owl's cry eerily echoes the rebel yell of the soldiers on their charge into oblivion.

The poem becomes more introspective in its final section, as the speaker asks himself what he should do, with night falling on him, and he thinks of himself wrapped in fruitless speculation, unable to act—unless to follow the action of an imaginary jaguar, who "leaps / For his own image in a jungle pool" and thus drowns himself. Tate's own illuminating commentary on the poem, "Narcissus as Narcissus,"[3] says that the jaguar is the central image of the poem, since it is intended as an ironic allusion to the Greek myth of Narcissus, who fell in love with his reflection in a pond and drowned trying to embrace himself. Narcissus is the mythical victim of self-love, and the myth is a warning against excessive human vanity, but Tate suggests that self-love is the only form of love left to modern man, since in his solipsism he can believe in no reality outside himself. Narcissism, or solipsism, trapping man in his own subjectivity and signifying the failure of human beings to function in society, is, Tate says, the main theme of the poem. The speaker finds no solution to his problem, no answer to his questions: he has "knowledge / Carried to the heart" of heroic human action in the past, but he cannot worship the dead, a form of psychological suicide, and he has no constructive choice to make, no way out of what Tate called "the modern squirrel-cage of our sensibility." His final thought, as he leaves the cemetery in growing darkness, is of the "gentle serpent, green in the mulberry bush," an ironic image of evil causing the Fall of man in the Garden of Eden. The speaker's only consolation is death itself, a common fate that will at last break the wall of separation between men and join them—ironically, of course—in the common grave of earth.

Tate's poem about the Civil War is a highly civilized poem about the collapse of civilization, the speaker a modern southerner who has lost touch with the past. Davidson's "Lee in the Mountains" is written from a quite different perspective: that of General Robert E. Lee, the defeated hero of the Confederacy, who speaks in the first person from his refuge in the Virginia

3. Allen Tate, "Narcissus as Narcissus," in *Essays of Four Decades*, 593–607.

mountains after the war is over, when he has accepted the presidency of what would become Washington and Lee University. This historical persona of the general most admired by southerners accepts defeat with a calm dignity, it seems, having retired from the bloody battlefields to a place of peaceful contemplation, a university campus set in the mountains, where he remembers the "lost forsaken valor" of the army that fought under his command and waits for death to come and claim him. Davidson's Lee is a more introspective character than is to be found in the history books, although his portrayal is historically accurate in every detail—even to the bitter memory of his father, Henry Lee, who left the family home in Virginia reluctantly, because, having fought bravely in the Revolutionary War, where he earned the nickname "Lighthorse Harry Lee," he did not wish to fight the British again in the War of 1812; his self-imposed exile to the West Indies left a scar on the memory of his son. Lee recalls that his father never heard "the long Confederate cry / Charge through the muzzling smoke or saw the bright / Eyes of the beardless boys go up to death," as he had to do, and he describes lovingly the scene around him now

> The Shenandoah is golden with new grain.
> The Blue Ridge, crowned with a haze of light,
> Thunders no more.

and he wishes that he could fight the lost battles once again, but knows it is impossible, because

> The rifle
> Returns to the chimney crotch and the hunter's hand.
> And nothing else than this? Was it for this
> That on an April day we stacked our arms
> Obedient to a soldier's trust? To lie
> Ground by the heels of little men . . . ?

Davidson's portrait of Lee is sympathetic yet distant; it pictures him as one who still agonizes over his defeat, refusing to accept its finality, but forced to recognize that he cannot change the course of history, that the war is forever lost, and that he is "alone, / Trapped, consenting, taken at last in mountains." What is left for Lee, before death comes to release him from life, is to teach the young men around him never to give up their belief in God, "the fierce faith undying," or their loyalty to their families, "the love quenchless," but to continue holding on to their land, "the hills to which we cleave" and "the mountains whither we flee" in the hope that they will be vindicated someday by a "just / And merciful God" who will, like the God of the Old Testament, honor "His children and His children's children forever / Unto all generations of the faithful heart." Davidson's portrait of Lee as an unreconstructed Southerner makes of him a figure much like himself, an unlikely Fugitive but a Fugitive nonetheless, for his "Lee is in mountains now, beyond Appomattox," an alienated leader who welcomes death as a respite from the defeats of life, and who in his attitude toward death is like the speaker in Tate's "Ode to the Confederate Dead," even if he is part of the historical past that Tate's speaker sought in vain to recover.

The Civil War poems of Tate and Davidson are their best-known works; they are about the South as a whole region, but there are also two excellent poems about Tennessee and Kentucky, the specific areas of the South the two poets came from, "Sanctuary" by Davidson and "The Swimmers" by Tate, which deserve to be better known. These two poems are as fine as any the Fugitives wrote, embodiments of the essence of the South as a historical region, fusing what was classical in their education with what was modern in their experience. These two poems can be better understood in conjunction with each other than separately, for "Sanctuary" is to Tennessee what "The Swimmers" is to Kentucky: a moving portrait of the natural landscape that is also a criticism of its human inhabitants.

Tennessee and Kentucky are part of the South, but not quite the Deep South—a phrase reserved, oddly enough, for northern Mississippi, Alabama, and Georgia, the territory most central to the Southeast as a region. Still, both Tennessee and Kentucky are clearly southern in the sense Allen Tate meant when in his essay "The New Provincialism" he wrote that "no literature can be mature without the regional consciousness." We think of Robert Frost as a New Englander first and a Vermonter second, just as we think of Robinson Jeffers as a westerner first and a Californian second (despite the fact that Frost was born in San Francisco, Jeffers in Pittsburgh). Similarly, we think of the Fugitives first as southerners, and second as natives of Tennessee or Kentucky, the two states nearly all of them came from. Wallace Stevens once remarked that "Mr. Ransom's poems are composed of Tennessee," without explaining what he meant by it, but undoubtedly there is "Tennesseeness" in the poems of Ransom and Davidson, as there is "Kentuckiness" in the poems of Warren and Tate. There is also something individual in each of these poets, along with what is local and regional, and it is the rich combination of qualities that makes for the originality of their poetry.

There is also something modern in each of the poets, despite their resistance to it, and it is historical as well as contemporary. Tate, who was as profound in his criticism as in his poetry, said of the whole southern renaissance in the twentieth century, "The arts everywhere spring from a mysterious union of indigenous materials and foreign influences." If the literature written in the South in this century was truly the sign of a renaissance, then something of the past was reborn in the present, and indeed southern regionalism was infused with the same Christian humanism that stemmed from the earlier European Renaissance, which brought Greek and Roman classicism to new life in the arts of Western Europe. "Regionalism without civilization—which means, with us, regionalism without the Classical-Christian culture—becomes provincialism,"[4] Tate believed, and none of the Fugitives could be accused of a narrow provincialism, that is, of preferring local values or customs to the universal values and manners by which civilized human beings are judged. Place and time are significant in the poetry of the Fugitives without being limited to their own place and time, for they take in the whole past of Western civilization.

Certainly Davidson's "Sanctuary" assumes by its very title that there are civilized values to preserve, ultimately deriving from religious beliefs, although the poem's setting is not a church but the wilderness of the woods and mountains. As Davidson wrote in his essay "A Mirror for Artists" in the agrarian symposium I'll Take My Stand, the artist who is dedicated to tradition will find that "the very wilderness is his friend, not as a refuge, but as an ally."[5] What Davidson meant by "wilderness" was not nature in a pure state undefiled by men, as it meant for the romantic poets, but nature as a "hermitage" (also the title of one of his best poems) for pioneer settlers and as a home for the native Indians—that is, a human habitation. The poem starts in the aftermath of what must be the Civil War, since it speaks of a "defeat" that drives the speaker and his family back to their homestead in the Smoky Mountains of Tennessee. They are obeying a remembered warning to "go to the wilderness / In the dread last of trouble," but in doing so, they are following familiar paths that "were your fathers' paths, and once were mine." Thus the poem starts with a historical memory of a time when civilized people lived in the wilderness and cleared it to cultivate their farms, before the formation of towns and cities. Davidson thinks of this pioneer society not as a plantation image of the South, with pillared white mansions surrounded by cotton fields, but as an extended family living close to nature on a farm in a clearing of the woods.

"Sanctuary" is a narrative in blank verse, the traditional unrhymed iambic pentameter inherited from Shakespeare and Milton and other English poets, but adapted to the American scene and language, for as Davidson wrote, "The Southern people have long cultivated a historical consciousness that permeates manners, localities, institutions, the very words and cadence of social intercourse."[6] The southernness of speech is certainly a feature of

4. Allen Tate, "The New Provincialism," in Essays of Four Decades, 542.
5. Donald Davidson, "A Mirror for Artists," 52.
6. Ibid., 53.

Fugitive poetry generally, and in this poem there is a detectable regional accent that might even be called Tennesseean in phrases such as "tall sons" and "dread last" and in place-names such as "Will's Ford" and "Chilhowee." There is the feeling of generations of the same family returning to the place of origin in their need, after their defeat by an unnamed enemy (as much "industrialism" as Yankees), and there renewing themselves in the freshness and vitality of nature. There is also the historical connection with an earlier war, the American Revolution, when Davidson says that "Tryon [a British colonial governor] raged / In Carolina hunting Regulators." And there is the recollection of the wilderness scouts who came to Tennessee from Virginia and Carolina after the Revolution, most notably Sam Houston, who later went west to lead Texas to statehood:

> Some tell how in that valley young Sam Houston
> Lived long ago with his brother, Oo-loo-te-ka,
> Reading Homer among the Cherokee. . . .

The description of Sam Houston among the Indians, reading his book of classical Greek poetry, is startling but historically accurate, depicting southern civilization carrying its classicism into the wilderness. Davidson goes even further back in history, to the Spanish explorers, who were the first Europeans in the South, to Hernando de Soto, who got as far east as present-day Memphis in his travels through what was then Indian territory. And even further back, he suggests, there is a primeval memory at work, for

> Men have found
> Images carved in bird-shapes there and faces
> Moulded into the great kind look of gods.

It is this southern sense of the land as sacred, of a mystique of locale, derived from the aborigines and passed on intact to the European ancestors who settled his native state of Tennessee, that Davidson makes the focus of his final descriptive images, giving the poem a memorable and moving close. He makes it seem that not only does nature offer a sanctuary to man, but man should offer a sanctuary to nature, for he is charged with protecting what is left of the wilderness and passing it on to the generations of people to come:

> This is the secret refuge of our race
> Told only from a father to his son,
> A trust laid on your lips, as though a vow
> To generations past and yet to come.

The theme of conservation of nature is as strong in this poem as in Faulkner's *Bear* or Thoreau's *Walden,* and what is most southern about it is the sense of mutual dependency of man and nature, Davidson's agrarian philosophy expressing itself. But there is also his modernism intruding itself, giving a touch of tragic irony to the final lines:

> Or else, forgetting ruin, you may lie
> On sweet grass by a mountain stream, to watch
> The last wild eagle soar or the last raven
> Cherish his brood within their rocky nest,
> Or see, when mountain shadows first grow long,
> The last enchanted white deer come to drink.

The sense of doom, of an apocalyptic vision taking over and annihilating all that is most precious in nature and most intimate to man, is implied in the repeated "last" that Davidson attaches to the eagle and the raven and the deer, all creatures threatened by the ravages, not of civilization, since the people who love the wilderness are certainly civilized, but of industrialization, which is polluting and destroying the landscape as no human enemy alone could do. The critique of "advanced" civilization in the cities and the factories is as strong as the theme of natural conservation in Davidson's poem, and it gives the whole work a poignancy that is realistic and prophetic at the same time.

For readers of Allen Tate's poetry, the poem that looms over all the rest is his "Ode to the Confederate Dead," the most famous of all southern poems. But that poem is less Kentuckian in its setting than his later masterpiece, "The Swimmers." There is no identification of the cemetery in the "Ode" with any particular battle of the Civil War, and the places mentioned in the poem are not in Kentucky but in Tennessee, Maryland, and Virginia. "The Swimmers" is unique among Tate's poems in that it is set near his birthplace of Winchester, Clark County, in the Kentucky Blue Grass region, whereas poems like "The Mediterranean" and "Aeneas in Washington" are set far away in Southern France and in the American capital. Even his Civil War novel, *The Fathers,* has its setting in Virginia and Washington, D.C., not in Kentucky. Place is generally symbolic for Tate, imbued with historical memory and literary allusion, but he said that his central theme was not place but religion, the negative theme of "man suffering from unbelief," its positive corollary being, as he said in one of his essays, that "the end of social man is communion in time through love, which is beyond time."[7] It was Tate's active principle that "the imaginative writer is the archeologist of memory," and "The Swimmers"

---

7. Allen Tate, "The Man of Letters in the Modern World," in *Essays of Four Decades,* 16.

is his most specific poem of memory, set in his native place in his boyhood time: "Montgomery County, Kentucky, July 1911."

The form of Tate's poem is terza rima, or rhyming triplets, derived from Dante's *Divine Comedy*, which Tate himself referred to as a "straightjacket" for a poet writing in English, since there are fewer rhyming words than there are in Italian. Technically, the poem is a virtuoso performance, a rare example of the three-line stanza in English that compares favorably with other equally rare examples: Shelley's terza rima in *The Triumph of Life* and Eliot's adaptation of it in a passage of "Little Gidding," the last of his *Four Quartets*. Although Shelley's and Eliot's are masterful poems, Tate's poem is technically the nearest English equivalent to Dante's terza rima.

The setting of "The Swimmers" is in a rural yet populated place, a pastoral scene in the woods that ends in a town square. It begins appealingly with water imagery, "Kentucky water, clear springs," calling up the freshness of nature and making "Kentucky" the equivalent of "unadulterated, pure, natural." It was not the way Tate originally began his poem, as we know from a special issue of *Poetry* magazine, which honored him posthumously in November 1979 by printing the manuscript of "The Swimmers" alongside the published poem. The first line originally read, "O fountain of joy, clear waters," and Tate transformed it into a symbolic place-name of his native state, leading from the excited innocence of a boyhood swimming adventure into the guilty knowledge of a brutal adult murder, with which the poem confronts the reader early and on which it centers to the end. The pastoral imagery is disturbed in the fourth stanza by "the cold dream of the copperhead," and the tension between "love and fear" builds up with phrases such as "Dog-days" and "poison-oak," and the heavy breathing of the boys above the swimming hole is jarred by the words "Borne on the copper air / A distant voice green as a funeral wreath / Against a grave: 'That dead nigger there.'" The rest of the poem irretrievably disrupts the peacefulness of nature, as we see the lynched corpse of the black man being dragged to the town square by the sheriff and his posse, where it is left alone in the public clearing, innocent nature disgraced by human violence and only acknowledged in the shamed silence felt by the boy, who was Tate himself at the age of twelve in an incident he said he remembered vividly the rest of his life.

Tate's poem is a meditation on a true story, that of the lynching of a man in his part of Kentucky early in the twentieth century, or rather the aftermath of it, which the young boys witness, the sheriff having come too late to stop the mob from its racial killing, the boys watching in shocked silence as the corpse is dragged away. The poem has a tone of restrained emotion throughout, the tension building in the boys' minds as they see the horrible fact of violence and brutality, ending with profound silence and shame, as the corpse lies disfigured in the public square and no one will acknowledge it: the whole last scene has a disturbing quietness about it. The theme of the poem is remembered guilt, tied to a boyhood incident that haunts his memory—he did not publish the poem until 1953, when he was fifty-four, and so he spent over forty years ruminating on the crime. The guilt was communal, not personal, since the boys were innocent witnesses of the aftermath of the lynching near Mt. Sterling, Kentucky, a town not far from Tate's birthplace of Winchester. He associates it in his memory, however, with a much older guilt, that of the crucifixion of Christ, and so makes the burden of racial persecution a matter of conscience for all who witnessed it, whether they participated in the lynching or not.

"The Swimmers" is thus not only a later, but in some respects a more mature, poem than "Ode to the Confederate Dead," because it assumes a collective guilt or tragic flaw in southern society that the more famous "Ode" is not concerned with, and it assumes a community that feels the guilt, whereas the "Ode" portrays individual isolation and suffering, lacking a sense of community. The point of view is that of Tate as a boy, laughed at by his playmates for having "water on the brain," but the narrator is an adult recounting the story, and the interpretation of it, especially the analogy with the crucifixion, is an adult viewpoint, as is the silent communication of shared guilt at the end. Thus the poem is a recollection that is also a confession, ritualized into art; it is painful but it is also purgative. Tate noted in one of his essays, "We have seen in our time a powerful attempt to purify ourselves of the knowledge of evil in man. Poetry is one of the sources of that knowledge." "The Swimmers" is certainly such a source of knowledge, embodying poetically the power of evil in men and the power of guilt resulting from it.

"The Swimmers" is a Kentucky poem, which makes of the setting a potent symbol both of natural innocence and of human guilt. Tate was a symbolist as well as a Fugitive, expressing as the French symbolists did the private experiences of an isolated modern consciousness, acute personal sensibility finding unique poetic expression. Tate translated Baudelaire's symbolist sonnet "Correspondences" and used the technique of what he called "the fused metaphor of Symbolism" effectively in such lines as "Savage as childhood's thin harmonious tear" and in the silent guilt felt at the end of the poem. To describe feelings beyond the normal range of perception is to reveal depths of reality that would otherwise be unknown, just as the nuances of light and color in an impressionist painting disclose otherwise imperceptible shades. Tate's poem is as sophisticated in its art as it is saturated in the reality of its native region, creating as a whole the southern renaissance motif, which Tate characterized as "a mysterious union of indigenous materials and foreign influences."

Together, Davidson and Tate were Fugitives who made the South resonate with poetry; whether they were treating the South as a whole in their Civil War poems or specific regions of the South, Tennessee and Kentucky, in "Sanctuary" and "The Swimmers," they were able to fuse modernism and classicism with a deeply felt southern regionalism.

16

ROBERT PENN WARREN
Portraits of the Artist as
a Young and an Old Man

Sometimes the most absorbing dialogues are not those that take place between older and younger generations, but those carried on by the same artist with his younger and older selves. One thinks of all the self-portraits that Rembrandt painted over a lifetime, which increased in interest and complexity year by year, as he aged and matured and was able to see more deeply into himself. Rembrandt's youthful portraits may be more dashing and handsome, more rakish in costume and expression, but the older portraits are richer in their expression of the inner self, in the artist's ability to put on canvas, along with the wrinkles and blemishes that inevitably come with age, the character lines surrounding the penetrating gaze, steadily looking into the mirror and seeing what seems to be the soul inside. So Robert Penn Warren worked portraits of himself into his poetry from early to late, and the Warren that is revealed in the earlier poems often seems a dark fatalist, haunted with the fear of some nameless evil inside himself and in other men, while the later Warren seems more hopeful and forgiving of himself and others, more joyful and affirmative.

Warren did become in his long lifetime something of an Old Master—an exemplar, in time almost the lone survivor, of an era of great literature we call modernism, and part of the satisfaction of reading through his work now is experiencing in it the dominant themes and techniques of twentieth-century poetry. Starting as the youngest of the Fugitive poets of the South in his teens, he lived to become the first poet laureate of the United States in his eighties, a figure revered by many younger poets not simply because of his longevity but because of his amazing creative vitality in old age. Warren did not write a single poem that could be considered his masterpiece, but he wrote many memorable poems through six decades, and some of his best poems were among his last: like those other American masters, Wallace Stevens, William Carlos Williams, Ezra Pound, he stayed abreast of his time, and he belongs in the rare company of writers who achieved as much in age as in youth. It may be Warren's lasting distinction that his portraits of the artist as an old man are more joyful and comic, less mournful and tragic, than his portraits of himself as a young man. Warren once said that when he was young he was shocked by evil, but as he grew older he became shocked by goodness, implying that his perception of man changed from seeing him in prevailing darkness to seeing him in increasing light. In fact, if Warren has any parallel among the major poets of the age, it would be with the later Yeats, and especially with those venerable Chinese whom Yeats described in "Lapis Lazuli":

> Their eyes mid many wrinkles, their eyes,
> Their ancient, glittering eyes, are gay.

The comparison with Yeats is apt in another way, for Robert Penn Warren was one of the most complete men of letters America has ever produced. Only Warren of all American writers of the century received Pulitzer Prizes both for his fiction and for his poetry, and along with fiction and poetry he published more than thirty books of biography, social history, literary criticism, and even college textbooks, each distinguished by unfailing originality and literary style. But he himself rated his poetry above all his other writings, saying in a 1977 interview that he began his career as a poet and hoped in the end he would be judged primarily as a poet: "I started as a poet and I will probably end as a poet. If I had to choose between my novels and my *Selected Poems*, I would keep the *Selected Poems* as representing me more fully, my vision and my self. I think poems are more *you*."[1] Of course, in his *Democracy and Poetry* (1975), Warren argued for the broadest possible definition of poetry, as art in general and as literature in particular, maintaining that human achievement depends more on poetry than on any other artifact. "For all my adult years," he said, "my central and obsessive concern has been with 'poetry,' and I scarcely find it strange that I should seek some connection between that concern and the 'real' world."[2] So to take Warren as first and foremost a poet, despite the many-sidedness of his talents, is only to take him at his word. Warren frequently liked to borrow from Randall Jarrell a homely metaphor for poetic inspiration, that of being struck by lightning while standing in the rain: "Lightning hits you once, you're good; hits you six times, you're great." A writer of astonishing versatility, Warren seems to have stood in the rain most of his life and to

---

1. Robert Penn Warren, *Robert Penn Warren Talking: Interviews 1950–1978*, 233.
2. Warren, *Democracy and Poetry*, xvi.

have been struck by lightning a number of times. Not every time, though: Warren did publish some mediocre works along with the good, resembling in that respect one of his literary heroes, Herman Melville, a writer of genius who could be embarrassingly clumsy at times. But in the end, an artist is judged by his masterpieces rather than by his failures, and Warren had the sort of persistence that kept him going through fallow periods as well as fertile, patiently standing in the rain until the lightning struck him again.

Of all his novels, only *All the King's Men* may prove solid enough to endure, if for no other reason than that it is the finest American political novel ever written, and of all his poems, perhaps a dozen or two at most are truly lasting, but with his inexhaustible energy he kept working always to produce new novels and new poems. Probably the best of his short critical essays is "Pure and Impure Poetry," and his best book-length essay is certainly *Democracy and Poetry,* one of the most original and comprehensive studies ever written on the relation between American literature and American society. He argued in it that poetry serves both a "diagnostic" and a "therapeutic" function, and that American poets have diagnosed the principal weakness of our democracy as "the progressive decay of the notion of the self," while they have provided at the same time therapy for that ailment in that American poetry manages "to affirm and reinforce the notion of the self." Warren went on to say, "I suppose that I do think of poetry as, if not a passion of the soul, then the voice of the passion of the soul—though that lingo is high falutin. Even a nourishment of the soul, and indeed of society, in that it keeps alive the sense of self and the correlated sense of community."[3]

Because Warren was singular as a critic in maintaining that the American poet attacked the faults of his society out of a sense of responsibility, becoming if need be the "bearer of *bad* tidings of great joy," there is reason to take his poetry as both social criticism and self-criticism, and the fact that some of his best poems were written late is cause for believing that not all the tidings were bad ones, and that the joy, when it came, was earned after long despair.

According to his own account, Warren's poetic career started when he was invited to join the Fugitives at age seventeen, when he was a student at Vanderbilt in 1922. He always believed that without that fortunate event, his life might have been very different. He had wanted first of all to be a naval officer, but a boyhood eye injury prevented his winning an appointment to Annapolis, and so he had enrolled at Vanderbilt with the ambition of becoming a chemical engineer. Writing was his third vocational choice, and then only because John Crowe Ransom happened to be his freshman English teacher, and told him, after reading his first essay, "I think you don't belong

3. Ibid., 92.

in here. I think I will have you go to my advanced class." Then, as a junior in college, he was invited by Ransom to attend his first Fugitive gathering:

> Greatest thrill I'd had in my life. By then it was mostly a poetry club—we read each other's poems and argued poetry. Everybody was an equal in that room; no one pulled his long gray beard. And it was a good time to be there: Ransom was writing his best poems then, and Tate was just finding himself. I myself was seventeen, and I said, "This is what I'm going to do."[4]

Having decided on his career, Warren began pursuing it with characteristic energy, and before he graduated from Vanderbilt, he had published poems in the *Fugitive* magazine that showed an already mature talent, among them one poem he would reprint in all his later *Selected Poems,* "To a Face in a Crowd."

The earliest of Warren's mature poems, "To a Face in a Crowd" shows most of the distinctive features of his poetic style: the form, rhyming pentameter quatrains; the manner of address, second-person familiar "you," that may in his use sometimes be a dramatic character, sometimes the reader, sometimes Warren himself, but always with a dialogue, not a monologue, implied; the narrative method, anecdotal or brief, here an encounter with a stranger in a crowd, greeted in passing but never to be seen again; the sharp, often grotesque or naturalistic detail—the "faint lascivious grass" pictured obscenely as it "Fingers in lust the arrogant bones of men"; and finally, the explicit moral theme, that all men are "Fugitives," lonely individuals in search of a lost community, haunted by a historical memory that binds them, in their alienated condition, to an "ancient band" of human beings.

Even in his earliest poems, Warren tended to write short parables based on common experience, placing himself as a modern Everyman at the center and expressing what he would later call the consciousness of the "yearner," which in his opinion was "rather a common type" of person who combines "a religious temperament" with "a scientific background" and whose condition is to "yearn for significance, for life as significance."[5] All of Warren's best poems, both early and late, embody this yearning for meaning in life, and their appeal is in the way they dramatize the essentially fugitive, or isolated, state of man, the naked self, while showing his longing to be drawn into communion with other lonely and naked selves: each poem is an appeal for companionship from one who suffers from its lack. The poems that Warren gathered into his first significant collection in 1942 were called "Eleven Poems on the Same Theme," and all shared the general characteristics of "To a Face in a Crowd." They

4. *Warren Talking,* 277.
5. Ibid., 205.

bore titles such as "Pursuit" and "Crime" and "Terror" and "Original Sin: A Short Story," and each was a graphic portrayal of the fate of modern man, endeavoring to escape from the prison of his self-consciousness by reciting aloud to himself the litany of his guilt and fear. He felt in "Crime" a strange envy for "the mad killer who lies in the ditch and grieves," because to be a real criminal would be to have committed an identifiable crime, whereas he is pursued by a nameless guilt that cannot be exorcised and that, in "Original Sin: A Short Story," takes the shape of a hideous nightmare "with locks like seaweed strung on the stinking stone" from which he cannot seem to wake up.

But the culminating poem of Warren's early period is that remarkable long narrative first published in 1943 called "The Ballad of Billie Potts," a short story in verse based on a frontier tale of Warren's native Kentucky that had been told to him as a boy by his great-aunt. The poem consists of alternating passages of naturalistic description and abstract speculation, telling the story of a backwoodsman whose family preys on travelers by offering them bed and board and then murdering them and robbing them. In the end, Billie Potts himself is murdered and robbed by his own parents, who fail to recognize their son when he returns home after years of wandering in the West. "The Ballad of Billie Potts" has a setting close to Warren's birthplace in western Kentucky, near the Tennessee border. The note at the beginning, as well as the frequently repeated refrain within the poem, tells us that it is set in "the land between the rivers," that is, the territory between the Cumberland and Tennessee Rivers, now known as "the land between the lakes" because dams have since converted the two rivers into Kentucky Lake and Lake Barkley, which serve today as recreational areas, though the area between them is still largely wilderness, as it was in the nineteenth century, when the action of the poem takes place.

The form of Warren's poem consists of loose, unrhyming tetrameter lines for the most part, but occasionally longer lines break the meter and there is a refrain in trimeter, "the land between the rivers." Behind the poem is the framework of the traditional ballad form; however, Warren's adaptation of the ballad is not traditional but idiosyncratic, and given that his subject is a wild outlaw tale rich with local dialect, it works very effectively, and its swinging— one could almost say galloping—rhythm suits the action, some of which is on horseback; it is also in striking contrast with passages of philosophical meditation, which seem like soliloquies meant for the eye rather than the ear. It is overall a ruggedly informal free-verse ballad.

The Kentucky setting is nature wild and untamed, not the pastoral setting of Tate's "Swimmers," and the refrain of "the land between the rivers" portrays the western frontier, where, in American history, man and man collided violently, as they do in Warren's poem. The characters of Billie Potts and his father and mother are all corrupt from birth, never innocent, and the descriptive imagery is deliberately crude: "his shoulders were wide and his gut stuck out / Like a croker of nubbins," we learn of Big Billie, and his wife's "eyes worked slow and narrow like a cat," and Little Billie is "a clabber-headed bastard with snot in his nose"—no wonder, then, that they make their living by preying on their guests, robbing and murdering them with no fear of punishment, since "the land between the rivers" is the Wild West that no sheriff has been able to tame. Warren uses the setting to convert the Kentucky frontier into outlaw territory, where evil reigns supreme in human form, until the villains murder their own kind in an ironic form of retribution entirely outside the law. Warren writes as the Kentucky "westerner" whose wilderness is like a mythical forest where only evil spirits live and which only the hardiest traveler would dare to penetrate.

The story Warren tells is of how an outlaw son is unknowingly—not innocently!—killed by his own parents, who discover after they have buried a hatchet in his head that he was their only child, who had gone out west for ten years and returned to "surprise" them, but was himself grimly surprised. Warren's tone is all bluster and vulgarity and hyperbole in the narrative, but the interspersed soliloquies allow the narrator to step back and contemplate the events, to suggest that the bloody ending of Billie Potts is what he deserves, a futile search for home and family become a shared condition of man in an alienated and unloving world. Warren puts his theme more explicitly in the meditative sections of "The Ballad of Billie Potts" than he does in the narrative passages, though it is implicit throughout the poem. It is, like the earlier "Eleven Poems on the Same Theme," a variation of the Christian doctrine of Original Sin. The murder of Billie Potts is brought about because he tried to escape his guilt by going west and finding a new identity, then bringing it home proudly to his parents, leading, inevitably though ironically, to his death. Time, in Warren's view, is the testing period for man, who can use it either to atone for his sin or to be damned by it. In Billie Potts's case, Time offers no redemption because he tries to recover his innocence by escaping his guilt rather than atoning for it, and he is trapped in his own desperate attempt to prove to his parents that he has overcome his failure and become their successful, prosperous son: they kill him out of greed, and damn themselves in the act. Time and the West become symbolic of man's self-love, his ambition to be his own redeemer from Original Sin:

> For Time is always the new place,
> And no-place,
> For Time is always the new name and the new face,
> And no-name and no-face.
> For Time is motion
> For Time is innocence
> For Time is West.

Billie carries with him a good-luck charm, a birthmark in the shape of a clover leaf, which after his death becomes the identifying sign his parents discover on his corpse. Billie and his parents think that there is fortune to be gained on earth, but it turns out to be misfortune for them, because love has been displaced by greed, and they are not able to recognize their own guilt; they are alienated from each other in an extreme form of self-love that makes them forever fugitives and wanderers, unable to find or establish a true home. As Warren says in *Democracy and Poetry,* "self is possible only in a community," and the solipsism of modern man makes him an isolated individual who searches vainly for his identity and becomes self-destructive without knowing it. Billie Potts in his crude frontier way typifies modern man, pitiable but unredeemed.

The tone of Warren's poem is melancholy, since there is not even a shared community of guilt at the end but a family destroyed by selfish greed. However—and this is the main defense of poetry, according to Warren—the poem itself is a unity expressing by its very form the counter-theme of self-fulfillment: he called poetry "a nourishment of the soul" that "keeps alive the sense of self and the correlated sense of a community." So far as the poem is a human embodiment of a universal moral truth, its relative artistic perfection complements the moral imperfection of human nature that it expresses, and its total effect is therefore not negative but positive: it is a "bearer of *bad* tidings of great joy." The argument is a subtle one, but Warren here as elsewhere is the "yearner," for whom poetry is always a religious expression, whether of Original Sin, as in earlier poems such as "Billie Potts," or of hope and joy, as in some of his later poems, such as the love poem for his daughter, "To a Little Girl, One Year Old, in a Ruined Fortress," in *Promises,* or the fine nature poem "Heart of Autumn," which ends *Now and Then.* And even "Billie Potts" is a more heartening treatment of the theme of human alienation than is to be found in its most notable contemporary parallel, Albert Camus's play *Le Malentendu [The Mistake],* where Camus uses a nearly identical plot—of a mother and daughter who mistakenly kill their own son and brother for his money—but expresses the existentialist theme of absurdity and final loneliness rather than implying the Christian doctrine of Original Sin that gives Warren's poem, for all its brooding desolation, redeeming value.

"The Ballad of Billie Potts" is more than a personal variant of the traditional ballad, for it is also a symbolist poem, in the international mainstream of modern poetry, as well as a Fugitive poem, regionally southern and Kentuckian. Without the symbolist discoveries of the "correspondences" of the senses, it is not likely that Warren would ever have invented such a revoltingly effective metaphor as "The testicles of the fathers hang down like old lace"—not simply a naturalistic image, but a symbolic description of the feeling of ancestral guilt. Warren's poem is as sophisticated in its art as it is saturated in the reality of its native Kentucky. The moral of Warren's early poetry is that man carries a burden of sin always with him that cannot be relieved by trying to move constantly away from his time and place, his home. As Warren put it in the memorable last quatrain of "Bearded Oaks," another of his "Eleven Poems on the Same Theme":

> We live in time so little time
> And we learn all so painfully
> That we can spare this hour's term
> To practice for eternity.

It may be said that the question posed in all Warren's later poetry is, How do we practice for eternity? The answer did not come easily, for though the religious temperament was deep in Warren's southern puritan upbringing, he was never able to find a solution in orthodox Christianity, and his yearning for significance in life remained strongly individualistic. He said that at one time he found great comfort in reading Dante, until he discovered that Dante was only another Protestant like himself. He went through a period of poetic "drought" that lasted for a decade, from the mid-forties, when he published "Eleven Poems on the Same Theme" and "The Ballad of Billie Potts," until the mid-fifties, when he wrote "To a Little Girl, One Year Old, in a Ruined Fortress," which was the first of his later poems. As he later spoke of this dry interval in his poetic (not his fictional) career,

> For about ten years, from 1944 to '54, I was unable to finish a poem—I'd start one, and get just so far and then it would die on me. . . . Then I got married, and my wife had a child, and then a second; and we went to a place in Italy, an island with a ruined fortress. It is a very striking place—there is a rocky peninsula with the sea on three sides, and a sixteenth-century fortress on the top. There was a matching fortress across the bay. We had a wonderful time there, for two summers and more, and I began writing poetry again, on that spot. I had a whole different attitude toward life, my outlook was changed. The poems in *Promises* were all written there.[6]

Promises, published in 1957, was well named, for it did mark a departure in Warren's poetry. The opening poem was dedicated to his daughter, Rosanna (now known as a poet in her own right), the "little girl, one year old" whom he carried up to the fortress for their private ritual of plucking a flower. The poem is a fairly long narrative, like "Billie Potts," but the central character this time is an innocent child, and the experience is a happy one, for when he

---

6. Ibid., 229–30.

plucks the flower for his daughter beneath the ruined fortress, "Recognition explodes in delight, / You leap like spray, or like light." His daughter's innocent joy in nature evokes the fatherly response with which the poem ends:

> I cannot interpret for you this collocation
> Of memories. You will live your own life, and contrive
> The language of your own heart . . .

In the affection between father and daughter, against a backdrop of natural beauty, symbolized by the flower, and the historical memory of human conflict, symbolized by the ruined fortress, Warren had discovered the possibility of human joy, "that joy in which all joys should rejoice," a decidedly new note in his poetry.

Between *Promises,* for which he won his first Pulitzer Prize in poetry in 1957, and *Now and Then,* which won him his second Pulitzer Prize in poetry in 1978, Warren published a number of new poems, some memorable and some forgettable, collected in one volume of *Selected Poems* in the mid-1960s and in another in the mid-1970s. They were evidence enough of a second flowering of his poetic talent, and of the affirmative spirit that was continuing, a sense that the hopeful tone of *Promises* was being fulfilled by further achievements. But it was *Now and Then* that confirmed that the later poetic period had reached the level of mastery evident in the early period of the *Fugitive* and the first *Selected Poems, 1923–1943.* There are several excellent poems in the later vein to be found in *Now and Then,* and they show the Old Master fully aware of his powers, ranging from the opening poem, "American Portrait: Old Style," about a boyhood friend, a baseball player whom he meets on a return trip to his native Kentucky, through "Love Recognized," a poem for his second wife, the writer Eleanor Clark (though she is not mentioned by name), and culminating in the final poem, "Heart of Autumn," which is a portrait of Warren himself in old age at the summit of his poetic powers.

"Heart of Autumn" is a poem about death, the poet's own anticipated death, and it is also a poem of exultation in life. The form is a looser quatrain than his earlier poems, without rhymes, but it has a strong and unmistakable rhythm that is in accord with the central image of the poem, that of the wild geese flying southward in autumn, a familiar sight to Warren from his Kentucky boyhood—though it might just as well have been seen on the farm in Connecticut where he lived during most of his later years. It is an image of flight, but not of fleeing from something menacing, as in his earlier Fugitive poems; rather it is a flight toward something attractive, "toward sunset," clearly a metaphor for death. Warren is picturing the soul's imagined flight into eternity, for which he had been practicing throughout his long career by writing poetry. As he once put it, poetry for him was a "prayerful state" in which much time is spent simply in being passive, waiting for inspiration to come. In the poem, he watches the geese following their "path of pathlessness, with all the joy / Of destiny fulfilling its own name," and he thinks, "I have known time and distance, but not why I am here," and yet this difference between nature's instinctive sense of direction and man's indeterminate fate does not leave him feeling desolate or lonely or separated from nature. The "heart of autumn" is finally the poet's own heart, mortal yet exultant, thrilling to the "imperial utterance" of the wild geese honking in the sky, and responding with "a fierce impulse / To unwordable utterance": he, too, is rising up and singing, "Toward sunset, at a great height."

None of the poems Warren published after 1978 quite rose to the level of "Heart of Autumn," though a few poems were worthy of collection into the final *New and Selected Poems, 1923–1985,* Warren's most complete anthology to date. The long poem *Chief Joseph of the Nez Perce* (1982) cannot be counted among Warren's best poetic achievements; like *Brother to Dragons* (1953) and *Audubon: A Vision* (1969) (except for its fine concluding section, "Tell Me a Story"), it is an extended poem about an American hero that is more significant for its subject than for its treatment. Warren was as ambitious as any American writer in the scope of his imagination, but as he said in *Democracy and Poetry,* "The form of a work represents, not only a manipulation of the world, but an adventure in selfhood,"[7] and he knew that only when the world and the self satisfactorily converge in a poem does it become "the made thing" that "stands as a perennial possibility of experience." If only a small number of Warren's poems have the finish of high art, all are touched with the unmistakable personality of an artist who matured from early premonitions of the terrifying presence of evil into later meditations on the prevalence of good, and who left us enduring portraits of the artist, young as well as old.

7. *Democracy and Poetry,* 72.

17

LAURA RIDING
Fugitive, Witch, or Goddess?

Laura Riding, née Reichenthal, remains one of the mystery figures of modern poetry. Born in New York in 1901 of an Austrian-Jewish father and a German-Dutch mother, she was educated at Brooklyn Girls' High School and won scholarships to Cornell, but before she graduated she enrolled in a history seminar with Louis Gottschalk as graduate assistant, married him, and moved with him to Louisville, Kentucky, where he taught at the University of Louisville and she sent in her first poems to be published in the *Fugitive* magazine in Nashville. It was because of her recognition in 1923 as the only significant woman Fugitive that she attracted the attention of Robert Graves, already widely known as a British poet, and late in 1925, reading her poems alongside his own in the *Fugitive*, Graves wrote and invited her to come to England to collaborate on a book. She had left her husband and returned to New York by then, joining company with Allen Tate and Hart Crane and other artists, but she accepted Graves's invitation and sailed to England to meet him. From there she went to Egypt with Graves and his family, and her first book of poems, *The Close Chaplet*, was published in 1926 in England by Leonard and Virginia Woolf.

In 1928, *A Survey of Modernist Poetry*, the result of her collaboration with Graves, was published, a book in which modernism was largely denounced except for a few poems by herself and Graves and, strangely enough, E. E. Cummings. In 1929, Graves left his family and took Riding, along with their private Seizin Press, to the Spanish island of Mallorca, where they lived until the Spanish Civil War drove them back to England in 1936. In all, their tempestuous literary and personal companionship lasted from 1926 to 1940, and Graves always considered her the better poet, eventually devoting his most original book, *The White Goddess*, to her in 1948, though by then Riding had

left Graves to marry another American, Schuyler Jackson, an editor of *Time*
magazine, and to settle down with him on a citrus farm in Florida. After her
"final" *Collected Poems* appeared in 1938, she wrote no more poetry and began
denouncing poetry altogether as "a lying word"; her reputation, which had
been high in both America and England during her fifteen-year career (she
was praised by Auden and later by Larkin, as well as by Graves), dwindled
away steadily until at her death in Florida in 1991, at the age of ninety, she was
hardly remembered any longer except as the muse of Robert Graves.

Nonetheless, Riding was one of the most accomplished of the Fugitives,
praised in editorial comments from the time Ransom and Tate and Davidson
accepted her poems in 1923, and when they awarded her their Nashville Prize
in 1924, they paid her the highest critical tribute she ever received:

> With a diverse play of imagination she combines in her poetry a sound
> intellectuality and a keen irony which give her work a substance not often
> found in current American poetry. Her poetry is philosophical in trend,
> yet not divorced from life, but generally tense with emotion and concerned
> with profound issues. Furthermore, she has developed her own idiom of
> expression,—an idiom which manifests itself in a variety of forms, conven-
> tional or unconventional, and which gives her poetry the stamp of an original
> personality.[1]

The Fugitives published a number of her poems in the three years from 1923
until 1925, when they ceased publication, and her work compared favorably
in quantity as well as quality with the work of the major Fugitives, Ransom,
Davidson, Tate, and Warren. Yet she remained an enigmatic outsider, not a
southerner, nor a classicist, nor a traditionalist, as they were, but a woman who
expressed in her own characteristic way the theme of intellectual alienation—
the modernism at the heart of Fugitive poetry.

Laura Riding in her Fugitive days was by her own admission "religious in
my devotion to poetry," and the poems she contributed to the *Fugitive* stood
out from those of other poets because they were often written in a tightly
controlled free verse more like that of the imagists. Her appealing voice could
be heard in the first poem they published, "Dimensions," even if it carried a
disturbing note of personal defiance that was strictly her own:

> Measure me by myself
> And not by time or love or space
> Or beauty. Give me this last grace:
> That I may be on my low stone
> A gage unto myself alone.

---

1. *Fugitive* (December 1924): 130.

From the first, then, Riding set herself apart from all others, emphasizing her singularity as if only she could understand herself. Her variations on the central Fugitive theme of intellectual alienation could be fierce at times, her velvet glove often showing that it held an iron fist, as in the ending of another Fugitive poem, "Virgin of the Hills":

> The violence will be over
> And an old passion,
> Before I leave these ancient hills,
> Descend abruptly into the modern city, crying
> Love!

It could even be said that in one of her Fugitive poems, "The Only Daughter," Riding gave a hint of the sort of witchcraft she could practice, particularly on Robert Graves, which led him in time to make her his "White Goddess" whose charm both inspired and entrapped him for the fifteen years of their stormy relationship.

> But it is dangerous to keep an only daughter
> Like Atlantis or an isle
> Sunken in green water
> Through which may rise a smile.

Laura Riding thus gave an early intimation of the role she could play, the fancied mermaid who could seduce men like a modern Lorelei (or like "Belladonna, the Lady of the Rocks, the lady of situations" in Eliot's *Waste Land*), and if she was unable to entice the Fugitives for long (Allen Tate had a brief love affair with her), she was able to engage Robert Graves for much longer, living for nearly two decades with a married man who had a wife and children, then leaving him abruptly for another man, Schuyler Jackson, who as editor of *Time* magazine had praised her in print even more extravagantly than Graves, bracketing her with Rilke as the only true poets of the age. She returned to America to marry a second time and take upon herself the new name of Laura Riding Jackson, settling down for the rest of her life—over half of it, more than fifty years—on a citrus farm in Florida, a semi-recluse who wrote no more poetry and delivered only occasional, highly polemical salvos in prose.

Given her undoubted intellectual and poetic gifts, clearly demonstrated in her early Fugitive poems, her motives for renouncing poetry after 1938 are hard to understand. She may have taken poetry too seriously for its value as truth, and not seriously enough for its value as art, leading her to view poetry not as an end in itself but as a means to an end, the sort of end she indicated when she wrote, "Existence in poetry becomes more real than existence in time—more real because more good, more good because more true," and, "To live in, by, for the reasons of, poems is to habituate oneself to the good existence."[2]

At any rate, for the latter half of her life she construed "the good existence" to mean, not continuing to write poetry, but living a very private life on a farm in Florida and publishing only occasional essays or fiction that did little to enhance her reputation. All that can be said for her now is that her poetry deserves a higher reputation than she seemed willing to grant it herself. Her early success as a poet and her influence on other poets seems summed up in the formidable figure Robert Graves made of her in *The White Goddess.*

She did bewitch a succession of men she knew, and she inspired a number of writers, including some she did not know, leaving the question still to be settled whether she was more the witch than the goddess. These apparently contradictory roles were evident enough to some who knew her during her sojourn with Graves on the island of Mallorca, and at least one of them (T. S. Matthews, a *Time* editor who would introduce Riding to Jackson later on) was moved to set down his observations in print:

> I thought then, as I do now, that Laura's was the most brilliant mind I
> had ever encountered. Her brilliance, or mental force, was so dazzling and
> lightning-like that there was something frightening about it. Julie and I
> agreed that Laura's mind was supernormal but that she used her extraor-
> dinary powers for good, not evil. The way we put it was: "She's a witch, but
> a good witch."[3]

So impressive was Riding's poetic intellect that W. H. Auden, who dominated the younger generation of British poets in the 1930s, admired her as "the only living philosophical poet," and told her so despite her patent disdain for his and his fellow writers' leftist politics. Auden also admitted that he was consciously influenced by Riding's "thin-lipped style," which was coolly intelligent, like his early poetry. It was her poetry above all that won her the renown she enjoyed in the early 1930s, and when in the late 1930s she renounced it, she was renouncing what was best in herself, for in retrospect her ideas about poetry seem less truthful than her poetry itself, whose truthfulness she came to doubt.

From her own perspective, as she expressed it in the introduction she wrote for the 1980 reprint of her 1938 collection, *The Poems of Laura Riding,* she had been persuaded at first of the value of "twentieth century literary

---

2. Laura Riding, original 1938 preface to *The Poems of Laura Riding,* p. 413 in 1980 edition.
3. T. S. Matthews, *Jacks or Better,* 156.

modernism" and had adopted its creed of individualism and experimentation: "In becoming a poet in the century's first quarter of poetic modernism, I assumed the character of a modern in the freedom with which I, cheerfully, dispensed with the literary conventionalities of poetic idiom,"[4] and finding in poetry an "absolute, life-purifying quality of spirituality" that was in her view "the secular twin of religion," she wrote the poems that made her famous, with the encouragement first of the southern Fugitive poets and then of the English poet Robert Graves.

She idealized the role of the poet to the limit at first, remembering later, "My sincerity as a poet was a sincerity of spiritual literalness of faith in the truth-potentiality of words embodied in the spiritual creed of poetry" (p. 3). But her very success as a poet in those early years began to raise doubts in her mind about what she was accomplishing, and she became more and more convinced that "the privilege of individual freedom of word that poetry bestowed could not be itself a warranty of truth of word." In short, she began to doubt the source of her own inspiration as a poet and to feel that there was too much difference between her poetic use of language and the ordinary uses of language, so that it seemed to her that all poetry was somehow artificial, not "natural," too much absorbed with what she called "conventionalities of form that restricted the operation of thought," and she began to take seriously the criticism that her poetry was—like much modern poetry—too abstract and obscure for common readers to grasp.

Her awareness of her public role as a poet made her more critical of the effect modern poets were having on Western culture, especially through their pessimism, and it occurred to her that she differed in sentiment from most of them, because "In my poetic work and critical writing, I have indeed flown a banner of moral hope" (p. 6), and so she took upon herself more and more the role of evangelist and less and less the role of poet, becoming an advocate of truth in words and a denouncer of lying in words, which for her meant giving up the elitist cultivation of poetic language and taking up instead what she called "my commitment to a universal linguistic solution befitting the general dignity of being human" (p. 8). It came home to her, she said, when "I put the final touches to *Collected Poems* for the 1938 edition that I had reached a limit in the possibility of holding these commitments within one frame of endeavor." Soon thereafter, she renounced poetry because, though she thought it carried the right message, that is, "it is the destiny of human beings to speak the meaning of being," she had come to believe that it does so too exclusively, since poetry "nurses it in itself as in a sacred apartness, not to be translated

4. *Poems of Laura Riding* (1980), 1, hereafter in this essay cited parenthetically in the text by page number alone.

into the language of common meanings" (p. 9). She now subscribed to a new creed that no longer gave prior place to poetry among the uses of language, but instead elevated truth-speaking to the level of the "linguistic best," which she defined in language that is, alas, much more abstract and obscure than her poetry: "Such a best in linguistic expression would unite the effect of truth, the essence of the good in language, with the effect of perfect sincerity of being, the essence of the good in the human, the personal, form of life" (p. 10).

It is still difficult to assess the full achievement of this remarkable but mysterious woman, Laura Reichenthal Riding Gottschalk Jackson. She became by her own efforts and talents a modern poet of high individual distinction, in spite of the fact that she opposed many of the tendencies of modernism in poetry and in time turned her back on it altogether, devoting the latter half of her life to a private investigation into the meanings of words, out of which she produced the makings of a book that, if it is finally published, will be called *Rational Meaning: A New Foundation for the Definition of Words.* The poetry, however, lasts. It is founded on a strong assertion of will, which in her practice was both a creative and a destructive force, a powerful motive for originality of style and yet a virulent agent of the egotism of the poet.

It may be that Laura Riding, in going to such an extreme of individualism both as poet and as critic of poetry, exposed more openly than any other modern poet the risks of self-love, or solipsism—that besetting sin that T. S. Eliot in his famous essay "Tradition and the Individual Talent" sought to expiate by advocating not self-expression but "the continual self-sacrifice of personality" and that Allen Tate, in another famous essay, "Narcissus as Narcissus," saw in his own "Ode to the Confederate Dead" and characterized as "the modern squirrel-cage of our sensibility." Certainly an acute self-consciousness is part of the intellectual alienation that the Fugitives made the principal theme of their poetry, and it is part as well of the individualistic experiments that led the imagists to carve unique personal styles out of words. Riding was described by some as a "madwoman," and she may have been just that, another case of the close link between madness and genius (the most celebrated case among modern poets being Ezra Pound, but Robert Lowell was another such case); she was right in her intuition, however, that the more individualistic the poet becomes, the more inevitably poetry becomes an antisocial force. Riding represents, perhaps better than any other poet of the century, an extreme instance of the individualistic artist whose very success leads to a logical impasse, where words in their poetic use become a threat to rational control. She may have sensed that her poetry was "a lying word" because it led in the direction of anarchy, the separation of human beings from each other into private worlds cut off from any community—that is, into pure idiosyncrasy, the ultimate form of intellectual alienation. She wrote an early book of prose expounding her ideas, *Anarchism Is Not Enough,* but she later forsook the public expression of her views and sought "the good existence" privately, probably feeling that it was more likely to be realized privately than publicly. It is impossible to know whether Riding realized how symptomatic of her age she was, but her rampant egotism led her to attempt suicide on the one hand and to renounce poetry on the other, and it is possible that at least intuitively she may have feared the role she had created for herself, which Graves called the "White Goddess," because she was aware of its destructive as well as its creative potential, its capacity for evil as well as for good. From an early religious devotion to poetry as the highest good, she was converted to a view that it was an obstacle to goodness, and in a statement published posthumously, in the spring of 1992, she declared:

> There is discoverable in poetry an unsoundness that spoils it as a typi-fication of the Good. Complacent though poets be about their calling, it is likely they will be the first to discover the unsoundness, not the public. . . . Only they, furthermore, can bring poetry to the end of itself. It will not pass without vision of something better. . . . But perception of the character of happiness will rescue them, and open up the joyful prospect of a use of words that is directly informed with the Good—the goodness of which inheres in its being the practice of truth in loving verbal detail, merely.[5]

Riding renounced poetry in favor of what she believed might be a more truthful and socially beneficial form of communication, but if we read her early poetry with her later renunciation in mind, we are aware of an emergent theme that is different from, and in many ways opposed to, what she believed to be the "banner of moral hope" she thought she was flying. What she flew, much more often, was the black flag of pessimism, as deep-dyed as that in any of her contemporaries' poetry, and the sense of painful isolation was so persistent in her poetry that she may well have renounced it as too truthful, not too "lying," as if she were possessed by demons who forced her to say things about herself and her life that were perhaps more truthful than she consciously willed.

For instance, one of her early poems, "Incarnations," expresses the theme of death taking over life and robbing her of selfhood:

> From what grave, what past of flesh and bone
> Dreaming, dreaming I lie
> Under the fortunate curse,
> Bewitched, alive, forgetting the first stuff. . . .

5. Laura Riding, "Poetry and the Good," 24.

> I grain by grain recall the original dust
> And, looking down a stair of memory, keep saying:
> This was never I.

It would be hard to see any hopeful meaning about human existence in this poem, for what it implies is the old biblical message that flesh is dust, and in death we return to the dust from whence we came, losing whatever self may have been contained in the flesh we once were. Another early poem, "Pride of Head," is equally scathing about the sin of intellectual pride, which surely must have been on Laura Riding's conscience all her life, and which eventually she tried to renounce along with her poetry:

> My head is at the top of me
> Where I live mostly and most of the time,
> Where my face turns an inner look
> On what's outside of me
> And meets the challenge of other things
> Haughtily, by being what it is.

No poet has expressed a keener sense of the power of mind at work in human beings, nor a more pained conscience about its arrogance and superiority to the rest of human nature, than did Riding in this poem. Again, in an early poem called "How Blind and Bright," she articulated the theme of alienation from others along with that of intellectual pride, and in so doing she described the figure of the Fugitive as well as any member of the group:

> Eyes not looking out for eyes
> Look inward and meet sight
> In common loneliness,
> Invisibility and darkness.

She was obviously haunted by the awareness of mortality, pride, and loneliness reflected in these early poems, which are so eloquent with gloom over the human condition, so descriptive of man trapped in his prison of self, that they provide reason enough for her to feel guilty about writing such poems—not because they were not truthful, but because they presented, through the eyes of a sensitive modern individual, such a hopeless human state.

Was Riding, then, a Fugitive, a witch, or a white goddess? She was all three during her career, but what matters most is that she was a fine poet. It is her message of intellectual alienation and cultural pessimism that makes her more the Fugitive than either the witch of her imagination or the white goddess of

Robert Graves, since Graves was a poet of a more traditional, humorous, and optimistic kind.

All in all, Riding may be viewed as a Fugitive, because she was a poet of early distinction whose best poems were published in the *Fugitive* in the twenties but were not included in her later collections until *First Awakenings: The Early Poetry of Laura Riding* appeared in 1992. She belongs among the most original poets of modernism, a position she earned during her fifteen-year career as a poet, which lasted from 1923, when her first (and possibly her finest) poem, "Dimensions," was published in the *Fugitive,* until 1938, when her final *Collected Poems* was published. Her subsequent renunciation of poetry was a courageous but foolhardy act of defiance that cost her much respect and loss of reputation, but despite her own denial of its worth, Riding deserves to be honored for the poetry she wrote. She once believed that "existence in poetry becomes more real than existence in time"; her existence in time ceased in 1991, but she continues to exist after death in her poetry, which is the best that survives of her long, controversial, ultimately tragicomic life.

18

W. H. Auden's Secondary Worlds

W. H. Auden was an English poet by birth (York, England, in 1907) who became an American poet by choice (moving to New York in 1939) and who died in Austria in 1973 as an international poet. His career was in some respects the reverse of T. S. Eliot's, as both later recognized, since Eliot had left the United States to become an English citizen and Auden had left England to become a United States citizen: both were Anglo-American writers with a strong European bent. Auden said of Eliot that he had been among the "discoverers" of modern poetry, who revolutionized the style of English poetry as no native English writer could have, because Eliot (like Pound and Yeats) was an outsider, and could deal with the English literary tradition independently. Auden counted himself among the "colonizers," or second generation of modern poets, whose style was by necessity a development of the new and prevailing style rather than a radical departure from it. Among his masters, in addition to Eliot, Auden counted Thomas Hardy, Yeats, and—surprisingly—Laura Riding, whose style of cool intellectual abstraction was closest to the early Auden.

Auden had been a student at Oxford in the twenties, when modern poetry was in its golden age, and his first poems were printed on a private press owned by his friend and fellow poet Stephen Spender, who in his autobiography described Auden at Oxford as the leading man of letters for his generation even when he was an undergraduate. The portrait he gives of Auden as a student at Christ Church College, Oxford, in the late twenties is remarkable:

> Calling on Auden was a serious business. One made an appointment. If one arrived early one was liable to find the heavy outer door of his room, called "the oak," sported as a sign that he was not to be disturbed. When with him, one was liable to be dismissed suddenly and told the interview was at an end.

On the occasion of my fulfilling my first appointment, he was seated in a darkened room with the curtains drawn, and a lamp on a table at his elbow, so that he could see me clearly and I could only see the light reflected on his pale face. He had almost albino hair and weakly pigmented eyes set closely together, so that they gave the impression of watchfully squinting. He jerked his head up and asked me to sit down. There followed a rather terse cross-examination in which he asked me questions about my life, my views on writing and so on. In all this there was on my side an element of self-betrayal. I tried to please, gave away too much, was not altogether sincere. "What poets do you like?" he asked again. "Blunden," I said. "Not bad. Who else?" I mentioned another name. "Up the wrong pole." Another. "Written ravishing lines, but has the mind of a ninny."

He then told me who was good. These included Wilfred Owen, Gerard Manley Hopkins, Edward Thomas, A. E. Housman, and, of course, T. S. Eliot. He had an excellent verbal memory and could recite poems with an intonation which made them seem obscure, and yet significant and memorable. He had the power to make everything sound Audenesque, so that if he said in his icy voice, separating each word from the next as though on pincers, lines of Shakespeare or of Housman, each sounded simply like Auden.[1]

In the sixties, Auden returned to Oxford to hold the Chair of Poetry, and he gave an inaugural lecture called "Making and Judging Poetry," which was a retrospect of his whole career. In it, he referred to the distinction Coleridge had made about the poetic imagination in his *Biographia Literaria*: there was the Primary Imagination, which deals with sacred beings and events and is inspired by forces outside human nature, and the Secondary Imagination, which deals with communications between men, is primarily social, and receives its inspiration from within the human sphere. Of the two, Auden recognized that the poetry of the "discoverers" such as Eliot and Pound and Yeats had come largely from the Primary Imagination, and that its strength was an authority that came from somewhere beyond human beings, ultimately from a religious source, whether Christian or pagan, whereas the poetry of "colonizers" like himself and his contemporaries had come largely from the Secondary Imagination, which was social in origin.

Much of Auden's best poetry was in fact satirical or occasional, deriving from his own interests in other writers and from his social and literary criticism, for he was one of the best critics of his age. He was the leader of the group of writers dominant in the thirties—including those he had known at Oxford such as Stephen Spender and Christopher Isherwood—whose social

1. Stephen Spender, *World within World,* 45–46.

philosophy was marxist, the fashionable intellectual position of the period between the two world wars. Auden spent a brief period in Spain driving an ambulance for the Loyalists during the Spanish Civil War, went to China as an observer during the clash between China and Japan, and then settled in New York in 1939, from which vantage point he wrote some of his finest poems.

It was in January 1939, after a trip around the world, that Auden, who had been to the United States in 1938 and said he had fallen "madly in love with it," decided to settle permanently in New York and to become an American citizen. It was the eve of World War II, and Auden was declaring himself to be an international citizen. In a statement he wrote at that crucial juncture in his career, called "My Belief," Auden declared that men are by instinct social animals rather than isolated individuals, but that "man's advance in control over his environment is making it more and more difficult for him, at least in the industrialized countries with a high standard of living, like America and England, to lead a naturally good life, and easier and easier to lead a morally bad one." In addition to changes in the world that made life more convenient but less satisfying, Auden felt that there were upsetting historical changes at work on human beings: "We have the misfortune or the good luck to be living in one of the great critical historical periods, when the whole structure of our society and its cultural and metaphysical values are undergoing a radical change. It has happened before, when the Roman Empire collapsed, and at the Reformation, and it may happen again in the future."[2] Auden took the view that at such a time the poet must speak for the private conscience of man, since civilization seems threatened with disaster. In an age when most poets felt alienated from their society, Auden welcomed the role of social poet, and with his great versatility he spoke to a wide audience, though he was most at home among poetry audiences on the metropolitan and college circuit, where his verbal sophistication, his mixture of formal diction, learned allusions, current slang, and even scattered clichés were most appreciated.

"The Unknown Citizen" is one of the most effective satires written on the collective welfare state, and Auden wrote it after he gave up his marxist sympathies and decided to join an ostensibly free society by settling in the United States. But American society was as much his target as Russian or any other, for his poem shows the disappearance of the individual into the crowd (a subject Robert Penn Warren explored seriously in "To a Face in a Crowd"), becoming a mere number on a list with no name:

> He was found by the Bureau of Statistics to be
> One against whom there was no official complaint,
> And all the reports on his conduct agree

2. W. H. Auden, "My Belief," 5, 12.

> That, in the modern sense of an old-fashioned word,
> he was a saint. . . .

There is comic pathos in the use of *saint* in this context, since the Unknown Citizen has clearly sold his soul for material comfort and social solidarity. Auden viewed this upside-down saint, this soulless consumer, with an amused pity, seeing him not as a monster but as the very type of the common man in a democratic state, serving the "Greater Community" until the day he dies and then being buried with an anonymous marker, because he had made no impact:

> Was he free? Was he happy? The question is absurd:
> Had anything been wrong, we should certainly have heard.

Acknowledging the secular world he lived in, Auden recognized only a few real saints, who were mostly writers. His strongest allegiance throughout his career was to writers and artists, since he felt they did whatever could be done to preserve individuality, to keep alive the belief in a higher destiny, and to defend spiritual freedom against all forms of political and social domination. He did not view writers as superhuman, but as finite beings who could speak to those who would listen, and who, if they could not change the world for the better, could at least make it more endurable. Poets spoke best, he believed, to an audience of only one other person, and he varied his highly personal lyrics from free verse to sonnets, from ballads to pastoral elegies, becoming by his virtuosity the poet's poet for his generation, as Pound had been for the previous generation. Of all his poems of tribute to other writers, "In Memory of W. B. Yeats," which he wrote after the Irish poet's death in January 1939, shows his fullest range as a poetic craftsman as it expresses the theme of human isolation and the poet's compassionate response to it.

The three sections of Auden's tribute to Yeats form the major parts of a pastoral elegy, placing his poem in the long tradition from the Greeks, who invented it, to English poets such as Milton, who used it in "Lycidas," and American poets such as Whitman, who adapted it in "When Lilacs Last in the Door-Yard Bloom'd." In the first part of Auden's pastoral elegy for Yeats, following the formal tradition, the poet depicts all nature mourning for the dead person; in the second, he eulogizes the dead poet; and in the final part, he affirms the immortality the dead man has achieved by his work, which will keep his memory enduringly alive.

Part I of Auden's poem is written in free-verse stanzas with a refrain:

> O all the instruments agree
> The day of his death was a dark cold day.

Part 2 is in blank verse, unrhymed iambic pentameter, for the most part:

> You were silly like us: your gift survived it all;
> The parish of rich women, physical decay,
> Yourself; mad Ireland hurt you into poetry.

Part 3 is in rhyming tetrameter quatrains, heavily accented in meter and with strong end rhymes, the force of which taken together gives it the drumbeat of a funeral march:

> Earth, receive an honored guest,
> William Yeats is laid to rest.
> Let the Irish vessel lie,
> Emptied of its poetry.

The effect of the changing form in each section is to emphasize the changing themes, from nature and man together in the first part, to the dead man himself in the second part, and then to his apotheosis in the third part, where he is pictured as transcending death by the immortality of his work. Although the pastoral elegy was used by the Greeks for celebrating heroes, Auden's modern version of it plays down the heroic or ideal side of Yeats and treats him as all too human, having many personal faults but having created in his work the heroic expression of a fallible man. In short, Auden converts the elegiac form into a celebration, not so much of the poet himself (Auden said he had never met Yeats and probably wouldn't have liked him personally if he had) but of his art: the poetry is the finer part of the man.

Looking at the poem in greater detail, in part 1, Auden emphasizes the appropriateness of the winter season as a setting for Yeats's death, giving the description distinctly modern and ironic touches ("the air-ports almost deserted, / And snow disfigured the public statues"), so that it is not really nature but the city that is the environment, reflecting death as measured by a hospital thermometer, a cold clinical instrument; in fact, Yeats's death itself is seen as the death of a city, by means of an elaborately extended metaphor:

> The provinces of his body revolted,
> The squares of his mind were empty,
> Silence invaded the suburbs,
> The current of his feeling failed: he became his admirers.

Auden says that nature will go on as before, indifferent to the poet's death, but that there will be a few individual human beings scattered about the world, readers of Yeats's poetry, who will be affected by his death—not dramatically, but "As one thinks of a day when one did something slightly unusual." Auden's tone is deflating throughout; it could be called anti-heroic, and his assumption that no more than "a few thousand" out of the millions of people in the world will notice that the poet is dead is a reflection of the hard fact that good poetry appeals to a very small audience. Yet the refrain insists that he died on "a dark cold day," as if indifferent nature were somehow in sympathy with the mood of mourning that the poet feels.

Part 2 is the most personal section of the elegy: it admits that Yeats was "silly," holding many foolish opinions and behaving foolishly at times, the pet of "the parish of rich women" (who included Lady Gregory and Olivia Shakespear, among others), a man tormented by old age and by his own exacting conscience, and plagued by his Irish patriotism as well, as Auden put it, "mad Ireland hurt you into poetry," no doubt a sweeping reference to the Easter Rising of 1916 and all that followed it, turbulent events of Irish history that play such a prominent part in Yeats's poetry. All of these are human weaknesses that the poet displayed, but they are transcended by his poetry, for though "poetry makes nothing happen," changing nothing in Ireland or the world, it gives men an expression of their public woes and their private sufferings, and as long as poetry survives, so does what is best in man: poetry keeps his feelings and his conscience alive. Yeats the man, Auden says, was no more admirable than other men, but his gift raised him above them, and his poetry still lives in them, a kind of truth that must be preserved.

Part 3 is the elegy proper: it places the ashes of Yeats in the grave, but says that though his body is an empty urn, the poetry he produced out of it lives on. Auden celebrates poetry as an expression of man's thirst for immortality, saying that not only Yeats, but many other equally eccentric individuals have their faults forgiven because of their poetry. Auden sees poetry as redeeming man in an age when he is estranged, separated from his fellow men, more capable of hatred than of love: "in the deserts of the heart"—that is, in the Waste Land of the modern city—it is poetry that still can sing of freedom and of life, despite entrapment and death. The view Auden expresses at the end of his elegy for Yeats is that the poet's role is to penetrate the darkness and loneliness in the heart of modern civilized man and affirm that all hope is not lost. Yeats played this role, and the poem suggests that other modern poets did so as well, since some of the language is reminiscent of Eliot, and it is evident that Auden himself hopes to follow them, expressing individual courage in one of the darkest moments of civilization, in 1939, the year when Yeats died and World War II began.

The poem with which Auden commemorated that later event was called "September 1, 1939," the date when the war began with the Nazi invasion of Poland. It remains one of his best, although he himself struck it from later collections of his poetry because he felt that some of the lines were insincere (in particular, "We must love one another or die"). It is a poem that clearly reflects Auden's new Americanism, for it is set in "one of the dives / On Fifty-Second Street," a New York bar. It characterizes the whole of the thirties, when Auden was the emergent leader among poets, as "a low dishonest decade," recognizing that the events that had led to the war came about because the menace of German and Italian Fascism was not seriously opposed. Auden traces the origin of Hitler's nationalism to Luther and the Reformation, when Europe split away from the Church into warring nationalities, as well as to Hitler's worship of "a psychopathic god," and he remembers the lesson of Greek history, that Athenian democracy fell to the Spartan totalitarians, as chronicled by Thucydides in his account of the decline of Athens in the Peloponnesian Wars.

Recognizing the historical parallels leads Auden to think that modern Western democracies also may fall before states ruled by dictators, such as Nazi Germany and Fascist Italy, though if they did, it would be from weaknesses within as much as from enemies without:

> Into this neutral air
> Where blind skyscrapers use
> Their full height to proclaim
> The strength of Collective Man,
> Each language pours its vain
> Competitive excuse

Auden even sees himself in his Fifty-Second Street bar as in retreat from responsibility, as are all those who seek solace in drink, since they are refusing to face the reality of the war that has erupted in Europe, indulging themselves in private pleasures while civilization is threatened with collapse:

> Faces along the bar
> Cling to their average day:
> The lights must never go out,
> The music must always play,
> All the conventions conspire
> To make this fort assume
> The furniture of home;
> Lest we should see where we are,
> Lost in a haunted wood,
> Children afraid of the night
> Who have never been happy or good.

Analyzing what has gone wrong with civilization leads Auden to examine his own heart first and to find it full of self-love, and so to condemn in himself what he believes to be the besetting sin of liberal democracy that contributes to its downfall, the tendency for each individual to think only of his own happiness and to ignore the rest of mankind; he includes even artists such as Vaslav Nijinsky, the Russian ballet dancer, and Sergey Diaghilev, the impresario of the Ballets Russes, because they too indulged themselves in the pleasure of their art and lacked a social conscience:

> What mad Nijinsky wrote
> About Diaghilev
> Is true of the normal heart;
> For the error bred in the bone
> Of each woman and each man
> Craves what it cannot have,
> Not universal love,
> But to be loved alone.

Auden sees his role as poet, in the time of crisis brought on by the war, as one of providing an honest assessment of the human conscience, "To undo the folded lie, / The romantic lie in the brain / Of the sensual man-in-the-street," of asserting against the self-indulgent attitude he finds in himself the truth that "There is no such thing as the State, / And no one exists alone," and of seeking ways to break out of the shell that isolates every human being from his fellow man: "We must love one another or die."

Though Auden later accused himself of insincerity in this desperate wartime plea, treating love as the only means of salvation man could trust, he was justified in putting the crisis in the strongest possible terms as the war began and in trying to be one of the "Ironic points of light" in a world plunging into darkness, since only "Ironic points of light" had any chance of illuminating the darkened consciences of men, and his last lines are a prayer to whatever gods may hear him (the Christian message is not yet firm on Auden's lips, though it is on the way):

> May I, composed like them
> Of Eros and of dust,
> Beleaguered by the same
> Negation and despair,
> Show an affirming flame.

It is fair to say that Auden saw his social role in 1939 more clearly than at any time of his life, since he wrote three of his best poems during the same year he decided to become an American: "The Unknown Citizen," "In Memory of W. B. Yeats," and "September 1, 1939." Auden responded to the coming of the war with the full weight of his European historical consciousness and his newfound freedom of expression as an American, which included using American slang words such as *dives* and *commuters*, giving his poetry a new raciness and contemporaneity.

Auden went on writing, through the war and after it, demonstrating again and again his skill at fashioning new poems, and continuing to assert the theme of his elegy for Yeats, that poetry was a means of helping man to be free. In some of the best critical essays of the age, collected in such books as *The Dyer's Hand* and *Secondary Worlds,* Auden argued that poetry was at its best a means of keeping religious faith alive, since he, like Eliot, had been converted to the Anglican Church, maintaining despite the secular age he lived in that there must always be a relation between the words of men and the Word of God, and that in so far as the poet expresses awe, wonder, mystery, and the ennobling emotions of men, as well as disgust, rage, and indignation at whatever degrades men, there will be reason to rejoice and not to give in to despair. As a poet, Auden continued to the end to practice both the art of praise and the art of satire, though many of his best poems are satirical, and no poem of his is without its touch of irony and wit, even when he is being most serious, since for Auden, the social poet, humor was as important an ingredient in poetry as beauty. His best religious poems are long sequences: *For the Time Being,* a play for voices that he called a Christmas Oratorio, and *Horae Canonicae,* or "Canonical Hours," a series of personal prayers at the traditional hours set aside for prayer in the medieval church. His most effective satires are shorter poems, such as "Under which Lyre: A Reactionary Tract for the Times," with its criticism of the intellectual fashions of the university, "On the Circuit," which is a wry glance at college poetry readings, and especially his "Prologue at Sixty," an irreverent poetic autobiography in which he looks at himself critically in old age:

> Who am I now?
> An American? No, a New Yorker,
> who opens his *Times* at the obit page

and thinks that he is hardly fashionable any longer, more and more aware of the bodily infirmities that advancing years bring with them, morbidly fascinated with death, and yet still believing that death is not the final end of human consciousness, and so concluding his amused self-examination with a prayer that is serious:

In *Acts* it is written
Taste was no problem at Pentecost.

To speak is human because human to listen,
beyond hope, for an Eighth Day,
when the creatured Image shall become the Likeness:
Giver-of-Life, translate for me
till I accomplish my corpse at last.

This poem was published in 1967, only a few years before Auden died in Kirchstetten, Austria, a suburb of Vienna, the home about which he had written a series of sketches called "Thanksgiving for a Habitat." His "Prologue at Sixty" came nearest to being the poet's own epitaph, with its mixture of self-critical humor and religious seriousness; it serves as Auden's final word about himself and his beliefs.

19

A WELSH SYMBOLIST
Dylan Thomas

It is natural to think of Yeats as an Irish poet, since he identified himself with the cause of Irish Nationalism, which succeeded during his lifetime in creating a separate state. However, Yeats's language was English, and he had an affinity for the French symbolists; therefore, he was as international a poet as any in the twentieth century. To call Yeats an Irish symbolist is only to recognize the influences he brought to bear on English poetry, which were both Irish and French. He wrote in English, not in Irish or French, and his tradition was English poetry, but his sensibility was unlike that of any native English poet, since the diction and rhythms of his poetry were derived from the distinctive way English was spoken in Ireland. He introduced Irish mythology into the English poetic tradition, and the conscious use of symbolism in his poetry came from his understanding of what French poets were doing in their language.

It is harder to place Dylan Thomas as a Welsh symbolist, because his poetry exhibits neither the strong nationalism nor the French influences evident in the poetry of Yeats; nevertheless, Thomas went beyond Yeats in stressing the spoken voice and the music of words, and in practicing the oral tradition, and for that reason alone Thomas qualified as a latter-day Celtic bard, singing his poems unaccompanied, but singing them all the same, and letting them be heard on radio broadcasts and phonograph records, so that audiences could go on listening to them long after he could no longer deliver them in his deeply resonant voice.

Thomas's poetic career was all too short, lasting barely twenty years, and when he died in 1953 at the age of thirty-nine—the result of a massive brain hemorrhage brought on by acute alcohol poisoning—he was on one of his highly successful reading tours of the United States, which had made his difficult, obscure poetry accessible to a wide audience. At the time of his death in New York, he was just launching a verse-play for voices called *Under Milk Wood*, a moving, sometimes hilarious drama about the small Welsh fishing village of Laugharne (pronounced "larn"), where he had settled with his family a few years earlier. The effect of the play, as with his readings and records, was magical, and Thomas did more to revive the sound of the spoken voice in modern poetry than even Yeats was able to do, for Thomas had the special gift of a marvelously rich voice, and he had been trained to read poetry when he broadcast over BBC radio during World War II. Though Thomas knew no more of the Welsh language than Yeats knew of the Irish language, after Yeats he was the poet who did most for the bardic tradition of the Celts, and he may even, by a stretch of imagination, be thought of as a Welsh bard in modern dress speaking English.

As for other influences on his poetry—Thomas joked, in introducing his readings, that he knew only English, "BBC and saloon," but wished he knew French, because then "maybe I would understand what some people mean when they say I have been influenced by Rimbaud"[1]—there are echoes in him of Hopkins and of Hart Crane, and he himself praised the World War I poetry of Wilfred Owen. But really, Thomas's poetic style was his own creation, for he was a celebrator of natural life, of "The force that through the green fuse drives the flower," that is, of the organic forces in nature. He used a singing, oratorical style full of complex and dark imagery, and made much of Christian symbolism without ever adopting the orthodoxy of his contemporary Auden or of the older Eliot. Thomas once described his poetry as "the record of my individual struggle from darkness toward some measure of light," and in fact the central imagery of his poetry has to do with birth, as when the plant breaks through the darkness of earth into the sun in "The force that through the green fuse drives the flower," or the painful and terrifying experience of the newborn infant being thrust out of the darkness of the womb into the light of day in "If my head hurt a hair's foot."

The essence of one of his most moving and mystifying poems, "Light breaks where no sun shines," is the internal working of the physical processes of the body, an inner darkness of unconscious instinct that Thomas—not without ironic touches—presumes to bring to light by means of verbal imagery. He begins with the metaphor of the blood as a sea and the heart as the source of energy, and lets the circulation of the blood through the body become a fantasy of "broken ghosts with glow-worms in their heads" which "file through the flesh" as the blood reaches every extremity. The second stanza of this tightly controlled yet free-verse poem pictures sexual energy originating from the

---

1. Dylan Thomas, "A Few Words of a Kind."

"candle in the thighs," or male organ, then impelling its "seed" to the "fruit" and "fig," or female organ, and so creating new life from the body, as a candle sheds light on the darkness. Stanza 3 then moves to the brain, with "Dawn breaks behind the eyes," and what is seen becomes what is unseen, where the emotions aroused in the body are transmitted by the nerves to a gushing of both happiness ("a smile") and grief ("the oil of tears"). Stanza 4 is filled with imagery of sleep and dreams, where the darkness of night engulfs the body "Like some pitch moon" and yet "Day lights the bone," and spring forms inside the body just as does winter, since the mind can produce light from its own thoughts, without any need for sun. The final stanza is a summary of all that is inside the body, insisting that "Light breaks on secret lots," that there are "tips of thought where thoughts smell in the rain," and above all that it is not logic but intuition that guides the interior life of man, and so it is possible that "The secret of the soil grows through the eye," even if what is outside is sterile, a Waste Land of the city, where "Above the waste allotments the dawn halts."

Thomas delighted in juxtaposing images in the manner of the French symbolists, using the "fused metaphor of Symbolism" in the manner of the American symbolist Hart Crane as a means of expressing private sensations that are otherwise beyond words. His most compelling description of his creative process was as a violent conflict of opposing images:

> I make one image . . . let it breed another, let that image contradict the first, make, of the third image bred out of the other two together, a fourth contradictory image, and let them all, within my imposed formal limits, conflict. Each image holds within it the seeds of its own destruction, and my dialectical method, as I understand it, is a constant building up and breaking down of images that come out of the central seed, which is itself destructive and constructive at the same time. . . .
>
> Out of the inevitable conflict of images—inevitable because of the creative, recreative, destructive and contradictory nature of the motivating center, the womb war—I try to make that momentary peace which is a poem.[2]

Having developed his complex poetic style at home in Wales, where he was the son of an English grammar school teacher, Thomas went from his native Swansea to London during World War II, and he wrote some of his most moving poems about the experience of London during the blitz, or Battle of

---

2. Dylan Thomas, letter to Henry Treece, quoted in *The Poetry of Dylan Thomas,* by Elder Olson (Chicago: University of Chicago Press, Phoenix Books, 1961), 34–35.

Britain, in the early forties, when he saw destruction and death constantly about him, yet found the capacity to sing joyfully amid the chaos. His poem, "A Refusal to Mourn the Death by Fire of a Child in London," came directly out of the firebombing of London by the Germans, when a small girl's body was uncovered in the ashes of a bombed house, inspiring him to write a defiant hymn of praise, one of the most memorable poems to come out of the war.

"A Refusal to Mourn" is about a death that becomes a birth. The source of the poet's defiance is his belief that all death leads back to birth: for him, every burial brings forth new life, not more death, as in Eliot's Waste Land. Thomas shapes his poem as five symmetrical free-verse stanzas, rhyming obliquely a-b-c-a-b-c, and to this formal symmetry he adds the rhetorical shape of a single long declarative sentence, which runs from the first line of the first stanza to the first line of the third stanza, followed by two more declarative sentences, each about one stanza long. The poem is thus highly organized, both rhythmically and rhetorically, and it is full of internal rhyming effects, such as frequent alliteration and assonance, increasing the overall harmony of the composition. What is even more impressive, though initially baffling, is the chain of conflicting images, which do not seem to be so much about the war and the child's death as about the mysterious processes of nature. What the poet is saying, literally paraphrased, is that until his own death comes, he will never stop celebrating the glory of the child's passage into nature, where she joins the dead of all the ages and goes on living in the elements of the earth and water, the fertility that never ceases to be regenerated, no matter how many individuals die. The poem does not describe a single physical process from death into birth, but is highly complex in its imagery and infused throughout with a tone of awe: the poet sees the darkness of death as a womb of nature, out of which all life springs—birds, beasts, flowers, and men— and the sea as a cyclical motion of nature, "tumbling in harness," because driven by powers of attraction and repulsion that are always at work, and the decay of the body at death as a rejuvenation of natural elements—the "round zion of the water bead" and the "synagogue of the ear of corn" are biblical allusions that make nature into a temple of worship, and even human tears become a "salt seed," which is "sown in the least valley of sackcloth"— literally, a pocket handkerchief. Everything in nature, as Thomas pictures it, is constantly converting death into life, mourning into joy, and the child's death in the firebombing of London is full of "majesty and burning," as if it were a funeral pyre, deliberately set to celebrate the passing of the little girl. Since the poet conceives of death as a glorious rather than a sorrowful experience, he refuses to "murder" her memory by writing an elegy, or funeral song; rather, he writes a hymn of joy and praise, picturing the little girl, in her "innocence and youth," asleep with the older dead of London, not merely in one war, but in all generations past, sharing their silent company and that of the elements of nature and her mother earth, beside "the riding Thames," an image of the river flowing through London like a giant rider on horseback. The last line of the poem is highly ambiguous—"After the first death, there is no other."—and demands to be taken in more than one sense, both as "each of us dies only once; therefore we should not grieve over death," and as "there is no death after the first one, but there is immortality in nature, hence we should not mourn but rejoice."

When Baudelaire in his seminal sonnet "Correspondences," the credo of French symbolism, conceived that "All nature is a living temple," he was foreshadowing such a poem as this one of Dylan Thomas, in which the very language becomes sacramental and filled with religious awe, and the experience of death is so interlocked with life that it is impossible to say where one ends and the other begins. In fact, most of Thomas's poems can be catalogued as either birth or death poems, or as a mixture of the two. A death poem such as "A Refusal to Mourn" may be transformed by Thomas into a birth poem, and a birth poem such as "Fern Hill" can just as readily become a death poem.

"Fern Hill" may be the most lyrical of all Thomas's poems, a celebration of childhood innocence comparable to Wordsworth's "Ode: Intimations of Immortality from Recollections of Early Childhood," but with the difference that in Thomas there is a constant war going on in the child's mind between immortality and mortality, and that in the end mortality wins. It is an autobiographical portrait of childhood, since Fern Hill was the name of a Welsh farm owned by Thomas's aunt, Ann Jones, where Thomas as a young boy often played. He makes it the setting for childish fantasies in which he imagines himself "young and easy under the apple boughs," as "prince of the apple towns," who "lordly had the trees and leaves / Trail with daisies and barley / Down the rivers of the windfall light." This blissful existence is extended in the second stanza (each stanza in controlled free verse of Thomas's own invention) to his becoming a "huntsman and herdsman" who can direct the calves on the farm and even the "foxes on the hills" and can believe himself a priest of nature, for whom "the sabbath rang slowly / In the pebbles of the holy streams." The young boy revels by day in the "hay / Fields high as the house" and in "the fire green as grass" (reversing the cliché, since fire is usually red but may appear green or yellow), and at night he hears the owls "bearing the farm away" into the darkness where the nightjars sing and the horses gallop through the dream world of the sleeping boy. Then, in the next morning of the fourth stanza, a birth miracle occurs, the cock crowing as the sun returns to shine like "Adam and maiden," as if this were the first day of creation—and it is, for he imagines

So it must have been after the birth of the simple light
In the first, spinning place, the spellbound horses walking warm
    Out of the whinnying green stable
            to the fields of praise.

In other words, the birth of Christ in the stable at Bethlehem was a day of
creation like that of Adam and Eve, and they are reborn in the eyes of the
young boy each day on the farm, when he sees the sun come up after a night
of darkness. Childhood innocence continues in the fifth stanza, with the boy
chasing about the farm "honored among foxes and pheasants" and pursuing
his "sky-blue trades," but beginning to feel that it all must end, for

                              time allows
    In all his tuneful turning so few and such morning songs
        Before the children green and golden
                him out of grace.

So as the poem of birth and childhood joy comes to its close in the last stanza,
the note of mortality has begun to be heard, and it grows louder as time comes
more and more to control the boy's carefree meanderings, for "time would
take me / Up to the swallow thronged loft by the shadow of my hand," and
the boy (who is now a man) must "wake to the farm forever fled from the
childless land." It is remarkable how the tone changes at the end of Thomas's
poem from the happiness of birth into the sadness of death, and the joyful
singing of the child becomes the mournful singing of the adult, looking back
on his lost childhood:

    Oh as I was young and easy in the mercy of his means,
        Time held me green and dying
        Though I sang in my chains like the sea.

As a Welsh symbolist, Dylan Thomas was able to make a rich verbal music
that could change birth into death and death into birth, and if his own life
was mercilessly short it was also mercifully blessed with song. Listening to the
recorded voice of Thomas reading "Fern Hill" aloud is perhaps the best way
of appreciating his poetry, for he used language as if it were symphonic form,
blending a subtlety of sense with a harmony of sound. "A good poem," he
once wrote, "is a contribution to reality. The world is never the same once a
good poem has been added to it." In his short lifetime, Dylan Thomas added
appreciably to the stock of good poems in English through his resonant voice
and his reverberating Welsh music.

20

PROPHETIC AND DEMONIC VOICES IN ROBERT LOWELL'S POETRY

> Ah, the swift vanishing of my older
> generation—the deaths, suicide, madness
> of Roethke, Berryman, Jarrell and Lowell,
> "the last the most discouraging of all
> surviving to dissipate *Lord Weary's Castle*
> and nine subsequent useful poems
> in the seedy grandiloquence of *Notebook.*"

That was how Robert Lowell summed up his poetic career in 1973, just four years before his death, in a poem called "Last Night," one of those informal free-verse sonnets that make up the collection rather grandly named *History*. *My History*, he might have called it, since, like his larger collection called *Notebook*, it is an almost daily account of his misfortunes, telling us all the worst about himself relentlessly, indulging over and over in the shocking self-exposure that was the hallmark of his later style. Here, he was confessing publicly that he had failed to live up to his early promise—largely true, as many readers of Lowell would agree, because *Lord Weary's Castle*, his Pulitzer Prize–winning collection of 1946, was an epoch-making book of poems that he never equaled again, but there was also some humorous exaggeration in speaking of his "seedy grandiloquence"—seedy, yes, but hardly grandiloquent, since Lowell's later style was as deliberately casual and downbeat as his early style had been formal and passionate.

Lowell was not joking, however, about being one of the longest survivors in a generation of self-destructive American poets—Roethke, Berryman, and Jarrell were his most brilliant contemporaries, and all were dead by the time he wrote the poem. He too was dead within a few years, but by then Lowell had come to see them all in historical perspective, as inheritors of a tradition that began with Paul Verlaine, who called his fellow symbolists in France in the late nineteenth century "les poètes maudits" [the damned poets], a tradition consciously continued by Yeats in his *Autobiography*, when he spoke of his friends in the Rhymers Club in London at the turn of the century as "The Tragic Generation." There was a difference, however, between the way Lowell saw himself and the way either Verlaine or Yeats had seen himself, for Lowell made his own self-destruction the subject of his poetry, deliberately translating his personal decline and fall into art. It was as if, having risen to the heights in the first decade of his career, Lowell turned against himself and, during his last two decades, subjected his readers to all the torments of mind, body, and conscience that he himself was suffering. As the acknowledged major poet of his generation, he felt free to inflict his personal anguish on the world, and he appeared to do so with increasingly morbid relish, if we can believe what he says about reading his own poems:

> Like millions, I took just pride and more than just,
> first striking matches that brought my blood to boiling;
> I memorized tricks to set the river on fire,
> somehow never wrote something to go back to.
> Even suppose I had finished with wax flowers
> and earned a pass to the minor slopes of Parnassus . . .
>
> this open book . . . my open coffin.

Poetry made from self-inflicted pain was nothing new—Baudelaire, after all, had written *Mon coeur mis à nu [My Heart Laid Bare]* a century before—but Lowell was arguably the first to make masochism fashionable, to influence other poets to write their excruciating confessionals in verse and to create an audience avid for any kind of degrading experience the poet might choose to describe, the more horrifying the better.

Of course high tragedy can be horrifying, too, since it involves us in the suffering of the hero, but high tragedy is always about a mythical hero, not about the author himself. Sophocles may well have suffered imaginatively the wounded pride of Oedipus, and Shakespeare may have endured vicariously the self-laceration of Hamlet, but neither Sophocles nor Shakespeare chose to mortify his own flesh, on stage, in person, as Lowell did. The bouts with insanity, the temptations to suicide, the marital woes he experienced with three successive wives, his failures both as a son and as a father—all these were Lowell's own, the ruins of his life, and his books became his open coffin, where he slowly and agonizingly died before the reader's eyes. Reading Lowell's later poetry is like voluntarily submitting to torture, and yet many readers seemed to love it, many poets imitated it, and many critics praised him above all other poets of his time. Is it possible now to understand how so much self-flagellation could have won him so much esteem?

Part of the answer is that Lowell was often his own best critic—in his poetry and also in his prose. An unfinished essay posthumously published in his *Collected Prose* (1987) tells us a great deal about the psychological strategy of Lowell's later poetry. His working title for it was "Art and Evil," and it begins with a quotation from T. S. Eliot's *After Strange Gods: A Primer of Modern Heresy,* a controversial set of lectures given at the University of Virginia in 1933 (which Eliot must have regretted, since he chose never to reprint it) in which he had spoken of "the intrusion of the diabolic in modern literature."[1] Eliot had attributed the powerful hold of evil on certain writers—Hardy and Lawrence were his major examples, and he called them "men of genius"—to the loss of moral conscience brought about by the decay of Christian belief. Eliot admitted that the diabolic might be hard to recognize in writers as widely read and admired as Hardy and Lawrence; Lowell quotes him as declaring, "I doubt whether what I am saying will convey much to anyone for whom the doctrine of Original Sin is not a very real and tremendous thing," but he contended that "a positive power for evil . . . may operate through men of genius of the most excellent character," and he used Hardy and Lawrence as examples of major writers in whom "the demonic powers found an instrument."

Eliot's views were delivered late in his career, after his conversion to Anglo-Catholicism; Lowell had been converted to Roman Catholicism early in his career, led at least partly by Eliot's example, but what he said in response to Eliot's discovery of evil in certain modern writers reveals much about the state of Lowell's mind at the time he was writing *Life Studies* in the 1950s:

> This passage at first struck many of us as a little stiff and silly, as being itself a bit diabolic. . . . And now, in 1956, we are older than the Eliot of 1933; we are older than the aged eagle himself; Original Sin has lost its shine for us; we no longer possess that simple faith, that straightforward sophistication, and that angry bounce that allowed T. S. Eliot to call Original Sin *tremendous.*

The difference between Eliot and Lowell, and between the earlier and later poetry of Lowell himself, can be fairly accurately adduced from these words. For Eliot had said that to recognize the diabolic means that one must be capable of being shocked by evil, and Lowell was saying that he had lost the capacity to be shocked. The poet of "Mr. Edwards and the Spider," of "The Quaker Graveyard in Nantucket," of "At the Indian Killer's Grave," who had

---

1. Robert Lowell, "Art and Evil," in *Collected Prose*, 129–44; Eliot, *After Strange Gods,* 61.

been able in his early poems to think himself back to Puritan New England, much as Hawthorne had done in his fiction, to share sympathetically its acute consciousness of Original Sin, and to voice dark prophecies about the future of the human race, now found that Original Sin no longer filled him with awe. Consciously, Lowell thought his new attitude more sophisticated than Eliot's, but unconsciously, he seemed to be proving Eliot's thesis that the diabolical flourishes as the moral sense atrophies. It is probably significant that Lowell never finished his essay "Art and Evil," but he went far enough with it to suggest that "one of the hopeful characteristics of our human nature is that we cannot even put up with *evil* for long, unless it is made exciting, and we cannot put up with excitement unless it is true."

Lowell in his essay tried to account for the perennial fascination of such great villains of literature as Milton's Satan, Shakespeare's Iago, and Faulkner's Popeye, characters recognized as powerfully and attractively evil both by the author and by his readers. He did not however, and probably could not, account for the kind of fascination Eliot was speaking of in *After Strange Gods,* when evil is unconsciously personified in the writer himself. Yet what Eliot professed to find in the fiction of Hardy and Lawrence—not so much in their poetry—might well be found in the later poetry of Lowell, in the strange demonic voice of a man helplessly obsessed with suicide, as in "Suicide":

> Do I deserve credit
> for not having tried suicide—
> or am I afraid
> the exotic act
> will make me blunder . . . ?

or possessed by insanity, as in "Fetus":

> Is getting well ever an art,
> or art a way of getting well?

or deliberately cruel, as in "St. Mark's, 1933":

> even now
> my callous unconscious drives me
> to torture my closest friend

or flippantly blasphemous, as in "Home":

> The Queen of Heaven, I miss her,
> we were divorced. She never doubted

> the divided, stricken soul
> could call her Maria,
> and rob the devil with a word.

In Robert Lowell's poetry, the prophetic and the demonic voices echo and re-echo; they speak for the author, directly or indirectly, and they have a way of making evil seem exciting and truthful at the same time, as he thought the artist must do. But there is a crucial difference between those voices that register shock at the evil in the world and those that express attraction toward it, and this difference to a large extent distinguishes the poetry of the early from that of the later Lowell. To put it simply, prophetic voices resound in the early poetry as often as demonic voices reverberate in the later poems, and understanding the changes in Lowell's voice is a key to understanding his poetic development.

I use the words *prophetic* and *demonic* to account for a metamorphosis in Lowell's poetry that might otherwise be seen as a character change, or as a change from character to personality, for all these words are closely related to what is sometimes called the authorial presence, the self projected by a writer in his work. *Prophetic* and *demonic* are both words with strong religious overtones, *prophetic* coming from a Greek word for "speaking forth," especially referring to inspired utterance or oracular pronouncements by people presuming to speak for gods, such as Tiresias in *Oedipus the King* or Cassandra in *Agamemnon,* while *demonic* also comes from Greek and means literally "possessed by spirits," especially in the sense of evil spirits taking human form, like the tempting Sirens in the *Odyssey* or the frenzied women in the *Bacchae.* So to speak of prophetic and demonic voices at all is to speak of invisible powers at work in human beings, and these powers may be for the better or for the worse, as the Greeks were quick to recognize, since their belief, at least as Plato expounds it in the Socratic dialogues, was that divine inspiration seizes the poet and causes him either to go mad or to appear mad. In Lowell's case, it would seem that poetic inspiration did lead directly to madness, because in little more than a decade he went from religious conversion to psychotic breakdown, a destructive process reflected in his poetry in the striking differences between the style and subject matter of *Lord Weary's Castle* in 1946 and *Life Studies* in 1959.

Critics have differed sharply on which of these is Lowell's best book, but all have agreed that a remarkable change took place in Lowell's poetry during the 1950s, so that it has become as customary to speak of the early and the later Lowell as it is to speak of the early and the later Yeats, or Pound, or Eliot. A change of style is often the mark of a major poet, but the difference that is generally regarded as a maturing of poetic power and wisdom in an older poet seems in Lowell more like a catastrophic degeneration of personality and loss of self-control—a clear case of the divine or demonic madness that led Plato to ban poets from his ideal republic.

I use the word *personality*—not the word *character*—to describe the change in Lowell's poetry, because it was the key word Eliot used in *After Strange Gods,* the book that provoked Lowell in mid-career to reflect on the relation between art and evil. *Personality* is not identical with *character,* even in origin, because *character* comes from the Greek verb "to engrave," as in carving words on a stone tablet, and we know that the Greeks regarded character as equivalent to fate, and hence the very substance of human identity, whereas *personality* comes from the Latin word *persona,* the mask that actors spoke through (*per* + *sona* meaning literally to "sound through"), and therefore personality signifies willed behavior that is not inherent but assumed. Eliot believed from the start, as he made clear in "Tradition and the Individual Talent," that poets who sought to be universal must strive to be impersonal, and in *After Strange Gods* he came down hard on the cult of personality in modern literature, saying that "when morals cease to be a matter of tradition and orthodoxy . . . and when each man is to elaborate his own, then *personality* becomes a thing of alarming importance." Observing that "it is fatally easy, under the conditions of the modern world, for a writer of genius to conceive of himself as a messiah," Eliot held that Hardy and Lawrence were writers who imposed their own powerful personality on everything they wrote, as if personal expression were in itself a guarantee of truth. "Where there is no external test of the validity of a writer's work," Eliot argued, "we fail to distinguish between the truth of his view of life and the personality that makes it plausible; so that in our reading, we may be simply yielding ourselves to one seductive personality after another." If the only test of a writer's truthfulness is the sincerity with which he expresses himself, Eliot concluded, then " 'sincerity' is considered more important than that the self in question should, socially and spiritually, be a good or a bad one," and "the personality which fascinates us . . . tends naturally to be the *unregenerate* personality, partly self-deceived and partly irresponsible, and because of its freedom, terribly *limited* by prejudice and self-conceit, capable of much good or great mischief according to the natural goodness or impurity of the man: and we are all, naturally, impure."[2]

That Eliot's remarks were more relevant to Lowell's case than Lowell himself perceived is to be judged, I think, from the amount of attention that has been given since his death to Lowell's tormented life, recognizing that the subject matter of his poetry became increasingly himself and his madness. He fictionalized his most humiliating experiences for the sake of his art, and the fact that he continued to draw readers into the vortex of

---

2. Eliot, *After Strange Gods,* 58–68.

his suffering shows that, as with Hamlet's feigned lunacy, there was method in his madness. As Monroe K. Spears notes in his essay "Life and Art in Robert Lowell" in *American Ambitions* (1987): "Lowell was a remarkable and fascinating personality; whatever his faults, nobody ever found him boring."[3] Indeed, Lowell may be seen as a further illustration, among writers of this century, of Eliot's criticism that in an age without any fixed moral principles it is not heroic character, but the unregenerate personality, that we find most fascinating.

However, it is important to remember that Lowell was not always mad; if he had not written a great deal of fine poetry before his mind cracked, it is doubtful whether the later poetry would have fascinated readers as much as it did. For in the early poetry, it was not the poet's own tormented personality that was dominant, but the character of earlier writers whom he was able to assimilate and whose voices he managed to modulate into what became a single prophetic voice denouncing the evils of his age. Such earlier American writers as Jonathan Edwards, Hawthorne, and Melville all speak through Lowell's words in the early poetry, giving authority to his dark vision of the apocalypse of Western civilization. Again and again, in *Lord Weary's Castle*, Lowell shows the ability to put New England history in touch with contemporary history, and so to see his age *sub specie aeternitatis*, that is, under the judgment of eternity. For instance, he adapted Hawthorne's voice to describe the massacre of the native Indian tribes by the zealous Puritan colonists in the seventeenth century, and he connected it with the waste land of twentieth-century Boston in "At the Indian Killer's Grave":

> Behind King's Chapel what the earth has kept
> Whole from the jerking noose of time extends
> Its dark enigma to Jehoshaphat;
> Or will King Philip plait
> The just man's scalp in the wailing valley!

Or he could speak in the terrifying manner of Jonathan Edwards, the spell-binding Puritan preacher of the Great Awakening of the 1730s in "After the Surprising Conversions":

> Content was gone.
> All the good work was quashed. We were undone.
> The breath of God had carried out a planned
> And sensible withdrawal from this land;

---

3. Monroe K. Spears, "Life and Art in Robert Lowell," in *American Ambitions*, 46.

Or he could appropriate the words of Melville, brooding on the Civil War in the 1860s in "Christmas Eve under Hooker's Statue":

> When Chancellorsville mowed down the volunteer,
> "All wars are boyish," Herman Melville said;
> But we are old, our fields are running wild:
> Till Christ again turn wanderer and child.

Whatever voice he used, Lowell built a consistent character in his early poetry, through a series of tightly constructed stanzas and lines packed with complex images and filled with dramatic tension, culminating in a devastating prophecy of the end of man in the closing lines of his long masterpiece, "The Quaker Graveyard in Nantucket," which in length and complexity compares with *The Waste Land* and is one of the best as well as longest of all Lowell's poems:

> Atlantic, you are fouled with the blue sailors,
> Sea-monsters, upward angel, downward fish:
> Unmarried and corroding, spare of flesh
> Mart once of supercilious, wing'd clippers,
> Atlantic, where your bell-trap guts its spoil
> You could cut the brackish winds with a knife
> Here in Nantucket, and cast up the time
> When the Lord God formed man from the sea's slime
> And breathed into his face the breath of life,
> And blue-lung'd combers lumbered to the kill.
> The Lord survives the rainbow of His will.

The early Lowell was strongly attracted to his New England ancestors—"Of New England Mr. Lowell has the ambivalent knowledge one has of one's damned kin," Randall Jarrell said in a review of *Lord Weary's Castle*, one of the earliest and finest essays ever written on Lowell,[4] and there is no more convincing contrast to be found, between the early and the later Lowell, than in his successive poems about Jonathan Edwards, the last great Puritan preacher and theologian.

We know that when Lowell went south in the summer of 1937 to be a disciple to Allen Tate, and in a famous episode pitched a tent in the front yard of Benfolly, the Tates' home near Clarksville, Tennessee, he was at work on a biographical study of Edwards. He never completed it, but he used the material

---

4. Randall Jarrell, "From the Kingdom of Necessity," in *Poetry and the Age*, 208–19.

very effectively in his poetry. One of the best early poems in *Lord Weary's Castle* is "Mr. Edwards and the Spider," and one of the best later poems in *For the Union Dead* is "Jonathan Edwards in Western Massachusetts." The differences between them are as interesting as the poems themselves, for they show how Lowell moved from internalizing the character of Edwards to externalizing the personality of Edwards, from speaking with the prophetic voice of Edwards in his most successful role as Puritan evangelist—roundly condemning sinners to hell during the revival period of the Great Awakening in order to bring thousands of lost souls into the church—to picturing Edwards as a failure in exile in western Massachusetts, preaching to the Indians after his congregation in Northampton, in eastern Massachusetts, who had supported him with enthusiasm throughout the Great Awakening, dismissed him because they could no longer tolerate his strict enforcement of the Puritan code of spiritual and moral discipline. To see how Lowell changed in his attitude toward Jonathan Edwards is to see graphically how he changed his own poetry.

Lowell based his early "Mr. Edwards and the Spider" on two main texts, Edwards's precocious childhood essay "Of Insects" and his famous Great Awakening sermon "Sinners in the Hands of an Angry God," and he interwove them so skillfully that one can hardly tell where Edwards is speaking and where Lowell is speaking. In fact, in a recorded reading of this poem, Lowell introduced it by saying that the point of view is that of Edwards, "who sounds like a fiend but was really a very great man." The poem begins:

> I saw the spiders marching through the air,
> Swimming from tree to tree that mildewed day
>   In latter August

Edwards himself, in "Of Insects," had written about spiders: "everyone knows the truth of their marching in the air from tree to tree . . . , nor can anyone go out amongst the trees in a dewy morning toward the latter end of August or at the beginning of September but that he shall see hundreds of webs made conspicuous by the dew that is lodged upon them." From this delightful natural scene, full of images of a warm New England summer day, Lowell turns in the next stanza to ask, "What are we in the hands of the great God?" and then in the third stanza to describe the black widow spider, that poisonous North American insect marked by a red hourglass on its belly, whose bite can bring death, and to assert ominously:

>   It's well
> If God who holds you to the pit of hell,
>   Much as one holds a spider, will destroy,
> Baffle, and dissipate your soul.

In his sermon "Sinners in the Hands of an Angry God," Edwards himself had used the spider image to terrify his congregation: "The God that holds you over the pit of hell, much as one holds a spider, or some loathsome insect, over the fire, abhors you and is dreadfully provoked; His wrath towards you burns like fire; He looks upon you as worthy of nothing else but to be cast into the fire." In the fourth stanza of his poem, Lowell goes on to describe the spider's death by fire as if it were the soul of a sinner cast into hell:

> On Windsor Marsh, I saw the spider die
> When thrown into the bowels of fierce fire . . .

And in the final stanza, the black widow spider becomes death itself, and the soul of the sinner is imagined burning forever in hell:

> Let there pass
> A minute, ten, ten trillion; but the blaze
> Is infinite, eternal: this is death,
> To die and know it. This is the Black Widow, death.

There is no consolation offered here; Lowell does not, as Edwards did in his sermon, offer the alternative to damnation, which was "to awake and fly from the wrath to come" by repenting and becoming a member of Christ's flock, the church. The poisonous black widow spider dominates Lowell's poem, whereas it was simply a rhetorical figure and a common spider in Edwards's sermon—though unforgettable, even to readers of the sermon today. What Lowell has done in taking on the character of Edwards and assuming his prophetic voice is to issue a warning that man cannot escape death nor the Last Judgment of God that will follow, not in Edwards's time nor in our own. The religious perspective of the poem is clear enough, even if the emphasis is upon damnation rather than salvation.

It is quite otherwise in Lowell's later poem "Jonathan Edwards in Western Massachusetts," and one can only assume that between writing the first Edwards poem in the forties and the second Edwards poem in the sixties, Lowell had undergone something like a fall from grace into the hands of an angry God. Furthermore, he had seen a similar pattern in Edwards's own career, from the enormously successful leader of the Great Awakening in the 1730s to the failed preacher whose flock has cast him out and exiled him to the Massachusetts frontier and the Indians, there to write his major theological work, *The Freedom of the Will*, and to find, when he was invited to become president of the newly founded Princeton College in New Jersey, that he hardly had the heart to accept it because of his extreme self-doubt. Edwards did accept the job, but he died after only two months in the office at Princeton, at the age of fifty-five, from the effect of a smallpox vaccination that proved toxic. Lowell in his poem deals only with Edwards's period of exile in Western Massachusetts, but he implies that the offer of the presidency at Princeton will not restore Edwards to his former self-assurance and hope of salvation. Thus the later poem presents Edwards as a pathetic and disillusioned figure, not a prophet of God, and it elicits sympathy for him in his weakness, but does not see him as a tragic hero who accepts responsibility for his own fall. In the later poem, Lowell is the narrator; the voice is no longer the voice of Edwards, and it is clear that Lowell shares the self-pity that he attributes to Edwards and that he sees Edwards descending at the end into bleak despair, as did Lowell himself at the time he wrote the poem.

The poem begins, in free-verse quatrains rather than rhymed stanzas—the looser poetic form goes with the change of heart—by describing the simple frontier setting where Edwards spent his last years, where "Faith is trying to do without / faith," the remnant of the faithful still living there, like sheep without a shepherd, having nothing to live for any longer. Lowell goes on to speak of his own generation in the same way:

> We know the world will end,
> But where is paradise, each day further
> From the Pilgrim's blues for England
> and the Promised Land.

And then he imagines himself meeting Edwards in heaven, as Edwards had often told his congregation he expected them to do:

> Ah paradise! Edwards,
> I would be afraid
> to meet you there as a shade.
> We move in different circles.

He remembers from Edwards's *Personal Narrative* that as a boy Edwards built a booth in a swamp for prayer, and there watched the spiders fly in the air, "swimming from tree to tree," as Lowell words it from his own earlier poem, adding, "You knew they would die." But this time he does not see the spider as an image of the sinner; instead, it is a part of nature that offers Edwards whatever consolation he may have felt on the wild New England frontier. Then Lowell brings to mind Sarah Pierrepont, the young Connecticut girl Edwards was to marry, who, when he first met her, seemed the perfection of innocent spirituality and a sure recipient of God's grace,

So filled with delight in the Great Being,
she hardly cared for anything—
walking the fields, sweetly singing,
conversing with some one invisible.

But Edwards, Lowell says, was able to give her only "a Negro slave and eleven children," and "people were spiders / in your moment of glory, / at the Great Awakening." He quotes from Edwards's farewell sermon, given when he was forced to leave his congregation in Northampton, where he leaves them with a warning:

Alas, how many
in this very meeting house are more than likely
to remember my discourse in hell!

And this monitory tone leads him to think of Edwards's fall from grace:

You stood on stilts in the air,
but you fell from your parish.

Lowell pities Edwards in disgrace and loneliness on the frontier, and he thinks of the final work of Edwards as a Puritan evangelist, "writing, writing, writing, / denying the Freedom of the Will." His concluding image is of an Edwards "afraid to be president / of Princeton" who confesses his own "deffects" and recognizes painfully that "I have a constitution peculiarly unhappy." The last words of the poem are Edwards's own, but they might almost be Lowell's, as he laments aloud, "I am contemptible, / stiff and dull." So the later Jonathan Edwards begins to resemble the later Robert Lowell, at least as Lowell depicts him, and though there is support for this despairing portrait in Edwards's writing, and though Lowell draws some striking quotations into "Jonathan Edwards in Western Massachusetts," just as he had in "Mr. Edwards and the Spider," the net result is certainly more personal and confessional in the later poem than in the earlier, and the tone and theme have changed drastically, from a terrifying denunciation of Original Sin and invocation of the wrath of God to a pitying description of a lonely old man beset by a sense of personal failure and the futility of his existence. Reading these poems together, knowing that they were written some two decades apart, it is possible to hear almost audibly Lowell's change of voice from the prophetic to the demonic.

I do not wish to overstate the case, yet we could go a step further down in Lowell's curious loyalty to Edwards the Last Puritan, so unlike himself and

therefore so complementary, for there is one more poem about Edwards in
the collection called *History* written in the last decade of Lowell's career. It is
"The Worst Sinner, Jonathan Edwards' God," and it reads in part:

> The earliest sportsman in the earliest dawn,
> waking to what redness, waking a killer,
> saw the red cane was sweet in his red grip;
> the blood of the shepherd matched the blood of the wolf.
> But Jonathan Edwards prayed to think himself
> worse than any man that ever breathed. . . .
>
> Each night I lie me down to heal in sleep;
> two or three mornings a week, I wake to my sin—
> sins, not sin; not two or three mornings, seven.
> God himself cannot wake five years younger,
> and drink away the venom in the chalice—
> the best man in the best world possible.

Lowell has extended his sympathy for Edwards in this very late poem beyond
hell and earth to heaven, where God sits in judgment on them both, as he
did in the beginning on Cain and Abel, and Lowell imagines that in that first
murder of brother by brother "the blood of the shepherd matched the blood
of the wolf," and man's fate was sealed for good, whether as criminal or as
victim: the alternatives for man, from the beginning, were equally unhappy.
Since Jonathan Edwards did indeed pray "to think himself worse than any
man that ever breathed," as he wrote in his *Personal Narrative*, Lowell wonders
whether any man can escape the wrath of God, and waking every morning
with a renewed sense of his sinfulness leads him, not to repent, but to blame
God for his suffering, and to question whether even God—or Christ, "the
best man in the best world possible"—can in the end forgive himself, "wake
five years younger, / and drink away the venom in the chalice." As the title
implies, it is God who is the worst sinner of all, and to call him "Jonathan
Edwards' God" is simply to credit Edwards with the terrible revelation that
God is man's eternal enemy, who created man as a sinner, as he created Cain,
and Edwards, and Lowell. It would be hard to find a more demonic poem
than this one in all of modern literature, since the transformation of God
into Satan, the creator of good into the creator of evil, seems the last cry of
despairing mankind, unless we take another line from *After Strange Gods* and
say with Eliot, "Where blasphemy might once have been a sign of spiritual
corruption, it might now be taken rather as a symptom that the soul is still
alive." Still, we would have to add about Lowell, as Eliot did about Lawrence,
"The man's vision is spiritual, but spiritually sick."

Lowell, like Lawrence (and like Hardy, despite Eliot's criticism), will go on being read for both his early and his late poems, for the prophetic as well as the demonic voices that he uttered, simply because at his best he was a great poet. But his poems in his *Selected Poems* reveal a large number of truly memorable poems in the first volume, as compared with the relatively sparse number in the succeeding volumes, thus bearing out Lowell's own late assessment of his work. If we continue to think of him as a major poet, we are likely to mean what he spoke of, "*Lord Weary's Castle* / and nine subsequent useful poems," rather than the vast bulk of forgettable poems—and some memorable poems we might wish were forgettable—written during his highly productive career. It is enough to say that Lowell was sometimes divinely inspired, sometimes simply mad, placing him in the company of other great modern poets such as Ezra Pound, whose works will endure because they are great, and Lowell will undoubtedly continue to be celebrated as the last major modern poet.

21

THE POET AS TRAGIC HERO:
Pasternak's *Dr. Zhivago* and the End of Modernism

The poets of the first half of the twentieth century made a new style of poetry out of many older styles, creating, by means of their poetry and their criticism, an expectation of great poetry that lasted through the remainder of the century, though it diminished slowly until, as the century drew to a close, great poetry was no longer being created nor fully appreciated. The "appetite for poetry" that Paul Valéry spoke about at the beginning of the century, when French symbolism was flourishing, was much less in evidence by the end of the century, when poetry had devolved into a period style that seemed increasingly derivative and into new "theories" of literature that had little to do with poetry at all.[1]

Modern poetic heroes, from Baudelaire's voyager to Yeats's visionary Irishman to Eliot's Prufrock to Pound's Mauberley to Pasternak's Dr. Zhivago, are alike in sharing a sense of heroic failure, the defeat of the artist or idealist who attempts to live for nonmaterial values and to strive for aesthetic or moral or spiritual goals in life. Such poets look at life tragically: to Baudelaire, "God is the eternal confidant in that tragedy of which each man is hero," and Yeats believed that "we begin to live when we have conceived life as tragedy," while Thomas Hardy wrote: "Tragedy. It may be put thus in brief: a tragedy exhibits a state of things in the life of an individual which unavoidably causes some natural aim or desire of his to end in a catastrophe when carried out."[2] Yeats's self-dramatization in his later visionary poems makes a tragic figure of the

---

1. See Frank Kermode, "Prologue," in *An Appetite for Poetry,* 1–46.
2. Charles Baudelaire, "My Heart Laid Bare," 52; William Butler Yeats, *The Autobiography of William Butler Yeats,* 128; Thomas Hardy, "Hardy Talks to Himself," in *The Portable Thomas Hardy,* 754.

poet, one who feels keenly that "an aging man is but a paltry thing / A tattered coat upon a stick" and sees himself as a "weather-worn marble triton among the streams," forced to recognize that his poems are of little consequence to "the bankers, schoolmasters, and clergymen that idlers call the world," because "Romantic Ireland's dead and gone, / It's with O'Leary in the grave." Yeats was not personally involved in the Easter Rising of 1916 out of which Ireland emerged as an independent nation, but he knew its leaders well and bore witness to their tragic deaths, which raised them in his eyes from "the casual comedy" of life to the fanatical, foolhardy courage of death, by which they were "changed, changed utterly" until "A terrible beauty [was] born."

And Pound in his *Cantos* projected himself tragically as a poet who followed Tiresias's prophecy to Ulysses, repeated in Canto 1, that he would "lose all companions" on his life's journey and would be forced much later, in Canto 74, to lament the deaths of those he had known best, the writers who were his closest friends:

> Lordly men are to earth o'ergiven
>   these the companions:
> Fordie that wrote of giants
>   and William who dreamed of nobility
>   and Jim the comedian singing:
>   "Blarrney castle me darlin'
>   you're nothing now but a StOWne"

A half-century after Yeats wrote his "Easter 1916" and Pound wrote his first canto, Pasternak's fictional alter ego, Dr. Zhivago, became another exemplary case of the poet as tragic hero, writing poems in a time of revolution and repression in Russia, being forced to descend into the disorder and squalor of his society, leaving only his poems behind as a memorial to private aspirations that were fulfilled though his other missions in life, as a doctor and lover and husband, had failed. The modern poet may be, like Pasternak's Dr. Zhivago, or like Pound in the prison camp at Pisa, a tragic hero, or may simply wear a tragic mask, like Wallace Stevens's "connoisseur of chaos," an ironic maker of order amid disorder, or like Rilke, who heard "the singing of things" despite the overpowering materialism of the age, and tried by his re-created Orpheus to redeem man even from death by his singing.

Pasternak's *Dr. Zhivago* seems to stand as the last great masterpiece of the entire modern period, from Baudelaire to the present, because it is unique in combining the modern novel and modern poetry at their best in a single book, a feat that no other writer has achieved. Pasternak's novel spans the major events of modern history, from pre-Revolutionary, Czarist Russia, through World War I, the Russian Revolution, and the Stalinist period, to World War II.

The novel is a fictional autobiography, with a poet as its hero, one who not only writes poems privately but is tragically involved in most of the major events of his time, who has both a public and a private career, like Pasternak himself. Pasternak must have realized that he had written a culminating work of modernism when he agreed, despite official Russian censorship, to let an Italian publisher bring his book out in 1957—exactly a century after Flaubert's *Madame Bovary* and Baudelaire's *Les Fleurs du mal* appeared in Paris—for though it was thoroughly Russian, it was also thoroughly international, in the twin traditions of the French realist novel and the French symbolist poem. Edmund Wilson, American critic and historian of the symbolist tradition, was among the first to recognize the place of Pasternak's poetic novel in modern literature; he hailed it in a *New Yorker* review as "an event in man's moral and intellectual history."

Any reader of *Dr. Zhivago* is immediately reminded of Joyce's *Portrait of the Artist as a Young Man,* of Pound's *Hugh Selwyn Mauberley,* and of Eliot's "Love Song of J. Alfred Prufrock." The heroes of Joyce's novel and Pound's poem were poets who wrote poems themselves, just as Pasternak's hero does; moreover, there is the same vein of irony running through Pasternak's novel as ran through Joyce's novel and Pound's and Eliot's poems, for his poet-doctor struggles to maintain his personal integrity against the destructive events of history. Yuri Zhivago tries heroically to be the public servant and patriot, the loyal husband and father, but he is broken on the wheels of war and revolution, separated from his family and forced to follow a degenerative course of action rather than to make a conscious self-sacrifice of his life. As early as 1936, during the Stalinist purges, Pasternak had said publicly at a Soviet Writers' Congress, "Art is unthinkable without risk and the self-sacrifice of the human soul." Dr. Zhivago's only real success is in his poetry, which comes out of his intensely private life as an artist, and which he leaves behind as his final legacy, the proof of his sincerity as a writer and of the authenticity of his existence in a time of human alienation and violence.

Pasternak had come to write his late masterpiece after a brilliant but shadowed career as a poet in Revolutionary Russia, one who miraculously survived all the bloody events of his lifetime and kept on writing, his early fame eclipsed by that of his friend Mayakovsky, who put his considerable gifts at the service of the Communist state and became Stalin's favorite poet, while Pasternak remained intensely private despite his reputation as one of the foremost Russian poets in a generation of outstanding talents that included Esenin, Gumilyev, Akhmatova, and Mandelstam. Esenin and Mayakovsky both committed suicide, Gumilyev was executed shortly after the Revolution, and Mandelstam vanished in a concentration camp during the Stalinist purges of the thirties, but Pasternak and Akhmatova continued as internal exiles in the Soviet state, Pasternak sustaining himself by his masterful translations of

Shakespeare when his own writing was too "decadent"—meaning modern and international—to be published.

Because of his artistic parentage, as a Russian Jew whose father was a portrait painter to the last Czar and whose mother was a concert pianist, and his advanced education, which included Moscow University as well as philosophical study at Marburg in Germany, Pasternak had always felt bound to what he called "the tangible unity of our culture." Believing that "the history of culture is the chain of equations in images," Pasternak wrote in his autobiography, "I loved the living essence of historical symbolism, that instinct by which, like house swallows, we have created our world—a huge nest, stuck together from earth and sky, life and death, and two times, time present and time absent."[3] Pasternak viewed art as the redemption of life, even in the worst times such as he knew in Russia under the Communists, and he felt long before he wrote his masterpiece of fiction and poetry that "the symbol of man is greater than man himself." After years of writing lyric poetry and translating poetry from other languages, Pasternak came to believe that "it is no longer possible for lyrical poetry to express the immensity of our experience," because life had grown "too cumbersome, too complicated," and that therefore a combination of prose and poetry was needed for the full expression of life. He said modestly of *Dr. Zhivago*, after its international fame had been assured by the award of a Nobel Prize for literature (which he had to decline to avoid being exiled from Russia): "I don't know whether my novel is fully successful, but then with all its faults, I feel that it has more value than those early poems. It is richer, more humane than the works of my youth."[4] Thus Pasternak deliberately chose to write a combined work of fiction and poetry that was unprecedented at the time his novel appeared, and that few writers in any language could even have attempted. He told the story of his poet-hero in a condensed, rhythmical prose and then placed the "Poems of Yuri Zhivago" at the end, as the last will and testament of this doctor whose life had paralleled his own life, from pre-Revolutionary to post-Revolutionary Russia, but who, unlike the author, died of a heart attack on a Moscow tram shortly after World War II.

Pasternak said that "the plan of the novel is outlined by the poems accompanying it," which he placed there, he said, "to give the novel more body, more richness"[5] and to enhance its religious symbolism. The poems of Dr. Zhivago come at the end of the novel, though we know he worked on them many times before, and they interweave symbolic parallels between Zhivago, Hamlet, and Christ, thus implying a thematic connection with these fictional

3. Boris Pasternak, *Safe Conduct*, 101.
4. Boris Pasternak, interview by Olga Carlisle, in *Poets on Street Corners*, 88.
5. Ibid., 84.

and real sacrificial heroes, with a further symbolic parallel in the character of
Lara, the dark mistress of Zhivago, who is compared with Mary Magdalene,
the fallen woman whom Christ redeemed.

Many of the poems are written by Pasternak's hero at that point late in the
plot of the novel when Zhivago, separated by revolution and civil war from
his wife and family in Moscow, has taken refuge with Lara in a winter cottage
in the Ural Mountains, and most of them are tragic love-poems with a strong
vein of irony running through them. As he writes in the solitude of a Russian
winter night, his life already in ruins, he affirms his belief in the redemptive
power of art that can make order out of chaos, beauty out of catastrophe, just
as Baudelaire, Yeats, Pound, Eliot, Stevens, Warren, and other modern poets
had done before him:

> As he scribbled his odds and ends, he made a note reaffirming his belief
> that art always serves beauty, and beauty is delight in form, and form is the
> key to organic life, since no living thing can exist without it, so that every
> work of art, including tragedy, expresses the joy of existence. And his own
> ideas and notes also brought him joy, a tragic joy, a joy full of tears that
> exhausted him and made his head ache.[6]

Pasternak thus agreed with the view of the later Yeats that the paradoxical
feeling of "tragic joy" is the highest emotion possible in art, and of all the
poems Yuri Zhivago writes during his life and leaves behind at his death,
perhaps the most tragically joyful is "Winter Night," a lyrical celebration of
the passionate though illicit love of the exiled doctor and his mistress. It brings
together symbolically three widely separated events in the novel, linking Yuri
and Lara at the beginning, the middle, and the end of the action, and therefore
serving better than any of the poems to outline the plot, as Pasternak said he
meant all the Zhivago poems to do.

The first episode of the novel that foreshadows "Winter Night" describes
the frozen window pane with a candle burning inside it, a scene that Yuri
as a young man sees on his way to a Christmas party in Moscow, without
knowing that in the room where the candle is burning is Lara, whom he is to
meet later. At that moment, when he sees the candle burning a circle in the
frozen glass, Yuri starts the poem in his mind with the refrain "Upon a table:
candle-flame . . ." He goes no further with it until much later in the novel,
when he begins working on it in the summer cottage in the Ural Mountains,
on a winter night when Lara is sleeping with her child in the bedroom, and
he completes it there in a sudden rush of inspiration that Pasternak fully and
dramatically describes:

6. Boris Pasternak, *Dr. Zhivago*, 378.

After two or three stanzas and several images by which he himself was struck, his work took possession of him and he felt the approach of what is called inspiration. At such moments the relation of the forces that determine artistic creation is, as it were, reversed. The dominant thing is no longer the state of mind the artist seeks to express but the language in which he wants to express it. Language, the home and receptacle of beauty and meaning, itself begins to think and speak for man and turns wholly into music, not in terms of sonority but in terms of the impetuousness and power of its inward flow. Then, like the current of a mighty river polishing stones and turning wheels by its very movement, the flow of speech creates in passing, by virtue of its own laws, meter and rhythm and countless other forms and formations, which are even more important, but which are as yet unexplored, insufficiently recognized, and unnamed.

At such moments Yurii Andreievich felt that the main part of the work was being done not by him but by a superior power which was above him and directed him, namely the movement of universal thought and poetry in its present historical stage and the one to come. And he felt himself to be only the occasion, the fulcrum, needed to make this movement possible.[7]

Zhivago presumably finishes the poem there in the remote cottage in the mountains on a winter night, but it is not read by others until after his death, and by then a third episode has occurred that is linked to "Winter Night." He has become separated from Lara as he had been separated from his wife and family earlier, and after his death by heart attack, his body lies in a room in Moscow, and Lara comes to view it; as she stands looking at the corpse of her lover, she recalls their love affair, against the snowy backdrop of the Ural Mountains, and suddenly she recalls the image of the candle burning in the window—without knowing that Yuri had seen it earlier, too. The burning candle in the frozen window has therefore become an unknown link between them through the course of their lives and has come to symbolize their passion.

Winter Night

Snow fell and fell. It filled the air,
the whole world claiming.
Upon a table: candle-flame,
a candle, flaming.

Like clouds of summer insects swarming
about a flame,
the white flakes flocked and swirled about
the window-frame.

7. Ibid., 363–64.

Circles and arrows on the glass,
the snow made, gaming.
And on a table: candle-flame,
a candle, flaming.

On the illuminated ceiling,
two silhouettes.
A cross of arms and legs, a feeling
of crossing fates.

Two slippers fluttered to the floor—
no other sound—
but soft, upon a dress, wax tears
came dropping down.

The world lay blanketed in snow,
grey-white and dreaming.
Upon a table: candle-flame,
a candle, flaming.

A sudden draft blew from a corner,
touched fever-springs:
a cross rose upward through the air,
like angel's wings.

The snow fell on, through February,
always the same.
And always on the table flared
the candle-flame.
                    (my translation)

This poem is symbolist in its use of the candle to represent the passion of the lovers, who are never directly seen, and imagist in its concentration on the single indoor winter scene that is dominated by the candle-flame. But it is also ironist in that the candle seems to go on burning month after month in spite of the winter cold, symbolizing the enduring love of Zhivago and Lara in the novel, and yet the reader of the novel knows their love will last only until Lara leaves once again and they are parted for good—the candle, still flaming with heat and light inside, while the world outside is dark and cold with snow, is a symbol of the brevity of life and the transience of their love. Thus, in Pasternak's novel, a fusion of the modern novel with the modern poem finally occurs, with a multiplicity of ironic contrasts typical of both the modern novel and the modern poem. The power of poetry and fiction united in Pasternak's novel is greater than either would be separately, and there has been no comparable masterpiece in the four decades since. More recent poets have been less critical of their age, less tragic in their stance.

The Zhivago poems stand as a highly significant group of poems by a modern poet, showing greater coherence, in their direct relation to the life of the fictional poet who wrote them, than other collections of poems, and since the story of Zhivago's life is contained in the novel, the poems do not need any further biographical context to be understood. They sum up his life and are the immortal part of him, as poetry tends to be the immortal part of any civilization, lasting longer on the whole than other literary forms. The poems not only attest to the enduring value of the poet's life, but they authenticate it, since by their high quality as symbolist-imagist-ironist poems they prove convincingly that the fictional Zhivago, like the real Pasternak, was a major artist of the modern tradition. They represent that tradition well, in its subjectivity and intimacy, its refinement of feeling and subtlety of expression, its irregular but musical rhythm. They are not greater, certainly, than the poems of Baudelaire, Yeats, Rilke, Pound, Eliot, or other major modern poets—no one of them by itself may be called a masterpiece—but in the context of the novel, a major work of fiction, they are major works of poetry. Their modernism, that is to say, their obscure symbolism and allusion, their ironic dualism, the subtleties of meaning that make modern poetry challenging to the reader, all are related to the life of their supposed author, the fictional hero Yuri Zhivago, and beyond him to the life of their creator, Boris Pasternak.

The Zhivago poems are also consciously related to two of the greatest tragic heroes in Western religion and literature: Christ and Hamlet. Pasternak opens the sequence of Zhivago poems with "Hamlet" and closes it with "Magdalene" and "The Garden of Gethsemane," linking his hero with Shakespeare's best-known tragic hero and with the God-man of the New Testament (Pasternak himself, a Jew by birth, had converted to Russian Orthodox Christianity). Thus it may be said that in the poems of Dr. Zhivago the figure of the modern poet as tragic hero achieved its fullest international expression.

Is modernism then at an end? The greatness of modernism may indeed be past, but we are still in the process of understanding what it means, and as long as that effort continues, we are not likely to see another movement of comparable greatness. Modernism has included symbolism and imagism in poetry, realism and naturalism in fiction, and irony in both forms of literature. Because of its pervasiveness, and because it expresses an inner duality, or ambivalence, within man—Baudelaire called it "the divided personality" of man, Yeats called it the Self and the Mask, and Faulkner spoke of it as "the human heart in conflict with itself"—modernism may well be called the Age of Irony. One of the ironies is that modernism has been a great age of literature, despite the fact that the writers who produced it profoundly criticized the age they lived in. Modernism has shown that a terrible age to live in may be a great age to write in, since the poetry that is most critical of the modern age forms the central tradition of modernism.

APPENDIX
A Brief Chronology of Modern Poetry, 1857–1957

1857   Charles Baudelaire publishes *Les Fleurs du mal [Flowers from Evil]* in Paris. The book is condemned, the author is tried on a charge of obscenity, and six poems are deleted by law.

1860–1880   Emily Dickinson writes over 1,500 poems in the privacy of her home in Amherst, Massachusetts. Gerard Manley Hopkins writes his "sprung rhythm" poems in England.

1880–1890   *Le Symbolisme,* the symbolist movement, is formed in Paris, with Stéphane Mallarmé at its center; Paul Verlaine publishes a collection of their poems titled *Poètes maudits [Damned Poets]*.

1895   Stephen Crane publishes *Black Riders and Other Lines* in New York.

1896   A. E. Housman publishes *A Shropshire Lad* in London. Edwin Arlington Robinson publishes *The Torrent and the Night Before* at his own expense in Boston.

1898   Thomas Hardy, discouraged by the public outcry over his last novel, *Jude the Obscure,* decides to devote the rest of his career to poetry and publishes *Wessex Poems.*

1900   Arthur Symons publishes *The Symbolist Movement in Poetry,* with translations of the leading French symbolist poets' work and an introduction by William Butler Yeats.

1902–1910   Rainer Maria Rilke, in Paris as secretary to August Rodin, publishes *Das Buch der Bilder [The Book of Images]* and *Neue Gedichte [New Poems].*

1909   A group of English poets in London, led by T. E. Hulme, secedes from the Poets Club and holds its first meeting on March 25 at the Eiffel Tower Cafe on Percy Street; in April, Ezra Pound, an American poet newly arrived in London, joins them. He later refers to them as "the forgotten School of Images."

1910   William Butler Yeats publishes *The Green Helmet,* and Ezra Pound hails him as the greatest poet now writing in English.

1912   Ezra Pound publishes a new collection of his poems, *Ripostes,* which contains as an appendix five short poems titled "The Complete Poems of T. E. Hulme" and a note: "As for the future, *Les Imagistes* have that in their keeping," the first appearance of the imagist name in print. In October, in the British Museum tearoom, Hilda Doolittle shows some new poems to Ezra Pound and Richard Aldington; Pound signs them "H. D. Imagiste" and sends them to Harriet Monroe, editor of *Poetry* magazine in Chicago; they are published in January 1913 as the first imagist poems.

1913   Robert Frost publishes his first book, *A Boy's Will,* in London, and Ezra Pound reviews it favorably.

1914   Ezra Pound, serving as contributing editor of *Poetry* in Chicago and the *Egoist* in London, also edits the first imagist anthology, *Des Imagistes.* Yeats publishes *Responsibilities,* and Pound in reviewing it proclaims "The Later Yeats."

1915   Pound publishes *Cathay,* his translations of Chinese poetry.

1915–1917   Amy Lowell edits yearly anthologies of *Some Imagist Poets* in Boston, without Ezra Pound but with three American poets: herself, H. D., and John Gould Fletcher, and three English poets: Richard Aldington, F. S. Flint, and D. H. Lawrence.

1917   T. S. Eliot's first book of poems, *Prufrock and Other Observations,* is published by the Egoist Press in London (financed by Pound). William Carlos Williams publishes his first book of imagist poems, *Al Que Quiere [To Anyone Who Asks]* in New York.

1918   Gerard Manley Hopkins's poems are published posthumously by Robert Bridges, his friend at Oxford and the English poet laureate. Wilfred Owen's *Poems* is published posthumously, edited by Siegfried Sassoon, his fellow officer and poet.

1919   Yeats publishes a new collection, *The Wild Swans at Coole,* showing the full maturity of his later style.

1920   Pound publishes *Hugh Selwyn Mauberley: Life and Contacts* as his poetic farewell to London and leaves for Paris. Paul Valéry publishes a long poem, *La Cimitière marin [The Cemetery by the Sea],* in Paris, the last major French symbolist poem.

1921   Marianne Moore's first *Poems* appears in New York.

1922   *The Waste Land,* by T. S. Eliot, is published simultaneously in the first issue of the *Criterion,* his new magazine, in London, and in the *Dial* in New York. It is both praised and damned.

1922–1925   The *Fugitive* magazine is published in Nashville, Tennessee, introducing a school of southern poets at Vanderbilt University that includes John Crowe Ransom, Donald Davidson, Allen Tate, and Robert Penn Warren.

1923   Wallace Stevens's first book of poems, *Harmonium,* appears, and so does

	E. E. Cummings's first book, *Tulips and Chimneys*. Yeats is awarded the Nobel Prize in literature.
1924	Robinson Jeffers's first important book, *Tamar and Other Poems*, appears.
1925	Thomas Hardy's *Collected Poems* appears. He is eighty-five.
1928	Yeats publishes *The Tower*.
1930	Hart Crane's *Bridge* is published in its complete form, and so is Eliot's *Ash Wednesday*, his first major religious poem.
1930–1940	W. H. Auden is the leading figure in a new school of poets originating at Oxford University, including Stephen Spender, Cecil Day Lewis, and Louis MacNeice.
1934	Dylan Thomas publishes his first book, *18 Poems*.
1935–1942	Eliot publishes a sequence of poems called *Four Quartets*, comprising "Burnt Norton" (1935), "East Coker" (1938), "The Dry Salvages" (1940), and "Little Gidding" (1942).
1939	Yeats's final work is published posthumously in *Last Poems*. Eliot calls him "the greatest modern poet in any language."
1947	Robert Lowell's second book of poems, *Lord Weary's Castle*, wins the Pulitzer Prize, and Lowell is identified as the leading younger American poet.
1948	Ezra Pound's *Pisan Cantos*, written while he was in an American prison camp in Italy charged with treason, is awarded the Bollingen Prize and arouses a storm of controversy. Eliot is awarded the Nobel Prize in literature.
1955	Wallace Stevens's *Opus Posthumous* is published.
1957	*Dr. Zhivago*, by Boris Pasternak, is published in Italy, a work of fiction and poetry; he is awarded the Nobel Prize in literature but declines when he is threatened with exile from Russia if he accepts it.

BIBLIOGRAPHY

Aiken, Conrad. "Ezra Pound: 1914," in *Ezra Pound: Perspectives,* ed. Noel Stock, 4–5. Chicago: Henry Regnery, 1965.

Auden, W. H. Introduction to vol. 5 of *Poets of the English Language,* xvii–xxv. New York: Viking Portable Library, 1950.

———. "My Belief," in *Essays of the Masters,* ed. Charles Neider, 1–13. New York: Rinehart, 1956.

Baudelaire, Charles. *The Mirror of Art: Critical Studies.* New York: Doubleday Anchor, 1956.

———. "My Heart Laid Bare," in *The Intimate Journals of Charles Baudelaire,* trans. Christopher Isherwood, 34–61. Boston: Beacon Press, 1957.

Blanshard, Brand. "Eliot at Oxford." *Southern Review,* Special Anniversary Issue: T. S. Eliot, 21, no. 4 (Autumn 1985): 889–98.

Bradley, F. H. *Appearance and Reality.* 1893. Reprint, Oxford: Oxford University Paperback, 1969.

Carlisle, Olga. *Poets on Street Corners.* New York: Random House, Vintage, 1970.

Crane, Hart. *The Complete Poems and Selected Letters and Prose of Hart Crane.* Ed. Brom Weber. New York: Doubleday Anchor, 1966.

———. *The Letters of Hart Crane, 1916–1932.* Ed. Brom Weber. New York: Heritage House, 1952.

Crane, Stephen. *Stephen Crane: An Omnibus.* Ed. R. W. Stallman. New York: Alfred A. Knopf, 1952.

———. *Stephen Crane: Letters.* Ed. R. W. Stallman. New York: New York University Press, 1960.

Cummings, E. E. *i: six nonlectures.* Cambridge: Harvard University Press, 1953.

Davidson, Donald. "A Mirror for Artists." In *I'll Take My Stand: The South and the Agrarian Tradition.* 1930. Reprint, New York: Harper Torchbook, 1962: 28–60.

Dickinson, Emily. *The Poems of Emily Dickinson.* 3 vols. Ed. Thomas H. Johnson. Cambridge: Harvard University Press, Belknap Press, 1955.

Donoghue, Denis. *Yeats.* London: Collins Fontana Modern Masters, 1971.

Doolittle, Hilda (H. D.) *End to Torment: A Memoir of Ezra Pound.* New York: New Directions, 1979.

Eliot, T. S. *After Strange Gods: A Primer of Modern Heresy.* New York: Harcourt Brace, 1934.

———. Essay I in *Revelation,* ed. John Baillie and Hugh Martin, 1–39. New York: Macmillan, 1937.

———. *The Idea of a Christian Society.* London: Faber and Faber, 1939.

———. *Knowledge and Experience in the Philosophy of F. H. Bradley.* New York: Farrar Straus, 1964.

———. *The Letters of T. S. Eliot, Volume I, 1898–1922.* Ed. Valerie Eliot. New York: Harcourt Brace Jovanovich, 1988.

———. "New Philosophers," omnibus review (unsigned) of *Elements of Constructive Philosophy,* by J. S. Mackenzie; *The Self and Nature,* by DeWitt H. Parker; and *Locke's Theory of Knowledge,* by James Gibson. *New Statesman* ii, no. 175 (July 13, 1918): 296–97.

———. "A Note on Poetry and Belief." *Enemy* 1 (January 1927): 15–17.

———. *Notes towards the Definition of Culture.* New York: Harcourt Brace, 1949.

———. *On Poets and Poetry.* New York: Farrar, Straus, and Cudahy, 1957.

———. "A Prediction in Regard to Three English Authors, Writers Who, though Masters of Thought, Are Likewise Masters of Art." *Vanity Fair* 21, no. 6 (February 1924): 29, 98.

———. "Religion without Humanism," in *Humanism and America: Essays on the Outlook of Modern Civilization,* ed. Norman Foerster, 105–12. New York: Farrar and Rinehart, 1930.

———. Review of *Conscience and Christ: Six Lectures on Christian Ethics,* by Hastings Rashdall. *International Journal of Ethics* 27, no. 1 (October 1916): 111–12.

———. Review (unsigned) of *Essays and Literary Studies,* by Stephen Leacock. *New Statesman* 7, no. 173 (July 29, 1916): 404–5.

———. *The Sacred Wood: Essays on Poetry and Criticism.* London: Methuen, 1920.

———. *Selected Essays.* New York: Harcourt Brace, 1950.

———. *Selected Prose of T. S. Eliot.* Ed. Frank Kermode. New York: Harcourt Brace Jovanovich, 1975.

———. "Sermon Preached in Magdalene College Chapel, Cambridge, 7 March 1948." Cambridge: Cambridge University Press, 1948.

———. *The Use of Poetry and the Use of Criticism.* London: Faber and Faber, 1933.

———. "What Dante Means to Me," lecture delivered at the Italian Institute, London, July 4, 1950. Reprinted in *Adelphi* 27, no. 2 (First Quarter 1951): 106–14.

———. "William James on Immortality," unsigned essay. *New Statesman* 9, no. 231 (September 8, 1917): 547.

Ellmann, Richard. "T. S. Eliot." In *The Dictionary of National Biography, 1961–1970.* Oxford: Oxford University Press, 1981.

Frost, Robert. "The Art of Poetry II: Robert Frost." Interview by Richard Poirier. In *Paris Review* no. 24 (Summer–Fall 1960): 88–120.

———. *Selected Letters.* Ed. Lawrance Thompson. New York: Holt, Rinehart and Winston, 1964.

Fussell, Paul. *The Great War and Modern Memory.* New York: Oxford University Press, 1975.

Gallup, Donald. *Ezra Pound: A Bibliography.* Charlottesville: University Press of Virginia, 1983.

———. *T. S. Eliot: A Bibliography.* New York: Harcourt, Brace and World, 1969.

Graves, Robert. *The White Goddess: A Historical Grammar of Poetic Myth.* New York: Farrar, Straus, and Cudahy, 1948.

Hardy, Thomas. *The Portable Thomas Hardy.* Ed. Julian Moynahan. New York: Viking Penguin, 1977.

Heisenberg, Werner. *Physics and Philosophy.* New York: Harper Torchbook, 1958.

Hopkins, Gerard Manley. *The Oxford Authors: Gerard Manley Hopkins.* Ed. Catherine Phillips. New York: Oxford University Press, 1986.

———. *The Poems of Gerard Manley Hopkins.* Ed. W. H. Gardner and N. H. MacKenzie. London: Oxford University Press, 1967.

Housman, A. E. *Selected Prose.* Ed. John Carter. Cambridge: Cambridge University Press, 1961.

Hulme, T. E. *Further Speculations.* Ed. Sam Hynes. Lincoln: University of Nebraska Press, 1956.

———. *Speculations.* Ed. Herbert Read. 1925. Reprint, New York: Harcourt Brace, 1961.

James, Henry. *The Art of Travel.* Ed. Morton Dauwen Zabel. New York: Doubleday, 1958.

———. *Henry James on Italy: Selections from "Italian Hours."* New York: Weidenfeld, 1988.

James, William. *The Varieties of Religious Experience.* 1902. Reprint, New York: Mentor Paperback, 1958.

Jarrell, Randall. *Poetry and the Age.* New York: Alfred A. Knopf, 1953.

Kenner, Hugh. *The Pound Era.* Berkeley and Los Angeles: University of California Press, 1971.

Kermode, Frank. *An Appetite for Poetry.* Cambridge: Harvard University Press, 1989.

Lawrence, D. H. *The Complete Poems of D. H. Lawrence.* Ed. Vivian de Sola Pinto and Warren Roberts. New York: Viking Press, 1964.

———. *Sons and Lovers.* New York: Random House Modern Library, 1913.

Lowell, Robert. *Collected Prose.* Ed. Robert Giroux. New York: Farrar, Straus, Giroux, 1987.

Mallarmé, Stéphane. *Mallarmé: Pages choisies.* Ed. Guy Delfel. Paris: Librairie Hachette, 1956.

Maritain, Jacques. *The Situation of Poetry.* New York: Philosophical Library, 1955.

Matthews, T. S. *Jacks or Better*. New York: Harper and Row, 1977.

Pasternak, Boris. *Dr. Zhivago*. Trans. Max Hayward and Manya Harari. New York: New American Library, 1958.

———. *Safe Conduct*. New York: New Directions, 1958.

Poe, Edgar Allan. *The Portable Edgar Allan Poe*. Ed. Philip Van Doren Stern. New York: Viking Portable Library, 1955.

Poulet, Georges. *Studies in Human Time*. Trans. Elliott Coleman. New York: Harper Torchbooks, 1956.

Pound, Ezra. *Collected Early Poems of Ezra Pound*. Ed. Michael John King. London: Faber and Faber, 1976.

———. *Guide to Kulchur*. New York: New Directions, 1938.

———. Interview by Donald Hall. In *Writers at Work: The "Paris Review" Interviews*, ed. George Plimpton. 2d ser. New York: Viking Press, 1965.

———. *The Letters of Ezra Pound, 1907–1941*. Ed. D. D. Paige. New York: Harcourt Brace, 1950.

———. *The Literary Essays of Ezra Pound*. Ed. T. S. Eliot. New York: New Directions, 1954.

———. *Pound/Lewis: The Letters of Ezra Pound and Wyndham Lewis*. Ed. Timothy Materer. New York: New Directions, 1985.

———. *The Spirit of Romance*. New York: New Directions, 1910.

———. "Vorticism." *Fortnightly Review* 96 (n.s.), no. 573 (September 1, 1914): 461–71.

Pratt, William. "The Metamorphosis of a Poem." Special John Crowe Ransom issue of *Mississippi Quarterly* 30, no. 1 (Winter 1976–1977): 29–58.

Pratt, William, ed. *The Fugitive Poets: Modern Southern Poetry in Perspective*. New York: E. P. Dutton, 1965; rev. ed., Nashville: J. S. Sanders, 1991.

———, ed. *The Imagist Poem: Modern Poetry in Miniature*. New York: E. P. Dutton, 1963.

Ransom, John Crowe. Introduction to *Selected Poems of Thomas Hardy*. New York: Macmillan, 1961.

———. "The Poems of T. S. Eliot: A Perspective." *New Republic* 127, no. 3 (December 8, 1952): 16–17.

———. *Selected Poems*. 3d ed., rev. and enl. New York: Alfred A. Knopf, 1969.

Richards, I. A., and C. K. Ogden. *The Foundations of Aesthetics*. New York: Lear Publishers, 1925.

Riding, Laura. *The Poems of Laura Riding*. 1938. Reprint, with new introduction by Laura Riding, Manchester: Carcanet New Press, 1980.

———. "Poetry and the Good." *PN Review* 18, no. 4 (March/April 1992): 20–24.

Rilke, Rainer Maria. *Rodin*. London: Grey Walls Press, 1946.

———. *Selected Letters of Rainer Maria Rilke*. Ed. Harry T. Moore. New York: Doubleday Anchor, 1960.

———. *Selected Letters of Rainer Maria Rilke, 1902–1926*. Trans. and ed. R. F. C. Hull. London: Macmillan, 1947.

Simpson, Eileen. *Poets in Their Youth*. New York: Random House, 1982.

Spears, Monroe K. *American Ambitions*. Baltimore: Johns Hopkins University Press, 1987.

Spender, Stephen. *The Struggle of the Modern*. Berkeley: University of California Press, 1963.

———. *World within World*. New York: Harcourt Brace, 1951.

Stevens, Wallace. *The Letters of Wallace Stevens*. Ed. Holly Stevens. New York: Alfred A. Knopf, 1977.

———. *The Necessary Angel: Essays on Reality and Imagination*. New York: Alfred A. Knopf, 1951.

———. *Opus Posthumous*. Ed. Samuel French Morse. New York: Alfred A. Knopf, 1957.

St. John, James H. "Some Reminiscences of T. S. Eliot." *Miami Dimensions* ii, no. 4 (Oxford, Ohio) (Summer 1965): 4.

Symons, Arthur. *The Symbolist Movement in Literature*. 1899. Reprint, New York: E. P. Dutton Paperback, 1958.

Tate, Allen. *Essays of Four Decades*. Chicago: Swallow Press, 1959.

———. *The Literary Correspondence of Donald Davidson and Allen Tate*. Ed. John Tyree Fain and Thomas Daniel Young. Athens: University of Georgia Press, 1974.

———. *Memoirs and Opinions, 1926–1974*. Chicago: Swallow Press, 1975.

Taupin, René. *The Influence of French Symbolism on Modern American Poetry*. Trans. William Pratt and Anne Rich Pratt, ed. William Pratt. New York: AMS Press, 1985.

Thomas, Dylan. "A Few Words of a Kind." In *Dylan Thomas*, no. 3. 1951. Read by author. Caedmon TC-1043. Record album.

Warren, Robert Penn. *Democracy and Poetry*. Cambridge: Harvard University Press, 1975.

———. *Robert Penn Warren Talking: Interviews 1950–1978*. Ed. Floyd C. Watkins and John T. Hiers. New York: Random House, 1978.

Weil, Simone. "Decreation." In *Gravity and Grace*, 78–86. New York: Putnam, 1952.

Weston, Jessie L. *From Ritual to Romance*. 1919. Reprint, New York: Doubleday Anchor, 1957.

Williams, Miller. *The Poetry of John Crowe Ransom*. New Brunswick, N.J.: Rutgers University Press, 1972.

Williams, William Carlos. *The Autobiography of William Carlos Williams*. New York: Random House, 1951.

Wilson, Edmund. *Axel's Castle: A Study in the Imaginative Literature of 1870 to 1930*. New York: Charles Scribner's Sons, 1931.

Yeats, William Butler. *The Autobiography of William Butler Yeats*. New York: Macmillan Collier Books, 1965.

———. *Essays and Introductions*. New York: Macmillan, 1961.

―――. *Letters on Poetry from W. B. Yeats to Dorothy Wellesley.* London: Oxford University Press, 1964.

―――. *Uncollected Prose.* Vol. 2. Ed. John P. Frayne and Colton Johnson. New York: Macmillan, 1975.

―――. *A Vision.* Rev. ed. New York: Macmillan Collier Books, 1965.

Index

CREDITS

Five of the essays in this book have been published separately: "Ezra Pound and the Image," in *Ezra Pound: The London Years, 1908–1920,* ed. Philip Grover (New York: AMS Press, 1978); "Eliot at Oxford: From Philosopher to Poet and Critic" (Summer 1995) and "To Doubt Yet Be Devout: The Lesson of the Later Eliot" (Winter 1992) in *Soundings* (University of Tennessee); and "Robert Penn Warren: Portraits of the Artist as a Young and an Old Man" (Fall 1990) and "Laura Riding: Fugitive, Witch, or Goddess?" (Fall 1995) in the *South Carolina Review* (Clemson University). Four of my translations of Rainer Maria Rilke's poetry originally appeared in the *Sewanee Review* (University of the South) (Autumn 1966): "Early Poem," "Archaic Torso of Apollo," "The Unicorn," and "The Panther."